New Perspectives on Human Security

New Perspectives on Human Security

EDITED BY MALCOLM McINTOSH AND ALAN HUNTER

Greenleaf
PUBLISHING

© 2010 Greenleaf Publishing Limited

Published by Greenleaf Publishing Limited
Aizlewood's Mill
Nursery Street
Sheffield S3 8GG
UK
www.greenleaf-publishing.com

Printed in Great Britain on acid-free paper by
Antony Rowe Ltd, Chippenham and Eastbourne

FSC
www.fsc.org
MIX
Paper from
responsible sources
FSC° C013604

Cover by LaliAbril.com

British Library Cataloguing in Publication Data:
A catalogue record for this book is available from the British Library.

ISBN-13: 9781906093419

Contents

Foreword

Ramesh Thakur
Waterloo University, Canada

Like several, perhaps even most, important concepts in political science and international relations—power, authority and legitimacy come readily to mind—security is an essentially contested concept. National security, no less than human security, is subjectively constructed and represented. The concept of security has been stretched both horizontally, to embrace issues beyond just the military, and vertically, moving up to embrace regional and global structures and down to local and individual identities. And from this flow the relevant policy prescriptions for action to be taken to address and defeat the security threats across the different issues at the relevant levels.

In the traditional framework, the individual is put at the service of the state, including killing others and being killed oneself, as and when called for duty by the government of the day. In contrast, human security puts the individual at the centre of the debate, analysis and policy. He or she is paramount, and the state is a collective instrument to protect human life and enhance human welfare. The fundamental components of human security—the security of *people* against threats to personal safety and life—can be put at risk by external aggression, but also by factors within a country, including 'security' forces. The reformulation of national security into the concept of human security is simple, yet has profound consequences for how we see the world, how we organise our political affairs, how we make choices in public and foreign policy, and how we relate to fellow human beings from many different countries and civilisations.

The states system, and the focus on state security, is a characteristic of the Westphalian system that emerged as the answer to the problem of order and violence in 17th-century Europe. The consolidation of the primacy of the state in the 18th and 19th centuries was accompanied by the monopolisation of security by the state. The state provided the solution to the security dilemmas of individuals who sublimated their quest for personal safety into the identity and security of the state. Once the underlying assumption began to fray, the fusion of individual and state security began to unravel.

According to Neil MacFarlane and Yuen Foong Khong, the rise of human security in the 20th century may be attributed to six factors.[1] First, the participants in armed conflict broadened from a narrow elite to mass conscripts. Second, the consequences of the industrial and scientific revolutions dramatically increased the range, lethality and accuracy of firepower, meaning that the state had to accept growing numbers of its own people being killed in the effort to protect them. The ultimate paradox came with nuclear weapons and strategies of mutually assured destruction. Third, many regimes took to murdering large numbers of their own people, for example in the Holocaust. Fourth, in the wake of decolonisation, many states emerged lacking the capacity to assure their citizens' security or exert authority over resources which were then captured by predatory groups who used the principle of sovereignty and the norm of non-intervention to shield themselves from external pressure. Fifth, the collapse of the Soviet empire and the end of the confrontational, militarised and state-centric cold war opened space for alternative conceptions of order and security. And sixth, globalisation has helped to reduce the salience of the state and of military threats and defences.

Analysts of the security *problématique* are likely today to be grappling simultaneously with problems of internal social cohesion, regime capacity and brittleness, failed states, economic development, structural adjustment, gender relations, ethnic identity, external threats and transnational and global problems such as HIV/AIDS, environmental degradation, drug trafficking, terrorism and so on. For example, malaria kills more than 1 million people around the world every year, 90% of them in Africa: 3,000 people, or the equivalent of 9/11, per day.

One 'leg' of human security is in the human rights tradition, which sees the state mainly, although not solely, as the problem and the source of threats to individual security. The other is in the development agenda, which sees the state as the necessary agent for promoting human security through improved social welfare. The emotional rod that connects both the protection and well-being agendas is solidarity across borders, the sense of shared affinity with fellow human beings qua human beings regardless of differences in nationality, race, religion or gender.

Of the handful of countries that have explicitly pursued a human security agenda in their foreign policies, Canada and Japan have emphasised a different leg each of human security. Canadians, especially during the tenure of Lloyd Axworthy as foreign minister,[2] gave priority to protecting citizens at risk of atrocities arising from failed or perpetrator states and set up an international commission to try to reconcile the imperative to render effective protection to at-risk populations with

---

1 S.N. MacFarlane and Yuen Foong Khong, *Human Security and the UN: A Critical History* (Bloomington, IN: Indiana University Press, 2006): 6-9.
2 See L. Axworthy, *Navigating a New World: Canada's Global Future* (Toronto: Vintage Canada, 2004).

the persisting reality of state sovereignty. The Ottawa Treaty banning antipersonnel landmines and the International Criminal Court were the other two operational-cum-institutional outcomes, along with the responsibility to protect as discussed in this volume by Vesselin Popovski, of Axworthy's human security agenda. Japan has prioritised the developmental leg of human security, and set up its own World Commission on Human Security.[3]

The reality of human insecurity cannot just be wished away. The 'soft' threats are neither unconnected to peace and security, nor can they be ignored until the 'hard' threats have been taken care of. This is why human security can be regarded as a foundational value, from which flow other individual and social values. To many poor people in the world's poorest countries today, the risk of being attacked by terrorists or with weapons of mass destruction is far removed from the quotidian yet pervasive reality of the so-called soft threats—hunger, lack of safe drinking water and sanitation and endemic diseases—that kill millions every year, far more than the so-called hard or real security threats.

Let us take some examples from India that run counter to the dominant narrative of the country as a rising power and wonderful success story. Its rapidly improving military capabilities through increased defence acquisitions include long-range maritime surveillance, maritime interdiction and patrolling, air interdiction and strategic airlift. The United States acknowledges sharing with India democratic values, an open political system, and commitment to global stability as demonstrated through peacekeeping, counter-piracy, humanitarian assistance and disaster relief efforts. Little wonder that the 2010 US Quadrennial Defense Review welcomed India's rising profile 'as a net provider of security in the Indian Ocean and beyond'.[4]

If we switch analytical focus from national to human security, however, a contrarian picture comes into the frame. For all of India's economic successes in the past decade, its child mortality reduction rates have not matched those of its poorer neighbour, Bangladesh. Had India matched Bangladesh, 732,000 fewer Indian children would have died in 2005.[5] Among children aged 1–5, girls are 50% more likely to die than boys. That is, 130,000 girls are discriminated to death every year in India.[6] In the 12-year period 1997–2008 inclusive, a total of 199,132 farmer suicides—this is not a misprint—were recorded by the National Crime Records Bureau, or an average of 16,594 per year.[7] One reason is the vicious debt trap caused by the removal of

3 Commission on Human Security, *Human Security Now* (New York: Commission on Human Security, 2003).

4 Secretary of Defense, *Quadrennial Defense Review Report* (Washington, DC: Department of Defense, 2010): 60.

5 UNDP, *Human Development Report 2005. International Cooperation at a Crossroads: Aid, Trade and Security in an Unequal World* (New York: Oxford University Press, 2005): 29.

6 Ibid: 31.

7 P. Sainath, 'Farm Suicides: A 12-year Saga', *The Hindu* (Chennai), 25 January 2010. See also P. Sainath, '16,632 Farmer Suicides in 2007', *The Hindu*, 12 December 2008.

quantitative restrictions under the World Trade Organisation (WTO) regime which has left the country's small and marginal farmers exposed to the volatility of international markets and prices. With no access to crop insurance, they are easy prey for usurious moneylenders.

Globally, on 2005 trends, the shortfall in the Millennium Development Goal (MDG) target for reducing child mortality will lead to 4.4 million avoidable deaths in 2015.[8] Some 2.3 million children could be kept alive through preventive and curative neonatal interventions at a cost of US$4 billion—just two days of military spending in the developed countries.[9] More than 1 billion people in the world lack access to clean water and 2.6 billion to sanitation. These deficits could be overcome through a decade-long annual investment of US$7 billion—less than what Europeans spend on perfume—which would save 4,000 lives *each day* from the resulting reduced exposure to infectious diseases.[10]

Realists who argue that only a 'lean' conception of security can provide an honest and effective policy tool to cope with the 'mean' enemies that prowl the international jungle should get real. Annual deaths, even on these massive scales, cannot be accommodated within the analytical framework of 'national security'; they can in 'human security'. To insist on national security at the expense of human security would be to trivialise the concept of security in many real-world circumstances to the point of sterility, bereft of any operational meaning. The best comment on this came from Michael Brown, the chief of the US disaster agency FEMA (Federal Emergency Management Agency) at the time of Hurricane Katrina. Testifying before a Senate committee on 10 February 2006, he insisted that he had informed the White House and Homeland Security on the day that Katrina hit that they were realising their worst nightmare and New Orleans was seriously flooding because the levees had been breached. But he could not get their attention because of the fixation with terrorism. Had there been a report that a terrorist had blown up the levee, said Brown, 'everybody would have jumped all over that'.[11] Just so.

The bottom line is that national security is more of a slogan for political mobilisation than an analytically useful concept. By contrast, human security directs our attention to the rationale, forms, techniques and measures of state and societal coercion: from the Holocaust and the gulags to the death squads of and disappearances in Latin America and the killing fields of Cambodia. The consolidation of state power can be used, in the name of national security and law and order, to suppress individual, group or even majority demands on the government, and to plunder the resources of a society. Internal security bureaucracies of many countries are dedicated to the protection of the state against dissident threats from within and can pose a major threat to the human security of the citizens of that state.

---

8 UNDP, *Human Development Report 2005* (New York: Oxford University Press, 2005): 41.
9 Ibid: 33.
10 Ibid: 93.
11 'Ex-Bush aide disputes late Katrina warning', *International Herald Tribune*, 11 February 2006.

National security is an artifice of the realists' imagination, a politically constructed concept, not an objective analytic tool. There are other ways of slicing the security cake. Ethnonationalism is the assertion of rights to sovereignty by ethnic nationalities and, by implication, a reconstruction of the international order on the basis of a system of nations. This makes 'nationalism' a key threat to state security. But this is just another way of saying that the sanctity of state sovereignty and its accompanying tenet of territorial integrity are the key threats to 'national' security. Ethnic minorities may perceive threats differently from majority communities: witness the conflict between the nation of Palestine and the state of Israel, or East Timor and Indonesia, or the Kurds and the many states across which they are divided.

Two conclusions follow. First, security is an essentially contested concept because it is an intellectual and cognitive construct, not an objective fact. Second, the standard referents of security are faced by many internal inconsistencies. 'National security' is itself riddled with conceptual confusion and policy problems stemming from its integral link to the state. Putting human safety at the centre of security concerns—the securitisation of individual life as a deliberate artifice of the liberal imagination—helps us to resolve some of these tensions. The rise in the proportion of internal wars, the use of small arms as weapons of choice and the emergence of irregular forces as the major combatants make today's violent conflicts less centralised and more brutal. Civilian casualties and displacement are no longer 'collateral damage', unintended by-products of warfare, but often the deliberate war aims of the fighting. At the same time, norms, instruments and regimes have proliferated for the advancement of human rights and humanitarian laws. The intersection of the two trends—of civilians as direct targets and growing casualties of warfare and rising normative standards of military behaviour during armed conflict—has created new and higher expectations regarding enforcement of human rights and humanitarian norms.

The primacy of the goal of state security does not withstand rigorous scrutiny, for it does not have privileged claim over such other needs for human beings as food, water and air. The operationalisation of human security in the practice of state and international organisations during the 1990s was evident in the changing and toughening mandates of peace operations, the training of personnel for such operations, the prohibition of particular types of weapon, the norm against the use of children in armed conflict, the terms of peace agreements, the international interventions in Kosovo and East Timor and the changed priorities of donors and humanitarian actors.

Human security thus gives us a template for national policy and international action, and that is its attraction. This can be usefully illustrated with the example of violence against women who can confront human insecurity that is direct (for example honour killing), or rooted in structural and cultural violence.[12] The way in

---

12 See G. Hoogensen and K. Stuvøy, 'Gender, Resistance and Human Security', *Security Dialogue* 37.2 (2006): 207-28.

which a society confronts the issue of violence against women defines the experience of security for women. Human security entails the enactment of protective laws and the creation of effective policing and enforcement machinery to ensure their implementation. While men suffer from the public violence of criminality and wars, the violence inflicted on women is mainly in the private realm of the household. Even war-related violence directed at women takes the form of public shaming and humiliation and is mostly suffered in silence. ' "Teach the bitch a lesson. Strip her in public." As one of the police officers told me, these were the orders issued by their bosses.'[13] The 'bitch' concerned was not just anybody; she was Asma Jahangir, head of the Human Rights Commission of Pakistan and the UN special rapporteur on freedom of religion.

Pakistan is not atypical of its region. Ruchika Girhotra was an aspiring 14-year-old tennis player in August 1990 when she was sexually molested by the president of the provincial tennis association in the Indian state of Haryana, senior police officer S.P.S. Rathore. On 21 December 2009—19 years after the sexual assault!—Rathore was convicted of the offence, sentenced to six months imprisonment but granted bail pending an appeal. In the meantime, Ruchika was expelled from her school attended also by Rathore's daughter, subjected to vilification and harassment, and committed suicide on 28 December 1993. Family members who pursued her case were repeatedly harassed and threatened with physical harm. Rathore, promoted to the top post in Haryana and awarded the Police Medal (since stripped) for distinguished service, retired in 2002.[14]

In the words of Sri Lanka's Radhika Coomaraswamy, now the UN Secretary-General's Special Representative on Children and Armed Conflict:

> Even before birth women suffer from sex selective abortion, at infancy they may face female infanticide, as young children they will have to put up with incest and son preference, as adolescents they may be sexually abused or trafficked, as young women they may suffer rape, sexual harassment, acid attacks; as wives they may experience domestic violence, dowry related violence, marital rape or honour killings, and as widows they may be required to self immolate or be deprived of property or dignity. The vulnerability to violence at every stage of their life-cycle makes VAW [violence against women] a terrible south Asian legacy that requires concerted regional, national and local level action.[15]

Policy measures in response include increasing state capacity to monitor and enforce laws against women-specific violence such as rape, national implementa-

---

13 A. Dayan Hasan, 'Pakistan's moderates are beaten in public', *International Herald Tribune*, 15 June 2005.

14 See R. Thakur, 'Corrupt India still has a long way to go', *Ottawa Citizen*, 9 January 2010.

15 R. Coomaraswamy, 'Human Security and Gender Violence', *Economic and Political Weekly*, 29 October 2005: 4,729-36, at p. 4,730.

tion machinery for international commitments signed by states and priority attention by humanitarian agencies to women's recovery from wartime violence.

Human security permits policy-makers to adopt a particular agenda for action that is distinctive from alternative ways of conceptualising security. The best guarantee of human security is a strong, efficient, effective, but also democratically legitimate state that is respectful of citizens' rights, mindful of its obligations and responsibilities and tolerant of diversity and dissenting voices. States that are too strong or, at the other end of the spectrum, too weak and failing, cannot provide human security to their citizens. At the same time, states by themselves cannot provide the full measure of human security, but instead must act in partnership with robust market forces and resilient civil society.

National security seeks to defend the state against external threats. Human security seeks to protect people from violence within states, including violence directed at civilians during international war and violence from their own states. It thus embraces the full complex of violent threats resulting from international, transnational and intrastate armed conflict, genocide, ethnic cleansing and population displacement.

Demarcating the boundary between national and human security, and also between the broad and narrow concepts of human security, is challenging and problematic. How do we distinguish analytically between insurgents who cultivate poppy to finance their fights and organised drug traffickers protecting their trade with guns? Between conflict-related disease and starvation and the denial of food and medicine—by burning crops or forcibly preventing the delivery of medical relief personnel and supplies—as a strategy of war? Between sexual violence directed by individual soldiers and rape as a deliberate instrument of warfare? When the military junta in Myanmar restricted international aid agencies' access to the victims of Cyclone Nargis in 2008, was that in defence of the country's national security (national sovereignty, regime security), an assault on the citizens' human security, both, or neither?

Within national systems, police forces are part of the security apparatus of the state, but are not normally included within the 'national security' apparatus; the latter refers to the defence forces. Yet civilian police, and indeed criminal justice packages, now constitute integral elements of international peace operations. Part of the Western and UN security operations in Afghanistan include building up the numbers and self-sustaining capacity of the Afghan National Police as well as the Afghan National Army. So the boundary between domestic and external is already blurred within the analytical framework of national security. In this volume, Bruce Baker takes this further in his discussion of African police as failing agents of human security. And Manish Jha argues that the state in India deploys police, paramilitary and militia forces to threaten the human security of its citizens.

How many people die unnecessarily each year owing to deficiencies in healthcare? The answer is in the tens or hundreds of thousands even in the United States, where 45 million Americans lack health insurance. As Deepayan Basu Ray argues, a social protection model of healthcare can help to mitigate the drivers of human insecurity. But what of the psychological safety that Marci Green talks about—is that stretching human security too far? What happens if a psychologically malad-justed person takes over the helm of government—does that make it into a security issue but not otherwise? What if a sociopath kills a large number of people in a shooting spree in a classroom or shopping mall?

David Roberts introduces us to the notion of biopoverty: the avoidable absence of resources such as food, water, sanitation and medicine which add to the toll of unnecessary civilian deaths. This would suggest that the pursuit of international security, not just national security, can be a threat to human security: for example, the UN sanctions regime on Saddam Hussein's Iraq that caused up to half a million excess deaths.[16]

The relationship between greed, grievance and conflict has been much studied. We are familiar with the notion of conflict diamonds and the need to regulate such trade. If conflict diamonds, why not conflict coltan mining as argued by Miho Taka? The role of oil in causing conflict, as discussed with respect to Angola by Liliane Mouan, requires little justification in any volume on security studies any more. But what of the role of business more generally? Should corporate good citizenship include codes of conduct for private sector operations in zones of conflict, as dis-cussed by Nicky Black? And if so, does human security provide a better conceptual or policy template for such prescriptions?

A number of authors point to the inadequacy or inappropriateness of the tra-ditional national security lens for capturing the complexities and texture of con-temporary global challenges and the web of global governance that has grown to address problems without passports. Human security has been criticised for being empty, trite, conceptually confused and promiscuous, theoretically incoherent, and far too elastic in practice to be of much policy use. The breadth and range of some of the chapters in this book under the omnibus concept of human security will be seen as vindication by both champions and critics, that it is far too vague and diffuse or that it is rich and comprehensive in focusing policy attention on problems of security, safety and dignity in the real world.

In short, whether readers agree or take issue with the theoretical arguments and empirical case studies assembled in this volume, they will find it hard to resist being stimulated and provoked by novel insights and fresh interpretations of what security means in a world that seems to be losing many familiar moorings.

16 See UNICEF, *Child Mortality: Iraq* (document GJ-99.8; New York: UNICEF, 1999).

Foreword

Human security and business: conflicts, human mobility and governance[1]

Mehrnaz Mostafavi
Human Security Unit, UN, USA

In this Foreword I will provide some brief observations on the human security concept and its added value in addressing the topics outlined for your consideration in this book on human security and business.

As increasingly recognised by both academics and practitioners, the complexity and interrelatedness of both old and new threats—from chronic and persistent poverty to ethnic violence, human trafficking, climate change, health pandemics and sudden economic and financial downturns—tend to acquire transnational dimensions and move beyond traditional notions of security threats that focus on external military aggressions alone.

And, while national security still remains pivotal to peace and stability, the need for an expanded paradigm of security that: draws attention to the multitude of threats that cut across different aspects of human life; that concentrates on the security of the individuals, their protection and empowerment; that highlights the interface between the lack of security, development and human rights; and that promotes a new integrated, coordinated and people-centred approach is also underlined by national and global challenges.

It is within this context that the international community has been working towards the broader concept of human security. So what is the added value of the

---

1 From a paper originally presented on 27–28 April 2009 at a conference organised by Tokyo University's Graduate Programme in Human Security and Cass Business School, City University, London (ochaonline.un.org/humansecurity, accessed 15 June 2010).

human security concept and how can it aid the international community, including the private sector, in creating sustainable peace and promoting greater stability at the local, national, regional and international levels?

First, by making the individual the centre of analysis, human security focuses the attention of all actors on addressing the root causes of insecurities in a given situation and engenders long-term solutions that build on local capacities and help prevent or mitigate the recurrence of identified threats.

Second, human security is based on a multi-sectoral and comprehensive understanding of insecurities that bring together the multiplicity of challenges faced by individuals and communities. As such, human security draws from the expertise and resources of a wide range of actors and seeks to establish synergies and partnerships that capitalise on the comparative advantage of each stakeholder.

Third, by promoting participatory processes, human security helps in establishing a social contract among the various actors in a given society and in this way it cultivates public discourse, promotes local ownership, and strengthens the bonds of mutual respect and responsibility that are important to resolving tensions in any given society.

And, last, by ensuring coherence and coordination across sectors and actors, human security allows for maximisation of impact by avoiding duplication of resources and expanding the space for cost-effective policies and approaches that often need to be considered together by those working at different levels, both geographically and sectorally.

All these elements can provide the framework with which the private sector, with its significant capacity for innovation, can forge partnerships with other stakeholders to find solutions to the most severe and widespread threats and vulnerabilities faced by the international community today.

Specifically, by:

- Building on the capacities of the affected individuals and communities

- Encouraging multi-actor collaboration, coordination and implementation

- Providing a contextual account of people's concrete needs and insecurities

The human security framework can ensure that efforts by the international community, including the private sector:

- Address the root causes of human insecurities

- Build on local capacities

- Emphasise early prevention rather than late intervention

- Capitalise on the comparative advantages of our rich humanity

While this brief outline certainly does not capture the rich context of the human security concept, let me say that, as the spectrum of risks and uncertainties increases in our globalised world, the advancement of human security is more relevant today than ever before.

At the Human Security Unit, we try to translate the human security concept into projects that are funded by the United Nations Trust Fund for Human Security and to date over 180 projects in approximately 70 countries have been supported. Through our efforts, we have seen the added value of the human security concept and its impact on laying the foundations for peaceful, well-functioning and sustainable communities where political, economic, social and other systems come together to give people the building blocks of survival, livelihood and dignity.

Acknowledgements

This book brings together divergent perspectives on human security from around the world. Our foremost thanks go to John Stuart and Dean Bargh at Greenleaf Publishing for having the wit and wisdom to publish in this emerging area. Second, thanks go to former UN Assistant Secretary-General Ramesh Thakur, soon to be resident in Australia, and third to friends and colleagues at the UN University in Tokyo, particularly Dr Vesselin Popovski, and to the University of Tokyo, particularly Professor Yasunobu Sato and Dylan Scudder—all of whom have offered and provided support and help with this project.

We would also like to acknowledge with gratitude the support of Coventry University for research and teaching programmes both in human security and in peace studies; and specifically for hosting an international seminar on human security and peace-building in December 20009, at which several of the papers in this collection were first presented. Alan Hunter and I started working together at Coventry University's Applied Research Centre for Human Security (ARCHS) some years ago but had unknowingly been connected through our links decades before to Alan Whitehorn, father of the eminent columnist Catherine Whitehorn. Forty years ago he was Alan Hunter's classics teacher and one of my father's and mother's closest friends and helped inspire a generation of pacifists and conscientious objectors, like my father, during the Second World War. Alan Hunter is now professor and director of the Centre for Peace and Reconciliation Studies at Coventry University, England, and I am professor and director of the Centre for Sustainable Enterprise at Griffith University, Queensland, Australia. We would also like to thank all those who have contributed chapters to this volume in the sincere belief that the idea and the practice of human security will become a dominant construct as the world understands that it is at a turning point. We must work together, think together, and act collectively, or perish. We have to learn to love each other, to show humility when we reflect on humanity's development, and be in awe of the wonder and complexity of the universe and the beautiful and delicate planet that we all share.

Malcolm McIntosh, Brisbane, Australia
Alan Hunter, Coventry, England

Section I
Introductions

1

Perspectives on human security
The emergent construct

Malcolm McIntosh
Asia Pacific Centre for Sustainable Enterprise, Griffith University, Australia

Alan Hunter
Centre for Peace and Reconciliation Studies, Coventry University, UK

This book is testimony to the emergent nature of human security as an idea, as a useful construct and as an operational strategy. Our aim is to showcase new directions that may, we believe, enrich the human security agenda at the time of writing in 2010. Some human security discourse is still rooted in the traditional language of the aid-agency/UN development/economic growth models that emerged from the 1950s onwards, often hostile to the corporate and business sector, and sometimes negligent of environment, sustainability and climate change issues. Another limited and, in our opinion, outmoded approach, is an exaggerated focus on Western interventions, especially military ones, as a 'solution' to problems in poor or conflict-prone areas. Various synopses and analyses of current thinking on human security have already been published, including an accessible account from the United Nations Development Programme (UNDP) (Jolly and Ray 2006). A report for the UN Centre for Regional Development from the early years of the millennium provides another good overview of human security (Mani 2002). Several major Internet-based resources provide regular updates: for example, the excellent Human Security Gateway maintained in Vancouver.

We believe that proponents of a human security approach should welcome efforts to remove the barriers between enterprise, corporates, aid and development agencies, government agencies, citizen groups and the UN; and work towards multi-stakeholder approaches to vulnerable populations. We also believe that such an approach is vital in responding to the imperative of action on climate change. There are several reasons why businesses may want to engage with the needs of vulnerable populations: companies need secure trading environments; they may also have corporate citizenship drivers which induce them to respond positively to customer, shareholder and employee concerns; and many consumers are interested in fair trade, peace and social justice as well as green issues.

The human security lens

The term 'human security' was first used by the UN in its *Human Development Report 1994*. In reality it was an idea whose time had come as a result of the evolution of thinking on *human* security, as opposed to international and state security: an evolution that gathered strength after the First World War, after the Depression of the 1930s, during the Second World War and as part of pre-post-industrial reckoning in democratic societies on both sides of the Atlantic and around the world. Looking back further, one can trace the origins of human security concerns to religious and early socialist ideals of community or commonwealth; and to Roman and Prussian, among other, state ideals of national security, law and order. In the UK such ideals formed the foundations of the National Health Service with the provision of healthcare free at the point of delivery to all, while in the US it led to the New Deal. On 6 January 1941 US President Franklin D. Roosevelt made a speech in which he talked about the 'Four Freedoms': freedom of expression and religion; freedom from want and fear. His wife Eleanor used the ideas and some of the language of this speech in the preamble to the UN's 1948 Universal Declaration of Human Rights when she said that these four freedoms were the 'highest aspirations of the common people'.[1] Many of the humanitarian concerns were indeed encapsulated in the Universal Declaration of Human Rights itself, Article 25:

> Everyone has the right to a standard of living adequate for the health and well-being of himself and of his family, including food, clothing, housing and medical care and necessary social services, and the right to security in the event of unemployment, sickness, disability, widowhood, old age or other lack of livelihood in circumstances beyond his control.

Human security is thus a potentially useful collocation: one word, security, carrying implications of realpolitik and law-enforcement; the other, human, with its connotations of the humanitarian tradition and a person-centred priority.

   Human security has three primary components: the sanctity of the individual; the relationship of the individual to the community; and the preservation of peo-

---

1   United Nations Declaration of Human Rights General Assembly Resolution 217A (1948).

ple and communities in the face of national, international and global interventions. In 2003 the UN Commission on Human Security, chaired by Sadako Ogata and Amartya Sen, reported that the world needed 'a new security framework that centers directly on people'. Human security, the Commission argued, 'focuses on shielding people from critical and pervasive threats and empowering them to take charge of their lives'. The necessity of paradigm shift is because there is:

> a consensus that the meaning of security is eroding; existing institutions and policies [are] unable to cope with weakening multilateralism and global responsibilities. The state has the primary responsibility for security, but the security challenge is complex and various new actors attempt to play a role.[2]

The Commission sought to develop a global framework focused on 'survival, dignity and livelihood; freedom from fear; and freedom from want'. Of particular concern were the most vulnerable individuals who need protection from violent conflict; those people who are on the move; those people who are economically insecure because the global economic system has failed them; or whose lives have been destabilised by forces far beyond their control (Commission on Human Security 2003).

The concept of security has until now tended to be shaped by the potential for conflict between states and this has often meant that security has been equated with the threats to a country's borders. Traditional approaches to security issues tend to focus on military security and are over-concerned with territorial issues. Now, however, economic globalisation and open, global, social networks mean that the professional worlds of humanitarianism, development, human rights, conflict and business must find space to meet and integrate. Human security therefore calls on all partners (business, government, civil society and individuals) to find ways to develop a new paradigm of sustainable human development. But the paradigm shift is from the nation to the individual. As the UNDP *Human Development Report 1994* states:

> For most people today a feeling of insecurity arises more from worries about daily life than the dread of a cataclysmic world event. Job security, income security, health security, environmental security and security from crime—these are emerging concerns of human security all over the world (UNDP 1994).

In the past decade, Canada, Japan, Norway, the Netherlands and several other states began to use the rubric of 'human security' to introduce a number of new emphases in foreign policy and international work. In summary, they tended to argue that:

- The main reference point for security should be the individual, or the individual in a group or community; and particularly vulnerable people.

---

2   For UN statements on human security, see McIntosh 2006.

Box 1.1 **Defining human security**

"survival, dignity and livelihood, freedom from fear . . . freedom from want . . .

a new security framework that centers directly on people . . . human security focuses on shielding people from critical and pervasive threats and empowering them to take charge of their lives . . . the consensus on the meaning of security is eroding . . . existing institutions and policies unable to cope with weakening multilateralism and global responsibilities . . . the state has the primary responsibility for security, but the security challenge is complex and various new actors attempt to play a role . . . so we need a shift in paradigm.

Protecting people in violent conflict; protecting and empowering people on the move; protecting and empowering people in post-conflict situations; economic insecurity—choices in a world of opportunity; health for human security; knowledge, skills and values—for human security; [and] linking the many initiatives.

The Report introduces a new concept of human security, which equates security with people rather than territories, with development rather than arms. It examines both the national and the global concerns of human security. The Report seeks to deal with these concerns through a new paradigm of sustainable human development, capturing the potential peace dividend, a new form of development co-operation and a restructured system of global institutions. For too long the concept of security has been shaped by the potential for conflict between states. For too long, security has been equated with the threats to a country's borders. For too long nations have sought arms to protect their security" (UN Commission on Human Security [2003] chaired by Sadako Ogata and Amartya Sen).

"A humane world where people can live in security and dignity, free from poverty and despair, is still a dream for many and should be enjoyed by all. In such a world, every individual would be guaranteed freedom from fear and freedom from want, with an equal opportunity to fully develop their human potential. Building human security is essential to achieving this goal. In essence, human security means freedom from pervasive threats to people's rights, their safety or even their lives" (UNDP 1994).

Military security of nation states remains important but is not always the overriding priority in every situation

- Individuals or groups are subject to a variety of threats, of which military threats from outside the state are only one and often not the most significant

- The international community has a responsibility in some circumstances to protect vulnerable individuals and communities

- The protection of vulnerable individuals and communities should sometimes take precedence over territorial issues, so in some cases there is possible tension between the security of the individual and that of the nation, the state or the regime

One influential official document reflecting these concerns was 'Responsibility to Protect', produced by an agency working for the Canadian government (Evan *et al.* 2001), which tried to evaluate the criteria by which cross-border interventions should be not only permitted, but morally obligatory. The discussion was informed by the perceived failure of the international community to intervene in genocides or near-genocides in Rwanda and Bosnia; and more lately in Darfur. The Responsibility to Protect doctrine was ultimately adopted as a United Nations Security Council Resolution, 1674, in 2006. Some recent publications focus mainly on similar issues (Kaldor 2007).

Human security in the 'developed world'

This collection also poses the question: is the concept of human security relevant to city, or indeed any, life in developed countries? Arguably it is, since citizens in any state may feel vulnerable to serious crime, marginalisation, terrorism or other problems. In August 2006, for example, Italians were shocked to discover the extent of marginalisation and mutual antipathy between immigrants and local residents in the affluent city of Padua . . .

> . . . renowned for its ancient university and medieval frescoes by Giotto. Yesterday, however, it acquired a less attractive claim to fame: a steel wall, 84 m long and 3 m high, blocking off a run-down housing estate with a high immigrant population and a reputation for drugs, violence and prostitution (Owen 2006).

Other EU states, among the most affluent countries in the world, had recently seen serious problems: violent riots in France, bombings in London.

Another issue in many countries, including developed ones, is the status of aboriginal peoples, for example in Australia, Canada and the USA among richer countries, and in Latin America, China and India among developing ones. Many communities in these countries were almost wiped out by policies close to planned genocides in some cases, and by neglect, displacement and disease in others. They often ended up demoralised, fragmented and with high levels of alcoholism and criminalisation. A particularly vicious sustained onslaught was that on native villagers in Guatemala between 1954 and 1995, conducted by militias and military with US assistance. Nevertheless, there have been some major improvements in the past decade, some of them proactively negotiated by governments, for example in New Zealand, and some concessions after years of pressure.

Thus the security agenda has extended beyond concerns with national borders to include 'non-traditional' security threats such as terrorism, organised crime, poverty, epidemics, drugs, hunger, natural disasters, illegal migration and refugees, environmental degradation, resource scarcity and poor governance. The view is sometimes expressed (although in our opinion it is a gross over-simplification) that

Box 1.2 **The origins of the UK National Health Service and human security**

"This report argues that we are at such a point in the world's history today that we should be thinking revolutionary thoughts that will shape the next one hundred years of social progress" (Beveridge 1942).

"The UK's National Health Service (NHS) came into operation at midnight on 4 July 1948, US Independence Day. It was the first time anywhere in the world that completely free healthcare was made available on the basis of citizenship rather than the payment of fees or insurance premiums. The service has been beset with problems throughout its lifetime, not least a continuing shortage of cash, but having cared for the nation for half a century, most Britons consider the NHS to have been an outstanding success" (BBC 1998), with the promise that 'everybody, irrespective of means, age, sex or occupation shall have equal opportunity to benefit from the best and most up-to-date medical and allied services available'. The services should be comprehensive and free of charge and should promote good health as well as treating sickness and disease. In purely medical terms the NHS has been an enormous success. One measure is in promoting longevity: men and women are living about 10 years longer on average than they did in 1948—men to 74 and women to 79. Despite its shortfalls, for the British it remains very popular and the top political priority.

The NHS was born out of the Dawson Report of 1920 which recommended a comprehensive system under the auspices of a single authority. The creation of the Emergency Medical Service in the Second World War added impetus and provided experience of how such universal healthcare, free at the point of delivery, might work in peacetime. In 1942 Sir William Beveridge, an eminent economist and first Director of the London School of Economics, identified a national health service as one of three essential elements of a viable social security system and pioneered the idea of human security at a time of threats to national security. War had brought the country together to focus on national priorities, just as climate change could be having the same galvanising effect today.

It is important to make the connection between social security, human security and national security. In his report, Beveridge makes the following comment:

"Organisation of social insurance should be treated as one part only of a comprehensive policy on social progress. Social insurance fully developed may provide income security: it is an attack on Want. But Want is only one of five giants on the road to reconstruction and in some ways the easiest to attack. The others are Disease, Ignorance, Squalor and Idleness (unemployment)" (Beveridge 1942: para 8).

Canada and Norway emphasise a definition of human security summarised as 'freedom from fear', stressing protection against violence and the effective implementation of human rights; while Japan, in line with other Asian countries including China, puts more stress on 'freedom from want': that is, assuring basic livelihoods and access to food, water and medical care. Some theorists, however, object that the very broad definitions of human security make the term amorphous, almost meaningless, or at least impossible to realise.

The current debate in the USA on the provision of universal healthcare provides a real contrast with Europe's experience in this area of positive peace building. Europeans had experienced at first hand the depression and two wars and were clear in their common understanding of collectivism, shown in a negative, destructive way in the shared fight for national objectives which had killed near neighbours, brothers, sisters and lovers. William Beveridge, the author of a report on social security in the UK in 1942, which set the foundations for the National Health Service (NHS), said: 'Now when the war is abolishing landmarks of every kind, is the opportunity for using experience in a clear field. A revolutionary moment in the world's history is a time for revolutions, not for patching' (Beveridge 1942).

It is no accident that the Europeans, Japan and New Zealand have by and large managed to develop the world's greatest economic global trade and social security nets (not for Japan) for all their populations with half the per capita carbon footprint of the USA, Canada and Australia and higher social cohesion, lower crime rate, greater democratic participation and greater longevity than the USA. After thousands of years of development and many centuries of war and economic recession some European nations have managed to develop a model of social democracy that delivers both quality of life and a high standard of living. Neither of the world's two largest economies, China and the USA, has so far managed to develop this level of sophistication and they may not even attempt to evolve in this direction unless the European model proves to be an irrefutably better system of organisation for a contemporary state and economy.

The Nobel Prize-winning economist Amartya Sen has written that 'to build a country, build a school' because the greatest acts of liberation and emancipation are derived from basic education and the enablement of access to information and democratic decision-making. In his writing over the last half century he has argued for fundamental rights as central to development (Sen 2002). Telling people they are free is not enough, telling people they can compete freely is not enough, and the absence of war is not enough. Positive peace is built on enabling structures and institutions that provide fundamental education and healthcare, founded on the principles of the rule of law, access to compensation and dispute resolution, and equal opportunities enshrined in human rights legislation. These aspects of community building can only be brought about by positive goals which seek to make resilience, social cohesion and mobility core characteristics of any civilised society. There are numerous examples of societies that have radically transformed themselves through applying these principles over the last century. Obvious post-Second World War examples are Japan, Costa Rica, Cuba and most of Europe—all places which now have high life expectancy, high life satisfaction, relatively high levels of social cohesion, and mid-to-low carbon footprints.

The chapters in *New Perspectives on Human Security*

Across all the chapters in this edited volume there are common foundational touchstones. Many make reference to the ideas of Roosevelt, Boutros Boutros-Ghali, Kofi Annan, Amartya Sen and Sadako Ogata, the UNDP Report of 1994, and Michel Foucault on bio-governance. And these are indeed good places for the student of human security to start their investigation of the idea. Chapter 2 by David Roberts is subtitled 'The calculated mismanagement of life' and carries a theme that resonates in all the chapters: almost all human tragedies are avoidable. Just this thought alone is enough to light the fire of debate across the many 'security' discourses. Witness Paul D. Williams's *Security Studies* (Williams 2008: 1): 'The concept [of security] saturates contemporary societies all around the world'. *Human* security is sometimes seen as a subset within the security debate but, as this book attests, it is at the heart of all the other debates with its unapologetic focus on the person, on people and peoples and community. But, as Roberts says: 'Human security has been a hard kite to fly. Perhaps its greatest value is as a measurement of our civilisational advancement; or perhaps as an end-point of cumulative development'.

Chapter 3 by Hitomi Kubo echoes another theme that runs through these chapters: that human security represents a paradigm shift as it focuses on the individual rather than traditional notions of security based on the sovereignty of the nation. We must be careful of misusing Thomas Kuhn's understanding of paradigm shift as, when it comes to human security, the shift may be true more in the thinking than in the practice. In a sense this is what Kubo writes about: the problems of recreating and operationalising security from national security to human security. Kubo also helps us understand human security by looking at the concept from different perspectives: people-centred, comprehensive, intersectoral, prevention-focused and context-specific.

Roberts argues that 'it is clear that more honest appraisals of cause and effect in the international system can be derived from elements of Foucault's work on power as framework for thinking about human security and insecurity'. Foucault's work on bio-governance is one of the themes that runs across these chapters and leads to Hazel Barrett's chapter on HIV/AIDS and 'the rise of biopolitics'. She argues that HIV/AIDS has played a central role in 'the incorporation of health security within the new human security paradigm'. While Barrett's chapter is mostly focused on healthcare issues in Africa, Deepayan Basu Ray's chapter takes the human security paradigm to the world's largest and most financially prosperous nation and critiques the lack of universal healthcare in the USA. In so doing Basu Ray and Barrett apply the human security paradigm to the richest and the poorest countries and show why this concept is so powerful in identifying individuals and communities within nation states who live in a state of fear and want. Also, in both their chapters they highlight the link between healthcare and governance, between fundamental human rights and GDP and governance and government.

Section III, on 'The environmental imperative, sustainable enterprise and human security', contains five chapters that make the link between business and human security with emphases on the natural environment, climate change, corporate responsibility and the emerging sustainable enterprise economy. Written in the immediate aftermath of the UN's Climate Change Conference in Copenhagen in December 2009, otherwise known as COP15, Chapter 6, by Malcolm McIntosh, seeks to learn some lessons from what has been described variously as a fiasco, a disaster and a missed opportunity by looking at the state of the world and trying to find new ways of co-creating a better future and developing a sustainable enterprise economy which incorporates the fundamentals of the human security paradigm.

Nicky Black's chapter runs through the development of voluntary corporate responsibility initiatives over the last decade and makes the link from them to the Millennium Development Goals (MDGs) and the concept of human security. She makes reference to Habermas's 'postnational constellation' and Zadek's 'civil market behaviour' and in doing so highlights once again one of the themes of this book: how we construct the post-state global governance given what we now know about ourselves, our success as a race and the state of the planet. The chapters by Black, and Yasunobu Sato and Dylan Scudder focus on one of the most imaginative but disputed voluntary initiatives of the past decade, that of the UN Global Compact (UNGC), which was designed to provide a learning space for business and the UN to think about how markets could help deliver the MDGs.[3] Sato and Scudder want to add an 11th principle to the UN Global Compact:

> Businesses should support concerted efforts by the United Nations and other international organisations to build and maintain peace and security; and support measures for conflict prevention and peacebuilding, and for protection of people in armed conflict, as well as empowerment of their capacity for human security at all times.[4]

The authors want to bring business and the UN together on human security by marrying the UN Global Compact to work being carried out in other parts of the

---

3 For background on the UN Global Compact and its history see McIntosh *et al.* 2004.
4 This working definition was first proposed by Professors Tatsuro Kunugi and Yasunobu Sato as an addition to the UNGC's ten principles and presented at a seminar held by the ARCHS (Applied Research Centre in Human Security) programme of Coventry University as part of the ESRC (Economic and Social Research Council) seminar series on human security in June 2008.

UN on human security. Heaven forbid, now there's an idea: that the UN should work non-tribally!

Liliane Mouan and Miho Taka's chapters on oil in Angola and coltan mining in DRC, respectively, highlight the links between international business and human security and what has come to be known as the 'resource curse'. In the case of oil, exploration requires significant expertise and investment to make extraction viable, while coltan mining tends to be artisanal, but the supply chain issues are not dissimilar. Both products are vital to the working of the current global economy, both are strategic assets, and both tend to be located in areas of the world where extraction is difficult. And, both exemplify the categorisations that Kubo lists in Chapter 3 of this book.

In Chapter 11, Marci Green writes on conflict and human relations and community with perspectives that are new to the human security discourse. Attachment theory—'a relational model of the mind and emotional development'—should, Marci Green argues, be part of the terrain of human security. This makes perfect sense when she reminds us that often development projects focus on hard infrastructure rather than soft emotional needs and social networks, which it is assumed will be delivered if children are sent to school, courthouses are built and clean water flows. Of course these things are important, indeed vital, in providing the infrastructure for human security, but how to build resilient, socially cohesive communities may be more to do with love than buildings. Which leads inexorably to Sarah Green and Alan Hunter's chapter on the disputed territory of reconciliation in Northern Ireland and a call for a better 'understanding of interface concerns to address the direct effects and disadvantages of violent conflict'.

Violence and keeping conflict at bay so that stability and positive peace become the norm are obviously central themes to human security, and Vesselin Popovski's introductory chapter to Section V on 'Human security and the responsibility to protect (R2P)' elaborates the links between this concept and human security. If, as Popovski says, human security broadly links a range of related issues which are common to all humanity at all times, then R2P 'only applies to [victims of] the most serious international crimes'. People might expect their state to protect them from genocide and mass murder, but the last 100 years has exposed this expectation as myth, since it is often the state that has committed these crimes. In these instances the world surely has a responsibility to protect innocent people; a commitment to protection of victims in such extreme circumstances, then, is a fundamental principle of human security and perhaps fundamentally challenges the legitimacy of the nation state and the UN's membership itself—although Popovski does not go as far as to state this conclusion.

Responsibility to protect (R2P) is the theme of the final three chapters by Bruce Baker, Manish Jha and Toru Sagawa. Baker's chapter analyses policing in Africa, or rather, the failure of policing. The police in many African states are part of an insidious culture of corruption where they fail to protect, fail to apply the law and act as a semi-lawless group dealing out arbitrary punishment. They are, Baker states, themselves often the perpetrators of human rights abuses. Manish Jha's chapter is set in the 'tribal hinterlands of India where the Maoists . . . are waging war against the state'. As he says, the human security paradigm calls on the state to serve the people, not the reverse, and in this conflict the state is found lacking in its ability to protect its people. Toru Sagawa's chapter is concerned with 'pastoralists in East Africa . . . operating under a state without the capacity or will to protect its subjects'. This chapter neatly rounds off the book and brings us back to the main themes: the sanctity of the individual, the pervasive threats to human life and well-being, and the inability of the state in many cases, whether in the USA, India or the DRC, to protect its own people and provide the basic necessities of life. The chapters highlight the fact that it is possible to prevent almost all human tragedies, as Roberts argues. They implicitly raise a key point, often overlooked in writing on human security, that there are also many states and communities that do manage to deliver freedom from fear and freedom from want to large proportions of their populations. Celebration of these exemplars, and more importantly learning from them, is a key task for the future of human security.

Conclusion: sustainable human security

The sustainability imperative is now perhaps more critical than ever before: both scientific and public opinion recognises that the impacts of climate change, resource depletion and environmental degradation may soon radically transform our way of life. It is possible to argue that sustainability is the fourth revolution for humanity after the revolutions of agriculture, industrialisation and information. The 'human security' agenda will surely have to engage with these issues with increasing urgency. There are many signs that businesses are engaging with them also. This is partly in response to consumer pressure for ethical trading and lower carbon emissions, partly to cope with regulation and higher fuel costs, and for a variety of other reasons. The term 'sustainable enterprise' is becoming more widely used to denote the strategies involved in these developments and changes in the wider economy. We need to engage with a dynamic for sustainable human security.

References

BBC (1998) 'The NHS: "One of the Greatest Achievements in History" ', news.bbc.co.uk/1/hi/events/nhs_at_50/special_report/123511.stm, accessed 23 September 2010.

Beveridge, W. (1942) 'Beveridge Report on Social Insurance and Allied Services' (Cmnd 6404; London: HMSO): para 7.

Commission on Human Security (2003) *Human Security Now* (New York: Commission on Human Security; www.humansecurity-chs.org/finalreport/English/FinalReport.pdf, accessed 22 September 2010).

Evan, G., M Sahnoun, G. Côté-Harper and L Hamilton, (2001) 'The Responsibility to Protect' (Report of the International Commission on Intervention and State Sovereignty, December 2001; www.iciss.ca).

Jolly, R., and B. Ray (2006) *The Human Security Framework* (New York: UNDP).

Kaldor, M. (2007) *Human Security: Reflections on Globalization and Intervention* (Cambridge, UK: Polity Press).

Mani, D. (2002) *Human Security: Concepts and Definitions* (Tokyo: UN Centre for Regional Development).

McIntosh, M. (2006) 'Human Security Solutions Require Sustainable Enterprise', *Compact Quarterly*, November 2006; www.enewsbuilder.net/globalcompact/e_article000688256.cfm?x=b11,0,w, accessed 23 September 2010.

——, S. Waddock and G. Kell (eds.) (2004) *Learning to Talk: Corporate Citizenship and the Development of the UN Global Compact* (Sheffield, UK: Greenleaf Publishing).

Owen, R. (2006) 'Ring of steel locks in immigrants', *The Times*, 11 August 2006; www.timesonline.co.uk/tol/news/world/europe/article605507.ece, accessed 22 September 2010.

Sen, A. (2002) 'To Build a Country, Build a Schoolhouse', *New York Times*, 27 May 2002.

UNDP (1994) *Human Development Report 1994: New Dimensions of Human Security* (New York: UNDP).

Vollebaek, K. (1999) 'A Perspective on Human Security', Chairman's summary at the *1st Ministerial Meeting of the Human Security Network*, Lysøen, Norway, 20 May 1999.

Williams, P.D. (2008) *Security Studies: An Introduction* (London: Routledge).

2

Human security and global governance

The calculated mismanagement of life

David Roberts

Social and Policy Research Institute, University of Ulster, UK

Human security, like all security, is a contested concept. That is, it is construed and represented in a subjective fashion, in parallel with all other matters claimed to be security issues by virtue of the language used. That we disagree about it routinely attests to its contested character. Even its claim to the apparel of security is contentious, since tradition and convention have rejected this 'pretender' not as a security concept but as a liberal nostrum that belongs in the ontologically distinct annals of development studies or human rights discourse. It has been considered and labelled more hot air than paradigm shift (Paris 2001); as intellectually incoherent and bereft of focus (Freedman 1998); and it is considered conceptually promiscuous (Stoett 1999).

From such schools and perspectives, themselves deeply divided, it is considered ontologically naive and epistemologically illegitimate. Commenting on this exclusionary discourse stemming from and protected by conventions of tradition, Kyle Grayson writes that 'cosmological realism functions as a gatekeeper, preventing the intrusion of anything that might unsettle [some] shared norms about what can count as knowledge' and what can and should count as security (Grayson 2008: 394). This gatekeeper practice has permitted a narrow understanding of human security, represented well by Andy Mack's *Human Security Report* (2005). But in defining the limits of the possible, it has also co-opted and subsumed human security within the bounds of the possible, according to Chandler (2008) and Roberts (2010). Given the inevitably and predictably illiberal nature of mainstream and tradition, and the intolerance and suspicion with which conservative paradigm owners treat challenge generally, this should not be surprising. Upendra Baxi understood this well when he wrote that political tradition serves to encode 'power and hierarchy, allocate competencies (who may speak), construct forms (how one may speak, what forms of discourse are proper), determine boundaries (what may not be named or conversed about), and structure exclusion (denial of voice)' (Baxi 1998: 129). Realism and tradition dictate what is and what may be considered matters of security.

If realism engages weakly with a narrow interpretation of human security, defined loosely as—but limited tightly by—the idea of damage to civilians occurring as a consequence of political violence, it effectively rejects the broader imaginings of what human security can and does mean. At this other end of the spectrum, human security stands for clearly stated but ill-conceptualised and defined—perhaps even abstract—notions such as 'freedom from want and fear'; the 'vital core' of human being; as 'vital freedoms'; or as human dignity. In some ways, one might sympathise with mainstream security for not engaging with a concept that no one has adequately defined or delimited beyond what mainstream security writers too numerous to recount have suggested is a fantasy of an unrealisable utopian ideal. But if we were to take from this that the broader human security project is well regarded beyond the canons and corridors of realism and other state-centric emphases on security, we would be wrong, for it has few friends presently in academia and fewer still in global policy-making circles.

Indeed, at times, it seems it cannot do right for doing wrong. If it is rejected from a conservative angle as incoherent, it is critiqued from a more critical and emancipatory perspective as being a means by which the liberal West dictates the evolution of the global South and as a control technology that sanctions intervention in the sovereign affairs of less economically developed countries while being primarily concerned in reality with the security of those in the economically more developed world (Duffield 2005; Chandler 2008; Roberts 2010). And from within, it is rent by divides over what human security can mean, with a range of participants variously proposing limits to the concept's breadth for purposes of practicability (Kaldor *et al.* 2007) or claiming the concept is constrained mainly by the permissions granted it by realist-dystopic discourses (Roberts 2010). It has thus been rejected by mainstream security, rendered unintelligible by definitional disagreements, disparaged as a means by which interventionary liberal imperialism is sanctioned, and vilified as a disguise for traditional security interests in the global North. Some have even suggested it should be dropped entirely and energy directed instead at instigating alternative approaches to reinvigorate a process whose value has been marginalised and undermined by the wrangling that has failed to evoke agreement even on a most basic meaning (Cooper 2009).

To circumvent these challenges, I present a consideration of human security revolving around **biopoverty**. Biopoverty is the avoidable absence of resources—nutrition, medicine, water, sanitation, vaccination—without which civilians die unnecessarily. It is remediable. It stands at the nexus of the biologically essential and the economically prohibited. It is structural and institutional in character, since it is socially constructed and mobilised around rules that determine the in/accessibility of available life-preserving resources. For brevity, it may be considered the remediable denial of physiological necessity. It encompasses a large enough number of lethalities to warrant being taken seriously and being prioritised on the grounds of avoidable civilian mortality, but it is also solvable.

The intellectual virtue of this approach is that it forces engagement with the elephant in the room, of power in global governance. As David Chandler (2008) and David Roberts (2008b, 2010) have noted, there is a persistent lacuna in the literature concerning power in the international system. If power is engaged with critically and constructively, it reveals avoidable and preventable institutional abuse of humans in their millions, as well as standing as a critique of realist ontology and epistemology. And when engaged with constructively, it also allows for solutions, since responses cannot be properly considered without an honest consideration of cause. Crucially, it cannot be disconnected from the notion of power in the international system. Not power in material terms, but the power of ideas and the priorities afforded them. This is the power of neo-liberal global governance.

Global governance

From a liberal-institutionalist perspective, global governance is largely a response to globalisation, or 'the deterritorialisation of traditional concepts, which are rhizomatically disaggregated from their indigenous contexts and re-synthesised in unanticipated ways that make them globally efficacious among types of people and groups with certain shared interests' (Eade 1997: 5). Mainstream views consider global governance as functional and necessary to manage the unevenness of tumultuous globalisation, since its range and scope far exceeds the capacity for regulation of the traditional unit of authority in the international system. James Rosenau and Ernst-Otto Czempiel (1992: 3) suggest that this 'governance without government' involved 'functions that have to be performed in any viable human system irrespective of whether the system has evolved organisations and institutions explicitly charged with performing them'. The idea that this process is beneficial is taken up by Yakub Halabi (2004: 21), who describes global governance as marking 'the acceptance of regulations at the global level out of a conviction that such regulations will enable actors to seek wealth in an orderly fashion and in accordance with the norms of the international system'. Global governance has thus been defined as 'the management of global political and economic space in the absence of a global state' (Solomon 2006: 327).

That it is technocratic, impartial, procedural and cooperative and aimed at mutual beneficence is a theme pursued commonly in this literature. Riordan Wilkinson notes:

how the steady development of international institutions and regimes
have, when taken in the aggregate, led to the emergence of a web of
international norms, treaties, and conventions that encourage sustained
co-operation among states and, in so doing, generate a measure of international governance (Wilkinson 2004: 4).

In a similar vein, James Rosenau (1995: 13) considers global governance as something 'conceived to include systems of rule at all levels of human activity—from
the family to the international organisation—in which the pursuit of goals through
the exercise of control has transnational repercussions'. And Robert Keohane and
Joseph Nye represent international institutions and governance as politically passive systems (2000: 37).

More recent scholarship has gone further. The incoming editorship of the prominent journal *Global Governance* declared in 2006 that there were many elements to
global governance; but while they briefly alluded to the notion of a planetary rules
regime being rooted in something called 'structure', the emphasis in the journal is
very clearly on what they describe as 'multilayered regulation' (Carin *et al.* 2006:
3). Like much of the literature on this subject, the respected *Global Governance*
journal largely conceives of its subject matter in neutral terms; identifies its core
elements as institutional in nature; and has little to say about global governance in
ideological and ideational terms (Diehl 1997). As Cornelia Beyer (2008: 23) notes,
'the concept remains empirical, is not normative or prescriptive and provides a
description of real processes of change in the international system'. Similarly, the
Commission on Global Governance (1995: 2-3) remarks that global governance is
'not founded on domination but upon accommodation'. And James Rosenau (1997:
1) is equally clear about the neutrality of global governance when he writes that 'the
organising perspective is that of governance in the world rather than governance
of the world. The latter implies a central authority that is doing the governing, an
implication that clearly has no basis in fact'. Global governance, in this view, relates
to a system of multi-level arrangements that exists to manage the fluctuations, dis-
tortions, accidents, trends, moods, transformations, traditional security dilemmas
and other disasters and developments that routinely punctuate and characterise
contemporary global life. In a sense, this literature tends to treat international institutions and regimes *as* governance.

Power in global governance

More recently, from alternative epistemologies and ontologies, another perspective recognises much of the technocratic determinism outlined in the liberal-institutionalist literature, but then departs radically from the claim that partisan and
ideational power is absent from global governance. According to Barnett and Duvall
(2006), persisting in considering power in terms of a liberal-institutionalist/state-

centric 'central authority' is not just intellectually moribund but also carries with it very real risks in the 'real world' of everyday human lives. They argue that 'failure to develop alternative conceptualisations of power limits the ability of international relations scholars to understand how global outcomes are produced and how actors are differentially enabled and constrained to determine their fates' (Barnett and Duvall 2006: 41). In short, they argue that 'concern with power . . . brings attention to global structures, processes, and institutions that shape the fates and life chances of actors around the world' (2006: 7-8; Lines 2008). There are inevitable implications for broad human security in observing the relationships between governance, power and outcomes: neo-liberal structure, institutional projection and human in/security.

Barnett and Duvall are not alone in this view. Others have considered power in global governance and identified a variety of forms. Kapstein (2005), for example, suggests that international institutions, as the heart of global governance, may change or maintain conditions or processes in ways that benefit some more than others. Thus, neo-liberal institutional architectures create and/or perpetuate hierarchies of advantage and disadvantage by dictating and maintaining uneven preferences and practices in a range of economic regimes which aggravate postcolonial asymmetries of relative prosperity and poverty. Affirming such a proposition is the wealth of qualitative critical international political economy scholarship that identifies distorted practices and uneven playing fields that challenge neo-liberal claims of free markets and fair practices (Williams 1994; Payne 2005; Greig *et al.* 2007). Of great importance also, Ian Johnstone (2005) identifies a second type of power present in global governance as 'productive'. This refers to the ability to represent a subjective concept as an objective, absolute and neutral truth. Economics, for example, is presented in the neo-liberal mainstream as a neutral science when the plethora of contending perspectives and priorities suggest it cannot be so; human nature is presented as universal and a scientific fact when no such scientific evidence has ever existed; common sense is claimed as an absolute when it is a subjective and shifting collection of prejudices and preferences. All claim a universality and reliability which none can prove, but they enjoy productive power since they are accepted and taken for granted by many, in part because they normally enjoy hegemony; they are dominant norms. A third form of power in governance, discussed by Barnett and Duvall (2006) involves structures, or transnational social rules systems which, when combined with the hegemony of productive discourses, are responsible for creating and perpetuating material and capability inequality. And, since these concepts of power permeate the institutions and practices of global governance and are projected by them, governance itself is a form of power. However, even from such an enlightened perspective, structure as power is still considered in relatively conventional terms, such as class and related social and economic divides.

Departing from such limitations, Felix Berenskoetter argues that power at the global level maintains the institutions, beliefs and practices that underpin it. Perhaps yet more importantly, Berenskoetter maintains that power can also be applied to challenge and change a given scenario, implying clearly that power is 'responsible for both change and continuity' in the international system (Berenskoetter 2007: 13). That is, intentional or unintentional agency is required both to maintain a status quo and to transform it. Berenskoetter (2007: 13) further contends that if the exercise of power makes a difference then 'identifying power is analytically indistinguishable with identifying cause'. 'This is significant', he argues, 'because it also means identifying who/what is responsible for the ways things are, or are likely, to be . . . Power can be made analytically responsible for phenomena of both change and continuity' (Berenskoetter 2007: 13). For this argument to be constructively pursued requires that traditional conventions relating to power and global governance be left behind, in search of a more nuanced framework in which to pursue human security.

Global governmentality?

Similar to Cox's (1983) elevation of Gramsci's analysis of hegemony from state to international level, the following section traces and further develops the adoption of Foucault's analysis of state power over national life (governmentality) to the international level (global governmentality). Governmentality as a concept refers to the notion that a state's power over its territorially bound population relates to particular forms of governmental practice that are extended through a society to achieve control (Foucault 2003). Foucault expressed government as the means by which population life was modulated: disciplined and punished, with the sovereign owning, ultimately, the right to end life in certain circumstances. He suggested that government power was not solely centralised but was 'capillary', in the sense that the power of the state circulated through a national territory by way of decentralised organs and instruments of states tasked with socio-biological management. Although initially addressing institutions such as schools and prisons as aspects of decentralised and omnipotent control, many other bodies extend this capillary power into human lives, from tax declarations to driving licence numbers to ID cards, allowing for the regulation of life-by-state. It was biopolitical in the sense that it represents the 'calculated management of life' (Foucault 1979: 140).

This approach can be applied to the level of global governance. Ronnie Lipschutz (2005) remarks that 'although Foucault wrote only about governmentality within states, with each separate [state] order constituting its own sphere of normality and discipline, the extension of his idea to the international arena is rather straightforward'. He continues that:

> Global governmentality is more than the sum of national governmentalities; it is more than the state system and its associated organs; it is more than the standard definitions of global governance. It is an arrangement of actors and institutions, of rules and rule, through which the architecture

> of the global articulation of states and capitalism is maintained . . . The management of human populations and their environments—the exercise of compulsory and institutional power—is the task of both the agencies of government and the populations themselves (Lipschutz 2005: 235-36).

Both national and global government and governance modulate life. Increasingly, Foucault's thought is being propelled into the global as a means of describing the processes of global governance, in terms of both neo-liberal virtuosity and liberal disciplinarity. Even though Foucault 'left us guessing as to what [his] analysis of the international would look like' (Albert and Lenco 2008: 265), we may reasonably extrapolate such a process. Michael Merlingen (2008: 272-73) argues that conjoining Foucauldian imaginings and global governance 'with a view to assembling a larger picture of the biopolitical character of the international' would facilitate 'a powerful critical sociology . . . for the exploration of world order'.

Taking this approach further, Michael Dillon and Julian Reid argue that 'global liberal governance' involves 'a varied and complex regime of power, whose founding principle lies in the administration and production of life'. They continue that global governance 'is substantially comprised of techniques that examine the detailed properties and dynamics of populations so that they can be better managed with respect to their many needs and life chances' (Dillon and Reid 2001: 41, 46). Biopolitical neo-liberalism, or global governance, is concerned 'with the detailed knowledgeable strategies and tactics that affect the constitution of life and the regulation of the affairs of populations, no matter how these are specified' (Sorensen 2002: 12-13). Jo Rowlands notes that governance of this kind 'affects us all', adding that this process 'refers to social, cultural and political phenomena that deeply shape and govern daily life and what happens within it' (Rowlands 2008: 801). It affects almost everyone on the planet in different ways, determined in part by the specific values of governance invoked at particular times, reflecting the numerous and varied manifestations and multifarious consequences of different imaginings of this means of extending power, control and direction over human life. Global governance at the international level, then, is as biopolitical as government at the national level. Governmentality and biopolitics can be understood to operate at the global level through:

> a pervasive, complex and heterogeneous network of practices. Structuring the desires, proprieties and possibilities that shape the operation of life, working on and through subjective freedoms, governmental rationalities typically develop around specific problematics, such as those of health, wealth, security, poverty, esteem, culture or migration (Dillon and Reid 2001: 48).

Global governance can be understood, then, as the means by which neo-liberal beliefs are authorised and projected around the world, with variations in policy being explained by state desire for homogeneity with neo-liberal precepts, or state capacity to resist or ignore that assimilation, which accounts for the paradox whereby more powerful Northern states may urge privatisation of public provision while delivering public services themselves. For example, the international financial institutions (IFIs) are part of the supranational capillary distribution system that subverts state sovereignty to dictate national social policy (Deacon *et al.* 1997). State acquiescence to or cooperation with such processes furthers capillary circulation, while neo-liberal propaganda asserting the absence of alternatives fuses national societies to global governance. The spread of neo-liberal diktat through capillary power and institutions is more pronounced in the global South, but this pattern of ideational neo-liberal power is also apparent in the global North, as neo-liberal ideation is hegemonic, even if its authority is challenged.

It is in this interpretation of power and global governance that we find the nexus of power and biopoverty, and the visible connection between variable rates of human security and insecurity in the North and South. I refer to human security and insecurity in this sense as produced by global governance. It reflects the outcomes of neo-liberal ideational hegemony and institutional authority, since it is neo-liberal prescription that is predominant in both hemispheres, but with greater capacity to resist its fiat normally found in the North, and greater submission by state authority to its will found in the South. This is due to the power of conditionality in very poor states—although Harrison (2007) makes it clear that some states in the South are able to resist or manipulate this process to varying degrees. Global governance is the modulation of planetary life by hegemonic neo-liberal ideation. Global governmentality projects its hegemony and priorities through the neo-liberal institutional architecture of the international system. This includes bodies such as the World Bank and the World Trade Organisation (WTO), Amnesty International, Transparency International, Lawyers for Human Rights and a plethora of smaller NGOs working at grass-roots level and invested with neo-liberal values and expectations.

Neo-liberal prescription treats the public sector as a matter for the markets. Global governmentality regarding water, sanitation and hygiene—the absence of which strike children hardest—dictates market provision and state subsidy termination in situations where people have no or insufficient money to pay for such provision when marketised, creating biopolitical contingencies experienced transnationally across sub-state populations. It proscribes state subsidies in public provision, and it prescribes marketisation of public services, including health, education, utilities and so on. The absence of clean water, sanitation and hygiene (WASH) is the greatest immediate and proximal cause of easily preventable death in the world. Medical epidemiology, unencumbered by ideological challenges to its natural sciences epistemology, reveals the true extent of child mortality. It notes the causes in terms of inadequate water treatment for public health needs, and it records this data in numerous globally recognised bodies such as the World Health Organisation (WHO). It discusses these matters among an increasingly concerned and involved medical science community (Taback and Coupland 2007; Piachaud 2008; Roberts 2008a), including venerable canons of medical scholarship such as *The Lancet* and its editorial (Black 2003; Victora 2004; Stoltenberg 2006). Science does not doubt the causal relationship between inadequate water treatment and avoidable mortality (Mackenbach 2007). It is the argument of this work that the absence of physiological necessity—the condition of biopoverty affecting tens of millions of people—is directly a consequence of global governance.

Confronting biopoverty and human security

R.J. Rummel famously refers us to the idea of deliberate 'death by government', or democide, in which he invites us to consider the state as the cause of death of millions of its own citizens (1997). In this process, the state exercises the ultimate in biopolitical governmentality. Most states function similarly in terms of control, with some still applying *in extremis* the traditional sovereign right to put offenders to death, as in Afghanistan, Botswana, China, Egypt, Japan, the Palestinian Authority, the US and Vietnam. 'Death by government' is therefore familiar. If we willingly accept the idea of global governance, as the literature plainly does, then it is only a small step to extending Rummel's notion to the international, where we are presented with the idea of **death by governance**, since some institutions of global governance plainly contribute to lethal, and avoidable, biopoverty and death en masse by selecting and applying policies and practices that ignore the avoidability of that mortality. A crucial distinction is, of course, that there is no evidence of deliberate intent attached to death by global governance. It is, rather, death by dogma.

We have observed global governance through a Foucauldian lens and seen government and governance as similarly biopolitical and regulatory. Furthermore, if, in the tradition of the social sciences, we are to accept that no social process is infallible, and if we are to accept that global governance preferences inevitably have positive and negative outcomes, then we may consider the downside of global governance more honestly, perhaps as death in the midst of life. Just as low mortality rates in Western Europe are a product of biopolitical governance, so too are high mortality rates in parts of Africa, Asia and elsewhere a consequence of biopolitical global governance, as this supranational hegemony directs and prohibits national policies and practices that determine biopoverty. Mass, avoidable mortality, especially among children under five and birthing mothers, is a proximal consequence of an unreflective and dogmatic liberal idealism, sustained in part through outmoded and sometimes outlandish adherence to falsifiable conclusions drawn from the unreliable and inappropriate application of Enlightenment scientific epistemologies and ontologies to the global social sphere.

There is, then, a connection between global governance, biopolitics and the regulation of human security. And, by continuing in a Foucauldian vein, we are presented with a means of protecting life in the midst of death. Just as his interpretations of power and governmentality help us understand and describe global governance more thoughtfully, we may also draw from some of his thinking on national population contingencies and consider them in a transnational context as the first step in making human security both meaningful and doable.

In the same way that I have built on Foucault's elevation to the international (above), I apply the same approach to Foucault's thinking on populations that exhibit shared behaviours, conditions, conditioning and contingencies, with a view to rendering operable the human security concept. Foucault referred to territorially bounded populations within sovereign jurisdiction which shared certain characteristics that were formed in part by the state, around which state policy evolved. These include matters of health or education provision, which empower, and institutions such as prisons, which repress. Governmentality was the outcome of concern with such contingencies (Foucault 1979). A familiar example is the common state response to dealing with water-borne disease in Europe towards the end of the 19th century. Recognition of the damage done by disease, coupled with the co-option of scientific thought on how to manage such crises, resulted in state policies such as public engineering programmes to increase sanitation provision and, later, appropriate healthcare and education strategies managed by the state.

It is this analysis of the biopolitical management of diverse populations around shared characteristics and contingencies that provides a template for thinking about global governance, biopolitics and human security. From this perspective, global governance becomes analytically indivisible from Foucauldian biopolitics, and determines life chances for human groups that are not state-defined but which can be mapped across sovereign boundaries of groups of humans experiencing similar contingencies and requiring, as a consequence, similar biopolitical interventions to maintain life, or, in the case of international war, to end it. It is such groups that may provide the basis and focus for a more coherent reorientation of human security directed not at the universal-individual but towards the 'calculated management of life' (Foucault 1979: 140) of human groupings not specific to territories 'with all the conditions that can cause these to vary' (Foucault 1979: 139). Simply put, when presented in biopolitical terms, global governance authorises and prescribes policies that threaten mortality en masse not only within groups of people within a sovereign boundary, but also in those groups of people mapped across many sovereign boundaries, among sub-state populations in many countries where those populations are similarly vulnerable from shared contingencies. Human security can be enhanced through reverse engineering: of the policies of global governance which preventably incur mass lethality.

Thus, to the adaptation of Foucault's concept of sovereign biopolitics from the national to the international, we may fuse this further adaptation of his work on sub-state populations with shared characteristics and contingencies around which state policy evolves. This involves the mapping of trans-state, intercontinental populations sharing similar characteristics and related contingencies which are functions of the practical and ideational authority of biopolitical global governance. The highest avoidable mortality rates among civilians derive from the absence of clean water and sanitation mechanisms in rural areas where income is routinely below US$2 per day and/or where conflict has ruined life. Mortality from inaccessibility to vaccines is similarly prevalent among the poorest people in the world. We may begin, then, by identifying as a priority the tens of millions of people who would live if state-subsidised WASH were not prohibited by fiat of global governance or as a result of prices being unaffordable following marketisation. And we are quite sure that people die in their millions from WASH problems because there is a wealth of scientifically verified data to tell us this (above).

What is at once puzzling, remarkable and ironic is that the solutions to these contingencies are both easy and cheap: purifying water is simple in non-conflict environments and sanitation education and provision is similarly unchallenging, while the impact of change in these areas is all but immediate as well as dispro- portionately extensive compared with inputs. How is this to be achieved? Global governance and neo-liberalism have long advocated and authorised, to the exclu- sion of local solutions, transnational corporations to privatise and render efficient otherwise inefficient state delivery of biopoverty essentials such as water (if it even exists). This has proven unsuccessful in terms of affordable pricing, since privatisa- tion in developing metropolises routinely raises water costs far above the prices paid by people in more developed capitals (Hall and Lobina 2008). Furthermore, according to Hall and Lobina, water TNCs (transnational corporations) demand taxpayer subsidies to even investigate start up costs because they have proven so inefficient and ineffective in the past, reflecting a similar departure from market practices to that facing taxpayers in the developed economies who are forced to subsidise the collapse of the Western banking system (Hall and Lobina 2008; Cam- dessus 2003; Hall 2004; Kenny 2008). Water TNCs are shying away from such ten- ders and contracts because risk is high and return is low

In some respects, this may prove to be a blessing, although this is not to say that privatisation should be ruled out. Indeed, privatisation may be a means by which aspects of biopoverty can be ended. But rather than pursuing the 'top-down' model enforced by IFIs, the UN and numerous others, some are advocating indigenous approaches. Although this has recently stemmed from a need to evolve post-con- flict situations, the approach is equally applicable to situations of biopoverty, since both require emergency recovery from disasters of often epic proportions, when measured from the perspective of people surviving war or inaccessible water, since both kill. A big difference, however, is that dirty water, either for drinking or sanita- tion, kills millions more than conflict.

The UN discusses the idea of 'indigenous drivers of economic recovery', which it classifies as 'the efforts and initiatives of local communities, individuals, house- holds and enterprises that stimulate and impel economic activity after war' (Ohior- henuan and Stewart 2008: 49). The notion is not complex. After war and/or in peacetime penury, there are almost always local people who know what communi- ties need for recovery and/or development and who have the basic skills for low- technology rebuilding. But in many places where people may well have the will and capability to rebuild their worlds, they too often lack cheap material resources. The UNDP report suggests that public development projects:

> Should use local capacities and inputs rather than imported ones in order
> to stimulate the economy in addition to providing work . . . Contracts ten-

dered to local organisations, associations and firms can help build local skills and knowledge and can also foster local enterprise capacities. Activities amenable to this approach include irrigation projects with a focus on smallholder farmers, water, sanitation and solid waste management in urban and rural areas, feeder roads and rural access infrastructure, and the reconstruction or rehabilitation of public buildings (Ohiorhenuan and Stewart 2008: 75).

The report concludes that 'economic recovery [or development] is quicker and more sustainable when it supports and builds on indigenous drivers because local actors are the best placed and have the strongest long-term incentive to engage in activities conducive to sustained economic recovery' (Ohiorhenuan and Stewart 2008: 89). Increasingly, this notion of entrepreneurialism is advanced as a means for generating development and recovery. Baumol (1990), Baumol *et al.* (2007) and Naude (2008) point to the importance of local entrepreneurialism and social responsibilities, although they are quite firm that such local industry should follow the standard neo-liberal ethos of openness to competition and accountability, as well as recognising that it can be destructive as well as creative (Baumol *et al.* 2007). But this can only be effective where external processes, institutions and ideas do not control the extent to which local agency can otherwise be realised. That is, local initiatives and ventures must not be dominated and/or constrained by rules and actors from outside; the pattern in this respect has been destructive, although not entirely.

The World Bank has intervened to facilitate such local initiatives at a small scale already, with some degree of success. In Bosnia and Herzegovina, the Bank funded two Local Initiatives Projects (LIPs) after the war of 1992–1995 which 'aimed to provide financial resources to people wanting to start their own small businesses and to take an active part in rebuilding their livelihoods instead of depending on state social welfare funds' or, presumably, doing without (Ohiorhenuan and Stewart 2008: 85; Bojicic-Dzelilovic and Causevic 2008). The Bank is also increasingly aware, at the very least rhetorically, that supporting women works for development, and it does not take a giant leap of the imagination to unite women and grant-making around, for example, WASH provision. A conceptually similar project in Ethiopia in 2000 lent US$7 million to women in the Women's Development Initiative Project (WDIP) and found that 'it is possible to empower poor, illiterate women socially and economically through small-scale and group-based micro-business initiatives' (World Bank 2007: 18).

While there should be no prizes for this conclusion, it is surprising that a project found to be 'highly successful in achieving its development objectives' should not be considered worthy of further expansion, which was the Bank's conclusion (World Bank 2007: 12). Importantly, it is evidence that the Bank has evoked tactical lending (local enterprise) already, even if the performance of the state stakeholder, rather than the beneficiaries, was a problem (World Bank 2007: 16). The potential is clear: local indigenous capacity linked to external funding determined by local priorities, rather than by externally driven development agendas that outsource development to TNCs and extract financial benefits to offshore banks, allows for an emancipatory form of human security.

A human security, sector-wide approach (SWAp)

The essence of a revised approach to biopoverty, water security and reduced child mortality, then, is to place the emphasis less on capacity-building and more on capacity-mobilising while removing the external barriers to enhancing human security and reducing biopoverty. The difference is that the human and material resources needed for WASH provision are often not absent and may not necessarily need to be 'built' or expanded dramatically, or with substantial foreign intervention. Agency is certainly present in such circumstances but it may be immobilised by structures and disconnects that can be overcome with small-scale local investment. People sometimes need money for resources or the logistical means of moving resources physically, but normally these resources are present in some form or can be fetched from nearby for cash. Furthermore, the knowledge necessary for this mobilisation is often well understood at the local level and, where it is not, there is room for consultancy contributions by the World Bank and water-orientated NGOs, such as WaterAid.

What very poor people in very poor communities often lack is the means to buy or rent, and then maintain, basic rebuilding equipment, such as earthmovers and diggers, trucks and cranes, and, as often as not, low-technology equipment such as wheelbarrows, spades and ladders. Local initiatives are wide-ranging, when people have the opportunity and support to self-mobilise, and basic projects often have substantial benefit. Building toilets near schools and villages, sinking boreholes, repairing existing facilities, connecting cheap plastic pipelines, building paths and roads to accelerate connectivity are all relatively modest exercises, compared with the transnational interventions that tend to focus on metropolises and which often result in extremely expensive water, as Hall and Lobina *et al.* have noted. But they have quite sudden and disproportionate returns. Rather than the years of investment associated with TNC activities for minimal internal benefits, locally mobilised exercises bring almost immediate reduction in foul water ingestion and intestinal diseases, while improved sanitation is similarly productive for health and mortality.

The role of interested providers in this approach would be characterised by low-key, in-country consultancy, relatively modest unconditional grant-making and lending aimed at existing local capacity, higher-end funding for distant resources, such as heavy earthmovers rentable from neighbouring provinces or countries, and communication facilitation for local private sector needs, such as radios and cell phones. International funding could support local and regional construction companies, the training and retraining of community engineers and car mechanics to maintain boreholes, and fund educators to demonstrate the efficacy of water treatment. One example might be to employ people to take basic microscopes, routinely found in children's play sets in Western countries, to communities unaware of basic hygiene rules and show the microbes in motion in their drinking water, and compare this with their absence in clean water.

The essence of provision and opportunity lies in micro-credits and grants for local people to self-mobilise, deploy their capabilities and connect with resources that lie beyond their immediate purview, to support the expansion of private sector provision of local water needs in areas worst affected by high infant mortality rates by sustaining emerging water-orientated business communities, and resource mobilisation from distant parties, where necessary. Lending would be directed through global water banks, organised at, for example, municipal level where child mortality rates are highest. These banks would act as interfaces between local need and global provision, with the former determining the latter, rather than the other way round, which is the present convention. That is, the nature of 'development' is routinely determined by trends in Western fundraising, the success or failure of particular advertising campaigns in Western countries, the interests and values of international NGOs, the changing priorities of public international bodies, and so on. Global water banks would instead communicate what was actually needed by people in stricken conditions of biopoverty (for example) and then direct those requests into the international community. Rather than a high-end, low-impact, transnational private sector neo-liberal approach to mega-projects that extract substantial profit to multinationals, this approach favours a low-end, high-impact (measured by decreases in child mortality), indigenous private sector focused on mini-projects that benefit local communities with water provision and profits for local entrepreneurialism. Conceptually speaking, this strategy can be applied across regions, since child mortality is a product of similar resource absences. Tactically thinking, different approaches in specific places would require particular localised responses undertaken within the wider strategic and sector-wide approach of WASH provision. Greater emphasis financially and tactically could be placed on under-exploited and already existing World Bank operations, such as the Local Initiatives Project (LIP). This approach also considers the different conceptions of what is and is not an impediment to human well-being as it is understood by those whose lives are always structured and often ended by water inaccessibility. According to Edward Carr, this 'poverties' approach 'does not necessarily signal the death of large-scale efforts to alleviate [water] poverty, nor does it require the abandonment of development itself. Instead, [it] forces us to seriously rethink development [and human security] goals and our means of achieving them' (2008: 727).

Conclusion

Human security has been a hard kite to fly. Perhaps its greatest value is as a measurement of our civilisational advancement; or perhaps as an end-point of cumulative development. Rather than being disparaged and dismissed as unrealistically utopian, it can instead be considered a departure from the preventable dystopia maintained and perpetuated by the unenlightened assumptions of its critics. As a means of rethinking security priorities, it lacks the consent of hegemonic security thinking and remains outside those boundaries. But, given wings big enough, it will work as more than narrow human security and less than the profound and worthy aims of its broadest imagining, a target at which we might aim. Understood with honest analysis as a function and consequence of asymmetric, ideational and hegemonic power, the institutions of its keeping can be adjusted. In workable form, it can accelerate the fixing of the truly unconscionable—the indifference towards child mortality and the adiaphoristic denial of ideational and institutional culpability globally—and it is clear that more honest appraisals of cause and effect in the international system can be derived from elements of Foucault's work on power as a framework for thinking about human security and insecurity. This honesty is essential for evolving human security; but it is also essential to understand the damage done to liberalism by its own hubris and narcissism.

Bibliography

Albert, M., and P. Lenco (2008) 'Introduction to the Forum: Foucault and International Political Sociology', *International Political Sociology* 3.2: 265-77.

Barnett, M., and R. Duvall (2006) 'Power in International Politics', *International Organization* 59: 39-75.

Baumol, W. (1990) 'Entrepreneurship: Productive, Unproductive, and Destructive', *Journal of Political Economy* 98.5: 893-921.

——, R.E. Litan and C.J. Schramm (2007) *Good Capitalism, Bad Capitalism and the Economics of Growth and Prosperity* (New Haven, CT: Yale University Press).

Baxi, U. (1998) 'Voices of Suffering and the Future of Human Rights', *Transnational Law and Contemporary Problems* 125.8: 125-70.

Berenskoetter, F. (2007) 'Thinking about Power', in F. Berenskoetter and M.J.W. Williams (eds.), *Power in World Politics* (London: Routledge): 1-23.

Beyer, C. (2008) *Violent Globalisms: Conflict in Response to Empire* (Aldershot, UK: Ashgate).

Black, R. (2003) 'Where and why are 10 million children dying every year?', *The Lancet* 361.9376: 2,226-34.

Bojicic-Dzelilovic, V., and F. Causevic (2008) 'Microfinance in Post-conflict Economic Recovery: Lessons from Bosnia and Herzegovina' (Bureau for Crisis Prevention and Recovery Background Paper; New York: UNDP).

Camdessus, M. (2003) 'Financing Water for All: Report of the World Panel on Financing Water Infrastructure' (Kyoto: World Water Council).

Carin, B., R. Higgott, J. Scholte, G. Smith and D. Stone (2006) 'Global Governance: Looking Ahead 2006–2010', *Global Governance* 1.6.

Carr, E. (2008) 'Rethinking Poverty Alleviation: A "Poverties" Approach', *Development in Practice* 18.6: 726-34.

Chandler, D. (2008) 'Human Security: The Dog that Didn't Bark', *Security Dialogue* 39.4: 427-38.

Commission on Global Governance (1995) *Our Global Neighbourhood* (Oxford, UK: Oxford University Press).

Cooper, N. (2009) 'Comments', *ESRC Human Security Research Seminar*, University of Bradford, UK, 27–28 January 2009.

Cox, R. (1983) 'Gramsci, Hegemony and International Relations: An Essay in Method', *Millennium: Journal of International Studies* 12.2: 162-75.

Deacon, R., M. Hulse and P. Stubbs (1997) *Global Social Policy: International Organizations and the Future of Welfare* (London: Sage).

Diehl, P. (1997) *The Politics of Global Governance: International Organizations in an Interdependent World* (Boulder, CO: Lynne Rienner).

Dillon, M., and J. Reid (2001) 'Global Liberal Governance: Biopolitics, Security and War', *Millennium: Journal of International Studies* 30.1: 41-66.

Duffield, M. (2005) *Human Security: Linking Development and Security in an Age of Terror* (Bonn: EADI).

Eade, J. (1997) *Living the Global City: Globalization as Local Process* (London: Routledge).

Foucault, M. (1979) *The History of Sexuality: An Introduction* (London: Allen Lane).

—— (2003) *Society Must be Defended: Lectures at the College de France, 1975–1976* (London: Penguin).

Freedman, L. (1998) 'International Security: Changing Targets', *Foreign Policy* (Spring 1998): 48-64.

Grayson, K. (2008) 'Human Security as Power/Knowledge: The Biopolitics of a Definitional Debate', *Cambridge Review of International Affairs* 21.3: 383-401.

Greig, A., D. Hulme and M. Turner (2007) *Challenging Global Inequality: Development Theory and Practice in the 21st Century* (London: Palgrave Macmillan).

Halabi, Y. (2004) 'The Expansion Of Global Governance into the Third World: Altruism, Realism or Constructivism?', *International Studies Review* 6: 21-48.

Hall, D. (2004) *Water Finance: A Discussion Note* (London: Public Services International).

—— and E. Lobina (2008) *Sewerage Works* (London: Public Services International).

Harrison, G. (2007) *The World Bank and Africa: The Construction of Governance States* (London: Routledge).

Johnstone, I. (2005) 'The Power of Interpretive Communities', in M. Barnett and R. Duvall (eds.), *Power in Global Governance* (Cambridge, UK: Cambridge University Press): 185-204.

Kaldor, M., M. Martin and S. Selchow (2007) 'Human Security: A New Strategic Narrative for Europe', *International Affairs* 83.2 (March 2007): 273-88.

Kapstein, E. (2005) 'Power, Fairness and the Global Economy', in M. Barnett and R. Duvall (eds.), *Power in Global Governance* (Cambridge, UK: Cambridge University Press): 80-101.

Kenny, C. (2008) 'Corruption in Water: A Matter of Life and Death', in H. Labelle (ed.), *Global Corruption Report 2008: Corruption in the Water Sector* (New York: Transparency International): 16-17.

Keohane, R., and J. Nye (2000) 'Introduction', in J. Nye and J. Donahue (eds.), *Governance in a Globalizing World* (Washington, DC: Brookings Institution): 1-44.

Lines, T. (2008) *Poverty: A History* (London: Zed Books).

Lipschutz, R. (2005) 'Global Civil Society and Global Governmentality: Or, the Search for Politics and State amidst the Capillaries of Social Power', in M. Barnett and R. Duvall (eds.), *Power in Global Governance* (Cambridge, UK: Cambridge University Press): 229-48.

Mack, A. (2005) *The Human Security Report 2005: War and Peace in the 21st Century* (Oxford, UK: Oxford University Press).

Mackenbach, J. (2007) 'Sanitation: Pragmatism Works', *British Medical Journal* 334.7: 1-3.

Merlingen, M. (2008) 'Monster Studies', *International Political Sociology* 3.2: 272-74.

Naude, W. (2008) 'Entrepreneurship, Post-Conflict', in T. Addison and T. Bruck (eds.), *Making Peace Work: The Challenges of Social and Economic Reconstruction* (London: Palgrave Macmillan): 251-63.

Ohiorhenuan, J., and F. Stewart (2008) *Post-Conflict Economic Recovery: Enabling Local Ingenuity* (New York: UNDP).

Paris, R. (2001) 'Human Security: Paradigm Shift or Hot Air?', *International Security* 26.2: 87-102.

Payne, A. (2005) *The Global Politics of Unequal Development* (London: Palgrave Macmillan).

Piachaud, J. (2008) 'Global Health and Human Security', *Medicine, Conflict and Survival* 24.1 (January–March 2008): 1-4.

Roberts, D. (2008a) 'The Science of Human Security: A Response from Political Science', *Journal of Medicine, Conflict and Survival*, January–March 2008: 16-22.

—— (2008b) *Human Insecurity: Global Structures of Violence* (London: Zed Books).

—— (2010) *Global Governance and Biopolitics: Regulating Human Security* (London: Zed Books).

Rosenau, J. (1995) *Along the Domestic–Foreign Frontier: Exploring Governance in a Turbulent World* (Cambridge, UK: Cambridge University Press).

—— and E.-O. Czempiel (1992) *Governance without Government: Order and Change in World Politics* (Cambridge, UK: Cambridge University Press).

Rowlands, J. (2008) Book Reviews: 'Good Governance and Development; Public Administration and Democratic Governance: Governments Serving Citizens; Learning Civil Societies: Shifting Contexts for Democratic Planning and Governance', *Development in Practice* 18.6: 801-04.

Rummel, R.J. (1997) *Death by Government: Genocide and Mass Murder Since 1900* (Piscataway, NJ: Transaction Press).

Solomon, M.S. (2006) 'Review: Power in Global Governance', *International Studies Review* 8.2: 327-29.

Sorensen, J. (2002) 'Balkanism and the New Radical Interventionism: A Structural Critique', *International Peacekeeping* 9.1: 1-22.

Stoett, P. (1999) *Human and Global Security: An Exploration of Terms* (Toronto: University of Toronto Press).

Stoltenberg, J. (2006) 'Our Children: The Key to Our Common Future', *The Lancet* 368.9541: 1,042-47.

Taback, N., and R. Coupland (2007) 'The Science of Human Security', *Medicine, Conflict and Survival* 23.1 (January–March 2007): 3-9.

Victora, C. (2004) 'Achieving Universal Coverage with Health Interventions', *The Lancet* 364: 1,541-48.

Williams, M. (1994) *International Economic Organisations and the Third World* (London: Harvester Wheatsheaf).

Wilkinson, R. (2004) 'Introduction', in R. Wilkinson, *The Global Governance Reader* (London: Routledge).

World Bank (2007) *Implementation and Completion and Results Report ICR134* (Washington, DC: World Bank).

3

Operationalising human security

A brief review of the United Nations

Hitomi Kubo
Sciences Po, France

The term 'human security' does not appear as such in the Charter of the United Nations. Despite early allusions to the concept, it does not appear in United Nations (UN) documents for nearly 50 years from the founding of the institution until the publication of the 1994 United Nations Development Programme (UNDP) *Human Development Report*. The charter defines the purpose of the UN by focusing on three primary themes including maintaining international peace and security, furthering social and economic development of all peoples and promoting respect for human rights. Human security similarly focuses on the same themes, yet emphasises the linkages among these three pillars of security, development and human rights. The UN and human security also share at least one objective of securing people from the tragic impacts of war, disaster and neglect.

One could argue that reflecting on the charter of the UN provides adequate evidence that human security has been an important goal for the institution from the outset. The more recent reform agenda put forth in the past two decades perhaps provides more direct support to this assertion. The reform agenda clearly recognises the need for greater coherence at both the conceptual and practical level among the goals of security, development and human rights. Human security promotes the same objectives—that is, the conceptual and practical linkages among these sectors—and, therefore, could be posited as an overarching objective of the UN, though not stated as such. It is therefore not surprising that the UN has been the primary international institution to grapple with the concept of human security. Although the concept is not born uniquely from the UN, it is the UN that has inaugurated it and continued to drive its development from theory into practice.

If we place human security within the set of objectives of the UN, it is important to evaluate the extent to which human security as both a concept and a practice has been operationalised to date. In order to assess the degree and type of operationalisation that has thus far taken place within the UN, it is necessary to establish an evaluative framework based on the concept of human security that can appraise its application both at a conceptual and a practical level. As human security can be viewed as both an end and a means, as an objective and a method, it is appropriate to develop an evaluative framework based on human security in order to determine the extent to which human security has been operationalised. This chapter thus presents an operational framework for human security and one of its various applications as an evaluative tool, which is then applied to the case of the UN.

Operational principles of human security[1]

Beginning from a broad definition of human security, such as that proposed by the Commission on Human Security (CHS),[2] the process of attempting to translate the concept into practical action appears daunting if not impossible. In doing so, we are confronted with a set of methodological questions: Can such breadth be accurately represented in order to provide meaningful guidance to human security policy and/or practice? What method would accommodate multidimensionality, while allowing for the necessary flexibility for contextualisation in specific circumstances of insecurity? In addition, we are faced with a set of ethical questions: What are the potential dangers of attempting to put such a broad concept into applicable form? Does the danger of manipulation through operationalisation surpass the potential positive impacts?

1 The operational principles presented in this chapter were first developed by Dr Shahrbanou Tadjbakhsh and Hitomi Kubo at the Center for Peace and Human Security (CPHS), Sciences Po, Paris, and later refined in collaboration with the Human Security Unit at the Office for the Coordination of Humanitarian Affairs (HSU/OCHA) at the United Nations and published in the handbook *Human Security in Theory and Practice: Application of the Human Security Concept and the United Nations Trust Fund for Human Security*. The process of developing the principles will be elaborated in other writings and does not appear in this chapter.

2 The CHS definition of human security referred to in this text: 'to protect the vital core of all human lives in ways that enhance human freedoms and human fulfilment. Human security means protecting people from critical (severe) and pervasive (widespread) threats and situations. It means using processes that build on people's strengths and aspirations. It means creating political, social, environmental, economic, military and cultural systems that together give people the building blocks of survival, livelihood and dignity' (CHS 2003: 4).

On the one hand, there is no doubt that scepticism is based on legitimate concerns regarding the utility and impact of a concrete operational approach for human security. On the other hand, there is also no doubt that the concept is ingrained with both analytical and practical characteristics. That is, while it promotes a new perspective on what constitutes security and potential threats to security, human security also calls for action. While recognising that the state remains the primary provider of security, human security acknowledges that the goal of securing the state does not necessarily provide for the security of individuals and communities within the state. At the conceptual level, human security implies a shift in the way we think about the essence of security. By placing the individual at the centre of analysis, it poses new questions relevant to the 'problem' of security: Security for whom? Security from what? Security by which means? (Tadjbakhsh and Chenoy 2007: 13). Human security also incites us to reflect on how we govern for security. The final question—security by which means—invites a re-evaluation of the foundations of security and the mechanisms used to achieve it. First, by promoting favourable social, economic and political conditions as fundamental aspects of attaining security at the individual level, human security expands the options of responses beyond solely military strategies. Second, recognising that institutional structures and processes related to security provision draw heavily from theoretical or conceptual perspectives and assumptions that prevail, human security calls for an examination of these institutions and structures in order to identify more effective mechanisms that are able to respond to an expanded security agenda and the reality of the interdependence of the various elements of the international security system, both threats and responses.

Developing principles of human security represents part of the process of marking and implementing the paradigm shift from traditional notions of security. Principles develop the concept with the goal of creating meaningful and relevant guidelines for strategies that aim to address the 'critical and pervasive' insecurities faced by individuals and communities. They can provide direction in answering the questions of why, when and how to address situations of insecurity in such a way that is at once flexible, while capturing complexity and dynamic changes without diluting the meaning and purpose of the concept itself. In applying to both the means and the ends of interventions, the principles guide the selection of the types of process and approach that can be employed to ensure that operational responses also reflect the nature and values of the concept. Complementary and mutually reinforcing they together put forward a holistic approach to human security in practice, which captures the different elements and characteristics of the concept.

Deriving operational principles of human security based on a broad definition, including but not limited to those proposed by the CHS and the UNDP framework of seven domains (UNDP 1994), requires identification of the core features of the concept. The following discussion presents a set of operational principles that effectively reflect the breadth of the concept and provide guidance for undertaking a human security approach.

People-centred

The first and perhaps most evident of the key features of human security is people-centredness. As Kofi Annan stated, 'no shift in the way we think or act is more critical than that of putting people at the centre of everything we do' (Annan 2002). People-centredness focuses attention on individuals and communities, the 'critical and pervasive' threats to their survival, livelihood and dignity, and the structures and processes that are or are not in place in order to provide for their protection and empowerment.

By placing the individual at the centre of analysis, human security gives voice to individuals and communities, providing space and importance to the perspectives of the people experiencing first-hand the situation of insecurity. It holds their perspectives as significant and attempts to define problems and solutions from the point of view of affected individuals and communities in collaboration with other actors, internal and external, when necessary. As a fundamentally people-centred approach, human security, in grounding situational analyses on processes based on people's own perceptions of fear and vulnerability, can yield accurate insights into the main sources of people's insecurities as well as the concrete needs of populations under stress. This type of analysis has the potential to generate in-depth and more complete pictures of the experience of insecurity than other types of traditional state-centric approach (Jolly and Basu Ray 2006). Moreover, analysis of human perceptions can help unveil mismatches between domestic and/or international policies and priority security needs at the local level, thus constituting a valuable guide in the development of appropriate—more customised—policy responses as well as for analysing the impact of global processes on particular national settings. Finally, human security considers people to be agents with capacities and knowledge that should be engaged in order to address insecurity in a sustainable manner and to promote prevention-oriented approaches that contribute to their longer-term security.

A people-centred approach requires the continued identification and development of alternative arrangements and strategies that are aimed at strengthening the security of people. Failures to protect people are due to a variety of issues, some of which may be the result of conceptual gaps and some of which may arise from structural or procedural gaps in security mechanisms at the international, national and/or local levels. Gaps in security infrastructure or responses can represent an absence of appropriate mechanisms or a mismatch between the nature of the security problem and the means used to address the problem. Therefore, by focusing attention on the sources of individual and community insecurity and how these sources may be related to insecurity at the national and international levels, human security also broadens the types of actor who may be central to security discussions, including the development and human rights communities.

Comprehensive

The second operational principle of human security is that it is comprehensive. Human security draws attention to the diversity and complex nature of threats in the 21st century. Threats are interconnected, often compound, and come from a wider diversity of sources than previously covered by traditional security concepts. Many of these threats do not respect national boundaries, or may be too overwhelming for a single state to manage and, therefore, may not be solely the concern of a single state.

The breadth of potential threats has been a contentious aspect of human security, with some proponents applying a limited definition constrained to issues of violence or issues of development. Another potent critique of human security concerns the securitisation of non-security issues. Recent actions on the part of national governments to curtail certain rights and liberties as a facet of their security responses to threats posed by international terrorism highlight the potential hazards of securitisation and should be considered carefully. If, however, the objective of human security is actually about securing individuals and communities (in addition to the state), how is it possible to delineate from the outset the types of relevant threat and insecurity considering their diversity and complexity depending on each specific context? Furthermore, how is it possible to address security problems in the longer term without addressing the root causes, which may be found in political, economic and social conditions that may not be considered through narrow approaches?

The breadth of human security simply requires us to consider the complex set of factors that could be interacting to produce a situation of insecurity; it does not imply that each and every factor will necessarily be engaged in the problem or potential solution. Focusing on 'critical and pervasive' threats places emphasis on those threats that affect core activities and functions of human life in addition to threats that are large scale, recurrent and/or abrupt (Alkire 2003: 8). From an operational perspective, comprehensive implies an extensiveness of analysis across domains and levels, including direct and indirect threats. Analysis needs to take into account the variety of factors converging in a specific situation of insecurity and assess, based on the relationships of threats and vulnerabilities, the most effective points of entry, which in some cases may be far from the initial assessment of insecurity.

Intersectoral

Perhaps one of the most promising, yet challenging, contributions of human security as an operational tool is its call for a true intersectoral agenda. Based on the recognition that achieving individual and community security is a result of a number of interlinked factors, human security requires a focus on the relationships between threats, how they interact and addressing them in conjunction with one another when appropriate (Tadjbakhsh 2007). By developing these links, human security represents a potentially powerful analytical tool that can provide new perspectives for concrete situations through approaches that combine analysis from diverse fields including security, development and human rights (Gasper 2004). It also introduces a framework of externalities to accommodate policy programming and implementation with a look to maximise positive and mitigate any negative impacts. As such, the human security framework can result in greater policy coherence and coordination to tackle interventions from a broad spectrum (Tadjbakhsh and Chenoy 2007).

Closely linked with the principle of comprehensiveness, an intersectoral approach implies addressing specific cases of insecurity, while also considering potential structural factors that created the environment for such insecurity to arise. Key challenges of an intersectoral approach are the current gaps in research examining the interaction of the social, political and economic conditions of insecurity. Despite the existing gaps, analysis that carefully considers the interaction of various threats, the enabling conditions in which such threats arise and that draws on expertise and knowledge across fields is necessary for the development of interventions or solutions that promise to alleviate insecurity in the longer-term and with minimal negative consequences or the creation of new insecurities. In order to do so, a human security approach requires the development of an interconnected network of diverse stakeholders, drawing on the participation of a wide range of actors across international, regional, national and local actors in both the public and private spheres. Such collaboration has the potential to lead to the establishment of synergies and partnerships that capitalise on the comparative advantages of each actor, minimising overlaps and/or gaps, and contributing to information sharing and new research discoveries.

Prevention-focused

Another key feature of human security is its explicit emphasis on preventive action in addressing insecurity. The element of risk reduction embedded in human security has important implications for its operational approach and distinguishes the approach from other closely related conceptual approaches such as human development and human rights (CHS 2003). The orientation towards protecting people from 'downside' risks stems from the 'belief that most, though not all, large-scale human tragedies should be preventable' (Mine 2007: 64).

An added value of human security as an operational approach relates to its dual policy framework resting on the two mutually reinforcing pillars of protection and empowerment (HSU 2009). The protection element provides a framework for 'foundational prevention',[3] aimed at addressing root causes of insecurity before they create the conditions for devastating human tragedy to occur. The protective

3 As explained by Lodgaard: 'Foundational prevention is premised on the belief that prevention cannot begin early enough. It tries to address deep-seated causes of human insecurity' (Lodgaard 2000: 15).

element necessary for a human security approach, however, is not solely based on top-down processes from the state towards its citizens, but also relies on bottom-up processes emphasising empowerment of individuals and communities to actively participate in creating and maintaining human security.

The operationalisation of human security's framework of protection and empowerment introduces a dual approach, which combines 'strategies, set up by states, international agencies, NGOs and the private sector, [to] shield people from menaces' and 'strategies [that] enable people to develop their resilience to difficult situations' (CHS 2003: 10). The orientation of human security towards prevention requires that norms, institutions and processes are in place for the comprehensive and systematic protection of individuals and communities before and during emergencies or disasters, not only in the aftermath.

Context-specific

Human security acknowledges that insecurities vary considerably across different settings and that few generalisations can be made about their causes or their expressions as they depend on a complex set of factors. This element of a human security approach has been the source of much of the hesitation and difficulty in developing the operational aspect of the concept; it is perhaps primarily this element that requires the elaboration of a set of principles rather than other operational approaches that may provide more directives. Human security aims to advance solutions that are firmly anchored in the local context and specific situation of insecurity and calls for the reduction of 'one size fits all' policies and strategies.

What is critical to note regarding the aforementioned operational principles—people-centred, comprehensive, intersectoral, prevention-focused and context-specific—is that they must be applied together as they are mutually reinforcing and complementary. Taken alone each principle may lead to a desired end, but individually they do not represent human security and, in some cases, they could represent a distinctly different field. For example, prevention-focused, applied by itself, may invoke frameworks and practices related to risk assessment and risk management. Perhaps these tools would aid a human security approach, but in and of themselves, they do not represent the approach in its entirety. The operational principles together aim to translate the human security concept into guidelines for human security practice.

Operational principles as an evaluative framework for human security at the United Nations

As a concept and operational approach, human security has profound and perhaps even daunting implications. Not only is it wide-ranging in the domains that it covers, it is also extensive with regard to the types of strategy, institution and process necessary in order to achieve its objectives of protecting individuals and communities from preventable and devastating impacts on their survival, livelihoods and dignity. With regard to international organisations, human security poses an additional set of questions: Are international organisations prepared to tackle an expanded security agenda? Are international organisations prepared for interdisciplinary work? What types of institution and process are necessary for representativeness, participation and responsiveness? To further examine human security at the United Nations, the various aspects of operationalisation can be examined separately as they indicate both the type and the extent of progression of the concept in addition to highlighting some of the key barriers. The three aspects of operationalisation assessed are: norm setting, institutionalisation and application at the programme/project level.

There remains much debate regarding the role of international organisations (IOs) in establishing and/or diffusing norms. Much of the literature has tended to focus on the role of IOs as transmitters of norms rather than their role in norm emergence (Park 2006); however, for the purposes of this argument, the assumption that IOs play a key role in setting new norms is accepted. Norm setting represents a critical step in the process of operationalising human security, at the United Nations and within national governments. As mentioned above, human security introduces significant changes in both how we view security and how we govern for security. Therefore, acceptance of the concept is the first step in the process of operationalising human security as it indicates a certain level of international consensus and political will on the part of a certain threshold of national governments. To what extent national governments share in the 'consensus' and which governments are party has important implications for norm setting, diffusion and transmission; however, this discussion is not within the scope of this discussion. Norm setting, however, is only the first of many steps that need to occur in order to apply a human security approach in its entirety. Institutionalisation refers to the application of human security at the level of structures and processes. Human security implies certain institutional and procedural changes, such as shifting or creating structures and processes that make possible a people-centred approach. The clear call for intersectorality and multidisciplinary approaches in practice translate into integration, networks, multi-agency and multi-actor approaches, for example. Additionally, a human security approach as presented here invokes the necessity of coherence not only of international policies and programmes, but also between local and international, and local and national. Therefore, in order for a holistic application of human security, it is necessary that systemic and procedural changes are implemented in addition to general political will in accepting the concept.

Finally, application at the programme and project level has another set of implications. Human security can be operationalised at the programme and project level, meaning that it can help frame new ways of undertaking programmes or projects that seek to address insecurity in a comprehensive and preventative manner. The emphasis on the perception of people and on the issue of vulnerability has important implications for the application of human security. These include foremost, the inclusion of individuals and communities and their perspectives as a fundamental element of analysis, planning, implementation and/or evaluation. Therefore, programmes or projects at the community level will always be a crucial ingredient of a human security approach, although the manner in which it is incor-

Table 3.1 **Operationalisation of human security at the United Nations**

	Norm setting (Security Council; Secretary-General)	**Institutionalisation (General Assembly)**	**Programmes and projects (Agencies)**
People-centred	Consider impacts of international action on people and the most vulnerable groups	Alternative institutional arrangements and strategies that can strengthen the security of people	Meaningful engagement of local actors and population in all aspects of interventions, programmes and projects
Comprehensive	Recognise broader range of security threats and solutions beyond solely military and diplomatic action	Structures and processes to address gaps in security mechanisms	Consider how local, state and international processes can be mutually supportive
Intersectoral	Consider requisite linkages between security, development and human rights	Thematically driven institutional collaboration	Multi-agency planning, implementation and evaluation based on assessment of externalities
Prevention-focused	Identify and reduce risk before major human tragedies occur	Structures and processes that provide early action for significant threats	Address root causes of insecurity
Context-specific	Comprehensive treatment on a case-by-case basis	Processes/structures that promote in-depth country/locality engagement linked with broader, relevant initiatives	Determined based on the needs and vulnerabilities in a specific situation, including the perspective of local actors and the local population

porated could vary dramatically depending on the type of intervention or process. The bottom-up process is not only about empowerment, although this is a fundamental element; the objective is also to ensure that micro-level approaches are not left in isolation from the national and international processes.

Table 3.1 provides examples of which types of general criteria that could be used to evaluate the operationalisation of human security at the United Nations. Each example would need to be further disaggregated for a rigorous analysis. As indicated in the table, the different bodies within the UN system have varying roles with regard to the three phases of operationalisation and, therefore, in assessing the progression of applying human security, it is necessary to examine these bodies separately; however, as is true with the set of operational principles, a complete picture on the level of operationalisation also requires a holistic assessment.

Norm setting of human security at the UN

The shift in security thinking proposed by human security, as discussed above, requires that human security attain the status as a norm or standard. The establishment of norms indicates a broad international consensus and, without some consensus at the level of national governments, a holistic application of human security will not be possible. Within the UN system, the Secretary-General and the Security Council represent two key bodies with respect to norm setting. Reviewing relevant documents and resolutions from these bodies reveals a relatively significant level of progression with respect to the operationalisation of human security at the conceptual level.

A certain threshold of high-level reports can indicate the emergence or standardisation of a norm (Goldstein *et al.* 2000: 386). A number of high-level reports have introduced various aspects of the concept including: then Secretary-General Boutros Boutros-Ghali's 'Agenda for Peace' (United Nations 1992) which called for 'an integrated approach to human security' in order to address the root causes of conflict that span economic, social and political issues; then Secretary-General Kofi Annan's report leading up to the Millennium Summit, *We the Peoples: The Role of the United Nations in the 21st Century*, which called on the international community to address the dual objectives of freedom from fear and freedom from want; the 2004 report of the *High-level Panel on Threats, Challenges and Change* (United Nations 2004), which recognised an expanded set of threats, their interconnectedness, and the importance of stronger international collaboration and partnership for successfully addressing these threats; and the 2005 report of then Secretary-General Kofi Annan, *In Larger Freedom: Towards Development, Security and Human Rights for All* (United Nations 2005), which established a set of policy priorities and proposed a number of institutional reforms to achieve the three objectives of freedom from fear, freedom from want and a life with dignity. The presence of the pillars of a broad definition of human security throughout the high-level documents indicates that, at a minimum, the notion of an expanded security agenda and increased attention on the lives of individuals and communities in addition to the security of the state has reached prominence within the international policy realm.

Further disaggregating human security into salient rubrics—the protection of vulnerable groups, the need for a more relevant security paradigm, an expanded set of threats and menaces to security, the call for more integrated and collaborative action across diverse actors within and across institutions, and the importance of greater emphasis on prevention—reveals the persistence and growing importance of key themes related to human security. A brief examination of the progression of human security and these related themes within the Security Council (SC) over the past ten years highlights small, yet promising, movement. Over this time, the SC has undertaken a wide range of consultations for the purpose of increasing the protection of people and, in particular, vulnerable groups. For example, provision 2 of the SC resolution 1674, adopted on 28 April 2006,

> *Emphasizes* the importance of preventing armed conflict and its recurrence, and stresses in this context the need for a comprehensive approach through promoting economic growth, poverty eradication, sustainable development, national reconciliation, good governance, democracy, the rule of law, and respect for, and protection of, human rights, and in this regard, urges the cooperation of Member States and underlines the importance of a coherent, comprehensive and coordinated approach by the principal organs of the United Nations, cooperating with one another and within their respective mandates [italics original].

Although not specifically referring to human security, the emphasis on prevention, the recognition that security is based on a broader set of social, economic and political conditions, and the call for coherence and integration of the organs of the UN system reflect some of the key aspects of human security at the conceptual and operational level. In addition, numerous other resolutions have passed the SC, which concern: the protection of civilians in armed conflict (S/RES/1674 [2006], S/RES/1738 [2006], and S/RES/1894 [2009]); the proliferation of small arms and light weapons (S/RES/1467 [2003]); children and armed conflict (S/RES/1460 (2003), S/RES/1539 [2004], S/RES/1612 [2005]); comprehensive post-conflict peace-building, which also calls on the need for a greater emphasis on conflict prevention (S/RES/1645 [2005], S/RES/1646 [2005]); women, peace and security (S/RES/1820 [2008], S/RES/1889 [2009]); and cooperation among the UN and regional organisations for the purpose of maintaining international peace and security (S/RES/1631 [2005]).

While these thematic resolutions are important indications of steps towards recognising and prioritising the human impact of security problems, they should not be overstated as evidence that the SC has in any manner adopted a human security approach. They at best represent a degree of change in perception regarding the types of threats to security, how various groups may be differentially impacted, and the promotion of alternative mechanisms for promoting peace and security. Incremental change is critical in the process of norm setting but, as will be discussed in the following section, structural and procedural changes would need to follow. For example, critiques regarding the transparency and accountability of SC decision-making processes highlight the challenges of adopting an approach that would holistically reflect the operational principles of human security. Structural and procedural changes that would be necessary for the SC to effectively tackle an expanded security agenda in an interdisciplinary, participatory and prevention-oriented manner, not to mention changes that would broaden the types of response to security challenges, are far from being realised.

Institutionalisation of human security at the UN

Institutional and procedural changes are just as important as norm setting to the application of a human security approach. A brief review of measures towards institutionalisation of a human security approach at the UN reveals important contributions as well as significant gaps. Parallel to the conceptual discussions occurring in 1999, human security found its first designated institutional home in the UN when the Government of Japan and the UN launched the United Nations Trust Fund for Human Security (UNTFHS),[4] which represents one of the most important contributions of the UN towards operationalising the concept. The UNTFHS began funding projects relating to key thematic human security areas with the objective to further translate human security into concrete activities that comprehensively address the threats to the survival, livelihoods and dignity of individuals and communities.

A second institutional change was the creation of the Advisory Board on Human Security (ABHS), established following the recommendation of the CHS at the conclusion of its activities, with the specific role of advising the UN Secretary-General on issues regarding the management of the UNTFHS, promoting the concept within the UN system and increasing the impact of programmes and projects funded through the UNTFHS. An essential contribution of the ABHS to the promotion of human security was its role in the establishment of the Human Security Unit (HSU) in the Office for the Coordination of Humanitarian Affairs (OCHA). In addition to managing the UNTFHS, the HSU plays a key role in highlighting the added value of the human security approach and mainstreaming the concept in concrete UN activities at the project level. Recent contributions including the revision of funding guidelines and the publication of *Human Security in Theory and Practice: Application of the Human Security Concept and the United Nations Trust Fund for Human Security* (UN HSU 2009) have been instrumental in the application of a human security approach at the level of programmes and projects (to be further discussed in the next section). The extent to which the HSU, the ABHS and the UNTFHS succeed in promoting the structural change necessary to mainstream human security within the institution and not solely its programmes or projects has not been assessed here; however, a bottom-up approach wherein micro-level activities reach a threshold that has an influence on the structures governing those

---

4 The UNTFHS has been primarily funded by the Government of Japan with additions in 2007 by the governments of Slovenia and Thailand.

activities is a fundamental part of the dual approach proposed by human security.

A third development that is important to mention with regard to the institution-alisation of human security is the creation of the Friends of Human Security (FHS). Although the FHS is an optional and informal group of member states[5] and, there-fore, does not have a formal role with regard to adapting structures and processes within the system to better reflect a human security approach, it does represent a commitment by states and international organisations to engage with the broad concept of human security. The FHS provides a forum for discussions concerning the concept and the avenues for mainstreaming a human security approach within the United Nations. More than 50 member states have been present at the informal meetings of the FHS, which indicates a moderately strong level of interest (and one that has grow since its inception in 2006) at least in examining the potential of the concept and its impact for the UN. Discussions among member states from FHS sessions also indicate reinforcement of the trend that human security as a concept and policy framework is gaining ground in the international arena. Mere numbers are not necessarily the best criteria for predicting potential change at the institu-tional level, and therefore these newer forums more strongly support norm emer-gence and standardisation than structural or procedural adaptations.

Furthermore, in May 2008, the General Assembly held a thematic debate on human security, indicating that the concept had reached a certain level of salience within the institution itself. Other institutional changes highlight the prominence of certain aspects of human security, such as the creation of the Peacebuilding Commission (PBC), tasked with comprehensive case-by-case support to coun-tries emerging from conflict or languishing in a fragile peace and underdevelop-ment after the cessation of violence. Additionally, the UN has made clear efforts to increase the role of civil society actors, businesses and other non-state actors. Many of the institutional changes mentioned are a part of the reform agenda of the UN and therefore cannot be attributed specifically to the application of a human secu-rity approach. They remain relevant for this analysis, however, because whether or not the reforms are directly related to its application, the types of reforms sug-gested refer to the aspects of the operational approach of human security.

The changes in the past ten years with regard to the institutionalisation of human security at the UN indicate important contributions. However, similar to the con-clusions regarding norm setting processes, does the establishment of the ABHS and the HSU actually indicate mainstreaming of the concept? Can the creation of these new entities override other structures and processes that remain tied to state-centred security assumptions? Is improvement in multi-agency planning, implementation and evaluation within the UN extensive enough to promote a holistic application of human security? Are appropriate institutional arrangements being created to deal with thematic areas of human security that require interna-tional and national collaboration such as migration and environmental disasters?

---

5   The FHS consists primarily of representatives from UN member states and international organisations working at the UN headquarters in New York.

Affirmative answers to these questions would be necessary in order to assert that a human security approach is reflected in the institutionalisation phase of operationalisation.

Application in programmes and projects

A primary contribution to the operationalisation of a human security approach at the level of programmes and projects has been through the UNTFHS-funded projects.[6] As outlined in the follow-up document to the outcome of the Millennium Summit (United Nations 2008), a number of UN agencies and departments have implemented more than 175 human security projects worldwide, covering a wide range of human security-related themes including: protection and reintegration of refugees, post-conflict peace-building, prevention of human trafficking, women's empowerment, food and health security, and socioeconomic security for vulnerable communities, as well as activities to further promote the concept of human security.[7]

The vast majority of these projects have been directly funded by the UNTFHS, sometimes in collaboration with bilateral and multilateral donor agencies and other partners. According to the HSU website, programmes have been funded in 75 countries, not including regional and global projects. As mentioned above, the UNTFHS has produced revised guidelines and a more structured framework for undertaking human security projects at the community level. The new guidelines mandate an approach based on the operational principles of human security and, therefore, aim to be multi-agency, to include local actors in the process, and to consider prevention. The extent to which local populations are included in the initial assessment process aimed at identifying the specific human security concerns to be addressed by funded initiatives remains unclear. Of perhaps more concern is whether or not achievements made through these local-level projects, which are significant, are linked directly to policy priorities at the national and international levels in order to ensure sustainability and coherence.

Conclusions

This brief review of human security at the UN through an evaluative framework based on the operational principles of human security indicates significant advance-

---

6 Several UN agencies have undertaken human security projects, including the UNDP human security-themed NHDRs; however, this analysis is limited to the projects funded by the UNTFHS.

7 The 25 February 2008 report to the General Assembly includes a comprehensive outline of human security activities by member states of the FHS and UN agencies, funds and programmes.

ments, particularly with regard to norm setting and the application at the level of programmes and projects. The most significant barrier that arises from this analysis is at the level of institutionalisation. Despite the creation of new bodies within the UN system dedicated to the promotion and development of human security, more significant structural and procedural changes would need to be advanced for the UN system to be prepared to undertake the people-centred, comprehensive, intersectoral, prevention-oriented and context-specific approach indicated by the operational principles of human security presented.

The primary challenge today rests at the level of national governments. It is equally, if not more, crucial for national governments to adopt a domestic human security agenda than for human security to be applied as a foreign policy objective or as part of official development assistance policy. 'Embracing the universality of the concept would [mean applying] domestic human security strategies and policies, even in Western societies' (Tadjbakhsh 2007: 10). States must take the next step in preparing themselves to manage an expanded and multidimensional security agenda based on a human security approach, otherwise international efforts to promote the operationalisation of human security will encounter the same challenges as the human rights community faces today.

Bibliography

Acharya, A. (2001) 'Debating Human Security: East versus West', paper presented at the *Security with a Human Face: Expert Workshop on the Feasibility of a Human Security Report* (Cambridge, MA: Harvard University).

Alkire, S. (2003) *A Conceptual Framework for Human Security* (Centre for Research on Inequality, Human Security and Ethnicity (CRISE) Working Paper; Oxford, UK).

Annan, K. (2002) 'Foreword', in R. McRae and D. Hubert (eds.), *Human Security and the New Diplomacy: Protecting People, Promoting Peace* (Ottawa: Carleton University Press).

CHS (Commission on Human Security) (2003) *Human Security Now: Final Report* (New York: CHS).

Fukuda-Parr, S. (2003) 'The New Threats to Human Security in the Era of Globalization', in L. Chen, S. Fukuda-Parr and E. Seidensticker (eds.), *Human Insecurity in a Global World* (Cambridge, MA: Harvard University Press).

Gasper, D. (2004) 'Securing Humanity: Situating the Human Security Discourse', paper presented at the *4th Conference on the Capability Approach*, Pavia, Italy, September 2004.

—— (2007) *Human Rights, Human Needs, Human Development, Human Security: Relationships between Four International 'Human' Discourses* (GARNET Working Paper: No 20/07; Rotterdam, Netherlands: Institute of Social Studies).

—— and T. Truong (2005) 'Deepening Development Ethics', *European Journal of Development Research* 17.3 (September 2005): 372-84.

Glasius, M. (2008) 'Human Security from Paradigm Shift to Operationalization: Job Description for a Human Security Worker', *Security Dialogue* 39.1: 31-54.

Goldstein, J., M. Kahler, R. Keohane and A. Slaughter (2000) 'Introduction: Legalization and World Politics', *International Organization* 54.3: 385-99.

Grayson, K. (2004) 'A Challenge to the Power over Knowledge of Traditional Security Studies', in P. Burgess and T. Owens (eds.), 'What is Human Security? Comments by 21 authors', *Security Dialogue* 35 (Special Issue, September 2004): 357.

Jolly, R., and D. Basu Ray (2006) 'The Human Security Framework and National Human Development Reports' (Occasional Paper 5; New York: Human Development Report Office).

King, G., and C. Murray (2001) 'Rethinking Security', *Political Science Quarterly* 116.4.

Lodgaard, S. (2000) 'Human Security: Concept and Operationalization', paper for UN University for Peace; www.upeace.org/documents/resources%5Creport_lodgaard.doc, accessed 23 September 2010.

Mine, Y. (2007) 'Downside Risks and Human Security', in G. Shani, M. Sato and M. Kamal Pasha (eds.), *Protecting Human Security in a Post 9/11 World: Critical and Global Insights* (Basingstoke, UK: Palgrave Macmillan).

Nef, J. (1999) *Human Security and Mutual Vulnerability: The Global Political Economy of Development and Underdevelopment* (Ottawa: IDRC Books).

Ogata, S. (2001) 'State Security: Human Security', paper presented at the *Fridtjof Nansen Memorial Lecture*, UN House, Tokyo, 12 December 2001.

—— and J. Cels (2003) 'Human Security: Protecting and Empowering the People', *Global Governance* 9: 273-82.

Owen, T. (2004) 'Human Security—Conflict, Critique and Consensus: Colloquium Remarks and a Proposal for a Threshold-Based Definition', *Security Dialogue* 35.3: 373-87.

Park, S. (2006) 'Theorizing Norm Diffusion within International Organizations', *International Politics* 43.3 (July 2006): 342-61.

Sen, A. (1999) *Development as Freedom* (New York: Random House).

—— (2000) 'Why Human Security?', paper presented at the *International Symposium on Human Security*, Tokyo, July 2000.

Stewart, F. (2004) 'Development and Security', *Conflict, Security & Development* 4.3 (December 2004): 261-88.

Tadjbakhsh, S. (2005) 'Human Security: The Seven Challenges of Operationalizing the Concept', paper presented at *Human Security: 60 Minutes to Convince*, conference organized by UNESCO, Paris, 13 September 2005.

—— (2007) 'Human Security in International Organizations: Blessing or Scourge?' *Human Security Journal* 4 (Summer 2007): 8-15.

—— and A. Chenoy (2007) *Human Security: Concepts and Implications* (London: Routledge).

Ul Haq, M. (1995) *Reflections on Human Development* (Oxford, UK: Oxford University Press).

United Nations (1992) 'An Agenda for Peace: Preventive Diplomacy, Peacemaking and Peacekeeping', Report of the Secretary-General Boutros Boutros-Ghali, 17 June 1992; www.un.org/Docs/SG/agpeace.html.

—— (2000) 'We the Peoples: The Role of the United Nations in the 21st Century', Report of the Secretary-General Kofi Annan, 3 April 2000; www.un.org/millennium/sg/report/full.htm, accessed 23 September 2010.

—— (2004) *A More Secure World: Our Shared Responsibility— Report of the Secretary-General's High-level Panel on Threats, Challenges and Change* (New York: UN).

—— (2005) 'In Larger Freedom: Towards Development, Security and Human Rights for All', Report of the Secretary General Kofi Annan, 21 March 2005; www.un-ngls.org/orf/UNreform/UBUNTU-1.pdf

—— (2008) 'Follow-up to the outcome of the Millennium Summit', General Assembly 62nd session, 25 February 2008; www.un.org/ga/62/plenary/millennium/bkg.shtml.

UNDP (United Nations Development Programme) (1994) *Human Development Report 1994: New Dimensions of Human Security* (New York: Oxford University Press).

UN HSU (United Nations Human Security Unit) (2009) 'Human Security in Theory and Practice: Application of the Human Security Concept and the United Nations Trust Fund for Human Security'; ochaonline.un.org/Reports/tabid/2186/language/en-US/Default. aspx.

Section II
Human security and health

4

The securitisation of HIV/AIDS
Human security, global health security and the rise of biopolitics

Hazel R. Barrett
Coventry University, UK

HIV/AIDS is a pervasive threat to the health and life of many individuals, especially in the high prevalence regions of sub-Saharan Africa, where 20 million people have already died from the disease and 22 million are currently living with the disease (UNAIDS 2009a). There is no question that this disease reduces the quality of life of those infected and those around them. It limits the socioeconomic development of those communities and countries where HIV/AIDS prevalence is high. It has resulted in declines in life expectancy of up to 25 years in the hardest hit African countries. While HIV/AIDS affects individuals, it is also having a negative political, social and economic impact on many communities and as such is undermining the human security of the region. The setting up of UNAIDS in 1996, the first and only United Nations organisation to deal with a single disease, is evidence that this disease has been recognised as a barrier to human development as well as a threat to human and health security, particularly in sub-Saharan Africa. In 2000 the UN declared HIV/AIDS a threat to peace and security in sub-Saharan Africa, thus acknowledging that health is linked to both human and state security. Since the securitisation of HIV/AIDS in 2000, a number of powerful international initiatives have emerged to fight HIV/AIDS. These include the Global Fund to Fight HIV/AIDS, Tuberculosis (TB) and Malaria (The Global Fund) and the US President's Emergency Plan for AIDS Relief (PEPFAR), which has led to the rise in biopolitics.

The incorporation of health security into the security agenda

Over the last quarter of a century the traditional view of security as state-led and related to military protection of territory and the maintenance of peace has been challenged by a human-centred view of security where individual rights and welfare are a priority. This shift in emphasis coincided with the break-up of the USSR, the end of the cold war and a deepening of the international health crisis associated with the HIV/AIDS pandemic. The global acceptance of the human development paradigm and the subsequent signing of the Millennium Development Goals by world leaders in 2000 have demonstrated that, in the 21st century, most governments and international organisations regard human security together with health security as essential elements of state security.

The term 'human security' was first officially used in the 1994 *Human Development Report* (UNDP 1994) (Fourie and Schonteich 2001; Chandler 2008). The report claimed that 'Human security is not a concern with weapons—it is a concern with human life and dignity' (p. 22). According to the *Human Development Report*, this meant ensuring safety for people from both violent and non-violent threats to their security and well-being; succinctly expressed as 'freedom from fear and freedom from want' (UNDP 1994: 24). The report suggested that six indicators could be used to provide an early warning of threats to human security: food insecurity, job and income insecurity, human rights violations, ethnic or religious conflicts, inequality and military spending. Thus the report conceived human security in terms of the security of individuals as well as nation states. With the discourse that followed, the term 'human security' quickly began to be associated with the individual rather than with the state. According to Hubert (1999, cited by Fourie and Schonteich 2001: 1) human security 'is an alternative way of seeing the world, taking people as its point of reference, rather than focusing exclusively on the security or territory of governments'. This is a view supported by Poku *et al.* (2007: 1155): 'security today is more widely accepted to embrace insecurities driven by non-military challenges. Central to this view is the challenge of meeting the basic needs and aspirations of millions of people in Africa, Asia and beyond'. By 2009, human security was regarded as 'protection from direct and indirect threats to the personal safety and well-being of the individual' (Iqbal 2009: 126). Reference to 'the state' has been dropped as 'security' has been bifurcated into 'state security' concerning sovereign rights and 'human security' focusing on the individual and human rights (Chandler 2008; Owen 2008). In short, human security is about protection of the individual and entails taking preventive measures to reduce vulnerability and minimise risk regardless of state citizenship (Tadjbakhsh and Chenoy 2007). Human security has become a 'fundamental and inviolable right of all individuals' (Tadjbakhsh and Chenoy 2007: 451).

The suggestion that health is part of human security can be traced back to the publication of the first *Human Development Report* in 1990 (UNDP 1990) and the unveiling of the Human Development Index. This alternative paradigm of development emphasised the role of good health and education in the development process. Within ten years the human development paradigm had become mainstream, informing development thinking and policy, which culminated in the international acceptance of the UN Millennium Development Goals (UNMDGs) all of which either directly or indirectly relate to improving the health status of people in the developing world.

The *Human Development Report 1994* (UNDP 1994) contained a discussion of human security, which suggested that, within the human development paradigm, human security comprises seven elements: economic, food, health, environmental, personal, community and political security (Glasius 2008). The report postulated that chronic threats such as hunger, disease and repression could undermine human security in the same way as sudden catastrophic disruptions such as war and internal conflict. While the authors of the report recognised that human security was a narrower concept than human development, they stressed that 'human development is the means through which human security is to be achieved' (Glasius 2008: 33). In May 2003, the Commission on Human Security's report *Human Security Now*, included health as one of its ten policy recommendations (Aldis 2008). The report stated that health security is 'at the vital core of human security . . .' and '. . . illness, disability and avoidable death are "critical pervasive threats" to human security' (Commission on Human Security 2003: 96). Many now recognise that health and in particular infectious diseases have national and global security implications (Bond 2008), as they are at the 'crisis end' of human development (Sen, cited by Glasius 2008) and are an integral part of human security.

Global health security and biopolitics

The unprecedented numbers of deaths caused by AIDS, the rapid global spread of SARS in 2003, the event of high-speed travel and the almost instantaneous reporting of health issues in the digital world have been some of the factors that have raised the profile of global public health. The WHO *World Health Report* 2007 (WHO 2007) addressed global public health security. This report defined global public health security as:

> the activities required . . . to minimise vulnerability to acute public health events that endanger the collective health of populations living across geographical regions and international boundaries . . . Global public health security embraces a wide range of complex and daunting issues, from the international stage to the individual household (WHO 2007: 1).

The report emphasises that global health security may have an impact on economic or political stability, placing public health very much within the human security paradigm. This is very much aligned to Foucault's concept of biopolitical rational-

ity, with international organisations such as the UN taking on the role of a biopolitical power protecting and ensuring global public health security (Elbe 2008).

The spread of infectious disease across regions and international borders is not
a new phenomenon and over the last 200 years various attempts have been made
to control the international spread of public health threats. In 1996 WHO introduced a global system of epidemic alert and response. It is based on the concept
of international partnership involving over 140 technical partners from more than
60 countries (WHO 2007). Known as the Global Outbreak Alert and Response Network (GOARN), its aim is 'the rapid identification, confirmation and response to
outbreaks of international importance' (WHO 2007: 8). Between 2000 and 2005
there were more than 70 GOARN international outbreak responses. GOARN has a
specialised surveillance network for dangerous pathogens including dengue fever,
influenza and the plague.

In the second half of the 20th century, the international community through the
WHO agreed a set of International Health Regulations (1969) to achieve the maxi-
mum protection against the global spread of disease with minimal disruption to
trade and travel. This was based on the notification of six diseases (cholera, plague,
relapsing fever, smallpox, typhus and yellow fever) and the imposition of international border controls. But compliance was patchy and rapid international travel
nullified many attempts to control disease at international borders. So in 2005 the
International Health Regulations were revised and brought into force in June 2007.
These revised regulations define a health emergency as an 'extraordinary event' that
could spread internationally or might require a coordinated international response
(WHO 2007). The regulations are no longer limited to the six notifiable diseases
listed above, but instead focus on illness or medical conditions that could present
significant harm to humans. Such threats to public health may include epidemics
of infectious diseases, as well as threats to human health from natural disasters and
chemical emergencies. States are still required to report significant public health
risks, but instead of the standard international border response, context-specific
measures to stop spread will be agreed with the WHO and applied to populations
deemed to be at risk. But these initiatives have come far too late to halt the global
spread of HIV/AIDS.

The securitisation of HIV/AIDS

Until January 2000, the global HIV/AIDS pandemic, which had killed millions of
people and had infected many millions more since the disease had been formally
identified in 1982, had been regarded as a medical problem associated with behavioural and cultural factors (Iqbal 2009). However on 10 January 2000 this was to
change. On that day the UN Security Council discussed the HIV/AIDS pandemic
and declared the disease a threat to international peace and security in Africa

(McInnes 2006; Elbe 2008; Selgelid and Enemark 2008). This meeting of the UN Security Council proved decisive in placing the global HIV/AIDS pandemic on the international security agenda, resulting in the 'securitisation' of HIV/AIDS (Elbe 2008). UN Security Council Resolution 1308 asserted that if left unchecked HIV/AIDS 'may pose a risk to stability and security' in Africa. It also stated that the spread of the disease was 'exacerbated by conditions of violence and insecurity'. The Resolution expressed concern for peacekeeping forces, as both victims and vectors of the disease. While the issue of HIV/AIDS and human welfare was identified as a threat to security by Resolution 1308, it was framed in the language of political and state security, thus demonstrating the tension evident at that time between state security and human security.

Resolution 1308 is historic as it was the first time that a health issue or disease had been officially framed as a risk to international peace and security. In the years since, the notion that HIV/AIDS is a threat to human security has become commonplace (Selgelid and Enemark 2008). This 'securitisation' of HIV/AIDS challenges traditional state-centred concepts of human security and has contributed to an alternative conceptualisation of human security which stresses human welfare and rights. As a result the international agenda on human security has been infused with what Foucault labelled 'biopolitical rationality' involving concern for the welfare of populations which is associated with strategies aimed at collectively increasing life expectancy and decreasing morbidity levels (Elbe 2008). Human security and in particular health security has become a fundamental right of all individuals regardless of state citizenship (Tadjbakhsh and Chenoy 2007).

By identifying an infectious disease as a security threat the UN not only challenged the existing security paradigm, but also raised the profile of global health issues. According to Selgelid and Enemark (2008: 457) an infectious disease can be branded as a security threat when it 'threatens the existence or stability of society and/or when emergency measures are required to address it'. The fear that infectious diseases engender among populations often leads policy-makers into rapid decision-making which is emotionally driven. This is particularly the case when the infectious disease is new, spreads rapidly and kills significant numbers of people in a short time, as happened with the SARS (Severe Acute Respiratory Syndrome) outbreak in 2003. Thus, acknowledging that an infectious disease is a security issue gives a sense of urgency to the health of communities with the expectation that both international and national policy-makers will give the disease a high priority and provide the necessary resources required to tackle it.

Yet it was 20 years after HIV/AIDS had been identified by the medical community as a new disease and its transmission routes understood that it was designated a security threat. This delay may be due to the fact that HIV/AIDS is 'the quintessential long-wave event' (Merson *et al.* 2008: 476), with the period from initial infection to acute illness and death of many years. It does not fit the profile of a new disease which kills people quickly and results in panic, often irrational, among the population. By contrast, HIV/AIDS can be considered an 'attrition' disease; the damage to individuals and society from the disease occurs over the longer term and affects all aspects of society, including the functioning of traditional state-led human security mechanisms, such as the operation of government, the military, police and legal system, and threatens human welfare and human rights. The UN and others consistently highlight the fact that HIV/AIDS is potentially politically destabilising; the profound economic impacts of the disease on communities are linked to social and political insecurity (Fourie and Schonteich 2001; O'Manique 2005; McInnes 2006). As Peter Piot, then executive director of UNAIDS, stated in 2001: 'By overwhelming Africa's health and social services, by creating millions of orphans and by decimating health workers and teachers, AIDS is causing social and economic crises which in turn threaten political stability'. For others, HIV/AIDS constitutes the biggest human security threat of the 21st century, as it poses a danger to the personal safety and well-being of the individual (Iqbal 2009). As HIV/AIDS threatens the security of both the state and the individual, many believe that 'this disease may be a special case worthy of securitization' (Selgelid and Enemark 2008: 462).

AIDS as a threat to state-level security in sub-Saharan Africa

Many suggest that the threat of HIV/AIDS to state-level security in sub-Saharan Africa has been overstated. While the UN has consistently highlighted HIV/AIDS as potentially destabilising (McInnes 2006), in the ten years since HIV/AIDS was declared a security issue by the UN it has become evident that it has not produced the instability and insecurity in sub-Saharan Africa that was expected. There has not been the collapse of state structures that many feared in the late 1990s. However it is clear that the HIV/AIDS epidemics coursing through sub-Saharan Africa are a major challenge to governance in most high prevalence countries, but this has barely been the subject of research (Barnett and Whiteside 2002). The impact of high morbidity and mortality rates from AIDS among members of parliament and ministers of state and the implications for good governance are unknown (Barnett and Whiteside 2002). But it is likely that the epidemic has weakened institutional structures and, in those countries most severely affected by the epidemic, may be responsible for creating 'fading' states rather than 'failing' states.

More is known about the impact of HIV/AIDS on the military and police. Until recently it has been accepted that rates of HIV infection are higher in the military and police forces than in the general population of sub-Saharan Africa (O'Manique 2005; Sagala 2008; McInnes 2009). The figures most often cited were that infection rates among the armed forces were between two to five times those of the general population (McInnes 2009). Such a high prevalence rate has two potential implications: first that high levels of HIV prevalence among military personnel would mean that the military could become a vector for the spread of the disease among the general population; and second that the high prevalence levels would be a threat to military effectiveness and might mean that some countries would not have enough healthy military personnel to deploy as peacekeepers. This led the UN General Assembly in 2003 to launch a global initiative to raise awareness of AIDS in armed forces across the developing world (McInnes 2006). However recent data suggests that the relationship between soldiers and HIV is not straightforward and studies have failed to show dramatically elevated levels of HIV infection among the armed forces in sub-Saharan Africa (McInnes 2006; Becker *et al.* 2008). This suggests that the perceived threat of HIV/AIDS to the security of sub-Saharan Africa as expressed in UN Resolution 1308 has, in hindsight, been exaggerated.

AIDS as a threat to human and health security in sub-Saharan Africa

While the threat of HIV/AIDS to state-level security appears to have been exaggerated, the threat to human and health security in sub-Saharan Africa has been underestimated. This is exemplified by the links between HIV/AIDS, agricultural production and food security. HIV/AIDS retards agricultural production and threatens food security, putting unique pressures on agricultural systems (Hunter 2007). The connection between HIV/AIDS infection and agricultural production is real. In sub-Saharan Africa women are responsible for producing over 75% of the region's food. With the feminisation of the HIV/AIDS epidemics in sub-Saharan Africa through the 1990s (females comprise approximately 60% of cases in the region; UNAIDS 2009b), food production has been severely compromised as women become ill and die, or find themselves caring for sick relatives.

The link between HIV/AIDS and food security came to the attention of the world in 2002 when the UN mounted an appeal to the international community for immediate food and relief supplies for 14 million people in southern Africa at risk of starvation (O'Manique 2005). While food security was under pressure in southern Africa before 2002, the drought of that year tipped the high HIV prevalence region into famine at an alarming speed. The high levels of morbidity and mortality associated with hunger and malnutrition among adults infected with HIV/AIDS meant it was very difficult for the region to return to full food production when the rains did return to normal. This unusual famine was subsequently labelled as a **new variant famine** which was HIV/AIDS induced (de Waal and Whiteside 2003; Hunter 2007). HIV/AIDS-induced food insecurity and famine are examples of how this disease is affecting the human and health security of this region, leaving millions of people vulnerable to malnutrition and at risk of poor health.

The securitisation of AIDS and the rise of biopolitics

The securitisation of HIV/AIDS by the UN in 2000 assigned to this disease the urgency and importance traditionally only afforded to wars between states (Owen 2008). For some the securitisation of HIV/AIDS appeared to be a political exercise undertaken by policy-makers, particularly those associated with UNAIDS, to attract resources and political support in controlling the spread of the infection (Selgelid and Enemark 2008). Whatever the motivation for Resolution 1308, the result was the inauguration of a number of international organisations to fight HIV/AIDS including The Global Fund and PEPFAR.

The Global Fund was set up in 2002 as a major tool in the fight against HIV/AIDS, TB and malaria in developing and middle income countries. It is a public–private partnership between governments, the private sector, civil society and affected communities dedicated to attracting and disbursing resources to prevent and treat HIV/AIDS, TB and Malaria. The fund supports prevention, care and treatment programmes in 137 countries. To date The Global Fund has invested US$7.2 billion and provides 23% of all international funding for HIV/AIDS. In total 60% of its funding went to programmes in sub-Saharan Africa.

PEPFAR is the USA's initiative to combat the global HIV/AIDS pandemic. Following the signing into law of the United States Leadership Against HIV/AIDS, Tuberculosis and Malaria Act of 2003, PEPFAR began its work in June 2004. The legislation approved expenditure of up to US$15 billion over five years. In fact spending over the period was US$18.8 billion. In July 2008, PEPFAR was re-authorised for a further five years, with funding up to US$48 billion over the five year period. PEPFAR focuses on 15 specific countries, all in Africa and the Caribbean (apart from Vietnam). Since 2008 PEPFAR has promoted a partnership framework model. The new partnership framework emphasises the role of host country governments in ensuring an effective and sustainable response to the HIV/AIDS pandemic.

UNAIDS, together with the Global Fund and PEPFAR, have implemented and coordinated a range of international HIV/AIDS interventions in what Elbe (2008) labels 'a kind of marketing strategy' which is associated with 'an epidemiological risk rationality' (Elbe 2008: 188) that has resulted in 'a risk-based bio-political security practice' (Elbe 2008: 189). Thus in Elbe's opinion the securitisation of HIV/AIDS has been responsible for the development of a global biopolitical economy of power dominated by the USA and other Western democracies, through these hugely powerful international organisations.

Conclusion

It is clear that in the last 25 years health security has become an important element of human security that mirrors the shift in development thinking and the dominance of the human development paradigm. The global HIV/AIDS pandemic has been instrumental in putting health at the centre of the human security debate as a consequence of the securitisation of the disease by UN Resolution 1308 in 2000. In 2000 the threat of the HIV/AIDS epidemic on state security appears to have been exaggerated; the predicted collapse in state structures in countries most severely affected by the disease did not occur. However the impact on human welfare and security was underestimated, with the impact on livelihoods little understood. An unexpected outcome of Resolution 1308 has been the rise to prominence of international biopolitical power concerning the health and well-being of populations in the developing world and in sub-Saharan Africa in particular.

The HIV/AIDS pandemic has changed the world we inhabit in many ways. For those living in high prevalence regions, the pandemic is not only a medical tragedy, it also retards human development and has produced fears of state insecurity and the reality of human insecurity including uncertainty of food production and in extreme cases famine. This disease connects human and health security at all scales and contributes to state insecurity. It has played a central role in the incorporation of health security within the new human security paradigm.

Bibliography

Aldis, W. (2008) 'Health Security as a Public Health Concept: A Critical Analysis', *Health Policy and Planning* 23.6: 369-75.

Barnett, T., and A. Whiteside (2002) *AIDS in the Twenty-first Century* (Basingstoke, UK: Palgrave).

Becker, J.U., C. Theodosis and R. Kulkarni (2008) 'HIV/AIDS, Conflict and Security in Africa: Rethinking Relationships', *Journal of the International AIDS Society* 11: 3-9.

Bond, K. (2008) 'Health Security or Health Diplomacy? Moving beyond Semantic Analysis to Strengthen Health Systems and Global Cooperation', *Health Policy and Planning*, 2008: 8-10.

Chandler, D. (2008) 'Human Security: The Dog that Didn't Bark', *Security Dialogue* 39: 427-38.

Commission on Human Security (2003) *Human Security Now* (Washington, DC: Commission on Human Security).

De Waal, A., and A. Whiteside (2003) 'New Variant Famine: AIDS and Food Crisis in Southern Africa', *The Lancet* 362: 1,234-37.

Elbe, S. (2008) 'Risking Lives: AIDS, Security and the Three Concepts of Risk', *Security Dialogue* 39.2-3: 177-98.

Fourie, P., and M. Schonteich (2001) 'Die, the Beloved Countries: Human Security and HIV/AIDS in Africa', paper presented at the *South African Association for Political Science (SAAPS) Conference*, University of Durban-Westville, South Africa, July 2001.

Glasius, M. (2008) 'Human Security from Paradigm Shift to Operationalization: Job Description for a Human Security Worker', *Security Dialogue* 39.1: 31-54.

Hunter, L.M. (2007) 'Understanding How HIV/AIDS, Agricultural Systems, and Food Security are Linked', Population Reference Bureau; www.prb.org/Articles/2007/UnderstandingLinksHIVAIDSAgricultureFoodSecurity.aspx, accessed 24 June 2010.

Iqbal, J.M. (2009) 'AIDS and the State: A Comparison of Brazil, India and South Africa', *South Asian Survey* 16: 119-35.

McInnes, C. (2006) 'HIV/AIDS and Security', *International Affairs* 82.2: 315-26.

—— (2009) 'HIV, AIDS and Conflict in Africa: Why isn't it (even) worse?' paper presented at the *Annual Conference of the International Studies Association*, New York, February 2009.

Merson, M.H., J. O'Malley, D. Serwadda and C. Apisuk (2008) 'The History and Challenge of HIV Prevention', *The Lancet* 372: 475-88.

O'Manique, C. (2005) 'The "Securitisation" of HIV/AIDS in Sub-Saharan Africa: A Critical Feminist Lens', *Policy and Society* 24.1: 24-47.

Owen, T. (2008) 'The Critique That Doesn't Bite: A Response to David Chandler's "Human Security: The Dog That Didn't Bark" ', *Security Dialogue* 39: 445-53.

Piot, P. (2001) 'Executive Director, UNAIDS, AIDS now core issue at UN Security Council', press release, TheBody.com, 19 January 2001; www.thebody.com/content/art642.html?ts=pf, accessed 12 November 2009.

Poku, N.K., N. Renwick and J.G. Porto (2007) 'Human Security and Development in Africa', *International Affairs* 83.6: 1,155-70.

Sagala, J.K. (2008) 'HIV/AIDS Prevention Strategies in the Armed Forces in Sub-Saharan Africa: A Critical Review', *Armed Forces & Society* 34: 292-313.

Selgelid, M.J., and C. Enemark (2008) 'Infectious Diseases, Security and Ethics: The Case of HIV/AIDS', *Bioethics* 22.9: 457-65.

Tadjbakhsh, S., and A.N. Chenoy (2007) *Human Security: Concepts and Implications* (London: Routledge).

UNAIDS (2009a) 'AIDS Epidemic Update'; data.unaids.org/pub/Report/2009/JC1700_Epi_Update_2009_en.pdf, accessed 24 June 2010.

—— (2009b) 'Fact Sheet: Sub-Saharan Africa: Latest Epidemiological Trends'; data.unaids.org/pub/FactSheet/2009/20091124_fs_ssa_en.pdf, accessed 24 June 2010.

UNDP (1990) *The Human Development Report 1990* (Oxford, UK: Oxford University Press).

—— (1994) *The Human Development Report 1994* (Oxford, UK: Oxford University Press).

WHO (2007) *The World Health Report* (Geneva: WHO).

5

Human security and healthcare in the USA

Deepayan Basu Ray
Independent Consultant

The concept of health as a fundamental human right has been enshrined in the Universal Declaration of Human Rights, and also the constitution of the World Health Organisation (WHO). On the other hand, health as a driver of insecurity has received comparatively little attention. Health-related insecurity has primarily been discussed as an epidemiological or crisis-related issue, with policy responses focusing on containing outbreaks and responding to the threats of disease in disaster conditions. Framed in this way, the all-encompassing impacts of poor health and weak health systems on human capability is not included in the policy analysis and potential opportunities for reform, and no amount of financial input can ever adequately address the resultant problems.

The US economy is the one of the most prolific in the world, generating annual per capita gross national income of US$45,850 in 2007—second only to Luxembourg (WDI 2009: 353). National health spending is expected to reach US$2.5 trillion in 2009, accounting for 17.6% of GDP (NCHC 2009a: 1). The combined daily public–private expenditure on healthcare in the US amounts to a staggering US$5.2 billion (Burd-Sharps *et al.* 2008: 5, 50). The US is one of the leaders in cutting edge and high-tech medical treatments; in 2004, the US had more MRI and CT scanners per million of population than any other OECD country (Ariana 2007: 3). 'The number of biotechnology firms in the US (3,154) far exceed those in other OECD countries and this is accompanied by a correspondingly high level of employees (73,520) and expenditure on biotechnology research and development' (Ariana 2007: 5).

Despite this innovation and immense financial investment and expenditure, the US continues to fall behind other OECD countries in most indicators of good health. The US ranks 24th globally on life expectancy (UNDP 2007: 261). The disparity between American states is also glaring. For example, there is close to an eight year difference in life expectancy between the population of Washington, DC (73.8 years), and that of Hawaii (81.7 years), despite the fact that Washington, DC, has the highest median income of all states (AHDR 2008: 51). Certain demographic groups within American society are also more at risk than others, with over 19 years separating African-American males (69.4 years) and Asian females (88.9 years) (AHDR 2008: 53). Over 45.7 million Americans (15.3% of the population), including 8.1 million children (11% of all children) are without health insurance, and therefore do not have access to any form of preventive medical treatment (DeNavas-Walt *et al.* 2008: 20). Shockingly, the US infant mortality rate is ranked 29th in the world, and on par with countries such as Poland, Cuba and Croatia, who spend far less per capita on health-related investments than the US (HDR 2008: 261).

It is therefore no surprise that healthcare reform has rapidly become one of the key barometers of success of Barack Obama's first term in office as the President of the United States. The issue has generated a lot of media and political attention, and illustrates the importance of health reform on the political agenda in the US. This chapter explores the current state of service delivery in the healthcare sector, and argues that a social protection model can help to mitigate the drivers of human insecurity in America. It does not attempt to outline the perfect system, but aims to illustrate where policy is creating gaps in service delivery, the impact of these policies and gaps, and the potential consequences of reform initiatives on the perception and experience of human security in America.

Impacts of health on human security in America

Health has a fundamental impact on human security and capabilities. Poor health prevents individuals from exercising agency over life choices, which in turn compromises their economic productivity and social mobility. As UNDP has noted,

> health is also essential to human security, since survival and protection from illness are at the core of any concept of people's wellbeing. Good health enables human choice, freedom, and progress. Poor health— illness, injury, and disability—undermines those essential human capabilities and can trigger potentially catastrophic reversals for individuals, communities and economies (UNDP 2009: 145).

In the US, poor health can trigger a downward cycle towards chronic poverty because access to healthcare is dependent on medical insurance—the majority of which is provided by employers. This generates significant insecurity, as without access to healthcare, an individual or family's ability to cope with medical emergencies significantly diminishes. Furthermore, the ability of these individuals and their families to access preventive care is also compromised, which potentially worsens the impact of an emergency.

One of the main drivers of health-related insecurity in America is the cost of medical assistance, in terms of both emergencies and long-term or preventive care. Treatment for 'neurologic illnesses such as multiple sclerosis were associated with the highest out-of-pocket expenditures (mean $34,167), followed by diabetes ($26,971), injuries ($25,096), stroke ($23,380), mental illnesses ($23,178), and heart disease ($21,955)' (Himmelstein *et al.* 2009: 744). There is a sufficient body of anecdotal evidence that illustrates cases of patients and families being denied treatment without proof of health insurance provided to health practitioners. Although in cases of life-threatening emergencies hospitals are obliged to provide care, the bill for services is usually presented back to the recovering patient or their family. In most cases, these amounts—typically US$11,800 or more—must be paid back in their entirety, often in one lump sum (AHRQ 2009).

It is therefore no surprise that more than 60% of all bankruptcies in 2007 were due to medical costs (Bates 2009: 7). A recently study entitled 'Medical Bankruptcy in the United States, 2007' estimates that medical bankruptcies affect about 2 million Americans every year, if both debtors and their dependents, including about 700,000 children, are counted (Fox 2005).

> 92% of these medical debtors had medical debts over $5000, or 10% of pre-tax family income. The rest met the criteria for medical bankruptcy because they had lost significant income due to illness or mortgaged a home to pay medical bills (Himmelstein *et al.* 2009: 741).

Hospital bills were the largest single out-of-pocket expense for 48% of patients who had claimed bankruptcy, with prescription drugs accounting for a further 18.6%, doctors' bills for 15.1%, and premiums for 4.1% (Himmelstein *et al.* 2009: 741). Uninsured patients and their families could expect a bill for services to be in excess of US$26,000. What is even more surprising is that most medical debtors were 'well educated, owned homes, and had middle-class occupations'. Furthermore, up to three-quarters of people declared medically bankrupt had health insurance, but it was the cost of co-payments or out-of-pocket expenses that pushed them to bankruptcy. The study found that the share of bankruptcies due to medical expenses and costs rose by 49.6% between 2001 and 2007 (Himmelstein *et al.* 2009: 741).

The US government has a medical insurance programme—Medicaid—set up to assist individuals and families on very low incomes, and this programme provided medical services to 39.6 million Americans in 2007 (DeNavas-Walt *et al.* 2008: 20). The programme is not, however, designed to systematically address the needs of those without insurance and, by its own admission, does not help all poor Americans either. Pending further reform, Medicaid remains a stop-gap solution which doesn't address persistent poverty or the need for health security. Furthermore, the programme is implemented at state level, which creates a lack of uniformity as eligibility thresholds are based on relative poverty in each state. This approach is not only more costly in the long run, but also does not address the drivers of poverty and human insecurity in a comprehensive and equitable manner. Medicaid and other types of public and private health insurance option are explored later in this chapter.

Having access to medical insurance is also no guarantee that individuals or families will be able to cope in the event of a crisis. There is a growing cross-section of the American population who, despite having some form of health coverage, find themselves under-insured in times of crisis. Many policies require customers to pay for a certain part of the treatment/process—for example, visitation fees for doctors—or to pay a medical bill in its entirety before making a claim. In a recent study exploring the role of health-related costs in bankruptcies, the authors found that out-of-pocket medical costs averaged nearly US$18,000 for all medically bank-rupt families. Despite having access to private or state-provided health insurance, patients or their families had to pay up front for services in the range of US$6,500 to upwards of US$17,500. For patients who initially had private coverage but lost it, the family's out-of-pocket expenses averaged $22,568 (Himmelstein *et al.* 2009: 744).

This evidence highlights the inability of poor Americans to absorb the cost of emergency medical care. This further reinforces the assertion of the UNDP *Human Development Report 1994* which notes that, 'in both developing and industrial countries, the threats to health security are usually greater for the poorest, people in the rural areas and particularly children' (UNDP 1994: 28). Providing public safety nets which enable all Americans to access affordable healthcare therefore becomes an even more pressing policy issue.

Box 5.1 **Glossary of key terms**

Medicare: The entitlement-based government-sponsored healthcare pro-gramme for all over-65-year-olds

Medicaid: A means-tested, needs-based social welfare scheme to assist very poor individuals and families

Premiums: The periodic (monthly/quarterly/annual) payment made on an insurance policy

Deductible: In an insurance policy, the deductible is the portion of any claim that is not covered by the insurance provider. These include co-pay-ments and coinsurance

Co-payment: A payment paid by the insured person each time a medical service is accessed. The thresholds are usually defined in the insurance policy. For instance, the insured person may have to pay the fees for each doctor's visit

Coinsurance: A percentage of the cost of medical service that the insured person has to pay on top of what the insurance policy covers. The thresh-olds are usually defined in the specific policy. For example, the policy may state that the insured person is responsible for paying 25% of all costs incurred in hospitals

---

Achieving health security through a social protection model

Health policy has mostly been defined in terms of reducing the burden of sickness and preventing premature death. In recent years, there has been a lot of work to refine this basic policy prescription by analysing the burden of ill-health and identifying interventions that reduce it (Bloom 2005: 1). In the US, demographic pressures and healthcare trends are increasingly forcing policy-makers to consider 'prevention and reduction of shocks, rather than merely assisting people to cope afterwards' (Norton *et al.* 2001: 16). The Medicaid system is inadequate, and does not address the chronic insecurity created by uncertainties and lack of preventive intervention. One of the main reasons for this is poverty in the US, which should be considered in relative terms: 'meaning deprivation based on what is considered necessary by most of society' (AHDR 2008: 19). Government responsibility and corresponding initiatives to assist those most in need therefore need to be developed along the model of social protection programming.

Norton *et al.* (2001: 1) define social protection as 'public actions taken in response to levels of vulnerability, risk and deprivation which are deemed socially unacceptable within a given polity or society'. In the context of the US it is therefore important to:

> read the definition of social protection provided above as referring to the protection of those who fall temporarily or persistently under levels of livelihood deemed acceptable, rather than the promotion of a general standard of opportunity and livelihood for all citizens (Norton *et al.* 2001: 10).

A social protection approach to service delivery in the health sector will help improve human security because it will help to target policy mechanisms (such as Medicaid) to address both shocks and stresses associated with ill health. Shocks can be understood as the sudden onset of crises such as accidents or exposure to contagious outbreaks of disease or viruses. As the data on bankruptcy has shown, the financial ramifications of these events can prove catastrophic for individuals and families, particularly those below or near the poverty line. Stresses, on the other hand, can be understood as structural barriers that impede access to care, both preventive and emergency. These can include the outright cost (or imposed limits) of insurance coverage, or the ability to access and secure employment through which *sufficient* medical insurance is provided to cover the individual or their family. Medicaid, it can be argued, is geared to a certain extent to address both shocks and stresses, but it is not an open policy, and does not come to the aid of every poor American who cannot access healthcare. Medicaid is, for all intents and purposes, an institutionalised zip-code lottery, where access to services and care is predicated on an individual's relative poverty in relation to the state they live in, and not a nationally derived threshold.

Furthermore, in a system where access to healthcare is intrinsically tied to employment, the financial crisis has presented an existential challenge to the existing medical insurance-based system in the US. Upwards of 14,000 Americans are losing their insurance coverage every day in the current economic climate (Obama 2009). Studies assessing the scale of the impacts of the current financial crisis predict that for every one percentage point increase in unemployment, the number of uninsured people increases by 1.1 million (Fish-Parcham and McAndrew 2009: 1). Facing recession, many small employers are finding it difficult to afford health-related benefits for their employees. The National Coalition on Health Care (NCHC) has recently noted that companies that do offer health insurance are now requiring employees to contribute a larger share of their salaries towards their coverage. This has put further pressure on families below or near the poverty line, and the increased cost of premiums is unaffordable for many Americans. On average, it costs employers approximately US$13,000 to provide health insurance to cover a family of four; of this cost, more than US$3,300 is directly borne by the employee (NCHC 2009a: 2). The cost of private insurance is also around US$12,000, and higher still if there is any previous history of illnesses such as cancer. It is clear that, for any family earning on or around the poverty threshold amount (US$21,027), the cost of this premium is simply not an option (AHDR 2008: 124).

The importance of a social-protection approach to ensure human security cannot be underestimated, particularly given the financial burden that emergency medical treatment (or indeed preventive care) places on millions of Americans. Although hospitals and other medical establishments are obliged to provide care in cases of emergency, the system continues to discriminate against those who are unable to afford the cost of services or have access to adequate insurance to address emergency needs. As statistics have illustrated, many Americans have no option but to simply forgo medical treatment if there is no state-sponsored assistance.

A lack of health insurance also has knock-on impacts on emergency services. Ostensibly, there is a greater risk of public health crises because people cannot take preventive steps to improve their health and perceptions of health security by simply visiting their local doctor. As noted by Hale (1996: 195-210), the inability to protect themselves . . .

> either because they cannot run fast, or lack the physical prowess to ward off attackers, or because they cannot afford to protect their homes, or because it would take them longer than average to recover from material or physical injuries . . .

has a profound impact on an individual's perceptions of insecurity. If these fears are compounded by a perception of inadequate government social protection mechanisms—particularly in a wealthy country such as the US—then the experience of security is dictated almost exclusively by levels of wealth, which is neither just nor sustainable.

An overview of the current system of health insurance

The current system of healthcare in the US is based for the most part on a partnership between public and private health insurance companies. The number of people with health insurance in 2007 was 253.4 million, of which 202 million people were covered by private health insurance, and 83 million were covered by government health insurance (DeNavas-Walt *et al.* 2008: 19). The Agency for Healthcare Research and Quality estimated that more than one in four Americans under the age of 65, was uninsured in 2007 (NCHC 2009b: 1). Although men are more likely to be uninsured (16% of all American men), some 13% of American women were uninsured in 2006 (Cohen and Martinez 2007: 14). Other indicators of capacity constraints show that some 30% of adults without a high school diploma remain uninsured. Their lack of health coverage could be traced back to their inability to secure jobs in sectors where health benefits are available, further reinforcing the cyclical nature of poverty (Cohen and Martinez 2007: 14). Among those persons aged under 65 years, 170 million (65%) had private health insurance, and 38 million (15%) had Medicaid; however, 44 million (17%) were uninsured (Cohen and Martinez 2007: 14). Some 35% of poor, working-age adults were covered by publicly provided insurance, and a further 25% were covered through private insurance (Cohen and Martinez 2007: 4).

Americans in the lowest income group were about five times as likely as persons in the highest income group to 'delay' medical care because of cost, and about ten times more likely not to access preventive care (HHS 2009: 32). Correspondingly, statistics from the Centre for Disease Control and the US Census Bureau found that the higher an individual or family's income bracket, the greater the coverage of health insurance (Pilkington 2007: 6). In 2007, nearly one in four Americans living in households with annual incomes of less than US$25,000 had no health insurance coverage. That figure reduced to less than 1 in 12 with annual household incomes of US$75,000 or more (DeNavas-Walt *et al.* 2008: 23).

As identified above, the majority of Americans rely on private or employment-based health coverage to meet their medical care needs. By way of assistance, the federal government provides tax deductions for employers and individuals. Over US$180 billion in tax revenue was forgone by the government to provide these exemptions; 180 million Americans were able to benefit from this process in 2004. The cost of private health insurance for a family of four has steadily increased each year. There is, as yet, no government-run insurance scheme that competes directly with private insurers—though this has become one of President Obama's main areas of policy reform in the first year of his term.

The introduction of a government-run scheme is not inconsequential—private insurance and other health-sector companies have made a lot of money in recent years. Though the profit margins of private insurance companies are relatively modest, the absolute value of their profits is staggering. UnitedHealth Group, one of the largest insurance providers, saw its revenue jump by 7% between January and March 2009 from US$20.27 billion to US$21.66 billion, 'helped by higher premiums and price increases' (NASDAQ 2009). This enabled the company to project a US$3 increase in the value of its shares for 2009, which is a substantial amount given the current economic climate. Private insurance companies have also been very active in lobbying the US government, having provided in excess of US$41 million as campaign contributions to current members of Congress—the majority of which has been provided to those politicians involved in preparing the collection of 2009 health-related bills (Fram 2009). 'Since the beginning of 2008 alone, they have spent $145 million on lobbying, led by Blue Cross-Blue Shield organisations and the AHIP trade group' (Fram 2009).

The current entitlement-based scheme that provides medical assistance to the over-65s and individuals with specific disabilities is the Medicare programme. This programme received in excess of US$400 billion in direct government funds, and provided assistance to 41.4 million people in 2007. Medicare still requires eligible Americans to pay monthly premiums for medical insurance, as well as having to pay deductibles, co-payment and coinsurance. Over and above these expenses, those eligible for Medicare must also pay for prescription drug coverage. The option is also provided to select a Medicare Advantage Plan, which is, for all intents and purposes a private health plan approved by the programme. Anecdotal evidence has suggested that the cost borne by the over-65s to access critical medication has created a lot of anxiety among patients, particularly given that certain types of age-related chronic illness such as Alzheimer's and heart disease require intensive medication. The bulk of the cost of prescriptions is still borne by the patient. The potential costs of co-payment have also put off many Medicare beneficiaries from undertaking preventive steps such as screening for diabetes, osteoporosis and prostate cancer (Rother 2009).

As discussed earlier, Medicaid is a means-tested, needs-based social welfare scheme, which provides medical assistance—not insurance—to the 'categorically needy, medically needy, or special groups' (CMS 2005: 1). The plan is administered at state level, and is not intended to provide medical assistance to all poor persons, nor does it make cash transfers to the poor for medical expenses. Instead, the programme makes payments on behalf of the patient to the medical practitioners. There continue to be ongoing concerns about the bureaucratic and administrative burden created by the paperwork to determine eligibility. There are also concerns that thresholds are not uniform across the country because it is administered by individual states. For instance, those likely to be ineligible for Medicaid assistance in Mississippi (where levels of absolute poverty are highest) would probably qualify for assistance in wealthier states such as Connecticut (where levels are low).

Another big concern with Medicaid is the costing structure, particularly in light of the growing numbers of Americans becoming eligible to receive Medicaid in the wake of the financial crisis. The federal government provides the majority of funds to states to implement the service; federal funds accounted for 75% of the funding base for the Mississippi Division of Medicaid (MDM 2009: 5). The conditions for eligibility (as noted above) are also set by each state, which means that the number of individuals receiving Medicaid varies greatly between states. This generates differential requests for federal funding between the states, making it difficult to predict year-on-year need and allocate the appropriate funds.

Other federal health insurance schemes include the State Children's Health Insurance Program (SCHIP), which assists an estimated 4.1 million children who are ineligible for Medicaid, while their families cannot afford private insurance. This programme accounts for US$7.9 billion of government expenditure annually (AHDR 2008: 75). The Military's TRICARE programme provides medical care to active duty service members, National Guard and Reserve members, retired veterans, their families and survivors. Those in active service do not have to pay any premiums, and those who have retired are expected to pay annual fees of US$230 for an individual or US$460 for a family (AFMS 2009). TRICARE, like other federally run programmes, offers individuals a choice of three tiers of service, with each tier providing progressively more services and lower deductible costs (TRICARE 2009). Approximately 9.4 million Americans are enrolled in this scheme which costs US$35.4 billion annually. Of all the federal programmes, TRICARE has been hailed as a model for government service delivery, and one that the Obama administration has been studying carefully.

Based on this evidence, the current system of service delivery in the US health sector has in effect developed a two-tier social welfare system which serves, primarily, the interests of those with money, and reinforces inter-generational transmission and geographies of poverty. A number of critical gaps have appeared in the delivery of healthcare and health systems. The cost of private insurance is preventing more than 15% of all Americans from accessing preventive and emergency care, and the political lobby continues to advocate strongly—and hitherto successfully—against major structural reform. In the wake of the recession, employers (who are the largest providers of health insurance) are being forced to pass on increasing costs onto their employees or deciding to do away with the provision of insurance altogether. The co-payments and deductibles associated with Medicare continue to place over-65s under acute financial stress. Medicaid's system of differential state thresholds continues to prevent poor Americans from accessing healthcare, thereby entrenching cycles of poor health, unemployment and chronic poverty. Given these concerns, the American government has a long way to go before the investment it makes annually into healthcare starts to produce the desired results.

Healthcare reform options and prospects for realising human security

A joint consortium of development donors (GTZ, ILO and WHO) has recently noted that:

a country's health financing system is a key determinant of population health and wellbeing. The question that remains of utmost importance is therefore, how national health systems can ensure universal coverage that is defined as access to key promotive, preventive, curative and rehabilitative health interventions for all at an affordable cost (GTZ-ILO-WHO 2009).

This challenge encapsulates the problem for healthcare reform in the United States. Healthcare reform is not a new topic of debate in American politics. Bill Clinton's first term in office was marked by a defeat of a comprehensive reform bill for healthcare in 1993–1994. Obama's popularity and rise to the presidency in 2008 provided an unprecedented opportunity to move healthcare reform high onto the political agenda. Incredibly, this momentum was sustained through the devastating impacts of the 2008/09 financial crisis that rocked the core of Wall Street, and resulted in a historic victory with the successful passage of the healthcare reform bill through both houses in March 2010.

The Obama administration's attempts to address the gaps identified above have been admirable. Predictably however, political concessions have significantly weakened the overall impact that the original bill envisaged. The comprehensive set of reforms proposed in the 2009 'America's Affordable Health Choices Act' had to be considerably edited down in order to garner the required support to pass into law. This notwithstanding, the subsequent 'Patient Protection and Affordable Care Act' of March 2010 was a historic achievement by the Obama administration, passing into law by the narrowest of vote margins (219–212) in the House of Representatives.

The healthcare reform bill is focused around two key premises: coverage and affordability. Expanding the coverage has been a key area of focus for the new bill. Despite its best efforts, political tradeoffs eventually forced the Obama administration to abandon a flagship initiative of the reform package—the creation of a government-run health insurance scheme that was meant to engender competition among insurance providers and increase choice for consumers. The issue of coverage was, however, addressed through a number of comprehensive and meaningful reforms—particularly on issues such as providing patients with more information on choices, and guaranteeing coverage without prejudice to past or chronic health-related problems. For example, the approved legislation now ensures that 'uninsured Americans with a pre-existing condition will have access to an immediate insurance program' (CEL 2010a: 1). Additionally, insurance companies are now barred from discriminating on based on pre-existing medical conditions (CEL 2010a: 1).

The second key premise of affordability was addressed through a number of measures, including but not limited to enabling MediCare patients to have access to more affordable prescription drugs, providing subsidies to low-income families wanting to purchase their own insurance, providing tax credits to small businesses, and developing an overall budget which reportedly reduces the deficit by US$138 billion over a period of ten years (BBC 2010; CEL 2010a). The reforms also included 'an expansion of federal subsidies to make insurance more affordable and more state aid for the Medicaid program for the poor' (Reuters 2010). The bill also strengthened preventative measures as a means of reducing the healthcare costs over time. To do this, 'the bill eliminates co-pays and deductibles for recommended preventive care', aims to improve education on disease prevention and public health, and works toward developing a national prevention and public health strategy (CEL 2010a: 2).

A closer scrutiny of the bill through a human security lens shows that though it goes a long way in addressing the service delivery gaps that the current system has created, a number of fundamental concerns are not adequately addressed by the package of reforms.

The first key point to emphasise is that access to health insurance remains predicated on an individual's or a family's ability to secure employment. Those who are out of work will likely find the premiums prohibitive—and the degree of coverage will depend on the type of work. This is problematic at a number of levels. Firstly, unemployment—which remains high as a result of the residual impacts of the financial crisis—will directly continue to affect the ability of the uninsured to access adequate coverage. Secondly, as the income bracket effectively dictates the levels of coverage, those families/individuals on low-paid jobs will likely receive a lower threshold of coverage than an executive or professional. This will continue to perpetuate the current two-tier system in practice, despite the bill's best efforts at reducing the gap between the rich and the poor in America.

The lowering of thresholds to expand Medicaid is also an important initiative in the new bill, as this step will ensure that over 33 million uninsured Americans are now able to access some form of healthcare. However, the thresholds themselves need to be revisited. Southern and western states are poorer, and the expansion of Medicaid needed to ensure that these states were able to receive proportionally more assistance in order to address both absolute and relative levels of poverty and deprivation. The bill fell far short of that mark. The only additional funds that poorer states are now able to access is through a fund aimed at 'expanding access to care' (CEL 2010b: 885) which will do little to address relative need in poorer states.

Of particular concern to the human security framework is the major failure of the bill to address the specific needs of women. Although a number of specific measures were adopted to ensure that the needs of vulnerable women were met through an expanded Medicaid service, political concessions made by the Obama administration ensured that no federal funds could be used to cover abortions (Herszenhorn and Calmes 2009). By removing the ability of the state to give women a real choice of a range of options—irrespective of the decision they ultimately make—the bill has ultimately failed to ensure the health-security needs of women.

A final area of potential future concern is the proposed cutting of US$500 billion from the MediCare budget over the next ten years. This decision could severely shortchange MediCare as the so-called 'baby-boomer generation' nears retirement and becomes eligible for the programme.

Conclusions

As explored earlier in this chapter, good health underpins human capabilities, which in turn comprehensively affect perceptions of security. It also boosts an individual's choices in terms of employment and income generation, both of which are crucial in mitigating the devastating impacts of shocks or crises. As individuals engender confidence in state institutions which are able to come to their assistance to mitigate the impacts of these shocks and stresses, the realisation of human security is that much closer to fruition.

Given the political capital dedicated to realising healthcare reform by the Obama administration—and indeed a number of former US Presidents—it has been clear for some time that the healthcare system in America has not adequately addressed health-security concerns of a considerable segment of the population. Judging by the embittered and polarised debate that resulted from the negotiations, and continues to generate news headlines many months after the bill was voted through, it is clear that this was a landmark and historic political victory for Obama. The reform package is likely to upgrade the service delivery model and will take a very strong step towards addressing the current gaps in coverage and affordability. This notwithstanding, there is a pervasive sense that perhaps the opportunity to deliver more on healthcare reform has potentially been missed. That perhaps a system that could be based on prevention, addressing human deprivation, social protection needs and, ultimately, human security could have been realised, but had to be compromised to survive the machinations of the Washington political process. Only time will tell if the package of reforms will affect the statistics, and make a difference in the lives of millions of Americans.

Bibliography

AFMS (Air Force Medical Service) (2009) 'TRICARE: General Information'; airforcemedicine. afms.mil/idc/groups/public/documents/webcontent/knowledgejunction.hcst?functi onalarea=ColumbusAFB&doctype=subpage&docname=CTB_041844, accessed 24 June 2010.

AHRQ (Agency for Healthcare Research and Quality) (2009) 'Statistics on All Hospital Stays'; hcupnet.ahrq.gov.

Ariana, P. (2007) 'Health Inequalities in America, Background Paper Commissioned for The Measure of America: American Human Development Report 2008–2009'; www. measureofamerica.org/wp-content/uploads/2008/07/health-paper.pdf, accessed 23 September 2010.

Bates, S. (2009) 'Why I'm so glad I broke my leg in Britain, not America', *The Guardian* G2, 19 August 2009.

BBC (2010) 'US House passes key healthcare reform bill', BBC, 22 March 2010; news.bbc. co.uk/1/hi/8579322.stm, accessed 23 September 2010.

Bloom, G. (2005) *Health and Social Protection: Meeting the Needs of the Very Poor* (Brighton, UK: Institute of Development Studies; www.eldis.org/fulltext/verypoor/2_bloom.pdf).

Burd-Sharps, S., K. Lewis and E. Martins (2008) *The Measure of America: American Human Development Report 2008–2009* (New York: Columbia University Press).

CEL (Committee on Education and Labor) (2009) 'America's Affordable Health Choices Act: Summary', US House of Representatives, 15 July 2009; edlabor.house.gov/documents/111/pdf/publications/AAHCA-BILLSUMMARY-071409.pdf, accessed 24 June 2010.

—— (2010a) 'Summary: Affordable Health Care for America', House Committees on Ways and Means, Energy and Commerce, and Education and Labor, 18 March 2010; docs.house.gov/energycommerce/SUMMARY.pdf, accessed 23 September 2010.

—— (2010b) 'The Patient Protection and Affordable Care Act', House Committees on Ways and Means, Energy and Commerce, and Education and Labor, 9 June 2010; docs.house.gov/energycommerce/ppacacon.pdf, accessed 23 September 2010.

CMS (Centers for Medicare and Medicaid Services) (2005) 'Medicaid At-a-Glance 2005: A Medicaid Information Source' (Department of Health and Human Services, Publication No. CMS-11024-05; https://www.cms.gov/MedicaidGenInfo/Downloads/MedicaidAt-AGlance2005.pdf, accessed 23 September 2010).

Cohen, R.A., and M.E. Martinez (2007) 'Health Insurance Coverage: Early Release of Estimates from the National Health Interview Survey, 2006', Centre for Disease Control, Atlanta, June 2006; www.cdc.gov/nchs/data/nhis/earlyrelease/insur200706.pdf, accessed 23 September 2010.

DeNavas-Walt, C., B.D. Proctor and J. Smith (2008) 'Income, Poverty, and Health Insurance Coverage in the United States: 2007' (Washington, DC: US Census Bureau; www.census.gov/prod/2008pubs/p60-235.pdf, accessed 23 September 2010).

Fish-Parcham, C. and C. McAndrew (2009) 'Squeezed: Caught between Unemployment Benefits and Health Care Costs', Families USA; www.familiesusa.org/assets/pdfs/cobra-2009.pdf, accessed 23 September 2010.

Fox, M. (2005) 'Half of Bankruptcy Due to Medical Bills: US Study', Reuters, 2 February 2005; www.commondreams.org/headlines05/0202-08.htm, accessed 24 June 2010.

Fram, A. (2009) 'The Influence Game: Health Insurance Lobby Uses Money, Allies to Fight Government Coverage', *Washington Examiner*, 6 August 2009; www.washingtonexaminer.com/politics/ap/52594887.html.

GTZ-ILO-WHO (2009) 'Social Protection in Health', GTZ-ILO-WHO Consortium on Social Health Protection in Developing Countries; www.socialhealthprotection.org/social_protection_health.php, accessed 24 June 2010.

Hale, C. (1996) 'Fear of Crime: A Review of the Literature', *International Review of Victimology* 4.

Herszenhorn, D.M., and J. Calmes (2009) 'Abortion Was at Heart of Wrangling', *New York Times*, 7 November 2009; www.nytimes.com/2009/11/08/health/policy/08scene.html.

HHS (US Department of Health and Human Services) (2009) 'Summary Health Statistics for the US Population: National Health Interview Survey, 2008', *Vital and Health Statistics* 10.243 (August 2009); www.cdc.gov/nchs/data/series/sr_10/sr10_243.pdf.

Himmelstein, D., D. Thorne, E. Warren and S. Woolhandler (2009) 'Medical Bankruptcy in the United States, 2007: Results of a National Study', *The American Journal of Medicine* 122.8 (August 2009): 741-46; download.journals.elsevierhealth.com/pdfs/journals/0002-9343/PIIS0002934309004045.pdf.

NASDAQ (2009) 'UnitedHealth Group Q2 Profit Jumps 155%', Dividend.com, 4 September 2009; www.nasdaq.com/newscontent/20090721/unitedhealthgroupq2profitjumps155unh.aspx?storyid=1395, accessed 24 June 2010.

NCHC (National Coalition on Health Care) (2009a) 'Health Care Facts: Costs', July 2009; nchc. org/facts-resources/fact-sheet-cost, accessed 23 September 2010.

—— (2009b) 'Health Care Facts: Health Insurance Coverage', October 2009; nchc.org/facts-resources/fact-sheet-coverage, accessed 23 September 2010.

MDM (Mississippi Division of Medicaid) (2009) 'General Presentation', The Office of the Governor, Division of Medicaid, August 2009; www.medicaid.ms.gov/Documents/FY09GenericPresentation.pdf, accessed 23 September 2010.

Norton, A., T. Conway and M. Foster (2001) *Social Protection Concepts and Approaches: Implications for Policy and Practice in International Development* (Working Paper 143; London: Centre for Aid and Public Expenditure, ODI; www.odi.org.uk/resources/download/2178. pdf).

Obama, B. (2009) 'Why We Need Health Care Reform', *New York Times*, 15 August 2009; www. nytimes.com/2009/08/16/opinion/16obama.html?pagewanted=2.

Pilkington, E. (2007) 'A State of Ill Health', *The Guardian*, 13 June 2007; www.guardian.co.uk/ usa/story/0,,2101547,00.html?gusrc=rss&feed=12, accessed 23 September 2010.

Reuters (2010), 'US Congress approves final health bill', printed in the *Financial Times*, 26 March2010;http://www.ft.com/cms/s/0/813de476-387c-11df-aabd-00144feabdc0,dwp_ uuid=b92c9d66-97df-11de-8d3d-00144feabdc0.html, accessed 23 September 2010.

Rother, J. (2009) 'Health Reform and a Strong Medicare Program', The Huffington Post; www. huffingtonpost.com/john-rother/health-reform-and-a-stron_b_278093.html, accessed 24 June 2010.

TRICARE (2009) 'TRICARE Costs'; www.tricare.mil/tricarecost.cfm, accessed 24 June 2010.

UNDP (United Nations Development Programme) (1994) *Human Development Report 1994* (New York: Oxford University Press).

—— (2007) *Human Development Report 2007/2008: Fighting Climate Change: Human Solidarity in a Divided World* (New York: Palgrave Macmillan).

—— (2009) *Arab Human Development Report 2009: Challenges to Human Security in the Arab Countries* (Lebanon: UNDP).

World Bank (2009) *World Development Report 2009: Reshaping Economic Geography* (Washington DC: World Bank).

Section III
The environmental imperative, sustainable enterprise and human security

6

'Radical change and unknown territory'
The sustainable enterprise economy and human security

Malcolm McIntosh
Asia Pacific Centre for Sustainable Enterprise, Griffith University, Australia

The impacts of climate change are not evenly distributed—the poorest countries and people will suffer the earliest and most. And if and when the damages appear it will be too late to reverse the process . . . Such temperature changes would take us into **territory unknown to human experience and involve radical changes in the world** around us . . . The analysis of climate change requires, by its nature, that we look out over 50, 100, 200 years and more (Stern 2007) [emphasis added]

92% of global thought leaders in business think that sustainability is important but the majority describe it as 'too complex' and while they think that business has a key role in solving global sustainability issues at present company action tends to be limited to regulatory requirements. 70% of companies have not developed a clear business case for sustainability but when companies look they find more opportunities than expected (Berns *et al.* 2009).

Post-Copenhagen: the second decade of the 21st century

This chapter is written with the intention of engaging the business community in helping to think about key strategic issues in what is termed here as 'the new economy', by which is meant an economy based on low carbon sustainable enterprise (SEE), which is more resilient and more hazard-adaptive. This chapter addresses the nexus between climate change, sustainable enterprise and change. What sort of society will the emerging new low carbon sustainable enterprise economy deliver? How are issues of equality and human rights affected by the fundamental changes caused by climate change?

An even more integrated globalised economy facing the climate change prognosis will see a need for greater emphasis on local solutions to problems and greater resilience in communities and businesses—what has been termed 'hazard-adaptiveness'. The need to balance global and local needs has been re-emphasised by the randomness of unexpected weather events and by the personal and institutional need to reduce risk through greater prudence in finance and resource throughputs.

This chapter is written in the immediate aftermath of COP15: the Copenhagen Summit (December 2009). We will have to wait and see what transpires but there are many who regard that conference as a missed opportunity, as a disastrous outcome and as having failed to deliver the results that are so needed if humanity is to survive on Earth. But, it is also possible to survey the wreckage and find hope and positive signals.

First, if the conference failed to deliver targets for GHGs (greenhouse gas emissions) it did succeed in forcing the major players into the open, and, in the middle of the night, tired and emotionally spent, to say what they really meant. So, the world's largest per capita emitter, the USA, failed to confront its own emissions in any significant manner. Indeed, President Obama's presence and position reminded the world that for all the hope, Nobel Peace Prize and rhetoric, he is still the President of the USA, the world's largest per capita emitter, the world's economic engine, and by far the world's largest military power. The US Constitution ensures that the President had less room for personal action than most other world leaders. So, Obama's rhetoric can only be realised if he can take a very conservative nation, wedded to what George Soros has called 'market fundamentalism', with a significant suspicion of the UN and a disbelief in science, with him. Similarly, China failed to recognise that the size of its population and land mass, the growth of its economy and middle classes force it to act responsibly for its own people and for humanity.

Second, the conference saw the limitations of trying to negotiate with 192 countries with equal UN voting rights. Here we saw US exceptionalism to the fore. Here, too, we saw China unable to manoeuvre on the world stage trying to be a member of G2, G20 and G77. Is China an emerging economy or a dominant global player? The truth is that it is both.

Third, we learnt a lot. Despite the failure to set legally binding emissions targets, it is worth noting the outcomes of COP15, otherwise known as Copenhagen 2009, and what the world learnt through this process:

- The science of climate change was recognised by all 192 countries. In particular there was consensus that global warming should be limited to 2°C above pre-industrial levels. Given the way in which climate change sceptics have been financed by the fossil fuel industry and supported by radical creationist extremists this is no mean feat—a real milestone. However, it is noted that, because of current emissions, unless a rapid decarbonisation effort is instigated, the world is bound to hit 3°C anyway

- Rich, industrialised countries (Annex 1 parties) are asked to submit their emission cuts by the end of January 2020. This is self-reporting and there are issues of monitoring, reporting and verification (MRV) but, as students of the transparency, accountability and reporting movement in the world of corporate social responsibility will know, this is a significant first step

- The 1997 Kyoto Protocol which established rich nations' legal responsibility for climate change was retained and will continue to work, despite some of those countries working to change this important legal point and in effect deny their legal responsibility

- Deforestation and agricultural degradation were recognised as significant causes of emissions—up to 20% globally—and cash will be forthcoming. This is important because it recognises the science and it recognises that those who rely on forest and agriculture for their livelihood need help in the change to a new economy

- New funding was established for developing countries to aid their transfer to low carbon economies. The amount on offer, initially US$30 billion and then US$100 billion a year by 2020, is about a third of the amount the UN thinks necessary, but again the principle has been established. Interestingly this funding is to be raised from government, business and other sources. This in itself is an interesting challenge for global governance: who will take the lead, how will the fund be managed, and how will projects be controlled? What will the role of business be?

- The final days saw leaders of most nations attending and taking part in the negotiations, in most cases face to face. In particular President Obama was photographed in hard talks alongside UN Secretary-General Ban Ki-moon, European leaders Gordon Brown from the UK, Nicolas Sarkozy from France and Angela Merkel from Germany. Given the antipathy among many Americans towards the UN and Europe this was a useful moment of unity

- Intelligence was to the fore and some leaders faded as it became clear that they did not have a full grasp of the complexity of the issues. This meant that the then Australian Prime Minister, Kevin Rudd, who both understood the issues and spoke fluent Mandarin, played a crucial role in building a new global governance around climate change. Similarly UK Prime Minister, Gordon Brown, having commissioned the Stern Review on *The Economics of Climate Change*, was in an authoritative position

- Just as President Obama made it clear that, whatever other high hopes he might represent, he is still the President of the USA, so China's stance *vis-à-vis* international relations became clear. When Obama called for increased monitoring, reporting and verification on emissions (MRV), referring obliquely to China, the Chinese Premier retired to his hotel room and sent a lower official to talk to the world's leaders—a very real insult to the US and the world. Just as the USA is the USA so we learnt that China is China and her borders are inviolable even when it comes to life-threatening climate change. But, this will change as the Chinese century advances and China embraces the world, and the world embraces it

- There was recognition of ideas and politics from developing countries and in particular significant interventions from Tuvalu, Ethiopia and India among others

How we got to the crossroads

It is conventional wisdom to say that we are entering a multi-polar world again as power slips from the United States and Europe towards the Asia–Pacific region. It is true that this is the Pacific century, with G2 (China and the USA) the most powerful marriage on the planet and the Asia–Pacific region holding most of the world's largest economies—Japan and India as well as China and the USA. It is also true that the politics of change, compassion, collectivism *and* exceptionalism are in the air. Both China and the USA think of themselves as exceptional, as special, as representing governance models that are identifiably different. But the birth of G2 has also witnessed the birth of G20, led by countries such as Australia, and the re-emergence of a powerful G77. G20 is a significant step in the direction of new global governance because it relegates G8's role and promotes a greater dialogue between industrialised, developed, emerging and other countries and recognises the way the world has changed since the end of the Second World War, the establishment of the Bretton Woods Institutions, and the birth of the United Nations.

The diffusion of power coupled with rethinking the international economic system and facing the twin challenges of economic collapse and climate change has encouraged many commentators to quote John Maynard Keynes on the role of government in balancing the extremism of the laissez-faire market economy. These commentators include James Speth in *The Bridge at the Edge of the World* subtitled

Capitalism, the environment, and crossing from crisis to sustainability, in which he reminds us that in 1933 Keynes said that within 100 years we would or should be able to put aside the god of economic growth and focus on universal well-being instead (cited in Speth 2008: 108). Indeed Keynes was scathing in his attack on economic growth and a love of money for itself:

> The love of money as a possession, as distinguished from the love of money as a means to the enjoyments and realities of life, will be recognised for what it is, a somewhat disgusting morbidity, one of those semi-criminal, semi-pathological propensities which one hands over with a shudder to the specialists in mental disease (cited in Speth 2008: 108).

We have *re*-learnt recently (2008/2009) that people are not always rational, that markets do not necessarily self-correct and that risk is often pushed on to those who can least afford to carry it. We have also *re*-learnt that there are some people who can always find the gap between our collective good intentions and making money, and that these people use their greedy, exploitative natures to defraud many in the pursuit of their own ends. Some of them work in perfectly legitimate areas of business and in fully incorporated business. J.K. Galbraith called this 'innocent' fraud (2004).

The fourth revolution

If the first revolution was agriculture, when we learnt animal husbandry, enclosure and harnessing the ability to grow our own food, the second was industrialisation, when we discovered that the rich resources that lay just beneath our feet could be used to provide new goods and services. The information revolution has arrived just in the last 30 years. The fourth revolution is what confronts us now: how to learn to live sustainably on planet Earth now that we know its limits, now that we are masters of our own destiny, now that we recognise our success. Re-seeing our world requires a real 'paradigm shift'—one that Thomas Kuhn, who invented the phrase, would understand.

We humans have been fantastically successful. We have conquered and controlled our environment and bred like rabbits such that some developing countries have birth growth rates that present extraordinary dilemmas for those countries and terrible threats to the environment and international peace. Now is the time to include population in the list of issues that must be faced if we are to develop the sustainable enterprise economy. These issues are universal and are relevant to all governments, companies and individuals whether they relate to governance, climate change adaptation, energy, water or population.

- Democratic, transparent, accountable **governance** mechanisms for all organisations and institutions in society that are based on the rule of law, an absence of corruption and respect for human rights. In 'leaving no one behind' and ensuring human security for all, and therefore stopping 'freedom from want and fear', we need governance mechanisms at the local and the international level that provide enabling frameworks that encourage enterprise, risk-taking, exchange and trade, recognise mobility as a human right, and deliver private wealth *and* public goods

- We must adapt to **climate change,** *now*. This is a process of adaptation and mitigation, although the latter will have a limited effect

- We must be more efficient with our *use* of **energy** and more intelligent in our *production* of energy

- We must be much more **water-efficient**

- We need to lower the total world **population** by discouraging families from having more than two children

If these issues are the most urgent in facing the fourth revolution at the end of first decade of the 21st century, there a number of other interacting factors that have caused a 'perfect storm', which, when considered systemically, should allow us to develop policies that advance social progress. The media tend to discuss each of these issues separately but conjoining them should help us to be innovative in public policy-making, in private business, in observing new organisational structures and in building more resilient communities. These factors are:

- The climate change prognosis

- The global financial system

- The diffusion of power towards Asia, the rise of the BRIC countries (Brazil, Russia, India and China) and the Asia–Pacific century

- The rapid development of social networking, global action networks, new hybrid organisational structures and access to instant information through the advancement of electronic communications media

The near collapse of the global financial system in 2008/2009 focused attention on the way in which the global economy had developed over the previous 20 and more years and, in particular, the transfer of uncertainty in financial speculation to risk management. The quantification of uncertainty into risk assessments allowed financial institutions to spread their bets in a world awash with cash that needed a home. In the final crash this private world, where a few individuals made risky decisions that rewarded them with millions beyond most people's dreams, was bailed out by the public world of governments.

The climate change prognosis rests on a similar principle: that of borrowing from the future to pay for the present. We have treated some goods as free and infinite and we have released into the atmosphere substances which have been stored in the Earth's surface for millions of years—and, most of this has happened in the last

200 years. The story of humanity's success is staggering but because we tend to see it only as a personal story and not as a collective bacchanalian feast we fail to appreciate how successful we have been—until perhaps now at this turning point in the history of humanity.

One measure of humanity's success is represented by the numbers 1–3–6–9. There were about 1 billion people on the planet at the birth of the industrial revolution in the mid-18th century. Mid-20th century there were 3 billion and by the end of that century the population had doubled to more than 6 billion. It is thought population growth could plateau at 9 billion by 2015 or so. Another measure of humanity's success is to be found in the figures 1–10–20. The poorest, and least 'developed' countries industrially, have per capita emissions of about 1 tonne per annum, while the highest emitters headed by countries such as Australia, the USA and the United Arab Emirates have per capita emissions of 20 tonnes per capita and between these two extremes are the Europeans on about 10 tonnes per annum per capita. These two sets of figures should cause us to rethink all our economic and development models because they are both based on growth—growth in population and growth in resource use and pollution. This is a moment to pause, to applaud ourselves, and to find new models that allow us, humans, to continue to live on planet Earth. If we don't find new ways we may not survive: the planet will go on, but we may not.

Later, this chapter discusses how to be on the front foot in the new economy, but this section finishes with one of many paradoxes. Between 1980 and 2008 global business improved efficiency significantly. In 1980 each US$1 of world output created 1 kg of carbon emissions but by 2008 that was reduced to 0.77 kg of carbon emissions per US$1 of wealth created. The benefits of this radical improvement have been wiped out by population growth and increased consumption, but the figures do prove that it can be done.

The climate change prognosis

The climate change prognosis forces humanity to confront its history. This moment of reflection comes as other issues, including the fragility of the global financial system, have also come to the fore. This should provide an opportunity to recognise that these times force us to forge a new society. But, to do so we must be a learning society. We have to learn like no other society before as we take on board the inescapable fact that we have been fantastically successful and very destructive. We have increased our population exponentially; we have developed technologies that can kill us all *and* that can save us all; technologies that have given us global electronic neural networks, eradicated smallpox and lengthened life spans beyond 100 years for many people.

That this century is going to be different there is no doubt. The world is entering a period of greater uncertainty than has been experienced heretofore because of the climate change prognosis. There is space for discussion on the size and shape of the coming changes and which measures are most appropriate in terms of adaptation and mitigation, but there is no doubt that climate change is happening and that human society must 'adapt or die'. But there is a paradox in the current situation. As electronics have improved, information flows and just-in-time have become the modus operandi in business and in our personal lives. We are now faced with having to make decisions about the state of the world for our grandchildren and their children. The science tells us that there is little we can do about the changes to the environment for the next 20–40 years, apart from adaptation, but that we can, by acting now, mitigate damage in the future through learning to tread more lightly on the planet.

November 2007 was a turning point for the people of planet Earth because in that month the vast majority of the world's climate change scientists put their names to the Intergovernmental Panel on Climate Change (IPCC) Fourth Assessment Report. The quotations in Box 6.1 from that report provide the background for this chapter and the need for all the organs of society to become vastly more hazard-adaptive.

The dilemma for humanity now is that we are so focused on the here and now, and in the case of business on short-term profit-making and survival, that it is impossible to even begin to think about making decisions that will affect the lives of people not yet born. We are asking for the ultimate moral decision based on the best of scientific evidence using current decision-making institutions and apparatus. As the Stern Review said 'policy must promote sound market signals, overcome market failures and have equity and risk mitigation at its core' (Stern 2007). And as the CEO of one of the world's largest mining companies, Rio Tinto, says:

> unfortunately the problem with carbon is that we will not really see the side effects of that for plus-30 years from now. So that means that someone in the next ten years has to begin to actually start addressing this problem, even though every bit of capitalism, every bit of net-present-value analysis, every bit of all the other tools you learn in the classrooms . . . I would say that this too far out a problem to have an economic payback (Albanese 2009).

The sustainable enterprise economy is not an economy that tells people you will live worse than your parents; it is not an economy where comfort is sacrificed; it is not an economy where mobility is denied; and it is not an economy that requires larger populations, indeed the world's population needs to shrink over the next two generations. The Optimum Population Trust asks people to pledge to have no more than two children but does not support enforced family planning. The trust's research shows that the world's population needs to halve to about 3 billion and it argues that, in the face of the climate change challenge, migration is the equivalent of 'moving the deckchairs on the Titanic'. Yet there are many countries seeking to increase their populations, most notably the UK from 60 million to 77 million and Australia from 20 million to more than 30 million by 2025. Given the impact of expanding populations on the planet and biodiversity the founder of the WWF, Sir

Box 6.1 **IPCC Fourth Assessment Report: selected quotations**

"Warming of the climate system is unequivocal."

"Global GHG (greenhouse gas) emissions due to human activities have grown since pre-industrial times, with an increase of 70% between 1970 and 2004."

"Most of the observed increase in global average temperatures since the mid-20th century is very likely due to the observed increase in anthropogenic GHG concentrations."

"There is high agreement and much evidence that with current mitigation policies and related sustainable development practices, global GHG emissions will continue to grow over the next few decades."

"Altered frequencies and intensities of extreme weather, together with sea level rise, are expected to have mostly adverse effects on natural and human systems."

"The impacts of climate change are not evenly distributed—the poorest countries and people will suffer the earliest and most. And if and when the damages appear it will be too late to reverse the process. Thus we are forced to look a long way ahead."

"Such temperatures changes would take us into territory unknown to human experience and involve radical changes in the world around us. With such possibilities on the horizon, it was clear that the modelling framework used by this Review had to be built on the economics of risk."

"The analysis of climate change requires, by its nature, that we look out over 50, 100, 200 years and more. Any such modelling requires caution and humility, and the results are specific to the model and its assumptions" (IPCC 2007).

Peter Scott, has been quoted as saying: 'I have often thought that at the end of the day, we [WWF] would have saved more wildlife if we had spent all WWF's money on buying condoms.'[1]

Global financial crisis

Most people around the world think that the role of government is to intervene to redistribute wealth, to enable access to the rule of law, to provide enabling

---

1 Sustainable Population Australia; www.population.org.au (accessed 25 June 2010).

structures that will allow for equal opportunity and human rights to be the norm. In the wake of the global financial crisis in 2008 and 2009 this popular perception was exemplified by a survey carried out by Globescan for the BBC World Service on the 20th anniversary of the fall of the Berlin Wall in 1989. It involved 29,000 people in 27 countries and showed that in 22 of the 27 countries people thought that the role of government was to increase wealth distribution. Only 11% thought the current model of capitalism was OK, and 23% thought it was 'fatally flawed'. Interestingly the largest percentage in this group were from France (43%) and the lowest from Germany (8%) with the USA on 12%.

The report on *The Economics of Climate Change* commissioned by the UK government and written by Nicholas Stern, former World Bank economist and now at the London School of Economics, said that climate change presented 'a unique challenge for economics' because 'it is the greatest and widest-ranging market failure ever seen' (Stern 2007). This should not be such a great surprise because even those who have benefited substantially financially recognise that free markets do not necessarily produce socially or environmentally good outcomes.

How wise will we be now that we need to learn from history? Will we be as wise as George Soros (see Box 6.2), as wise as Alan Greenspan who for 18 years was Chairman of the US Federal Reserve, or as wise as Jack Welch, who, as Chairman of GE, one of the world's largest companies, espoused the theory of increased shareholder value at all costs. Greenspan, reflecting on the crash of 2008 and 2009, admitted he had made a serious error:

> While I was aware a lot of these practices (sub-prime mortgages) I had no notion of how significant they had become until very late . . . I really didn't get it until very late in 2005 and 2006 . . . We knew there were a number of such practices going on, but it's very difficult for banking regulators to deal with that (Aversa 2007).

Jack Welch, regarded as the main spokesperson for business focusing solely on shareholder value after he made a speech in 1981 on that subject, said after the crash:

> On the face of it, shareholder value is the dumbest idea in the world . . . Shareholder value is a result, not a strategy . . . Your main constituencies are your employees, your customers and your products . . . It is a dumb idea, the idea that shareholder value is a strategy is insane. It is the product of your combined efforts—from the management to the employees.

The US and the UK adopted and benefited most from the last 30 years of the Chicago School of free market economics and it is those economies that are suffering most now. But, given the enormous differences between the rising economies of Brazil, Russia, India and China, the so-called BRIC countries, do they offer any useful insights for a new model of capitalism or should we turn to those economies that have combined the creation of private wealth with egalitarianism, the distribution of public goods and social welfare, and protection of the environment and

Box 6.2 **George Soros lectures: selected quotations**

"Financial markets are inherently unstable and there are social needs that cannot be met by giving market forces free rein. Unfortunately these defects are not recognised. Instead there is a widespread belief that markets are self-correcting and a global economy can flourish without any need for a global society. It is claimed that the common interest is best served by allowing everyone to look out for his or her own interests and that attempts to protect the common interest by collective decision making distort the market mechanism. This idea was called laissez faire in the nineteenth century . . . I have found a better name for it: market fundamentalism. It is market fundamentalism that has rendered the global capitalist system unsound and unsustainable . . . it was only when Margaret Thatcher and Ronald Reagan came to power around 1980 that market fundamentalism became the dominant ideology."

"The functions that cannot and should not be governed purely by market forces include many of the most important things in human life, ranging from moral values to family relationships to aesthetic and intellectual achievements. According to market fundamentalism, all social activities and human interactions should be looked at as transactional, contract-based relationships and valued in terms of a single common denominator, money. Yet the truth is that market fundamentalism is itself naive and illogical and is profoundly and irredeemably flawed. Marx and Engels gave a very good analysis of the capitalist system 150 years ago, better in some ways, I must say, than the equilibrium theory of classical economics. Unfortunately we are once again in danger of drawing the wrong conclusions from the lessons of history. What we need is a correct balance between politics and markets, between rule making and playing by the rules . . . the common interest does not find expression in market behavior. Corporations do not aim at creating employment; they employ people (as few and as cheaply as possible) to make profits. Health care companies are not in business to save lives; they provide health care to make profits. Oil companies do not seek to protect the environment except to meet regulations or to protect their public image. Full employment, affordable medicine, and a healthy environment may, under certain circumstances, turn out to be the by-products of market processes, but such welcome social outcomes cannot be guaranteed by the profit principle alone" (Soros 2009).

---

eco-efficiency? Many of these elements, but certainly not all, can be found in the political economies of Scandinavia, some European countries such as Germany and France, Australia and New Zealand, and Japan.

What is clear is that it is not capitalism or enterprise that is at fault but the rules that have been built to manage investment, risk-taking, entrepreneurialism and profit taking. In other words what is needed is to rebuild the foundations of capitalism taking into account all the capitals involved, not just financial, and ensuring that those who would commit evil are confounded at every step of the way. We need locally built sustainable enterprise economies everywhere that can knit together globally and are founded on the principles of people, planet and well-being. Indeed the most important topic that can be tackled by a new academic research and teaching centre is that of local and global governance of people, planet and well-being. But this means understanding local and global governance, climate change adaptation, energy conservation, production and use, water management and use, and population control.

Population

Population control is an area not often visited by those standing for public office. Without the Chinese government's one-child-per-family policy it is estimated that world population would have risen by approximately 300–400 million. As in all discussions about sustainable development, discussions on population are fraught with paradox. The most affluent countries tend to have the lowest birth rates, and in some cases have negative growth, but tend to have the largest carbon footprints. The less affluent the country, the higher the birth rate, often to counter high infant mortality and a lack of provision in old age and to provide labour for agriculture and manufacturing. However, as developing countries become more affluent and there is increased healthcare provision, there is a lag in the drop in the birth rate; hence the estimate of a 9 billion peak just when perhaps the world should be discussing reducing the total size of the global population.

The rise of the BRIC countries

The BRIC countries (Brazil, Russia, India and China) are experiencing economic growth rates of between 5 and 10% despite global economic downturns and, because of this, their populations' per capita carbon footprints are increasing dramatically such that they will near those of the people in the most polluting countries such as the USA and Australia. The comparison is useful because, while one-third of the world, the poorest, have per capita emissions of between 1 and 5 tonnes per annum, the comparable figure for Europe is approximately 10 tonnes, and the figure for the worst polluters is in the region of 20 tonnes per person per annum.

There is much discussion on the role of China this century and the relationship between China and the USA, a relationship which is so close that Niall Ferguson has called the new nexus 'Chimerica' (Ferguson 2007). Originally described by Ferguson as 'a marriage made in heaven' he is now of the opinion that China 'owns' too much of the USA and that in order to play a real leading role on the world stage China should revalue its currency, the renminbi. China's economic growth, which has seen some 400 million people lifted out of absolute poverty, has been based on exports, the same model which led Japan and Germany out of destitution at the end of the Second World War. But now it is also recognised that China's growth, based as it is on the industrial revolution of the West, has fuelled global, and particularly US, overconsumption, massive natural resource use and is an increasing cause of global warming through the emission of GHGs.

Just as all of us now have some contact with the world's second largest economy, Japan, through electronics, cars or other daily consumables, so now there is some part of China in our lives often through contact with the smallest of manufactured goods and through their recycling of cash into the global banking system. Between them Japan, China and the USA account for some 15% of the world's land surface, a quarter of the world's population, and about 50% of global economic output. As major producers and consumers, between them these countries also determine any negotiations and outcomes on climate change but each has a very different starting point. While international cooperation is absolutely vital there is recognition of local politics and states of development. Japan has a remarkably egalitarian society with recognised wealth distribution across a densely populated citizenship. The story in the US is radically different, with significant differences in income between rich and poor, while for the China the dilemma is even more focused as growth has created vast income differentials. Of the 1.4 billion Chinese citizens about a third still live on less than US$1,000 a year and about 15% live on salaries comparable with an average European wage. So, it is likely that China will continue to concentrate on lifting all of its people out of poverty at the expense of the environment and will not invest heavily in overseas military projection. At the end of the first decade of the 21st century about 30% of global economic activity is performed by the USA and, while this will diminish as the Chinese economy grows, this figure coupled with the fact that it still means that economically the US will be less dominant, most people will continue to live 'Americentric' lives as that country spends more than 50% of all defence spending annually and maintains over 500 overseas forward projection basis across Europe and the Pacific. The US does this by controlling the world's seas, air and space. Its policy is one of disruption when going to war rather than peace-building, except when the target country can become a forward security base and when part of US economic trade interests—as in the case of Japan and Germany's post-war development.

All this is important in understanding 'the new economy' because for most of this century, and certainly until mid-century, the world's banker will be China and the world's security will be 'maintained' by the USA, which means that Roosevelt's description of the military–industrial complex will continue to be the largest industrial sector by far.

How has the world changed? As former Australian Prime Minister Bob Hawke observed, the most significant event in the 20th century was Deng Xiaoping's market reforms in China, which turned it from an agrarian economy to an industrial giant in a matter of decades. Because of the economy's sheer size, it dominated global economics and increasingly manufacturing. For the US its rise has arisen partly through having a relatively low population density in a fertile country but mostly because after 500 years the Europeans first couldn't stop fighting and then when they did stop fighting they couldn't quite get their collective act together. This is as true at the end of the first decade of the 21st century as it was 50 years ago. If Europe could overcome its nationalistic chauvinism it could challenge the US and China to become a global power and provide a bridge between two very different economic and political systems.

The sustainable enterprise economy

The challenge for society and for communities all over the world is enormous but we have no choice. It has been argued in the past that the information age and our understanding of complex systems would mean we were able to ride the waves of change. In a book entitled *The Collapse of Complex Societies* Joseph Sainter argued in 1990: 'Complex societies are characterised by central decision-making, high information flow, great coordination of parts, formal channels of command, and pooling of resources. Dealing with adverse environmental conditions may be what complex societies do best' (Sainter 1990).

Jared Diamond's 2005 monumental study into communities that have disappeared said something completely different. His book was similarly titled to Sainter's, but in *Collapse: How Societies Choose to Fail or Survive* Diamond said there were four main reasons why peoples had stopped flourishing in various communities around the world over the last few thousand years:

- **'Creeping normalcy'**. Change is slow enough for people think that how it is now is how it always was

- **'Landscape amnesia'**. People forget how the land used to look, or where the trees used to be, when the birds used to sing

- **'Rational behaviour'**. Stop being emotional or spiritual or scared because we are bound to find a techno-fix or a sensible way out

- **'It's someone else's problem'**. What can I do anyway? (Diamond 2005)

We need to ask ourselves how many of these conditions exist for us today. Here is a parable. In 1991 a man's body emerged from a melting glacier on the Austro-Italian border in the Alps. Ötzi, as he became known, turned out to be more than 5,000 years old and had been quick frozen which meant that he had been perfectly preserved such that all his clothes and body were beautifully intact and his stomach contained the remains of his last meal. In his book, *The Man in the Ice*, the leader of the scientific investigation, Konrad Spindler, highlighted the world that Neolithic

man inhabited, and in doing so highlighted our modern dilemma—we are so dis-
tanced from the environment that sustains us:

> In the agricultural society of the Neolithic an individual would possess the
> total knowledge of his period, as well as all the skills necessary to perform
> his daily tasks. He would know how to hunt, fish and gather food, how to
> till his field, look after his livestock and build huts. He would make his own
> pots, prepare his food and manufacture the tools and implements needed
> for all these activities (Spindler 1995: 188).

There is no suggestion that we should return to this way of life or that we should
lose our sophistication but it is clear that we have lost our connection to the origins
of our sustenance. If the lights go out how many of the world's population can last
for how many hours or days? The answer is probably only those who are close to the
Earth and living natural lives, educated in living systems and life-cycles.

So the first priority in developing a sustainable enterprise economy is to recognise what Keynes said just before the Second World War, that economic growth is
not an end in itself but a means to 'the enjoyments and realities of life' (cited in
Speth 2008: 108). And the best way to reach this understanding is to hear Barbara
Ward (1972) when she reminded us in the 1950s that we have 'only one earth', not
two or four. The Christian Bible refers to the four horsemen of the apocalypse as
pestilence, war, famine and death. For many people—one-third of the world's population—these are the day-to-day realities of life, but they will become the realities
for all of us if we do not tackle head on the better local and global governance of
people, planet and well-being, climate change adaptation, energy conservation,
production and use, water management and use, and population control. These
five issues are the priorities for humanity today, not just in the Asia–Pacific region,
but worldwide.

We need to be careful not to be miserable because there is a very real danger
that the size of the task will overwhelm our ability to tackle the issues head-on.
The revolution that is just beginning to occur and the shift that is now necessary
are signs of our success. Recently, conferring with a colleague who is a reviewer for
the Intergovernmental Panel on Climate Change, we agreed that the question we
are asked most often, both of us having been talking about these subjects for some
20 years, is: 'are you optimistic or pessimistic about our chances of surviving?'. We
agreed that we have developed nuanced answers to this question. First, as individuals we are all going to die anyway. Second, many people in the world currently
live marginalised, uncomfortable lives and for them and succeeding generations
this revolution is an answer. Third, the human race has been fantastically successful—we have substantially increased our population, most of us live longer than
previous generations and modern medicine, housing, healthcare and nutrition has
made us the over-dominant species on planet Earth. So now is the time to accept
that and take the next step. Fourth, in terms of the history of the universe our life
on Earth has been a wondrous miracle of perfect conditions, but a mere flash in
time. Fifth, my scientific colleague and I *are* pessimistic about our future on Earth

because of our rapacious and greedy capacities which are the legacy of having to survive under difficult conditions in the swamp, on the land and as a minority. But now that we are dominant what shall we tell our young children? So, the only real question is: now that we have found ourselves, and the limits of our home, what shall we do next?

In the 1950s Barbara Ward was talking about the Earth's limits and in 1962 coined the phrase 'spaceship earth'. In 1972, prior to the world's first environment conference in Stockholm, she and René Dubos wrote in *Only One Earth* (Ward 1972) about sustainable development, not knowing that this would become a totemic phrase that would galvanise many to see a link between people, planet and well-being and lead to the publication of *Our Common Future*, commonly known as the Brundtland Report in 1987 (WCED 1987) and the United Nations Conference on Environment and Development in Rio de Janeiro in 1992, popularly known as the Earth Summit. She thought that the distribution of wealth and care for the planet were both moral *and* rational propositions.

At the end of the first decade of the 21st century it has taken the world more than 30 years to catch up with Ward, and more than 75 years to begin to realise Keynes's understanding of well-being. So now we have the emerging concept of the sustainable enterprise economy as the next moral and only logical step for humankind. But what is it? How shall we show that it is a natural development of two rapidly merging fields of enquiry: corporate social responsibility and sustainable development?

John Hendry has described what he calls 'the bimoral society' or the space 'between enterprise and ethics' that has moved from a world that Adam Smith probably would not have recognised where, as Hendry (2004: 17) says, 'selfish or exploitative behaviour' would be 'the exception not the rule' to a world where Jack Welch, one of the gods of shareholder value, now tells us that 'shareholder value was a dumb idea' (Guerrera 2009)! Hendry points out that it was the development of economics as a science that caused a disconnection between enterprise and ethics, where long-distance investment cares little for human welfare or the state of the planet. The growth of the global economy driven by many out-of-touch investors, long distance investment, and socio-pathological investment analysts rewarded by a bonus culture, is at the heart of the 'contemporary decline in all forms of moral authority' (Guerrera 2009). 'Civilized society has always been characterized by the co-presence of two contrasting sets of principles governing how people live their lives. One of these is associated with traditional morality, or the morality of obligation, and the other with self-interest' (Hendry 2004: 252).

A sustainable enterprise economy (SEE) is an economy that sees no conflict between self-interest and obligation to community, where any enterprise—corporate, social, public, state-owned or individual—aims to have as little impact on the environment as possible *and* is mindful of its social impact. In an enterprise economy the spirit of the community is geared to risk-taking, innovation, creativity, problem-solving, entrepreneurialism and enthusiasm for life but also recognises that mobility, exchange and trade are part of what it means to be human. A *sustain-*

able enterprise economy uses these human characteristics to create wealth and nurture well-being within a framework of peace and social justice which includes income distribution, the provision of fundamental public goods such as health and education, the observance of the rule of law, and the upholding of human rights. The SEE preserves natural capital and creates social and human capital.

The SEE builds on the concept of natural capital (Hawken *et al.* 1999) and the five capitals model to a new, more complex and sophisticated model of economics, one that allows for the management of the trade-off and the space between financial capitals, manufactured capital, natural capital, social capital and human capital (Porritt 2006). The five capitals model comes with some qualifications and caveats. For instance, in using this model it is necessary to acknowledge that the concept of 'capital' is useful and that, while traditionally these capitals have been land, labour and capital (financial), in the new model these capitals are both tangible and *in*tangible, some hard and some soft, some to be used and spent and some to be preserved, cherished and left untouched as totems of our learned wisdom about the state of the world.

The idea of sustainable enterprise is a progression from largely voluntary corporate social responsibility and corporate citizenship ideas and practice that have developed in the loosely regulated economy over the last few decades to a more inclusive model of the economy. It is an inclusive model that recognises that the old separations of business, government and civil society should not be applied too rigidly and are not necessarily as valid or useful as they once were. It is a model that acknowledges the growth over the last few years of stakeholder engagement, new social partnerships and strategic alliances, and recognises that many of our largest economic institutions and multinational corporations are state-owned institutions. And this model recognises that many of the gains in accountability, responsibility, transparency and sustainability (ARTS) were a precursor to a new economy which delivers private wealth *and* public goods.

The greatest threats to humanity come, first, from our inability to tackle climate change and bring about sustainable development, and, second, an inequitable global economic system that focuses too much on private wealth at the expense of well-being for all, believing, à la Adam Smith, in the invisible hand. All enterprises have a part to play, but our largest organisations and economic institutions (businesses and governments) have a greater responsibility to accept the challenge and seize the opportunities. The new economy is demonstrating every day that there are great opportunities for risk-taking and entrepreneurialism and for delivering the goods and services which we now need to live within the Earth's carrying capacity.

Enterprise, risk-taking, innovation and creativity, like conversation, caring and sharing, are part of what it means to be human and this century needs to recognise and reward these human characteristics more than any before if we are to make the transition to a sustainable future on Earth. This way of thinking about our futures is a step towards Mahatma Gandhi's vision of the meaning of life, or the purpose of humanity:

> I am convinced that a non-violent society can be built on the foundations
> of harmony and cooperation, without which society is bound to remain
> violent. If we argue that this cannot be done it will mean that a non-vio-
> lent society can never come into being. In which case our entire culture
> would be meaningless (quoted in Rees 2003: 156).

Bringing together the principles of sustainable development, which include eco-efficiency and social justice, with the principle of allowing enterprise and innovation
to blossom provides the best possible milieu for a wholly new model of capitalism
to be born out of the current wasteful and inequitable model of wealth creation.

Our current way of thinking and seeing the world has created global warming,
global terrorism and economic collapse. We must now use our new-found knowledge to create a paradigm shift to a more equitable global socio-ecological situation.

The sustainable enterprise economy requires a better understanding of complex
dynamics and systems, particularly fragile Earth ecosystems, but also an increasingly continuously connected and boundary-less social world. Both transcend traditional territorial boundaries and established institutional social mechanisms.
Two examples serve to illustrate this recent phenomenon. During a meeting of
the group of the 20 largest economies (G20) in London in April 2009 a man died,
apparently after being hit several times by the police, even though he was not part
of the good-tempered anti-globalisation and anti-banking demonstrations that
were taking place across London during the week. The subsequent inquiry elicited
numerous still photographs of the police action and many minutes of video foot-
age, all of which shows that the surveillance society watches you and me, but also
watches agents of the state and the status quo and that this evidence can be made
available worldwide instantaneously—to those who have electricity and the electronic means. In the same week Facebook announced that it had 200 million users
worldwide, causing the *New York Times* to describe it as 'the Web's dominant social
ecosystem and an essential personal and business networking tool in much of the
wired world' (*New York Times* 2009).

The new economy is for business but it is inclusive of all enterprises and organisations. The challenge is for all institutions to change the way they relate to local
and global environmental and social issues. This means government departments
rethinking the way they work, community organisations and local government
reorganising themselves, global corporations aligning their mission, purpose and
practices with the realities of climate change and sustainable development and
individuals making this happen by actively participating in the change.

How to make rapid progress

First, new ways of knowing, learning and sharing perception are necessary to find
solutions to the humanitarian and ecological situations that face us all and the

planet. Through conversational learning on sustainable enterprise it is possible to devise a way of working that is based on co-sensing, co-inspiring, co-enacting and co-creating knowledge. This means that we always try to break the rules by working across sectoral, professional and intellectual boundaries and reach into the past, the present and the future in sorting the current flood of ephemera and lose information to create knowledge. This creates surprise, the unexpected, ambiguity—and laughter—in the process.

Second, the world that we want to investigate requires knowledge creation that sees hard and soft edges, that can sense the tangible and the intangible, that is left and right brained, that is founded on what is known but also reaches into the energy of chaos for new ideas. We live in an age of reconfiguration, of decay and resurgence, a state where new value clusters are being created through the realignment of social networks and public–private–civil partnerships. Enterprise, innovation, creativity and action are creating a new economy that is at once local and global founded on a greater understanding of organisations as living social systems nested within living organic ecosystems. With this understanding not only is the way we learn changing, but also what we think is useful is challenged. This is best described by David Cooperrider, the originator of 'appreciative inquiry' who inspired the following approach in his colleagues:

> We have become so locked within a problem-centered, critique-driven worldview that we have severely limited our potential for innovation and transformation . . . New understanding emerges when we begin our capacity building through welcoming the unknown as an opportunity for discovery and innovation. It means suspending our confidence in old certainties (Barrett and Fry 2005).

Third, there are some imperatives. While understanding the past is essential, there *is now* something to learn about, to come to terms with. The planet on which humans depend for survival is by most reasonable accounts in need of more loving care and attention than humans have heretofore given it. On this small, delicate, beautiful Earth more than 6 billion people now live: exploiting and exploited, caring and uncaring, rich and poor, men and women, old and young, well and not well. The imperatives form the sustainable enterprise agenda, an agenda that calls for all to be made free from want and fear. This means addressing issues such as poverty, violence, inequity, discrimination and human rights within our enterprise models. It means finding positive ways to build socially just and peaceful societies. It means showing leadership which is life-enhancing and based on the principle of co-creation; hence our emphasis on knowledge creation through conversational learning, which draws on experiential learning, action research and appreciative inquiry.

There are those who insist on maintaining the myth that there is an incompatibility between green growth and comfort, or between economic wealth creation and sustainability. Significant work is now going on to incentivise change to what is loosely termed the 'green economy'. In the most enlightened cases economic recovery per se is linked to moves towards a low carbon, sustainable enterprise economy. Some of the best research is being carried out by those global institutions that are most affected by the current revolution. Among these is one of the world's largest banks, HSBC, one that has not been carrying toxic debts to any substantial degree; its team, led by Nick Robins, published in February 2009 a study of 20 national economic recovery plans. The leaders turned out to be the US and China and the research identified 18 investment themes that can be identified with 'stabilising and then cutting global emissions of greenhouse gases' representing 15% of the US$2.8 trillion in fiscal measures to restart national economies (Robins *et al.* 2009).

This is what Rajendra Pachauri, Chairman of the Intergovernmental Panel on Climate Change and winner of the Nobel Peace Prize in 2007, had to say in March 2009 about the link between the possibility of sustainable enterprise economics and well-being:

> The beauty of (the) desirable changes lies in the fact that they would pro-
> duce a huge range of so called co-benefits which if anything will enhance
> the welfare of human society such as through higher energy security,
> lower levels of pollution at the local level, stable agricultural yields and
> additional employment. I wonder why we are dragging our feet in the face
> of such overwhelming logic (Pachauri 2009)?

The answer to Pachauri's own question lies in the lack of real leadership among politicians and business leaders. As he says:

> The answer lies in forward looking policies on the part of governments,
> which of course, will cause some discomfort in certain sectors and to cer-
> tain actors. A complete reorientation of thinking among the leadership of
> the corporate sector and a significant change in lifestyles of people across
> the globe, most importantly in the rich countries, is now overdue. If a per-
> ceptible shift in all these three respects can be initiated adequately and
> soon perhaps Copenhagen December 2009 will be a success, for which
> future generations would have reason to thank those that bring about
> such a movement (Pachauri 2009).

Pachauri has a six-point plan of action, starting yesterday:

- Invest heavily in energy conservation, eco-efficiency and sustainable design
- Introduce comprehensive carbon pricing
- Dramatically improve water efficiency
- Induce lifestyle and behavioural changes
- Adapt to climate change now
- And, in doing so, leave no one behind (Pachauri 2007)

Business confusion and uncertainty

If the world was hoping for a clearer outcome from COP15 at Copenhagen, then business expectations were even more specific. The emerging low carbon sustainable enterprise economy requires that carbon and other GHGs are priced. Knowing that price is crucial to both business and government planning, but the world will have to wait a year or so even though there are numerous price signals through trading regimes. Setting legally binding carbon emission targets would have provided greater certainty of the distance that has to be travelled over the next few decades. The UK is legally committed to cuts of 80% by 2050 and the EU is committed to targets of between 20 and 30% by 2020. All countries' targets should become clear by the end of January 2010 under the Copenhagen accord.[2]

There has been significant leadership and initiative in the business–civil society nexus on issues of environmental management and corporate social responsibility since the 1970s, some of which has been led or followed by increased regulation by individual governments. Generally those countries that have led on legislation in the areas of environmental management and corporate responsibility have tended to see significant gains in exports of clean technology and associated trade and to see a clear link between innovation in public policy and community cohesion, and social resilience. Similarly countries with tight controls of banking, such as Australia, were more resilient in the face of the 2008/2009 global financial crisis as they were less exposed to toxic assets such as sub-prime mortgages.

A useful example of this combination of public policy and the new economy comes from research carried out in the UK, USA, China, India, Germany, Brazil, Australia and South Africa, which shows that bold public policy to promote rapid climate-friendly innovations creates new jobs and a low carbon economy. This specific piece of research, while calling for concerted and coordinated investment in low carbon technology across the G20 countries, showed, for example, that China stood to gain 40 million jobs and lose 10 million by 2020, and the UK could gain 70,000 jobs in the offshore wind industry.[3]

Making the link between public policy, fiscal incentives and the new economy has been easier for some governments than others. After the 2008/2009 global financial crisis many governments invested heavily in their economies to provide liquidity for business to continue. But some forward-looking governments made strategic investments into the new economy. China led this charge targeting 40% of its fiscal incentive of US$576 billion to low carbon innovations, while the US targeted just 12% of its US$775 billion investment. Similarly some Asian economies have signalled significant cuts in emissions levels led by South Korea with 30% by 2020 and Japan with 25% by 2020. It is worth noting that these economies will find it much harder to make these cuts than, for instance the US and Australia, because

2 In reality by this date some countries had supplied the necessary data and many had not.
3 www.globalclimatenetwork.info

South Korea and Japan are already relatively efficient while the US and Australia will benefit from significant low-hanging fruit as they are extremely inefficient economies which have relied on cheap and plentiful energy sources during their development. China and Australia both rely for their wealth on coal, the former's economic growth being based on using 'the black stuff' and the latter's economy significantly based on selling it and other extractive products cheaply to China.

Enlarging on the idea that domestic policy and regulation can lead competitiveness there is clear evidence that California, Germany and Japan have led in clean technology because of proactive environmental management regulations which raised the bar in those countries. In the 21st century that advantage has been taken by China which now has the majority of production in wind turbines, solar and PV production as well as the world's largest electric car factory.

From environmental management in the 1970s and the first corporate social accounting in California in the same period, came the introduction of what John Elkington termed 'triple bottom line' reporting in the 1980s and 1990s involving a matrix of reporting against financial, environmental and social criteria. This innovative work is still ongoing and has taxed the minds of many in business, not least chief financial officers for whom quantifying soft issues such as human capital and human rights against the apparently hard numbers of finance has proved difficult. Today it is the combination of environmental, social and governance (ESG) issues that are the subject of discussion in enlightened boardrooms and in the international public policy debate.

The measurement and understanding of the relationship between economic performance and social progress has been at the heart of the corporate social responsibility movement for the last 30 years and is central to the new economy. If we cannot find a way to live within the Earth's limits and to know human well-being when it is met then we will continue to base our economic system on greed, exploitation, consumption and waste. In 2009 a commission, headed by Professors Sen and Stiglitz and established by President Sarkozy of France, reported:

> Increasing concerns have been raised for a long time about the adequacy of current measures of economic performance, in particular those based on GDP figures. Moreover, there are broader concerns about the relevance of these figures as measures of societal well-being, as well as measures of economic, environmental, and social sustainability (Stiglitz *et al.* 2008).

There is not space here to evaluate all the conclusions of the commission but there is a direct link between economic growth, well-being and social progress, and corporate social reporting. The report says: 'It has long been clear that GDP is an inadequate metric to gauge wellbeing over time particularly in its economic, environmental, and social dimensions, some aspects of which are often referred to as *sustainability*' (Stiglitz *et al.* 2008: 8).

So the moves in the business world to engage with a range of stakeholders beyond shareholders, employees and customers on issues of accountability, transparency and reporting are mirrored in the field of public policy. There is much work to be done on the links between the two as it might be argued that the private policy world has developed numerous voluntary codes, initiatives and management systems around ESG and the triple bottom line that have lessons for public policy development, and vice versa.

The work that has been ongoing in the corporate responsibility and responsible investment communities over the last few decades has found purchase with some enlightened companies, as is witnessed by the 6,000 or so signatories to the UN Global Compact (UNGC), but there is much work to be done to translate ESG into performance. When questioned about implementation of the ten UN Global Compact principles and beyond, major signatories to the UNGC gave similar responses: 'There is no clear path from ESG to performance' and 'CSR professionals "do not know" how to how to translate ESG into financial performance figures'. One survey of this group showed that '50% of chief financial officers in large UNGC signatories in North America said that ESG only creates 2–5% shareholder value and 21% of CFOs said it creates no financial value'. The solutions, the respondents said, were to be found in 'moving from risk management to opportunity capture', 'embedding ESG into strategy, organisation, culture', in 'changing boards from the current 11 white men, 1 woman in a red dress and one black man' and 'ensuring that companies have oversight of ESG on the board'—currently only 25% of UNGC signatories in North America have such board-level oversight.

A similar survey, reported in the *Sloan Management Review* in November 2009 showed that, among 'global thought leaders in business', 92% 'thought that sustainability was important' but the majority described it as 'too complex' and while they thought that 'business has a key role in solving global sustainability issues' at present 'company action tends to be limited to regulatory requirements'. Echoing the UNGC survey, 70% of 'companies have not developed a clear business case for sustainability' but 'when companies look they find more opportunities than expected' (Berns *et al.* 2009).

IBM's 2009 Global CSR Survey presented to the European Academy for Business in Society (EABIS) showed that 60% of companies in the survey said that 'CSR has increased in importance in last 12 months' but there is 'confusion between desire and action'. 'Only 30% collect data on sustainability-related performance' and 30% 'have never done so' and only 35% 'understand their customers' concerns'. European companies outperform all others, Asian companies are worst and US companies in between. The report highlighted the lack of business leaders: 'executives are uncomfortable to engage in sustainability discussions as the area is so complex' (Hittner 2009).

On the front foot in the new economy

International multi-stakeholder Roundtables on Sustainable Enterprise

The Roundtables on Sustainable Enterprise which were convened by Coventry University and held in London, Cape Town, Sydney, New York and Beijing between 2007 and 2009 involved more than 400 people drawn from all sections of society and culminated in two conferences at the Eden Project in Cornwall, UK, in October 2008 and at Wessex Water, UK, in November 2009. This engagement showed that, at all levels, in all continents, and in all professions the questions are the same:

- Scientific illiteracy: How do we counter the current scientific illiteracy so that people understand the way the planet works and the relationship between human behaviour and the environment?

- Market failure: How do we develop an economic system that internalises externalities and makes a link between economic performance and human well-being?

- Institutional inertia: Are our current institutions, public and private, able to adjust to the new realities or are these institutions inertia led?

- Leadership deficit: Where are the leaders in all areas of society to show the way to the new economy?

- On being human: What does it mean to be human given what we now know about our success and the state of the planet?

- Sustainability: What should our relationship with the planet be?

These fundamental questions are central to the current debate over the emerging low carbon sustainable enterprise economy. The language of that debate is fascinating and reflects the uncertainties, the complexity and the contradictions inherent in thinking about systems and managing risk, uncertainty, new science and working within limits. The language of the current debate includes references to the 'low carbon economy', the 'zero carbon economy', the 'carbon economy' and the 'carbon-constrained economy'. This leads to new models with titles such as the 'ecological growth economy', the 'ecological enterprise economy' and the working hypothesis in this chapter: the 'sustainable enterprise economy' or SEE.

Rewiring the brain for the paradigm shift

The challenge, and the opportunity, for business, and society as whole, is to rewire our brains:

- **Paradigm shift**. We are at a moment when, according to Thomas Kuhn's definition of a paradigm shift, 'one conceptual world view is replaced by another'. Kuhn argued that scientific advancement is not evolutionary, but rather is a 'series of peaceful interludes punctuated by intellectually violent revolutions'.[4] We are at such a moment

- **Think flows**. Instead of thinking of static relations, start seeing all relations and all materials as in a state of change, flux and movement. This leads to the expectation of difference, to spotting turbulence, to navigating as in a river and to being able to understand and absorb random events

- **Decarbonisation and dematerialisation**. This new language will become the language of private and public policy for this century. How can we do more with less?

- **Efficiency**. Fossil fuel-based economies are inefficient because these materials have been cheap and were thought to be unlimited, but with a reduction in availability and the introduction of carbon pricing this old model of industrial capitalism is passing rapidly—see 'paradigm shift' above

- **Rationing and excess**. The end of mass consumption is heralded by carbon constraints, by developed countries reining in spending at both public and individual levels and by their adoption of the Asian model of saving before spending. We all also have to get used to understanding that the emphasis on well-being, resilience and social cohesion is a return to collective action and the distribution of resources through a mixture of public policy and market behaviour

- **Localisation**. Carbon pricing and rationing coupled with an emphasis on food and energy security means that there will be an even greater emphasis on 'buy to last' and 'buy local'

- **Travel less**. The cheap travel economy has run its course and carbon pricing plus a realisation that cheapness often means extreme discomfort and low quality will lead to a search for quality nearer to home, especially for Northern Europe where summers will in the main get warmer

- **Resilience and social cohesion**. All business and communities should have learnt the lesson of the global financial crisis that liquidity is all and over-extension leads to crashes. This reality is already forcing people in developed countries to pay off their debts and save more than they spend. The growing understanding that the climate change prognosis is that there will be an increase in dramatic, random, extreme local weather events—fires in Australia, floods in the UK, droughts in Africa—also requires all elements of society to become more hazard-adaptive and resilient. Collective action

4 en.wikipedia.org/wiki/Paradigm_shift.

to embrace greater resilience and reduce risk should lead to greater social cohesion as we all understand that our lazy, greedy, ever-expanding lifestyles require individual, community, national and international action to reduce our waistlines, reduce our pollution, be more efficient and engage in adaptation work to tackle climate change

- **Distributed response**. Since men landed on the moon in 1969 and took pictures of the Earth we have known that the world is one. The climate change science is a greater impetus to concerted, coordinated international action and a new role for global governance, which is not to be confused with global government. International action will be connected to distributed response mechanisms as it is understood that the world is a continual state of flux, the idea of central control is no longer tenable and that the way to manage unstable situations is to have coordinated responses from a variety of centres. So, just as a call from a mobile phone may take a number of possible routes to reach its destination, so too will resilient communities know that there must be a variety of possible solutions to any given problem

- **Consumption**. In developed economies the emphasis is moving from economic growth to harmony and well-being. This has led to the development of happiness economics and initiatives such as French President Sarkozy's Commission on the Measurement of Economic Performance and Social Progress (Hittner 2009) and the development of carbon footprinting techniques

Refocusing business, societal and public policy priorities

Away from systems-level thinking and strategising at the level of individual businesses, there are many ways to approach the new economy. In 'Why Sustainability is Now the Key Driver of Innovation', C.K. Prahalad, one of the people behind the 'bottom of the pyramid' strategy, and others, in the *Harvard Business Review* have presented a straightforward approach for business:

- See compliance as opportunity

- Make value chains sustainable

- Design sustainable products and services

- Think about new business models

- Next-practice platforms (Nidumolu *et al.* 2009)

At the level of society how might we effect the change we wish to see for the birth of the low carbon sustainable enterprise economy? Benjamin Lichtenstein, John Sterman and Peter Senge from MIT and New York University (Lichtenstein *et al.* 2009) have suggested a nest of eight options starting with personal change through to mass social transformation. This model can be entered at any level and is particularly useful for businesses that may be looking for a starting point which suits their governance, organisation, culture or leadership model:

- Individual aspiration
- Peer affiliation
- Process optimisation
- Entrepreneurial innovation
- Value chain collaboration
- Sector coordination
- System integration
- Social transformation

In the development of public policy designed to create the new economy there are a number of instruments for change:

- Leadership
- Incentives, rewards and breaks
- Markets
- Penalties
- Regulation
- Enabling structures
- Mass social movement

Learning, unlearning, network and action (LUNA)

If humanity is tenuously embarking on the fourth revolution, as has been argued in this chapter, then it is also a period of great learning. Indeed it might be apposite to say that the fourth revolution is as much concerned with learning as it is with sustainability because sustainability is a continuous process of learning, unlearning, networks and action (LUNA). In other words, building SEE means continuous LUNA. At the heart of this process is a set of characteristics which will be dominant in the transition, or the great transformation. They are:

- A love of innovation and experimentation which involves understanding that, while we cannot make too many mistakes, mistakes are often the best way to learn; that discontinuity is at the heart of paradigm shift and that tolerance and learning by failing is important

- The ability to embrace randomness as this will be a key characteristic of climate change effects

- Reworking the balance between free markets and collective action to produce sustainable social democracies

- New employment patterns with an emphasis on enterprise and innovation, on re-use, rethink, reduce, recycle, return and longevity—not just upskilling but also sideways skilling to use existing skilled workforces that can be adapted to the new economy

Conclusions

Climate change is already causing significant disruption to many communities across the world as random severe weather events force people from their homes, create energy and food security problems, and highlight the fragility of many poor people's lives—those that will be affected by climate change most and earliest.

The rise of the BRIC countries and in particular India and China mean that manufacturing costs and output will be determined by those countries' policies and growth trajectories. Expect almost everything we use on a daily basis to have a Chinese connection.

Population growth must be halted and reversed as this would see one of the greatest improvements in well-being for the vast majority of the world's poorest people and significantly reduce carbon emissions. These people are not just in developing countries but also in cities in every country in the world. If we are to focus on resilience and community cohesion this is an issue that political leaders must not shy away from.

The global financial crisis has led to some countries virtually bankrupting themselves as private debt has become public liability, and yet the systems are not being reformed. This will lead to severe political instability and cuts to the very public services that keep the poorest communities alive.

The US will continue to dominate the planet economically and militarily but will have to be gentler in its relations with other countries as they jostle for a voice in a crowded world.

But, to survive in business or government this century the astute leader has to be totally conversant in climate change science, international economics, Chinese politics, population control and conflict resolution. These are the issues that are determining the challenges and opportunities as the new economy—the low carbon sustainable enterprise economy—develops. Expect a very bumpy flight, tighten your seat belts and work now to build resilience, community cohesion (in communities and organisations) and hazard-adaptiveness into policy and strategy.

Bibliography

Albanese, T. (2009) 'The Future of Capitalism: Building a Sustainable Energy Future', *McKinsey Quarterly*, December 2009.

Aversa, J. (2007) 'Greenspan failed to spot seeds of mortgage mess', *The Seattle Times*, 14 September 2007; seattletimes.nwsource.com/html/businesstechnology/2003883764_greenspan14. html.

Barrett, F.J., and R.E. Fry (2005) *Appreciative Inquiry* (Chagrin Falls, OH: Taos Institute Publications): 33-35.

Berns, M., *et al.* (2009) 'The Business of Sustainability: Findings and Insights from the First Annual Business of Sustainability Survey and the Global Thought Leaders' Research Project, *MIT Sloan Management Review*; sloanreview.mit.edu/special-report/the-business-of-sustainability, accessed 26 October 2009.

Diamond, J. (2005) *Collapse: How Societies Choose to Fail or Survive* (London: Allen Lane).

Ferguson, N. (2007) 'Not two countries, but one: Chimerica' *The Telegraph*, 4 March 2007; www.telegraph.co.uk/comment/personal-view/3638174/Not-two-countries-but-one-Chimerica.html, accessed 23 September 2010.

Galbraith, J.K. (2004) *The Economics of Innocent Fraud* (London: Penguin).

Guerrera, F. (2009) 'Welch Condemns Share Price Focus', *Financial Times*, 12 March 2009.

Hawken, P., A. Lovins and L.H. Lovins (1999) *Natural Capitalism* (New York: Little, Brown).

Hendry, J. (2004) *Between Enterprise and Ethics: Business and Management in a Bimoral Society* (Oxford, UK: Oxford University Press): 17, 252.

Hittner, J. (2009) 'IBM's 2009 Global CSR Survey', presented at the *EABIS Seminar*, October 2009.

IPCC (Intergovernmental Panel on Climate Change) (2007) *IPCC Fourth Assessment Report: Climate Change 2007 (AR4)* (Cambridge, UK: Cambridge University Press).

Lichtenstein, B., J. Sterman and P. Senge (2009) presentation at the *Academy of Management Annual Meeting*, Chicago, August 2009.

New York Times (2009) '200 Million And Counting', *The New York Times* in association with *The Observer*, 5 April 2009: 1.

Nidumolu, R., C.K. Prahalad and M.R. Rangawami (2009) 'Why Sustainability is Now the Key Driver of Innovation', *Harvard Business Review*, September 2009: 57-64.

Pachauri, R.K. (2007) Speaking at the *UN Global Compact Leaders Summit*, Geneva, 9 July 2007.

—— (2009) 'Why Copenhagen is important for the future of human civilization', 16 February 2009; blog.rkpachauri.org/blog/13/Why-Copenhagen-is-important-for-the-future-of-human-civilization.htm, accessed 26 May 2009.

Porritt, J. (2006) *Capitalism as if the World Matters* (London: Earthscan): 111-94.

Rees, S. (2003) *Passion for Peace* (Sydney: UNSW Press): 156.

Robins, N., and Charanjit Singh (2009) 'A Climate for Recovery: The Colour of Stimulus Goes Green', HSBC Climate Change; www.globaldashboard.org/wp-content/uploads/2009/HSBC_Green_New_Deal.pdf, accessed on 23 September 2010.

Sainter, J. (1990) *The Collapse of Complex Societies* (Cambridge, UK: Cambridge University Press).

Soros, G. (2009) 'Capitalism versus Open Society', The Soros Lectures, *Financial Times*, 30 October 2009; www.ft.com/cms/s/2/d55926e8-bfea-11de-aed2-00144feab49a,dwp_uuid=90bc6a02-bf0b-11de-8034-00144feab49a.html.

Speth, J.G. (2008) *The Bridge at the End of the World* (New Haven, CT: Yale Books): 108.

Spindler, K. (1995) *The Man In The Ice* (London: Phoenix): 188.

Stern, N. (2007) *The Economics of Climate Change: The Stern Review* (Cambridge, UK: Cambridge University Press).

Stiglitz, J.E., A. Sen and J.P. Fitoussi (2008) 'Report of the Commission on the Measurement of Economic Performance and Social Progress', Commission on the Measurement of Economic Performance and Social Progress; www.stiglitz-sen-fitoussi.fr/en/index.htm, accessed 26 January 2009.

Ward, B., and R. Dubos (1972) *Only One Earth* (New York: W.W.Norton).

WCED (World Commission on Environment and Development) (1987) *Our Common Future* (Oxford, UK: Oxford University Press).

7

Sustainable enterprise and human security

Nicky Black
University of Waikato, New Zealand

For human security proponents and scholars, the millennium marked the reinvigoration of the human security framework at the highest international level. In launching the Millennium Development Goals, a set of eight targets for reducing poverty, the Secretary-General of the United Nations, Kofi Annan, specifically called for attention to the twin aspirations of 'freedom from fear' and 'freedom from want', the basis of the human security paradigm. With the establishment of the United Nations Commission on Human Security in 2001, these aspirations achieved a greater profile than they had enjoyed since the 1994 United Nations Development Programme's *Human Development Report* (UNDP 1994), which had taken human security as its main theme. The Commission subsequently published its framework to support the realisation of greater human security in *Human Security Now: Protecting and Empowering People* (UNCHS 2003), the key reference point for most subsequent treatments of the concept.

Less well known by the human security community, another initiative—the United Nations Global Compact—was also launched in the millennial year. Established to allow participants to 'advance their commitments to ... corporate citizenship', the Global Compact is a 'policy framework for the development, implementation, and disclosure of sustainability principles and practices'.[1] Signatories to the Global Compact commit to implementing ten principles of responsible corporate activity related to human rights, environmental stewardship, labour rights and corruption.

1 www.unglobalcompact.org, accessed 12 November 2009.

The Global Compact specifically aims to catalyse business action in support of broader UN goals, as discussed by Professor Yasunobu Sato in Chapter 8, through innovative partnerships between businesses, UN agencies and civil society organisations. With over 7,700 corporate participants from over 130 countries, the Global Compact was the largest corporate citizenship and sustainability initiative in the world in late 2009. It stands among a growing body of policy frameworks, corporate initiatives and civil society action, through which the roles and responsibilities of business in our increasingly integrated global economy are being challenged and developed.

Over the last decade these two discourses—of corporate citizenship and human security—have developed in parallel worlds. As illustrated below, many of the aspirations and activities within this emerging field of corporate citizenship align with those of human security. Yet corporations are almost entirely unaware of the human security framework. Equally, human security researchers and practitioners have yet to engage with corporate action on sustainable development, conflict-sensitivity and human rights.

In this chapter I consider the emerging, and rapidly developing, discourse of corporate citizenship, and highlight its relevance for human security proponents and practitioners. I begin with a brief description of these two discourses, highlighting the similarities in their espoused aspirations. Within the broad range of corporate citizenship activities I then focus on business activity in relation to areas and instances of violent conflict: areas of particular concern to the human security community. Expanding the scope to briefly consider corporate citizenship in relation to broader governance and development issues, I conclude with reflections on the tensions in this movement to transform commercial practice towards supporting greater human security.

Parallel conversations for a better world? Sustainable enterprise and human security

Given the breadth and depth of the collection presented in this book, I do not offer a critical analysis of the content or uptake of human security discourse here (for examples, see Paris 2001, 2004; Buzan 2004; Timothy 2004). Recognising the concept of human security to be an initiative aimed at systemic change, both as an attempt to align the aims and operations of the United Nations family of organisations, and to generate material change in situations of insecurity, I take the definition of human security offered by the Human Security Commission as being dynamic, comprehensive and aspirational. The Commission's definition of enacting human security is 'to protect the vital core of all human lives in ways that enhance human freedoms and human fulfilment' (UNCHS 2003: 4). The dynamism of this definition comes from its emphasis on protecting the 'vital core of life'—the 'set of elementary rights and freedoms people enjoy' and its recognition that what people consider to be essential and crucially important in this 'vital core' varies across individuals and societies. The comprehensive nature of human security—its integration of the international community's main policy agenda items of peace, security and sustainable development—is described by Kofi Annan (UNCHS 2003: 4):

> Human security in its broadest sense embraces far more than the absence of violent conflict. It encompasses human rights, good governance, access to education and health care and ensuring that each individual has opportunities and choices to fulfil his or her own potential. Every step in this direction is also a step towards reducing poverty, achieving economic growth and preventing conflict.

Two general and mutually reinforcing strategies are offered by the Commission to realise these freedoms: protection and empowerment. Protection is given to mean shielding people from critical and pervasive threats and situations, and requires concerted effort to develop norms, processes and institutions that systematically address insecurities. Empowerment is described as the creation and use of processes that intend to build on people's strengths and aspirations, to enable them to develop their potential and become full participants in decision-making. The combined emphasis of these two strategies is on the creation of 'political, social, environmental, economic, military and cultural systems that together give people the building blocks of survival, dignity and livelihood' (UNCHS 2003: 4).

As the primary organisations of global economic practice, transnational corporations (TNCs) are being increasingly targeted, and have become more active, in attempts to create systems that support the aspirations of human security. At the global level, the World Business Council for Sustainable Development, a CEO-led global business association of some 200 companies, has a mission 'to provide business leadership as a catalyst for change toward sustainable development, and to support the business license to operate, innovate and grow in a world increasingly shaped by sustainable development issues'.[2] TNCs are increasingly involved in social and environmental issues. For example, in the global South many companies have become involved in the provision of education and health services in their areas of operation. Beyond these material activities, corporations are also assuming a more open role in norm- and institution-formation in new processes of global governance. The role of business intermediaries (termed BINGOs in UN speak, Business and Industry NGOs) at the climate change negotiations held in Copenhagen in December 2009 (COP15), provides one example of business engagement in global governance. BINGOs such as the International Chamber of Commerce's Commission on Environment and Energy had a formalised role in the COP15 negotiations, in being allowed to offer 'interventions'—brief prepared statements—on the negotiating floor. Interventions took two forms: they stated general positions or were geared to specific expertise or agenda items. Beyond institutional inclusion

2 Our Mission Statement, www.wbcsd.org, accessed 12 November 2009.

in global governance systems, TNCs are also claiming a more active role in the support of universal norms that support better governance. In defending its operations in Myanmar, a state ruled by a military government accused of pervasive human rights violations, the French oil company Total has argued that it provides a 'model for business and political leaders looking for ways to address the country's human rights issues' and to enhance the well-being of the local people through its 'defense of common values' (Total 2007).

TNCs increasingly refer to these types of activity as evidence of their 'corporate citizenship', and this is a term used by some large corporations to describe their position and positive contributions *vis-à-vis* society. Many companies use corporate responsibility interchangeably with corporate citizenship, and generally use the phrase corporate social responsibility, often shortened to CSR, to refer to the subset of corporate responsibilities that deals with a company's voluntary or discretionary relationships with societal and community stakeholders (Waddock 2004). The term corporate citizenship is also used, and heavily debated, within academic communities (see Zadek 2001; Matten *et al.* 2003; Morrison 2003; Waddock 2004).

Corporate citizenship is one of a number of streams of inquiry into how enterprise, writ large, can contribute to sustainable development and human security. Within the management academy and in international development practice, social enterprise is a topic of great interest and investment. Social enterprises are 'driven by a social or environmental purpose',[3] and arguably include both well-known TNCs such as The Body Shop and the range of both for- and not-for-profit organisations within the fair trade and micro-finance movements. Broader attention to the relationships between commercial activity and sociopolitical processes are also seen in the focus on business in conflict-prevention and post-conflict reconstruction (Schwartz 2004; UNSC 2004), and on the adoption of sustainability and social justice practices by small-to-medium enterprises (SMEs). As argued by Professor Malcolm McIntosh in Chapter 6, the breadth of this interest in the forms, aims and activities of enterprises in pursuit of environmental sustainability and greater social justice, and in the policy frameworks that support their development and proliferation, can be better captured in the term 'sustainable enterprise'. I agree that sustainable enterprise more fully reflects the systemic nature of the movement to incorporate social and environmental issues into commercial activity than corporate citizenship. However, given that I highlight actions taken by and regarding corporations in this chapter, and that the term has considerable purchase in academic, policy and business circles, I use corporate citizenship in this chapter.

3 Social Enterprise Coalition; www.socialenterprise.org.uk, accessed 22 November 2009.

Corporate citizenship and 'sustainable capitalism'

Corporate citizenship has largely been generated as a response to challenges to the principles and practices of contemporary globalisation processes, currently dominated by the economic philosophy of neo-liberalism. Among other things, this philosophy favours the global expansion and integration of market activity, and the reduction of government involvement in the commercial and social spheres. Critics of neo-liberal globalisation (for example Pilger 2006; Klein 2008; Monbiot 2008) express concern that global institutions governing commerce and trade favour corporate freedom of competition and the movement of capital, reducing the ability of states to regulate corporate action to ensure environmental protection and social security. Challenges to the forms of global integration under this philosophy have been widespread, including from former proponents of the approach. Joseph Stiglitz, former Chief Economist of the World Bank argues (2002: 214):

> Globalisation today is not working for many of the world's poor. It is not working for much of the environment. It is not working for the stability of the global economy . . . what is needed is a policy for sustainable, equitable and democratic growth. That is the reason for development.

Global public protests also indicate that concerns are held by significant numbers of people. An 'alter-globalisation' movement first became globally visible at the World Trade Organisation Ministerial Conference in Seattle in 1999, and at the G8 summit in Genoa in 2001 (Klein 2002), reflecting the less visible work of the World Social Forum[4] and other alter-globalisation and global justice movements (Humphries *et al.* 2006; Hawken 2007).

Contemporary political-economic arrangements are understood by many within the alter-globalisation movement as a form of 'corporate capitalism'. As Fisher and Ponniah (2003: 10-11) note, 'The perception is that corporate dominion has been organised across global space by the most powerful Northern states in the world, in collaboration with Southern economic and political elites'. Multinational corporations are a site of challenge to these arrangements: for not meeting widely held principles of democratic governance or social orientation (Korten 2001; Bakan 2004); as beneficiaries and agents of the financialisation of capitalism (Perkins 2004); and for the 'suppression of political, economic, cultural, racial, gendered, sexual, ecological and epistemological differences' (Fisher and Ponniah 2003: 10-11) through their promotion of consumerist market practices (Klein 2000). From this Birch (2003: 1) concludes that demands for 'corporate responsibility' are calls 'upon contemporary capitalism (as expressed through business) to be environmentally and socially responsible; to be accountable and transparent; to be inclusive; to be ethical and stable; to be more equitable—to be sustainable'.

---

4 www.forumsocialmundial.org.br, accessed 20 February 2009.

The corporate response

Global civil society demands for corporate responsibility are often framed as calls for greater corporate accountability through the creation of mandatory legal regulation mechanisms. The corporate and policy response has been to promote voluntary corporate social responsibility and corporate citizenship (Fox and Prescott 2004; Halme and Laurila 2009), often with reference to the difficulty of establishing effective regulatory frameworks in the 'postnational constellation' (Habermas 2001) of globalisation. A landmark in the adoption of the term corporate citizenship by large transnational corporations was 'Global Corporate Citizenship: The Leadership Challenge for CEOs and Boards', a joint-statement by 34 CEOs of global companies at the World Economic Forum in 2002. While governments have latterly become involved in corporate citizenship, many of the most notable initiatives have been developed in the international arena in collaborations between multiple stakeholders in corporate activity. The Global Compact, as mentioned above, is the largest of these, providing a learning network through which businesses commit to align their operations and strategies with ten universally accepted principles in the areas of human rights, labour, environment and anti-corruption.

Companies may claim a range of activities as evidence of their corporate citizenship. Halme and Laurila (2009) identify **philanthropy**, **innovation** and **integration** as three discrete types of corporate responsibility activity, based on the activity's relationship to the core business, its target and expected benefits. Philanthropy approaches emphasise charitable corporate activity, including sponsorship and employee voluntarism. Innovation approaches attempt to re-cast social or environmental problems as business opportunities. This 'win–win' approach, in which companies seek to 'cater for the poor or to benefit the environment' as a profitable enterprise has been most fully developed (Hart 2002; Hart and Christensen 2002; Prahalad 2004; Prahalad and Hammond 2002) in 'bottom-of-the-pyramid', pro-poor business models. The examples of corporate citizenship discussed in this chapter largely relate to integration activities, particularly as they relate to corporate activity in conflict regions. Integration approaches emphasise conducting core business more responsibly towards primary stakeholders such as customers, employees and suppliers. Companies characterised by this approach (Prahalad 2004: 329):

> [Take] actions like ensuring high product quality and investments in R&D (responsibility towards customers), paying just wages and avoiding over-compensation to top managers at the cost of other employees, taking diversity-oriented measures (responsibility towards employees), paying suppliers on time, supplier training programmes, supporting responsibility in the supply chain (e.g. no child labour; responsibility towards suppliers) and applying environmentally benign practice and policies.

A number of voluntary accountability mechanisms have been developed to support the adoption of an integrated approach to corporate responsibility. These include the development of reporting systems (e.g. the Global Reporting Initiative)[5] and management certification systems (e.g. the labour and environmental management standards, SA8000 and ISO 14001, respectively). The Global Compact explicitly supports the integration of corporate citizenship activities through the learning network it provides for companies to share their implementation of the ten Global Compact principles. The focus of these principles on responsible corporate activity through the protection of human rights and labour rights, environmental stewardship, and the reduction of corruption, clearly commits companies to promoting human security, even if not in name.

The business of armed conflict

Areas of violent conflict, widespread human rights violations and political repression are of particular concern to both the human security and the corporate citizenship communities. Armed conflicts cause incalculable human suffering and economic damage. Recent decades have seen genocides or near-genocides, campaigns of mass murder and rape, bombings of modern and ancient cities, forced displacements to atrocious camps, a proliferation of small arms, and numerous other sequelae of violence. Along with these human disasters there have, inevitably, been economic opportunities; for those in the arms trade or who trade in 'conflict goods' such as diamonds and coltan, or for those who secure lucrative reconstruction contracts, among others. But overall the impact of war is devastating, especially for poorer populations who frequently see their livelihoods vanish, environments destroyed, and health and education systems collapse.

The last decade has seen a growing interest in the role of enterprise in conflict management, resolution and peace-building. The relationship between enterprise and conflict has drawn the attention of NGOs such as Global Witness and International Alert; policy institutes such as the International Institute for Sustainable Development and the International Peace Institute; and intergovernmental bodies such as the World Bank and the United Nations. Notable among these efforts is the work of Paul Collier (2000) and others (Collier *et al.* 2003) at the World Bank on the economic causes of civil wars.

Global civil society has been instrumental in mounting challenges to the responsibilities of corporations in conflict or weak governance states for complicity in human rights abuses. For example, a global movement drew attention to the potential complicity of the Dutch-UK oil company Shell in the execution of Ken Saro-Wiwa and eight other Ogoni people by the Nigerian Government in 1995 (Chandler 2003). Attention has also been drawn to the role of TNCs in particular conflicts or around particular resources, such as coltan mining in the Democratic Republic of Congo (UN 2002).

5 www.globalreporting.org/Home, accessed 12 August 2009.

More recently, through the actions of industry and international business associations or multi-stakeholder projects, attention has turned to how global business enterprises can be engaged in peace-building activities. Corporations are engines of enterprise; they provide employment and revenue, import new technology and introduce new business or cultural practices. For these reasons they are also highly political actors in weak governance states and conflict regions, although this is more frequently denied by those who argue that the 'business of business is business'. Since early 2000 there has been a concerted international effort to shift this perspective, and to promote the 'Business of Peace' (coined by Nelson 2000, in his book of the same name). Apart from the evident humanitarian concerns, analysis of and engagement with conflict issues are becoming an increasingly critical area of management for most large companies, either as part of the risk profile in their direct operations or in the corporate citizenship arena. With over 60,000 TNCs operating in more than 70 conflict regions (Bais and Huijser 2005), TNCs can have a direct and wide-ranging influence on the nature and dynamics of conflict. This impact is only just beginning to be explored and understood.

Key business sectors in conflict

Work on the role of international business in conflict and peace has been concentrated in two main areas. First, those companies **directly involved in the practice of conflict**: arms manufacturers and suppliers and private security companies (whose current role in the Iraq and Afghanistan conflicts has raised their profile on the international stage). Most contemporary armed conflicts are fought in states with a small or non-existent arms industry; in almost all cases, all parties to the conflict are likely to purchase their weapons from large businesses in a handful of key countries: the USA, the UK, Russia, Israel and China are among the leaders. There are vigorous campaigns, mainly led by NGOs such as Saferworld, for export bans or at least restrictions, and for a code of practice in the international arms industry, but by all accounts, arms traders have little difficulty in circumventing the codes, even in countries such as the UK, which claim to adhere to them.

The global security industry provides another example of the interplay between national and commercial interests in some enterprise activities, particularly related to conflict areas. The global security industry comprises private military and security companies (PMSC); the industry has expanded dramatically with the military campaigns in Iraq and Afghanistan. The lack of effective regulation of PMSCs became notorious with an incident in 2004 in Fallujah, Iraq, involving employees of Blackwater, an American PMSC. These companies are contracted to provide an increasing number of services, including: guarding and protection; operational support in combat, intelligence, interrogation, and prisoner detention services; and advice to, training and reform of local forces and security personnel. The main clients of PMSCs are state militaries, but they are also contracted by other companies to protect their assets and personnel, and by humanitarian actors in zones of conflict and elsewhere.

Second, many of the world's worst armed conflicts take place in regions of **resource scarcity** or **resource abundance** or, paradoxically, a region that combines both. For the former, analysts may highlight the extreme population pressure on limited land resources as an explanation for the atrocities and continuing tensions in the Great Lakes area of Africa. Extreme poverty has long been identified as a causal factor of social violence. Evidently, economic growth, or at least significant assistance, may be an alleviating factor. Equally important, many conflicts arise as a struggle for control over precious resources, especially mineral wealth. 'Conflict diamonds' in Sierra Leone, and the location of reserves of coltan in the Kivu provinces of the Democratic Republic of Congo, provide two salient examples. The international private sector is directly involved in the extraction and sale of these resources, and companies involved in the extractive industry may directly exacerbate or ameliorate conflict between warring parties or divided communities through the conduct of their operations, the tax revenues they provide to whoever is in control or through their financing of these projects.

In general terms, almost any business sector could be involved in peace and conflict issues, and directly affected by the outbreak of open, violent conflict. The experiences of Heineken Breweries in Rwanda during the genocide in 1994 (see Bais and Huijser 2005), or the terrorist attacks on Taj Mahal Palace and Oberoi Trident hotels in Mumbai in November 2008 provide examples. It is clear that in areas of raised ethnic or political tension, which are legion, companies can become involved and play a role in how the conflict unfolds.

Action on business in conflict-affected areas

Significant action to promote more 'responsible' business engagement in contexts of weak governance and conflict has, to date, concentrated on: (i) clarifying the legal and normative responsibilities of companies for human rights violations; (ii) developing voluntary mechanisms to integrate this responsibility into business activities; and (iii) altering financial practices which facilitate business operations in these areas.

Legal and normative responsibilities

A number of recent efforts have focused on clarifying the legal obligations of TNCs operating in conflict regions. The International Committee of the Red Cross is working to reinforce the rights and obligations of business under international humanitarian law (ICRC 2006). International Alert recently released 'Red Flags', an online compendium of the growing number of cases under which companies and their executives have been taken to court, and in some cases held liable, for human rights violations and other malfeasance in high-risk contexts such as wars, areas of widespread violence and human rights abuses, or in states ruled by repressive regimes.[6]

Particularly notable and far-reaching has been the work of Professor John Ruggie as the UN Secretary-General's Special Representative on Business and Human Rights. Appointed in 2005 and with an extended mandate until 2011, Professor Ruggie was charged with establishing the landscape of business action on human rights, in both law and practice for states and businesses. In 2009, Ruggie released a report detailing the 'Protect, Respect, Remedy' framework (Ruggie 2009). This framework clarifies that it is the duty of states to protect human rights, it is the responsibility of businesses to respect those rights, and that there needs to be effective access to remedy mechanisms when rights have been violated. Extensive documentation on the research and consultation conducted under the auspices of the Special Representative, within which conflict zones are a special focus, is available from the online Business-Human Rights Resource Centre.[7]

Voluntary integration mechanisms

A number of TNCs have been particularly active in promoting more responsible corporate engagement in conflict regions and developing voluntary mechanisms to integrate this approach into TNC activities. In 2000, the International Business Leaders Forum published *The Business of Peace* (Nelson 2000), a seminal report promoting the business and societal benefits of conflict-sensitive business practice. Subsequent multi-stakeholder initiatives have advanced the discussion at the Global Compact (in the Zones of Conflict policy dialogue [UNGC 2009], and in an initiative from 2009–2010 to promote the implementation of the Global Compact's principles in conflict-affected areas) and at the International Labour Organisation, the World Bank and the Organisation for Economic Co-operation and Development.[8] An industry of consultants and civil society organisations now provides assessments of the environmental, social, human rights and conflict impacts of business activity in a range of contexts to support this integration.

Engagement by resource extractive industries in weak governance contexts

---

6 www.redflags.info, accessed 22 November 2009.
7 www.business-humanrights.org, accessed 20 November 2009. The website is an excellent resource, providing a platform for civil society organisations and companies to engage publicly on particular human rights issues and allegations.
8 See for example, the ILO report *Business and Decent Work in Conflict Zones: A 'Why?' and 'How?' Guide* (de Luca 2003); *Deciding Whether to do Business in States with Bad Governments* (2001) from the World Bank; and *The DAC guidelines: Helping Prevent Violent Conflict* (2001), *Multinational Enterprises in Situations of Violent Conflict and Widespread Human Rights Abuses* (2002) and *OECD Risk Awareness Tool for Multinational Enterprises in Weak Governance Zones* (OECD 2006) from the OECD.

receives particular attention given the large environmental and social impacts of their activities, and their record of involvement in rights violations in host countries (ESCR-NET 2005). Self-regulatory initiatives in the extractive sector include the Voluntary Principles on Security and Human Rights,[9] the Extractive Industries Transparency Initiative[10] and the Kimberley Process Certification Scheme.[11] The Voluntary Principles were first released in December 2000, the result of a sector-wide initiative involving the US and UK governments, companies in the extractive and petrochemical industries, and non-governmental organisations. The Voluntary Principles provide criteria to be considered by a company to assess the human rights risk in forming security agreements with state security or private armies, in order to avoid complicity in abuses such as of the right to life, freedom from torture, arbitrary arrest, and freedom of assembly and speech (Leipziger 2003: 95-105). The Extractive Industries Transparency Initiative (EITI) is a coalition of governments, companies and civil society organisations that seeks to set a standard for companies to publish what they pay for extractive activity, and for governments to disclose what they receive. The initiative aims to 'make natural resources benefit all'. Launched in 2002, as of September 2009, 30 countries and 42 of the largest extractive-industry companies were active in the EITI. Another example of multi-stakeholder efforts to reduce the negative impacts of trade in conflict-fuelling resources is the Kimberley Process Certification Scheme which aims to certify the origin of diamonds, to prevent extraction from fuelling conflict.

There are also moves to improve the regulation of private military and security companies (PMSCs). In September 2008, the Montreux Document was agreed by 17 states (notably including Afghanistan, China, France, Germany, Iraq, the UK, the US, Sierra Leone and South Africa), reaffirming existing international law obligations and outlining 70 good practices for states in contracting and regulating PMSCs, complemented by a number of industry initiatives.[12]

In this arena, and other attempts to integrate corporate citizenship practices in non-conflict affected areas, a number of companies are entering into novel partnerships with NGOs to ameliorate their negative impacts on the population in a conflict. While these partnerships can be difficult in themselves, with problems of trust, conflicting interests and organisational and cultural differences, NGOs are increasingly playing roles other than provocateur or adversary. Organisations such as Amnesty International and Save the Children have worked closely with some companies to try to deepen understanding of these issues and to support the organisational changes necessary in companies and the frameworks—legal, political, social, economic—within which they operate.

---

9 www.voluntaryprinciples.org, accessed 13 August 2009.
10 eitransparency.org, accessed 13 August 2009.
11 www.kimberleyprocess.com, accessed 12 August 2009.
12 For an excellent study of the current regulatory limitations in relation to PMSCs, see *Beyond Market Forces: Regulating the Global Security Industry* (International Peace Institute 2009).

The role of business in peace has also recently begun to receive attention within the Academy of Management (Wessel 2006) reflected, for example, in George Washington University's 'Peace Through Commerce' initiative.[13] Empirical descriptions of companies adopting a conflict-sensitive business approach are few but increasing in number. In *The Profit of Peace*, Bais and Huijser (2005) present interviews with executives in Afghanistan, Myanmar and Rwanda about corporate responses to conflict, and the attributed commercial and societal benefits of attempts to contribute to conflict transformation. In a significant contribution to the field, the Collaborative Development Association (CDA) has recently published a volume of reflections on its Corporate Engagement Project (Zandvliet and Anderson 2009). Since 2000, CDA has worked with companies on 'deepening their engagement in challenging operating environments'.[14]

Responsible investment in conflict-affected areas

While the business sectors which operate in areas of conflict and their role and impacts are most easily identifiable, a growing 'socially responsible investment' movement is also drawing attention to the role of financial institutions in supporting this activity. In 2006, a partnership of the Global Compact, the UN Environment Programme Finance Initiative and a wide group of institutional investors launched the Principles for Responsible Investment.[15] Almost 650 asset owners, investment managers and professional services were signatories to the six principles in late 2009, some with over US$1 billion under management. Through this initiative and the broader movement for socially responsible investment, the political and operational risks for businesses with operations in conflict-affected regions are being reframed.

Corporate citizenship and human security beyond the battlefield

Some corporations are increasingly involved in cross-cutting sustainable development issues, as the statement from the World Business Council for Sustainable Development cited above illustrates. Many, if not all, of these issues resonate with the aspirations of human security. Food security provides one example. The UN has been scaling up efforts to involve the private sector, with the Global Compact recently releasing a *Guide to Private Sector Action on Food Sustainability* (2008).

---

13 www.peacethroughcommerce.com, accessed 31 July 2009.
14 www.cdainc.com/cdawww/project_profile.php?pid=CEP&pname=Corporate%20 Engagement%20Project, accessed 22 November 2009.
15 www.unpri.org/principles, accessed 22 November 2009.

The World Food Programme has also launched a five-year project with business partners including DSM, Heinz, Kraft Foods, Unilever and the Global Alliance for Improved Nutrition (GAIN) to address malnutrition with specific focus on issues such as hygiene, nutrition and sustainable agriculture (Jerbi 2009). The World Food Programme has also partnered with logistics corporations, including Dutch logistics company TNT, in improving the efficiency of its crisis-response activities (Lariche 2009).

Similarly, in 2007, at the Global Compact Leaders Summit, the CEO Water Mandate was launched, through which CEOs committed to undertake voluntary actions to manage the resource more judiciously. Through the significant developments in supply chain management practices and certification systems (i.e. SA8000) during the first decade of the 21st century, corporations have become increasingly drawn into, and actively involved, in the protection and promotion of labour and environmental rights.

In efforts to alter the core operations of corporations through the integration of social and environmental concerns, and through activities corporate actors undertake outside the organisation to fulfil their 'social responsibilities', corporations are increasingly involved in the development of institutions and systems that may promote greater human security. This involvement does not come without tensions.

Concluding reflections

Corporate citizenship, as a set of activities taken by corporations in order to enact their 'social responsibility', is the subject of extensive criticism. The societal benefits of CSR to sustainable development (and by extension increased human security) claimed by its proponents are challenged by critical scholars and some quarters of civil society (Springett 2003). These critiques especially take aim at: the extent to which corporate citizenship/CSR addresses the challenges put to globalisation, particularly around the further extension of the market paradigm into the social and political worlds; the failure to address the democratic deficit in global governance and corporate action; and the favouring of voluntary mechanisms of corporate responsibility over regulatory systems fostering accountability.

A number of critics see CSR as a further extension of the neo-liberal philosophy which they identify as being the central set of organising principles within the current phase of global integration. In *CSR and Development: Is Business Appropriating Global Justice?*, Blowfield (2004: 67) argues that a critical analysis of CSR reveals global corporations 'to have a very particular set of norms, values and priorities that are projected as universal, and that define the boundaries which circumscribe any other negotiation of justice and well-being'. As such, 'The starting point for any debate about whether CSR is of benefit . . . is therefore to consider if we accept these norms, values and priorities; in other words, the social, moral and economic dimensions of global capitalism.' Continuing this structural analysis, Shamir (2008: 1) describes and theorises CSR as 'the moralisation of economic action that accompanies the economisation of the political'. In this process local, national and transnational authorities—both state and non-state—increasingly follow the logic of 'economic sustainability' and operate in a corporate-like form, while commercial enterprises increasingly perform tasks once considered 'to reside within the civic domain of moral entrepreneurship and the political domain of the caring welfare state' (Shamir 2008: 2). Through this process, Shamir sees CSR as an evolution and adaption of the 'neo-liberal imagination', through its reframing of socio-moral concerns from *within* the instrumental rationality of capitalist markets.

A second set of criticisms levelled at CSR challenges it as a response to the 'democratic deficit' engendered by globalisation. As corporate entities have become trans-territorial, they are inadequately bound by the current, state-bound regulatory framework, taking them beyond the control of politically determined populations. Within the Academy of Management, Matten and Crane (2005), and Scherer, Palazzo and associates (Scherer *et al.* 2006, 2009; Palazzo and Scherer 2006, 2008; Scherer and Palazzo 2007) are leading a collective inquiry into the corporation as a political actor, in order to support the development of new processes of democratic control. Following Fung (2003), Scherer *et al.* (2006: 520) argue, 'Only the democratisation of corporate activities, through continuous discourse participation and enlarged mechanisms of transparency, monitoring, and reporting, can close the legitimacy gap of the corporation as a political actor in a globalised economy'. While some may see the participation of corporations in initiatives such as the Global Compact as contributing to this end, the involvement of corporations at the UN, including through the Global Compact, is heavily criticised by individuals and organisations who feel that this confers the legitimacy of the UN on ill-deserving corporations.[16]

Further, critical analyses of CSR in the development literature (see Fox 2004: 30) and from civil society organisations in the global South (see *Corporate Social Responsibility: Whose Voice is Heard?* by Bais 2008) challenge CSR as a 'Northern' project in which companies undertake CSR activities in the developing world mainly for the benefit of stakeholders in developed economies. These challenges, which resonate with the social justice concerns above, are supplemented by a lack of empirical research on the social and other impacts of CSR activities, particularly in developing countries (Blowfield 2007; Halme and Laurila 2009). According to these scholars, it is not yet clear who CSR is for, and what good it does. In addressing these shortfalls, Idemudia (2008: 103) suggests that assessment of the contributions of CSR to development would be enhanced by attention to outcomes over processes, and by privileging the voices and concerns of the intended beneficiaries of CSR initiatives.

Finally, CSR is heavily criticised for being, as yet, a body of voluntary mecha-

---

16 See Global Compact Critics; www.globalcompactcritics.blogspot.com, accessed 1 July 2010.

nisms. However, the CSR movement is founded on the premise that norms around the appropriate terms of corporate activity can be transformed, and that this requires the active engagement of business owing to the difficulties of regulation in the 'postnational constellation'. While criticised for being a 'learning platform' with no effective sanction beyond de-listing members, the Global Compact is built around this core principle. As Zadek (2001: 221) argues, 'corporate citizenship will only be effective if and when it evolves to a point where business becomes active in promoting and institutionalising new global governance frameworks that effectively secure civil market behaviour'. As the examples we have cited in this chapter illustrate, some companies have become active participants and leaders in developing the institutions and norms that may engender greater human security. In areas where there is limited government presence, or where that presence undermines the enjoyment of freedom from fear and want, companies are under increasing pressure to use their material and political resources to respect and support the enjoyment of those freedoms.

Over the past decade the corporate social responsibility movement has reflected and played a central role in challenges to the contemporary division of business and society. While the movement combines a number of different foci and priorities—both environmental and social—it is of particular relevance in areas of conflict and weak governance. Through its roles in shaping and supporting the economic conditions under which conflict and oppression occur at the individual, state and regional level, its direct and indirect provision of material or other support to warring parties, its production and supply of the tools and weapons of war, and its potential political influence for all of these reasons, the private sector is involved in conflict formation and resilience. It is hoped that through a deeper understanding of these activities and their dynamics, it can be engaged as a partner in conflict transformation and peace-building.

Bibliography

Bais, K. (2008) *Corporate Social Responsibility. Whose Voice is Heard?* (Amsterdam: MVO Platform).

—— and M. Huijser (2005) *The Profit of Peace: Corporate Responsibility in Conflict Regions* (Sheffield, UK: Greenleaf Publishing): 15.

Bakan, J. (2004) *The Corporation: The Pathological Pursuit of Profit and Power* (New York: Free Press).

Birch, D. (2003) 'Corporate Social Responsibility: Some Key Theoretical Issues and Concepts for New Ways of Doing Business', *Journal of New Business Ideas and Trends* 1.1: 1-19.

Blowfield, M. (2004) 'CSR and Development: Is Business Appropriating Global Justice? *Development* 47.3: 61-68.

—— (2007) 'Reasons to be Cheerful? What We Know about CSR's Impact', *Third World Quarterly* 28.4: 683-95.

Buzan, B. (2004) 'A Reductionist, Idealistic Notion that Adds Little Analytical Value', *Security Dialogue* 35.3: 369-70.

Chandler, G. (2003) 'The Evolution of the Business and Human Rights Debate', in R. Sullivan (ed.), *Business and Human Rights* (Sheffield, UK: Greenleaf Publishing).

Collier, P. (2000) *Economic Causes for Civil Wars and their Consequences for Policy* (Washington, DC: World Bank).

——, V.L. Elliott, H. Hegre, A. Hoeffler, M. Reynal-Querol and N. Sambanis (2003) *Breaking the Conflict Trap: Civil War and Development Policy* (Washington, DC: World Bank/Oxford University Press).

De Luca, L. (2003) *Business and Decent Work in Conflict Zones: A 'Why?' and 'How?' Guide* (Geneva: International Labour Organization).

ESCR-NET (2005) *Joint NGO Submission: Consultation on Human Rights and the Extractive Industry* (Geneva: International Network for Economic, Social & Cultural Rights Corporate Accountability Working Group).

Fisher, W.F., and T. Ponniah (eds.) (2003) *Another World is Possible: Popular Alternatives to Globalization at the World Social Forum* (London: Zed Books).

Fox, T. (2004) 'Corporate Social Responsibility and Development: In Quest of an Agenda', *Development* 47.3: 29-36.

—— and D. Prescott (2004) 'Exploring the Role of Development Cooperation Agencies in Corporate Responsibility', paper presented at the *Conference on Development Cooperation and Corporate Social Responsibility*, Stockholm, 22–23 March 2004.

Fung, A. (2003) 'Deliberative Democracy and International Labour Standards', *Governance* 16: 51-71.

Habermas, J. (2001) 'The Postnational Constellation and the Future of Democracy', in J. Habermas (ed.), *The Postnational Constellation* (Cambridge, UK: Polity Press).

Halme, M., and J. Laurila (2009) 'Philanthropy, Integration or Innovation? Exploring the Financial and Societal Outcomes of Different Types of Corporate Responsibility', *Journal of Business Ethics* 84.3: 325-39.

Hart, S.L., and C.M. Christensen (2002) 'The Great Leap: Driving Innovation from the Base of the Pyramid', *MIT Sloan Management Review* 44.1: 51-56.

Hawken, P. (2007) *Blessed Unrest: How the largest movement in the world came into being and why no one saw it coming* (New York: Viking Press).

Humphries, M., D. Fitzgibbons and N. Black (2006) 'A Relational Ethic for Beneficial Business Engagement', paper presented at the *Business as an Agent of World Benefit (BAWB), E-Conference*, Ohio, 22–25 October 2006.

ICRC (2006) *Business and International Humanitarian Law: An Introduction to the Rights and Obligations of Business Enterprises under International Humanitarian Law* (Geneva: International Committee of the Red Cross).

Idemudia, U. (2008) 'Conceptualising the CSR and Development Debate', *Journal of Corporate Citizenship* 29 (Spring 2008): 91-111.

International Peace Institute (2009) *Beyond Market Forces: Regulating the Global Security Industry*; www.ipinst.org/media/pdf/publications/beyond_market_forces_final.pdf, accessed 12 June 2010.

Jerbi, S. (2009) *Security and the Private Sector: Thinking about Human Rights?* (London: Institute for Human Rights and Business).

Klein, N. (2000) *No Logo: Taking Aim at the Brand Bullies* (New York: Picador USA).

—— (2002) *Fences and Windows: Dispatches from the Frontlines of the Globalization Debate* (Toronto: Vintage).

—— (2008) *The Shock Doctrine: The Rise of Disaster Capitalism* (London: Penguin).

Korten, D. (2001) *When Corporations Rule the World* (Bloomfield, CT: Kumarian Press).

Lariche, B. (2009) 'Humanitarian Logistics', *The CSR Digest*, 11 May 2009; www.csrdigest. com/2009/05/humanitarian-logistics, accessed 12 December 2009.

Leipziger, D. (2003) *The Corporate Responsibility Code Book* (Sheffield, UK: Greenleaf Publishing).

Matten, D., and A. Crane (2005) 'Corporate Citizenship: Towards an Extended Theoretical Conceptualization', *Academy of Management Review* 30: 166-79.

——, A. Crane and W. Chapple (2003) 'Behind the Mask: Revealing the True Face of Corporate Citizenship', *Journal of Business Ethics* 45.1: 109-20.

Monbiot, G. (2008) *Bring on the Apocalypse: Six Arguments for Global Justice* (London: Atlantic Books).

Morrison, J. (2003) 'Corporate Citizenship: More than a Metaphor?' *Journal of Corporate Citizenship* 10 (Summer 2003): 89-103.

Nelson, J. (2000) *The Business of Peace* (London: Folium Press).

OECD (2001) *The DAC Guidelines: Helping Prevent Violent Conflict*; www.oecd.org/dataoecd/15/54/1886146.pdf, accessed 12 December 2009.

—— (2002) *Multinational Enterprises in Situations of Violent Conflict and Widespread Human Rights Abuses*; http://www.oecd.org/dataoecd/46/31/2757771.pdf, accessed 12 December 2009.

—— (2006) *Risk Awareness Tool for Multinational Enterprises in Weak Governance Zones*; www.oecd.org/dataoecd/26/21/36885821.pdf, accessed 12 December 2009.

Palazzo, G., and A.G. Scherer (2006) 'Corporate Legitimacy as Deliberation: A Communicative Framework', *Journal of Business Ethics* 66.1: 71-88.

—— and A.G. Scherer (2008) 'Corporate Social Responsibility, Democracy, and the Politicization of the Corporation', *Academy of Management Review* 33.3: 773-75.

Paris, R. (2001) 'Human Security: Paradigm Shift or Hot Air?', *International Security* 26.2: 87-102.

—— (2004) 'Still an Inscrutable Concept', *Security Dialogue* 35.3: 370-72.

Perkins, J. (2004) *Confessions of an Economic Hitman* (San Francisco: Berrett-Koehler).

Pilger, J. (2006) *Freedom Next Time* (London: Bantam Press).

Prahalad, C.K. (2004) *The Fortune at the Bottom of the Pyramid: Eradicating Poverty through Profits* (Upper Saddle River, NJ: Wharton School Publishing).

—— and A. Hammond (2002) 'Serving the World's Poor, Profitably', *Harvard Business Review* 80.9: 48-57.

Ruggie, J. (2009) *Promotion of All Human Rights, Civil, Political, Economic, Social and Cultural Rights, including the Right to Development. Business and Human Rights: Towards Operationalizing the 'Protect, Respect and Remedy' Framework* (New York: UN General Assembly).

Scherer, A.G., and G. Palazzo (2007) 'Toward a Political Conception of Corporate Responsibility: Business and Society Seen From a Habermasian Perspective', *Academy of Management Review* 32.4: 1,096-120.

——, G. Palazzo and D. Baumann (2006) 'Global Rules and Private Actors: Towards a New Role of the Transnational Corporation in Global Governance', *Business Ethics Quarterly* 16.4: 505-32.

——, G. Palazzo and D. Matten (2009) 'Introduction to the Special Issue: Globalization as a Challenge for Business Responsibilities', *Business Ethics Quarterly* 19.3: 327-47.

Schwartz, J. (2004) *The Private Sector's Role in the Provision of Infrastructure in Post-Conflict Countries: Patterns and Policy Options* (Washington, DC: World Bank Conflict Prevention & Reconstruction Unit).

Shamir, R. (2008) 'The Age of Responsibilization: On Market-embedded Morality', *Economy & Society* 37.1: 1-19.

Springett, D. (2003) 'Business Conceptions of Sustainable Development: A Perspective from Critical Theory', *Business Strategy and Environment* 12: 71-86.

Stiglitz, J. (2002) *Globalization and its Discontents* (New York: W.W. Norton & Company).

Timothy, K. (2004) 'Human Security Discourse at the United Nations', *Peace Review* 16.1: 19-24.

Total SA (2007) 'In light of recent events unfolding in Myanmar, Total would like to restate its position regarding its presence in the country', 26 September 2007; birmanie.total.com/en/news/p_5_4.htm, accessed 1 July 2010.

UN (2002) *Final Report of the Panel of Experts on the Illegal Exploitation of Natural Resources and Other Forms of Wealth of the Democratic Republic of Congo* (New York: United Nations).

UNCHS (United Nations Centre for Human Settlements [Habitat]) (2003) *Human Security Now: Protecting and Empowering People* (New York: United Nations Commission on Human Security).

UNDP (United Nations Development Project) (1994) *Human Development Report 1994: New Dimensions of Human Security* (New York: UNDP).

UNGC (United Nations Global Compact) (2008) 'Guide to Private Sector Action on Food Sustainability' (UNGC).

—— (2009) 'Business and Peace'; 66.109.24.102:8080/opencms2/export/unglobalcompact/Issues/conflict_prevention/index.html, accessed 12 August 2009.

UNSC (United Nations Security Council) (2004) 'The Role of Business in Conflict Prevention, Peacekeeping and Post-Conflict Peace-building', paper presented at the *Security Council, Fifty-Ninth Year, 4943rd Meeting*, New York, 15 April 2004.

Waddock, S. (2004) 'Parallel Universes: Companies, Academics, and the Progress of Corporate Citizenship', *Business & Society Review* 109.1: 5-42.

Wessel, R. (2006) 'Business Schools' New Mission: Promoting Peace', *Wall Street Journal*, 2 June 2006.

World Bank (2001) *Deciding Whether to do Business in States with Bad Governments* (Washington, DC: World Bank).

Zadek, S. (2001) *The Civil Corporation: The New Economy of Corporate Citizenship* (London: Earthscan).

Zandvliet, L., and M.B. Anderson (2009) *Getting it Right: Making Corporate–Community Relations Work* (Sheffield, UK: Greenleaf Publishing).

8

The UN Global Compact as a catalyst for human security

A proposal from Japan for CPR (corporate peace responsibility)

Yasunobu Sato and Dylan Scudder

Graduate School of Arts & Sciences, University of Tokyo, Japan

Defining human security

The concept of human security is an attempt to treat the issue of security as an issue of individuals rather than as an issue between nations. As shown in Figure 8.1, human security can be seen as the nexus bonding the two concepts of human development[1] and positive peace.[2] This is because the goal of human security is located within the overlap of the development of individual capability as discussed by Amartya Sen (2001), and a society without structural violence, as discussed by Johan Galtung (1969). Here, we will consider the meaning of human security.

1 Human development is the basis of the United Nations Development Programme's (UNDP) human security theory, which is referred to below and derives from Amartya Sen's capability theory.
2 As defined by Johan Galtung, a situation in which there is not only no direct violence but also no structural violence such as poverty, oppression or discrimination.

Figure 8.1 **The nature of human security**

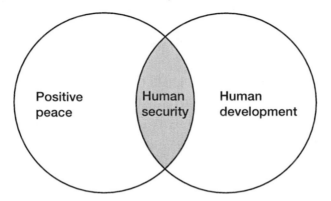

It was the United Nations Development Programme (UNDP) that identified human security as a new development issue in its *Human Development Report 1994*.[3] This emerged from a paradigm shift in development theory from development through the economic growth of nations to human-oriented development (human development), the goal of which is the advancement of human rights of individuals. Sen's argument of capability is the theoretical backbone of human development. According to the *Human Development Report 1994*, 'human security' has seven dimensions: (1) economic security, (2) food security, (3) health security, (4) environmental security, (5) personal security, (6) community security, and (7) political security. These are identified as typical areas in which human security is threatened, but it is recognised that human security is not limited to these seven. In other words, the problems of employment, income, food and so on are not only problems of development, but also of the basic security of individuals.

On the other hand, the paradigm of peace and security studies has also shifted from the cold war's balance of power to peace-building in order to address regional conflicts, introduced by Mary Kaldor as 'new wars' (Kaldor 1999). In 1992, then UN Secretary-General, Boutros-Ghali, proposed preventive diplomacy in his report *An Agenda for Peace*, including peacemaking, peacekeeping, post-conflict peace-building, and cooperation with local organisations as ways of strengthening the United Nations after the cold war. Drawing on the awareness that peace and development are inseparable, and taking lessons from the UNPKO (United Nations Peacekeeping Operation) in Somalia, discussion shifted away from peace imposed by force to a realisation that peace-building through development assistance is necessary and that peacekeeping and peace-building operations are consecutive issues.[4]

3 The World Summit for Social Development's Programme of Action confirmed that social development/social justice and peace/security are inseparable. Underpinning these ideas is the UNDP theory of human security, which regards social injustice as a structural problem threatening peace and development—a problem that must be addressed.

4 cf. Brahimi Report (Report of the Panel on United Nations Peace Operations; Durch 2003); www.un.org/peace/reports/peace_operations/report.htm, accessed 2 July 2010.

The Development Assistance Committee (DAC) of the Organisation for Economic Co-operation and Development (OECD) released its *DAC Guidelines on Conflict, Peace and Development Co-operation* in 1997 based on Canada's concept of comprehensive peace-building. In the guidelines, the DAC confirms the importance of the role of development assistance at each phase: pre-conflict, mid-conflict, immediate aftermath of conflict and post-conflict. The DAC also makes proposals at each phase regarding the goal of development assistance in strengthening the rule of law and in promoting civilian participation in the democratisation process. In this way, current discussions address the concretisation of comprehensive peace-building, making efforts towards further cooperation in development assistance with the aim of preventing armed conflict.[5]

The Japanese Government's contribution to human security

At the initiative of the Japanese Government, responding to the former Secretary-General of the United Nations, Kofi Annan's call at the Millennium Summit, the Commission on Human Security was established in June 2001 with co-chairs Sadako Ogata, President of JICA and former United Nations High Commissioner for Refugees (UNHCR), and Amartya Sen, Nobel Laureate in Economics and Professor at Harvard University. *Human Security Now*, the final report of the Commission on Human Security defined human security as the vital freedom of individuals consisting of the freedom from fear and freedom from want. They were two of the four freedoms mentioned in another era by President Franklin Roosevelt in the Atlantic Charter, which was the blueprint for the world after the Second World War and which served as one of the first steps towards the formation of the United Nations. The UN Charter was in turn reflected in the new Japanese Constitution, which renounces war as a means of settling international disputes and prohibits the maintenance of armed forces and other war potential. Interestingly, the key concepts of 'freedom from fear' and 'freedom from want' are embedded in the second paragraph of the preamble of Japan's Constitution, where it states that: 'We recognise that all peoples of the world have the right to live in peace, free from fear and want.'

This paragraph is reflected in the famous Article 9 of the Constitution, which articulates the prohibition of armaments in renouncing war.

---

5 DAC released a supplement to the guidelines in 2001, and in 2003 incorporated them in its guidelines *Helping Prevent Violent Conflict* (OECD 2001). In these guidelines, conflict prevention is dealt with as the core issue and new viewpoints such as gender and business are added.

Article 9: Aspiring sincerely to an international peace based on justice and order, the Japanese people forever renounce war as a sovereign right of the nation and the threat or use of force as means of settling international disputes. (2) In order to accomplish the aim of the preceding paragraph, land, sea, and air forces, as well as other war potential, will never be maintained. The right of belligerency of the state will not be recognised.

Japan is supposed to contribute to peace through non-violent means. Thus, Japan created the United Nations Trust Fund for Human Security in 1999 with the express aim of promoting human security through the protection and empowerment of people and communities threatened in their survival, livelihood and dignity. The fund finances grass-roots projects for human security in collaboration with UN organisations and non-UN entities rather than through governments. Along this line, the Japanese Government is promoting human security as its diplomatic principle, backed by its peace constitution that grew out of the UN Charter.

The Commission's report is concerned mainly with establishing security in place of conflict, poverty and disease, and the education needed to attain this security, and refers to 'protection' and 'empowerment' as strategies to this end.

Peace-building, on the other hand, means building a society in which positive peace—peace without structural violence such as poverty and discrimination—is secured, or a society in which human security is guaranteed. In other words, it is a society in which individual human rights and social justice are respected. This is where the concept of human security offers theoretical support for peace-building. The discussion on human security in general and on peace-building in particular is about how to transform a 'conflict society', characterised by competing interests, terrorism and violence, into a 'peace society' in which human beings can live free from fear and want; and how to create the conditions to bring about such a transformation.

In this spirit, Japan contributed to the establishment of the United Nations Peacebuilding Commission through the resolution of the UN World Summit in 2005. The outcome document from the summit also provides one paragraph on human security.[6] In this sense, human security and peace-building have been supported by the Japanese Government from the outset as twin concepts and as two sides of the same coin. Japan cannot take a military approach to peace-building. Thus, Japan's ODA in 2003 adopted human security as a policy principle and as a prioritised issue to be tackled. To this end, Japan is now seeking to expand civilian contributions to human security and peace-building.

6 As an initiative of the Japanese Government, the UN published the UN Secretary-General Report on Human Security on 8 March 2010. The report provides an update on developments related to the advancement of human security since the 2005 World Summit and takes stock of discussions on human security, its various definitions and its relationship to State sovereignty and the responsibility to protect.

Business and civil society as core actors for human security

At the heart of human security are the human-centred objectives of peace and development. Given the scale of the challenge, it follows that those playing a role in providing human security are not only states or state-made institutions but also non-state actors at both local and global levels: namely civil society and the private sector. Under the sovereign state system, each state pursues its own national security based on national interests and deems the security of its population to be an internal affair. Nevertheless, as complexities such as climate change or so-called failed or fragile states emerge, they are taken up as globalisation issues at a global level.

As these issues remind us, the framework of national security provided by states has proved to be inadequate for addressing threats that go beyond national borders. Meanwhile, global business has become increasingly powerful by expanding the market economy to all corners of the world. Under the so-called Washington Consensus, not only transitional countries, but developing ones, too, continue to promote the market economy through the free trade frameworks of the WTO (World Trade Organisation) and FTA (free trade agreement) regimes. At the same time, the market economy itself is the target of increasing criticism for exacerbating social instability and legitimising a commercial form of structural violence. Likewise, the WTO is regularly denounced as another symbol of globalisation because of the market economy's perceived role in increasing the economic dependency of vulnerable people and the myriad consequences thereof.

Against this background, the CSR (corporate social responsibility) movement arose in response to dissatisfactions with corporate governance, and with an interest in exploring more socially and environmentally sustainable business models. One of the drivers of corporate accountability and the CSR movement has been the recognition that the international community, as a collective of sovereign states, cannot effectively control global businesses that extend far beyond the borders of their individual states. Neither the United Nations nor any other international organisation is capable of addressing the transnational misconducts of global business as they, too, are restricted bodies of the same nation state system. Civil society on the other hand, represented by NGOs, has long been involved in shaping UN policy, while a good number of multinational corporations themselves have also adopted a range of certification systems such as SA8000 and ISO 26000, and voluntary standards such as the OECD Guidelines, the Global Reporting Index, and the Voluntary Principles on Security and Human Rights.[7] It was within this constella-

7 The Voluntary Principles on Security and Human Rights (VPSHR, commonly referred to as the VPs) are a set of non-binding principles developed in 2000 to address the issue of balancing safety needs while respecting human rights and fundamental freedoms. The VPs are seen as genuinely filling a critical void for companies seeking guidance about managing potential exposure to risks related to their security and human rights prac-

tion of corporate responsibility initiatives that the UN Global Compact established itself as a now well-known learning network where businesses meet and discuss best practice.

The UN Global Compact as a catalyst for human security

In addition to the Commission on Human Security, Kofi Annan also initiated the United Nations Global Compact (hereafter Compact) at the World Economic Forum on 31 January 1999 in Davos, Switzerland. It was then officially launched a year and a half later at the UN Headquarters in New York on 26 July 2000.

The Compact is a UN initiative to encourage businesses worldwide to adopt sustainable and socially responsible policies, and to report annually on their implementation. The Compact provides a value-based framework for businesses, promoting ten principles in the areas of human rights, labour, the environment and anti-corruption. Under the Compact, companies are brought together with UN agencies, labour groups and civil society to discuss how to apply the principles in day-to-day business operations. With some 5,200 corporate members, it is currently the world's largest corporate initiative. As a voluntary undertaking it has two objectives: 'Mainstream the ten principles in business activities around the world', and 'Catalyze actions in support of broader UN goals, including the Millennium Development Goals (MDGs).'

Though the principles could be read as a loosely worded code of conduct for Compact member companies, the Compact sees its role more as that of a value framework for encouraging innovative partnerships through dialogue on best practice. It does not set out to be a regulatory instrument, but rather a forum for discussion and a network of governments, companies and labour organisations, whose actions it seeks to influence, with civil society organisations playing a key role in the ongoing discussion on corporate responsibility and ensuring that their concerns are given a voice.

The Compact's principles encourage companies to refrain from doing harm to society or the environment, and to contribute to public goods and interests. As such, in theory at least, the Compact is well positioned to serve as a catalyst for human security. A closer look at the principles and the MDGs, however, suggests that they address the human development dimension of human security more

---

tices, especially in countries that are often associated with conflict or alleged abuses. The Principles also provide guidance for companies on identifying human rights and security risk, as well as engaging and collaborating with state and private security forces. The principles were developed through multi-stakeholder participation from governments, extractive industry and NGOs (www.voluntaryprinciples.org, accessed 16 December 2009).

than the positive peace dimension. Although Principles 1 and 2 regarding human rights, and Principle 10 regarding anti-corruption, all show links to peace in their aim to reduce structural violence, the remaining seven principles and eight MDGs express concerns that are more in line with Sen's capabilities approach.

Annan's oft-quoted statement summarises the overall aim of the vision he had at the Compact's inception in 1999: 'Let us choose to reconcile the creative forces of private entrepreneurship with the needs of the disadvantaged and the requirements of future generations'.[8] With a view to advancing this vision, the Compact Office is funded by six UN agencies that make up its current support base: the United Nations High Commissioner for Human Rights; the United Nations Environment Programme; the International Labour Organisation; the United Nations Development Programme; the United Nations Industrial Development Organisation; and the United Nations Office on Drugs and Crime.

Though focused primarily on promoting its ten principles, the Compact members have expanded their scope of commitment to include industry-specific guidelines such as the Equator Principles for the finance industry, the Principles of Responsible Management in Education (PRME) for management schools, and the Global Reporting Index as a reporting mechanism that Compact members can use to communicate their progress towards implementing the principles. Another example of Compact members going beyond their basic commitment to the principles is their adoption of the Geneva Declaration on corporate responsibility at the second Global Compact Leaders Summit, chaired by Secretary-General Ban Ki-moon, on 5–6 July 2007 at the Palais des Nations in Geneva, Switzerland.[9] Essentially an expression of intent on behalf of the private sector to adhere to the principles, the declaration also expresses their intent to advocate for their implementation throughout their businesses and among their partner companies.

Yet while stepping up its voluntary commitment to the principles and beyond, the Compact disengages at the same time from any commitment to monitoring its membership's de facto adherence to any of these initiatives. To the disappointment of some of its critics, in place of holding its membership accountable through independent auditing, the Compact explains that it simply accepts members' annual reporting in good faith. The Compact's disclaimer goes on to say that, although companies may declare their support for its principles, this does not imply recognition or certification that these companies have adhered to the principles. This makes it difficult to know what the Compact's contribution to human security has been, given the dearth of reliable data. In its defence, the Compact has made it clear to the public since its launch, however, that its goals and processes are not

---

8 UN Secretary-General, Kofi Annan, at the World Economic Forum in Davos, January 1999.

9 See www.unglobalcompact.org/docs/summit2007/GENEVA_DECLARATION.pdf, accessed 16 December 2009.

monitored and that they are intentionally flexible and open-ended.[10] In this sense, in pursuing its objectives, it attaches less importance to 'naming and shaming' or other forms of sanctioning. Instead, the Compact seeks to take a neutral stance and operates in four areas of general activity: policy dialogues, learning, local networks and projects.

Many civil society organisations are concerned, however, that without any monitoring and enforcement provisions, the Compact fails to hold corporations accountable. Moreover, many of these organisations argue that companies can misuse the Compact as a public relations instrument for 'bluewash' (Bruno and Karliner 2000), as an excuse to oppose any binding international regulation on corporate accountability, and as a means of increasing corporate influence on the policy discourse and development strategies of the United Nations.[11]

Antonio Vives of Stanford University offers five points of criticism that summarise many of the concerns about the Compact's overall credibility:

> While the principles constitute a useful guide, they only impact on companies that would have carried out responsible practices either way—regardless of the Global Compact—but wish to benefit from the additional public exposure.
>
> The activities are not specified beyond the general principles, which are voluntary, and there is no obligation to do anything in particular.
>
> There is no penalty for omitting to comply with the principles.
>
> The Global Compact lacks the capacity to verify companies' activities, let alone to determine whether they are actually contributing in any form.
>
> The only penalty consists in being expelled for not complying with the duty to inform, and this only occurs after THREE consecutive years of failing to report (Vives 2008).[12]

The Compact is quick to remind critics, however, that it was never intended to be a 'watch dog', but more of a 'guide dog'.[13] But critics asking for more accountability would be justified in wondering where this guide dog is leading us when the Compact appears to make the 'halo effect' of UN affiliation available to any company that wishes to have it. The current Compact member list includes, for example,

---

10 The Compact explains that 'The Global Compact is not a performance or assessment tool. It does not provide a seal of approval, nor does it make judgments on performance.' See www.unglobalcompact.org/AboutTheGC/faq.html, accessed 16 December 2009.

11 Those who have written on the subject include senior UN officials and advisers: Maude Barlow, senior adviser on water issues to the President of the United Nations General Assembly, David Andrews, senior adviser on food policy and sustainable development, Peter Utting, deputy director of UNRISD, and Ann Zammit, development economist (Utting and Zammit 2006).

12 Antonio Vives is a consulting professor in the Department of Civil and Environmental Engineering at Stanford University. He is the former manager of the Sustainable Development Department of the Inter-American Development Bank, IDB.

13 See www.unglobalcompact.org/AbouttheGC/faq.html, accessed 16 December 2009.

some of the world's largest weapons producers such as EADS France, EADS NV and International Armored Group, and even private military companies such as Aegis and DynCorp, both major contractors in the US attacks on Iraq and Afghanistan, which some may argue safeguards neither the autonomy nor the integrity of the UN.

Taking this line of reasoning to its logical conclusion, we would also have to ask about companies that provide material support to armed groups or who are involved in the trade of conflict goods such as timber and rare minerals, and to what extent their parent companies and subsidiaries are complicit in these activities. And if it is a company's investors and customers who enable it to engage in human rights abuses, how should the extent of their complicity as enablers be measured? The Compact has acknowledged these enabling factors through its initiative on PRI (Principles of Responsible Investment), which outlines suggested practices for preventing the funding of activities that may lead to environmental degradation or social injustices such as people being forced to evacuate their native lands. But how does one attribute proportionate responsibility to specific actors along the value chain across so many different industries and product lines? For example, if a large Japanese trading company imports timber products from South-East Asia that in turn fuel conflicts in Indonesia and elsewhere in the region, who exactly in the company is to be held accountable, and for what? And what about their investors, the end-users who knowingly or unknowingly buy the products, and the media's role in shaping consumer awareness?

Though at first glance the discussion on membership eligibility in the Compact may seem limited to a mundane issue of merely defining principled screening criteria, these same criteria soon prove to be inextricably bound up with fiercely debated issues of ethics and political philosophy. Asking, for instance, whether weapons producers merit their role as UN partners and to what extent their values are aligned with those of the UN opens up the long-standing contention about the potentially peaceful role of military threat in so-called 'big stick' diplomacy. On the other hand, as Michael Walzer's (2000) *Just and Unjust Wars* reminds us, the long-term effectiveness of military intervention remains highly debatable. Some may argue that the big stick approach could be abused to present even weapons of mass destruction as legitimate instruments of peace, thereby making those who produce and sell them agents of a peace process. At the centre of this controversy stands Chapter VII of the UN Charter, under which '[. . .] the Security Council can take enforcement measures to maintain or restore international peace and security. Such measures range from economic and/or other sanctions not involving the use of armed force to international military action.'[14] If the UN itself accepts Chapter VII as a justification for the use of force in fulfilling its own goals, and if the Compact sees its role as supporting these goals, then it could also be argued that having weapons producers among its membership is perfectly consistent with its principles.

14 See www.un.org/sc/committees, accessed 29 August 2010.

If we assume that fulfilling its objectives would make the Compact a catalyst for human security, does its controversial stance and the debate surrounding it drive or hinder the Compact in achieving its objectives and living up to its reason for being? From its own account, it simply provides a set of values and a visible space for global debate; that is, it fulfils an awareness-raising function. From this we can deduce that the Compact is not here to end the discussion. In contrast, it would seem that its role is only strengthened by stoking the flames of heated debate as a means of contributing to its stated objective of supporting the broader UN goals. So the question remains, could the awareness raising that results from the debate around the Compact's high tolerance policy serve as a justifiable means of reaching its ends?

Integrating corporate peace responsibility into the UNGC

The pragmatic view is less concerned with the means by which the Compact pursues its objectives and more with the extent to which it is actually achieving them. It explains that one of its main objectives is 'to catalyze actions in support of the broader UN goals, including the MDGs', and the first sentence on the UN's homepage reminds us that 'The United Nations is an international organisation founded in 1945 after the Second World War by 51 countries committed to maintaining international peace and security . . .'[15] Given that the UN's core goals are maintaining peace and security, and if *this* is what the Compact is catalysing action for, then the need for including a peace and security principle in the current set of principles would seem most urgent if not long overdue.

This view is further supported by the recent revision of the 'Guidelines between the United Nations and the Business Sector' (Guidelines) issued by UN Secretary-General Ban Ki-moon on 20 November 2009. According to the UN Press Office, as part of the SG's efforts to modernise the UN, the new Guidelines' purpose is to facilitate the formulation and implementation of partnerships between the UN and the business sector in a way that safeguards the integrity and autonomy of the UN. This raises the question of what sort of partnership 'safeguards the integrity and autonomy of the UN'.

In partial response to this, the new Guidelines set out six general principles describing the UN's expectations of its corporate partners. Point 12(a) shown in Figure 8.2 elaborates on what is meant by a company that helps to advance UN goals.

---

15 See www.un.org/en/aboutun/index.shtml, accessed 29 August 2010.

Figure 8.2 **Excerpt from revised Guidelines between United Nations and the Business Sector, 2009**

IV. GENERAL PRINCIPLES

12.   Irrespective of the situation-specific nature of cooperative arrangements, they should be guided by the following general principles:

> a)   Advance UN goals: The objective needs to be articulated clearly and must advance UN goals as laid out in the Charter. Chapter 1 of the UN Charter outlines key UN goals such as: maintaining international peace and security as well as solving international problems of an economic, social, cultural or humanitarian character, and promoting and encouraging respect for human rights and fundamental freedoms for all.

Though the Guidelines are unambiguous about the need for an explicit commitment to peace and security and though these are paramount among the broader UN goals, they are noticeably absent from the principles. There are two ways to read this, and both are problematic from a peace and security perspective. First, even if the Compact meets its first objective of mainstreaming the principles far and wide, there is currently no peace principle among them. Second, even if peace is somehow *implied* within the description of 'broader UN goals' (it would be 'un-UN' if not), what justification is there for marginalising a goal so central to the UN mandate and so explicit in the Guidelines?

Based on the SG's revised UN–Business Guidelines, UN Millennium Summit Resolution 55/2 (2000), and UN World Summit Resolution 60/1 (2005) mentioning the private sector's role in contributing to peace and security, the currently absent principle might be called the principle of corporate peace responsibility (CPR) and would be understood to be a private sector approach to ensuring human security as a general guideline by contributing to the peace and security of all those affected by its operations. Concretely, it would declare that:

> Businesses should support concerted efforts by the United Nations and other international organisations to build and maintain peace and security; and support measures for conflict prevention and peacebuilding, and for protection of people in armed conflict, as well as empowerment of their capacity for human security at all times.[16]

Thus, CPR promotes conflict prevention and peace-building for human security through business activities, and it demands due diligence in not hindering peace or human security by adding to any escalation of violence. And it takes a wider view in

---

16 This working definition was first proposed by Professors Tatsuro Kunugi and Yasunobu Sato as an addition to the UNGC's ten principles and presented at a seminar held by the ARCHS (Applied Research Centre in Human Security) programme of Coventry University as part of the ESRC (Economic and Social Research Council) seminar series on human security in June 2008.

that it also addresses businesses with no direct involvement in conflict or arms production. Rather it is more concerned with conflict economies driven by the global market economy. Though including CPR in the Compact's principles would help to align them with the revised Guidelines, it would also raise new questions about the consequences for current Compact members that might not be in compliance with the Guidelines.

To demonstrate the point with an extreme case, some may ask then if a company that manufactures landmines would qualify under this description as a corporate partner that shares the Compact's values and 'safeguards the autonomy and integrity of the UN'. If the CPR principle highlights the question of whether a given company is helping or hindering human security, then its definition should be clear enough to allow for a straightforward response: that is, the questions it poses need to be answerable. From a CPR perspective, the decisive criterion by which to assess whether a company is a human security driver or barrier would focus on whether the company was taking measures to reduce the amount of suffering caused by its products, and whether participation in the Compact would likely strengthen these efforts.

Applying the CPR principle to this extreme case also sheds a new light on the debate over the Compact's ability to foster a norm of non-violent business practice and by extension its potential as a catalyst for human security via the private sector. CPR discourages a zero-tolerance approach, which would deny the hypothetical landmine producer an opportunity to reduce its collateral damage 'footprint'. Expressed in terms of a moral trade-off, CPR would see potentially preventing the death or injury of one group of would-be landmine victims as a higher priority than preventing a company from getting potentially undeserved publicity as a UN partner. In this sense, CPR recognises that it may be unrealistic to expect an arms producer to operate in a way that 'does no harm'. Instead, it seeks to establish a middle ground that might be called the principle of 'doing less harm' as a first step in the process of becoming a more conflict-sensitive business. To sum up by highlighting the values shared by the Compact and proponents of the CPR principle, one of the more obvious points of agreement is that both believe a conflict-sensitive norm is better fostered through peer influence that requires inclusion than through a shaming approach that requires exclusion.

As evidenced by the cases of the oil companies Shell in Nigeria and Talisman in Sudan, among many others, and by diamond mining and the Kimberley Process, companies do respond to exclusionary measures. But these measures have been taken by stakeholders other than the Compact: namely NGOs, consumers and investors. This is not to say, however, that the Compact has no role to play. To the contrary, it has a crucial role to play, and that role is to support those of its members that take the initiative to promote peace as an explicit addition to the current set of principles. Japan, with its constitutional commitment to peace by non-violent means, is in the best of positions to seize this opportunity and to assume leadership in pioneering the CPR principle under the Compact's ongoing initiative. Japan's private sector, operating under an already strict code of conduct that bans the arms trade, can serve as a standard-setting example. But in this fast-growing field of challenges and opportunities, there is room for improvement for Japanese businesses, too. Japanese dual-use technology for instance might be used by third parties for unforeseen acts of aggression that could contribute to unintended and disastrous effects. Against this background, it would seem that building the *Made in Japan* label as a peace-friendly brand is an idea whose time has come.

Conclusion

The UN Global Compact is a soft-law approach to establishing a norm of ethical business practice by inviting the private sector as a positive force in a multi-sector pursuit of human security. Though confronted with valid and significant criticism related to living up to its ambitious promise of catalysing actions toward the achievement of the MDGs and the broader UN goals, the Compact has solidified its identity as a policy platform on which to host an ongoing debate within the values framework it has formulated.

As the UK-based NGO Global Witness notes, '[. . .] the limitations of the frameworks themselves—the self-selecting character of their membership and the lack of sanctions for non-performance—mean that their impact cannot go far beyond what individual members are willing to do'. But this report also concludes that 'Such voluntary frameworks are far from worthless: they have led some companies to improve their policies on human rights protection and have helped a wider debate between companies, governments and civil society groups'.[17]

The Compact remains a nexus of competing value systems that seem to achieve only partial consensus at the best of times. It is perhaps thanks to this constant tension that it remains a platform through which difficult discussions on policy can be held, and a mechanism through which action can be taken, though not monitored, in a multitude of spaces by a wide range of diverse actors from the public and private sectors in countries around the world. One of the Compact's more visible contributions to human security is possibly its awareness-raising of corporate impact on social and environmental issues. To establish that this is indeed the case, however, would require further research in the form of empirical impact assessments of Compact members over the past decade alongside a broad, perhaps intersubjective, investigation into how and how much member companies' potentially positive contributions can be attributed to their membership in the Compact.

Finally, from a human security perspective, the Compact points to a constructive way forward for the private sector. By continuing to invite companies to join, and by keeping its policy of not policing its members' commitments, more and more

---

17 See www.globalwitness.org/media_library_detail.php/580/en/oil_and_mining_in_
violent_places, accessed 29 August 2010.

companies are likely to commit to the Compact's principles. Essentially, we are faced with the dilemma of asking less of a growing pool of companies versus asking more of a shrinking pool. That being said, this assertion rests on the assumption that there is at least a certain minimum response from companies to these requests for ethical adherence. If there is none, then it hardly matters whether membership is growing or shrinking or whether they are asked to adopt a demanding or just symbolic set of principles.

Giving the Compact the benefit of the doubt in assuming that an increase in its membership's awareness leads to some form of behavioural change among them, its current catalyst potential may then be best understood as the plausible net impact of incremental change across its global membership, now some 5,200 strong. A question that remains is how these incremental changes are to support the 'freedom from fear' dimension of human security. Japan may soon provide a response to this question, but as the world's second-largest economy, the under-representation of its private sector in global efforts toward human security has been as conspicuous as its silence on the topic of conflict-sensitive business. Meanwhile, its membership in the Compact has recently grown to a critical mass of nearly 100 companies, giving this group the power to further galvanise the emerging norm of corporate peace responsibility, thereby equipping the Compact with the means to contribute to this underserved aspect of human security.

Bibliography

Bruno, K., and J. Karliner (2000) 'Tangled Up In Blue: Corporate Partnerships at the United Nations'; www.corpwatch.org/article.php?id=996, accessed 16 December 2009.

Durch, W.J. (2003) *The Brahimi Report and the Future of Peacekeeping Operations* (Washington, DC: Henry L. Stimson Center).

Galtung, J. (1996) *Peace by Peaceful Means: Peace and Conflict, Development and Civilization* (Oslo: International Peace Research Institute).

Kaldor, M. (1999) *New and Old Wars: Organised Violence in a Global Era* (Cambridge, UK: Polity Press).

OECD (Organisation for Economic Cooperation and Development) (1997) *DAC Guidelines on Conflict, Peace and Development Co-operation* (Paris: OECD).

—— (2001) *The DAC Guidelines: Helping Prevent Violent Conflict* (Paris: OECD Publications Service).

Sen, A. (2001) *Development as Freedom* (Oxford, UK: Oxford University Press).

UNDP (United Nations Development Programme) (1994) *Human Development Report 1994: New Dimensions of Human Security* (New York: Oxford University Press).

—— (2004) 'Corporate Citizenship in the World Economy'; www.unglobalcompact.ch/SiteCollectionDocuments/UNGC-brochure-en.pdf, accessed 28 August 2010.

—— (2009) 'Cooperation between the United Nations and the Business Community'; www.un.org/partners/business/otherpages/guide.htm, accessed 29 August 2010.

UNGC (United Nations Global Compact) (2010) 'Overview of the UN Global Compact'; www.unglobalcompact.org/aboutthegc/index.html, accessed 28 August 2010.

Utting, P., and A. Zammit (2006) *Beyond Pragmatism: Appraising UN–Business Partnerships* (Geneva: UNRISD).

Vives, A. (2008) 'Pacto Global: ¿esto es todo?'; cumpetere.com/Documents/Pacto%20Global. pdf, accessed 18 December 2009 (in Spanish).

Walzer, M. (2000) *Just and Unjust Wars: A Moral Argument with Historical Illustrations* (New York: Basic Books).

9
Human security and oil in post-conflict Angola

Liliane Mouan

Centre for Peace and Reconciliation Studies, Coventry University, UK

The purpose of this chapter is to expose some of the weaknesses of international policy-making towards African oil states. It draws from the experience of transparency campaigns in the Angolan post-conflict setting—as interpreted and understood by both domestic and external actors—to assess ways and the extent to which further petroleum-related policies aiming at addressing the 'resource curse', which analysts say is persisting in Angola, might be implemented.

In so doing, the chapter uses the human security framework. It espouses the idea that human security—that is, the absence of insecurity and threats (Shahrbanou 2004) to peoples' and communities' survival, livelihoods and dignity—is a prerequisite for sustainable development, and should be ensured prior to the implementation of larger social, political and economic development programmes (Stites and Leaning 2002). As such, it argues that the sustainability of such programmes can only be ensured if and when actors at the international, regional, national and local level work together and develop strategies that not only strongly emphasise good governance of the economic sector, but reconcile this with the promotion of the human security dimensions of food security, health security, environmental security, personal and community security, and political security, the latter requiring democracy and protection of human rights.

The chapter begins with a brief overview of the role that oil has played in Angola's war.[1] It goes on to look at various human security challenges that have been

---

1 For the purpose of this chapter, unless otherwise stated, the terms 'war' or 'conflict' will refer to the civil war. Comments can be sent to Liliane.mouan@coventry.ac.uk

reported in Angola since the end of the war and examines the ways in which the revenues from the oil sector are used to sustain the post-conflict reconstruction process and the impact that this has on human security. In a later section I discuss some of the reasons why transparency initiatives have had little impact in Angola and, most importantly, some of the lessons learned will follow.

Because of the scarcity of accurate data on local people's views of these policies, this chapter relies substantially on interviews conducted between March and September 2009, and on previous studies done on the topics discussed here, notably the 2008 *Drivers of Change* reports commissioned by the British Department for International Development (DFID) (Shaxson *et al.* 2008a, b) and the 2009 Idasa study on *Civil Society and Oil for Development in Angola* commissioned by the Norwegian Embassy in Luanda, Angola (Govender and Skagestad 2009).

Oil and conflict in Angola: a background

The Angolan civil war that started soon after the war for independence from Portugal in 1975 was a three-way war fought between the Movement for the Liberation of Angola (MPLA), the National Union for the Total Independence of Angola (UNITA) and the National Liberation Front of Angola (FNLA)[2] 'for power and domination' (Hare 1988: xvii, cited in Shankleman 2006: 96), rather than the greed-driven explanations given during the early 1990s. Despite numerous attempts to implement peace agreements, first in 1992 and then in 1994, the conflict intensified again in 1999—when oil accounted for about 90% of Angola's total exports and foreign exchange (Cilliers 2000: 9)—and only came to an end with UNITA leader Jonas Savimbi's death in 2002. This intensity did not, however, affect the oil sector, which was allowed to operate, and indeed to flourish, offshore. The remoteness of the oil industry from the rest of Angolan society, as the following paragraphs demonstrate, will determine the extent to which oil has or has not been linked to the conflict in Angola.

Early studies (Collier and Hoeffler 1998; Collier 2000) have pointed to the negative correlation that exists between mineral wealth and armed conflict, meaning that mineral resource endowment is more likely to cause civil war, among other things.[3] However, a close look at various case studies, including but not limited to those of Sudan, Sierra Leone, Nigeria, Cambodia and Angola, certainly points to the conclusion that the sheer nature of this correlation depends on a number

2 These parties all benefited from external support. The MPLA was supported by the Soviet Union and Cuba while UNITA and the FNLA were initially backed by the United States, France, the People's Republic of China and South Africa.

3 There will be a discussion on some of the other negative elements associated with resource abundance in subsequent sections of the chapter.

of factors, such as the types and abundance of the resource, as well as the type of conflict.[4]

In Angola, oil and diamonds (analysis of the latter is beyond the scope of this chapter) not only financed and influenced the duration of the war, they also determined its course and, accordingly, its outcome.[5] Angola's case is peculiar because, unlike most resource-rich countries such as Nigeria, the interaction between oil and the conflict was limited. This is mainly because the overwhelming majority of the oil fields were offshore,[6] which set the industry free from strikes, local insurrection and crime, with the exception of Cabinda where FLEC (Front for the Liberation of Canada) was reported to use kidnappings of expatriates, including oil workers, to attract the attention of the international community to its demands. As a matter of fact, it is Angola's offshore oil, analysts say, which led to increased production up to a point where, in 1973, oil became the country's principal export in spite of a robust colonial agricultural and manufacturing sector (Soares de Oliveira 2007a; Alexander and Gilbert 2008; Shaxson 2008).[7]

Having said that, three main factors speak of the ways in which oil wealth was linked to Angola's conflict: the conflict in Cabinda, the (mis)use of oil revenues and external influence.

Cabinda

Since the discovery of oil in Angola, Cabinda has produced about 60% of Angola's oil production, estimated at about 900,000 barrels a day and worth an equivalent of US$100,000 per annum for every Cabindan (Gomes Porto 2003), and generates the

---

4 For a brief overview of the arguments put forward on this debate, see, among others, Le Billon 2000; Ross 2003, 2006; and Samset 2009.

5 It is wrong, however, to think that the link between violence and natural resources in Angola is confined to the 27-year civil war, for, as many experts say, violence in Angola has mostly been associated with the abundance of resources (and wealth accumulation) over the 500 years of the country's historical development. Nevertheless, it seems that it is this civil war—reportedly 'one of the worst in the world'—that attracted most attention from the international community. For a discussion on this, see, among others, Le Billon 2000; Sogge 2006; and Newitt 2007.

6 Although oil was first discovered onshore in Angola in 1955 by a Belgian oil company Petrofina (which later merged with Total in 1999 to form TotalFina) in the Kwanza Valley, the greatest impetus to expansion came from the Cabinda Gulf Oil Company (CABGOC, a subsidiary acquired by the American oil major Chevron in 1984) which discovered oil offshore from Cabinda in 1966 (see Murison 2004: 51).

7 It should be noted here that oil exploration by CABGOC was put to a halt when, in November 1975, the company exited the country as the war raged followed by other companies such as Petrofina and Texaco that were operating in Angola at the time. These companies soon returned by 1976 (see Soares de Oliveira 2007a: 599). Angola's offshore is considered a 'world-class' area for oil production; some two-thirds of exploration wells strike oil, compared with a 50% success rate for Nigeria's deep offshore and a global average of around 15% (Global Witness 2002).

majority of the government's revenues. The enclave, located in the north of Angola and separated from Angola by a strip of land in the DRC (Democratic Republic of Congo), was the scene of much violence during the independence struggle, violence which intensified after independence, analysts say, because of its oil wealth (Shankleman 2006).

Undeniably, although the civil war in mainland Angola was about control of the entire country, the conflict in Cabinda was a secession conflict involving groups fighting for the independence for the enclave, claiming that Cabinda has a distinct and separate identity, history and culture from mainland Angola, unlike which it was never a colony, rather a protectorate (Gomes Porto 2003).

These claims have been disregarded by the ruling party, the MPLA, which has accused oil companies in general, and France's Elf in particular, of colluding with neighbouring countries and the secessionist movement to control Cabinda's oil wealth, and possibly annex the enclave to one of the two Congos with which Cabinda shares its borders. This latter belief, Jean-Michel Mabeko-Tali (2001: 50-51) explains, is the reason why the MPLA decided not to consider the question of Cabinda's autonomy, which was initially taken into consideration in the 1960s.

(Mis)Use of oil revenues and role of external actors

The use and control of oil revenues played a significant role during the conflict, and arguably, in the outcome thereof. There is consensus among analysts that the control of oil revenues by the MPLA helped the party come from a state of relative weakness, during the independence struggle, to one of political and economic hegemony (Marques 2004; Shankleman 2006; Messiant 2007). It is claimed that oil was:

> a key component in the regime's ability to gain access to political and material resources beyond Angola's borders: not just to markets but also to diplomatic channels and more politically connected commercial networks that directly advance the regime's security strategy (Reno 2002).

Many reports and studies confirm Reno's view. Some also suggest that oil rents were used to finance the war economy and satisfy the aspirations of the corrupt elite at the centre of power, often with the (tacit) complicity of foreign actors and companies (Global Witness 1999; Human Rights Watch 2004a; Sogge 2006).[8] It would appear that the *nomenklatura*[9] operated in such a way that the return to peace, and indeed the 'risk' of democratic political change associated with it, as Le Billon (2002) stated, was not necessary for the belligerents' interests.

8 A well-known example is the 'Angolagate' scandal which broke in December 2000, and implicated the Angolan government, members of the French political establishment and prominent international arms dealers in money laundering and illegal arms-for-oil deals.

9 Le Billon (2000) defines *nomenklatura* as a number of state and private companies and privileged sections of the population.

The aforementioned factors, among others, contributed to exacerbate and sustain the civil war, the consequences of which tell the story of the magnitude of human security challenges that face post-conflict Angola.

Human security in post-war Angola and the impact of oil

Ramifications of the war

As it emerged from the 27-year civil war, Angola was faced with enormous challenges. No aspect of life had been unaffected. The civil war not only destroyed roads, water supply systems, telecommunications and electricity systems, railways, schools, agricultural infrastructure and bridges built during Portuguese rule, it also took the lives of an estimated 1.5 million people, and displaced about a third of the population, over 4 million people. Many children were affected either directly or indirectly by the conflict, prompting UNICEF to declare Angola 'the worst place to be a child' (UNICEF 1999).[10] Clinics and hospitals had been destroyed, leaving only a small percentage of people with access to the most basic health services, while the majority relied heavily on the international community to provide their basic social services (International Crisis Group 2003). Landmine infestation—especially in the central highlands—was among the worst encountered in any post-conflict situation globally, and arguably represented the biggest challenge to resettlement (International Crisis Group 2003). Land had also emerged as a critical point of potential conflict as displaced people have sought settlement sites in both rural and urban districts (Cain 2007). Violence further undermined what is considered Angola's 'most glaring wealth disparity', that which exists between the rural and urban areas (Stites and Leaning 2002). This social disruption, it is said, stands as evidence of the trauma and widespread nature of the conflict (International Centre for Transitional Justice 2009).

As one senior analyst pointed out, Angola is an 'unusual post-conflict setting'.[11] In contrast with other countries in the region such as Namibia, Mozambique and

---

10 Angola's children, it is said, remain the most vulnerable in post-conflict society. Many children were maimed and separated from their families. Some children died as a result of the absence of basic services such as clean water and health facilities. However, while many children willingly took part in the fighting—either because of insecurity, vulnerability, boredom or lack of food (Honwana 2002)—other children were reportedly forcibly recruited by both UNITA and the MPLA (Wanduragala 2000). Subsequently, notes a report by Human Rights Watch, these children, many of whom carried out the same duties as adults during the conflict, had been 'forgotten' in the demobilisation programme that was initiated after the signing of the peace agreement in April 2002 (Human Rights Watch 2003).

11 Interview with the author on 24 July 2009.

South Africa—where peace came through negotiated settlement—Angola's transition from war to 'peace' was the result of a clear and definitive military victory by the MPLA and the government of Angola (International Centre for Transitional Justice 2009). 'Peace' came about without justice. The intensity and scope of the conflict, with Angolans implicated as victims and perpetrators and the government's use of amnesty as the strategy for national reconciliation, left many people with a total lack of trust between them and towards the authorities, thereby disrupting family and community networks. The somewhat abrupt end to the conflict also meant that local civil society groups already suffering from a difficult operating environment—restricted mainly by the increasing dominance of extractive industries—were even more unprepared for the future (Lari and Kevlihan 2004).

The conditions cited above definitely point to low levels of human security in the aftermath of the war. More to the point, as Tvedten *et al.* (2003) remarked, 'inequalities are increasing in Angolan society . . . implying that national resources are not channelled into the alleviation of poverty but to the enrichment of the better off'. How then could oil wealth particularly be used to serve the common good?

The role of oil

Angola has undergone a substantial transformation in recent years, moving from a state of complete disarray mostly caused by many years of war, to being one of the fastest growing economies in the world.[12] This transformation has been possible largely because of the rising production and revenues from the oil sector.[13]

As Shaxson *et al.* (2008a) reported, the Angolan Government strongly believes that oil can be used as 'a bridge to launch other sectors of the economy which can generate employment for Angolans'. The problem here, however, is twofold. First, as a highly capital-intensive industry, the oil sector provides relatively few jobs, estimated at about 15,000 at the beginning of the century (Hodges 2007). Second, it has very few linkages to the rest of the economy, since the majority of goods and services are imported. As a result, the potential benefits of the oil industry for broader economic development and poverty reduction lie primarily in the resources available to the state from the high taxation of the industry (Hodges 2007). The key question, therefore, has been whether, and most importantly how, the revenues from the oil sector can be used to serve ordinary Angolans.

Oil in Angola: a blessing or curse?

Angola is often thought to be suffering from the 'resource curse', which refers to the paradox that many resource-dependent countries face: an abundance of mineral

---

12 The World Bank estimates that Angola's economy was growing at 26% in 2005 and 41% in 2007.

13 Angola has recently taken over Nigeria as sub-Saharan Africa's largest producer of crude oil (Maidment 2008).

wealth, but slow long-term economic growth, wider inequality, massive poverty, higher risk of conflict, more corruption, and a more authoritarian regime than in other countries.[14]

Many reports and studies on Angola point to Angola's low ranking in the United Nations Development Programme (UNDP) Human Development Index. As a matter of fact, one out of every four children born in Angola is expected to die before the age of five from malaria, diarrhoea or other preventable diseases (UNDP 2008). Life expectancy is just over 40 years, one of the lowest in the world (UNDP 2008). The majority of the population lives on less than US$2 a day without access to basic healthcare, clean water or sanitation (Global Witness 2004, 2008). Of those living in rural areas, 90% are estimated to live below the poverty line; despite this, the shares of the government budget allocated to health and education, respectively, accounted for 4.4% and 3.8% of GDP in 2006, lower than average in the Southern African Development Community (SADC) area (Marques 2006).

Since the end of the war in 2002, the government's vision of Angola has been that of a 'modern' state, a vision that many note has often been seen as excluding the poor (Shaxson *et al* 2008a: 34; Amnesty International 2009; Human Rights Watch 2007; Foley 2007).[15] As a result, economic resources, most noticeably Chinese oil-backed loans, have been dedicated to physical and economic reconstruction, at a time when what many Angolans say they desperately need is lasting peace, social justice and national reconciliation (Marques1999; International Centre for Transitional Justice 2009: 15).

Cabinda also remains a critical issue in the transition from 'military' peace to 'sustainable' peace. The enclave has been a scene of political and military violence not seen in other parts of Angola since the end of the conflict in 2002 (Human Rights Watch 2004b, 2009; Mabeko-Tali 2008). There are reports, for instance, that sporadic guerrilla attacks have prompted the government to use systematic military arbitrary detentions and torture to retaliate (Human Rights Watch 2009: 2). Although many experts do not envisage another conflict in (mainland) Angola, there have been concerns about the increased likelihood that the low-level conflict in Cabinda will turn into a violent conflict because of Cabinda's importance for the oil sector (Aguilar 2005: 6; Shankleman 2006); and this, despite the signing of a

14 There are several existing explanations for the resource curse. The most notable explanation is that the exploitation of natural resources triggers the so-called Dutch disease, which increases the dependence of the country on these resources, while undermining other sectors. The second explanation focuses on fluctuation of commodity prices over time. The third element is the effect on political systems: oil like most natural resources, tends to create a state of **patronage politics** whereby only the elite, the rulers, allocate the resources in exchange for political support.

15 Amnesty International, for instance, recently reported that the government had forcibly evicted about 10,000 families living in informal housing areas since 2001, allegedly to make way for infrastructure for public good and housing projects (Amnesty International 2009; see also Human Rights Watch 2007; Foley 2007).

Memorandum of Understanding of Peace and Reconciliation between the Angolan Government and the Cabinda Forum for Dialogue (FCD) in 2006.[16]

However, inasmuch as it is important to recognise that natural resources are and have been a significant impediment to Angola's sustainable development, it is even more crucial to realise that the 'Angolan' predicament is not so much one of mere abundance of natural resources, especially considering, as explained above,[17] that Angola's history has mostly been marked by war and wealth accumulation by a few. Instead, Angola's problem could be seen as one of lack of good governance—and of lack of responsible leadership, as argued by one Angolan human rights activist[18]—both at the local and national level and at the international level, as Angola shares close links with the global economy as discussed above. In reality, as the next section suggests, there have been very few incentives for the Angolan government to significantly change its oil governance mechanisms in order to improve the lives of the majority of Angolans.

Better revenue management: responses to Angola's post-war challenges

Overall, the international community's policy prescriptions for Angola's challenges have been petroleum-related. The general belief is that 'Angola's petroleum sector would contribute to economic growth and that a "trickle-down" effect would contribute to a reduction in poverty, if good governance and control of corruption were established' (Govender and Skagestad 2009).

The international development community has often proposed four policies to resource-rich developing countries suffering from the 'resource curse': diversification of the economy away from the oil sector; greater revenue transparency; creation of oil funds; and direct redistribution of oil rents to the country's citizens. We shall concentrate here on the lessons learned from the experience of transparency campaigns in Angola—as seen by both external and internal actors—to assess whether the 'Western approach' to solving the 'resource curse' is appropriate for

16 The Memorandum included five main points: an amnesty law, an end to hostilities, demilitarisation of the armed opposition groups from Cabinda, reduction in the number of military troops in the oil region and its gradual return to a normalised situation, and reintegration of FCD members into civilian life (see Fisas 2009). It is argued that the peace agreement has enjoyed little credibility in Cabinda because it was not inclusive of all the actors involved, and was not supported by the people. Human Rights Watch note that the most active FLEC wing, FLEC-FAC, as well as other members of FCD had been excluded from the talks, and no political concessions were made to the separatists (see Human Rights Watch 2009: 7; see also De Queiroz 2006).

17 See footnote 5.

18 Interview with the author on 16 March 2009.

Angola's particular context. Revenue transparency has been chosen because of its prominence in Angola, and among Angolans.

Revenue transparency

Transparency has been viewed as a key to reducing corruption, an issue which is central in explaining why resource-rich countries perform badly in terms of socio-economic development (Kolstad *et al*. 2009: 521). As such, there have been many initiatives, some promoted by governments and business such as the EITI (Extractive Industries Transparency Initiative), others by NGOs such as the Publish What You Pay Campaign (PWYP), and others from international institutions such as the International Monetary Fund's (IMF) Code of Good Practices for Fiscal Transparency, or the World Bank's EITI++. Among these initiatives, the EITI has been particularly commended as a way to advance transparency of the petroleum and/or mineral sector in resource-rich countries like Angola.

As a matter of fact, revenue transparency could be a vital ingredient to transform people's lives. Analysts argue, among other things, that transparency can ensure that corruption is risky and less attractive; it can provide incentives that make leaders (more) accountable to their people; encourage public participation in democratic processes; and strengthen cooperation and trust (Kolstad *et al*. 2009). For this to happen, it is said, companies and governments need to provide more and better quality information on the scale of revenues derived from the extractive industries and on how these revenues flow from producers to governments. This should be coupled with civil society organisations' demands for greater accountability from their respective governments (Transparency International 2008).

However, transparency initiatives are not without controversy. Many studies (Macmillan 2005; Human Rights Watch 2004a; Global Witness 2004; Kolstad and Wiig 2009) have shown, for example, that in countries like Angola, transparency initiatives have failed to reduce corruption and generate political accountability. One of the reasons why these initiatives have failed to have the expected impact in Angola in particular is the lack of external and internal incentives.

External incentives

The first challenge that comes with the implementation of some transparency initiatives, and the EITI particularly, is their very nature: the EITI, for example, is a voluntary initiative, which means that member countries and companies can decide to opt in and out as they please, and this can be done without major consequences. A 2006 evaluation of the initiative revealed that, of the 20 countries that had committed to the EITI principles and criteria, only two had published fully audited and reconciled EITI reports; eight had yet to take even the initial step of appointing an individual to lead the EITI process; ten had not yet formed the required multi-stakeholder committee and 11 did not have a drafted and approved work plan (cited in Kolstad and Wiig 2009). It is also unclear what the implications are or could be for countries that follow the EITI principles. One argument often put forward is that many countries already publish what they receive and have not joined the initiative. So, as many may ask, what is the purpose of such an initiative? This point makes the EITI particularly unattractive to Angolans, many of whom see it as a 'Western box-ticking exercise' (Shaxson *et al.* 2008b: 23), or again, a 'useless initiative, which has nothing to do with complying with international regulations'.[19]

The implementation of transparency initiatives has faced other challenges in Angola, and this is also because there has been no real coordination of the international community, which in turn has resulted in a lack of international leverage on Angola's rulers. Lari and Kevlihan (2004), for instance, remark that, despite the increased international prominence of donor (political) conditionality in the 1990s especially in Africa, donors have maintained a relatively low profile in Angola. In fact, there is a consensus that traditional instruments of conditionality of the IMF and World Bank on lending with the purpose of increasing transparency in accounting for oil revenues have not worked in Angola, as the government was able to use its oil reserves to acquire private lending.

There is evidence that, despite a breakdown of what might be considered a critical relationship with the international financial institutions (IFIs), especially considering the scope of the challenges that Angola faced, several foreign governments were willing to provide Angola's elite with the cash they needed, first to finance the warfare, and subsequently to address the country's reconstruction needs; rather than pursuing a concerted debt renegotiation with the IMF. Many Angolans cite the examples of Portugal, Germany and the United States which continued to sign bilateral agreements with Angola despite Angola's tense relationship with the IMF and World Bank (Shaxson *et al.* 2008: 18).[20]

Most noticeable, though, is the case of China's relationship with Angola, which has burgeoned since 2004. Although highly contentious,[21] China's involvement in Angola has been playing an important role in assisting Angola's post-war reconstruction needs, for it allowed Angola to use oil-backed loans for Chinese financial

19 This point was made by an Angolan during an interview on 19 March 2009.
20 Other observers have referred to countries such as the US through USAID, and Norway through its Oil for Development (OfD) Initiative, which have adopted 'petroleum-related aid activities aiming to improve the development impact of oil and gas reserves, while promoting the commercial activities of their respective national companies in the implementation of such programmes' (Kolstad and Wiig 2009).
21 China's involvement in Angola has been singled out particularly because of its scale and political relevance (Ferreira 2008). Angola has been among the largest recipients of Chinese investment on the (African) continent (Davies 2009). One of the main criticisms of Chinese involvement in Angola and in Africa in general is that, without China's investment and tacit support, many African governments would be forced to change their behaviour. This sentiment is, however, not shared by some Africans and Angolans who put it that China's relationship is simply business as usual, perhaps with a slight difference that China tends to treat African leaders as equal partners as opposed to the Western approach of 'master–servant'.

assistance for key public investment projects in infrastructure, telecommunications and agri-businesses under the National Reconstruction Programme (Vines *et al.* 2009). Some critics also argue that it is this relationship, besides Angola's relationship with other Asian countries, record high oil prices and concerns over energy security, that increased Angola's global strategic importance and in return, led to the Bretton Woods institutions' abandonment of their transparency and accountability campaigns (Vidal 2007).

The analysis given above proves that there has not been a concerted approach to dealing with Angola's alleged grand corruption and egregious human rights record, which perhaps could have led to a change of attitude by the regime, but instead resulted in a lack of credibility and integrity on the part of the international community. It also supports the view given by Farouk *et al.* (2008) that the 'likely consequences of a contradiction between aid policy and commercial interests is a tendency for donors to operate in an imprecise foreign policy towards all producing countries'. More to the point, the analysis suggests two things: first, that transparency seems not to have been a *necessary* precondition for Angola's 'success'; and second, it demonstrates how exceptional Angola's officials have been at 'playing off' the international community. As many claim, oil-backed borrowing has been an effective alternative tool in allowing Angola's rulers to withstand international pressure while at the same time guaranteeing Angola's solid, long-term engagement with the international economy (Soares de Oliveira 2007b; Vines *et al.* 2009). Suffice it to say that this factor has earned the country the 'special' status of a 'successful failed state' (Soares de Oliveira 2007b; Sogge 2009): one characterised by weak institutions, loss of life and decrease in living conditions for the survivors but, at the same time, with 'successful'[22] leaders for whom oil revenues ensure legitimacy and the support of the international community.

A third point to mention is the focus of transparency campaigns on revenues. This, we posit, has failed to consider the global context within which Angola's political economy is situated. The influx of commercial diplomatic aid, just like petrodollars, and covert donations often provided by foreign oil companies have long been said to encourage corruption in resource-rich countries such as Angola. However, this supply side of corruption has been left off the hook, especially by the EITI. As Mo Ibrahim asked in an interview:

> Why is it legal for a large oil company to sign a multibillion dollar contract in Angola or somewhere without disclosing it? That should be an added requirement by [international accountants], if that is a legal requirement by the auditors. And it should be reported. Everybody would be forced to do it. Why aren't we introducing that? If we're convinced that's important, why aren't we doing it (Council on Foreign Relations 2009)?

---

22 'Successful', explain Prunier and Guisselquist (2003), as measured against their own parameters and judged by the standards of the state's political programme.

The sentiment among Angolans and some external observers interviewed so far is that it is indeed hypocritical of 'Westerners' to dictate rules to others when they themselves are not obeying them. This reaction appears to have been noticed by some Western governments such as that of Norway, which, on 2 October 2007, became the first wealthy country to implement EITI.[23]

A more fundamental mistake has been to assume that the local context is favourable to the implementation of transparency initiatives, as prescribed by Western analysts. On the contrary, it is argued here that the preconditions that would have made the use of the information effective have not been met in Angola, as the following paragraphs explain.

Internal incentives

We argue that the 'unusual post-conflict setting' marked by an absence of justice for victims, coupled with a lack of trust and capacity of civil society organisations as described above, among other conditions, meant that transparency could have been an additional tool in strengthening cooperation and trust, but not necessarily the most urgent, and certainly not the most important. It would appear from the background discussed above that the 'harmonisation of the minds'—as talked about by the Vice-Minister for Education Reform (*Imbondeiro* 2008)—with a truth-seeking mechanism might have been crucial starting points. Besides low literacy and high poverty rates, the weakness of opposition political parties, coupled with numerous efforts by the ruling party to harness the media as a tool of social control (see, for example, Marques 2009a) reflect the inability of local actors to demand accountability from their rulers; a condition which, even advocates agree, is crucial to the effectiveness of transparency campaigns. There is evidence for instance of the (limited) publication of data on the production of, and revenues from, oil that the government receives (block by block) on the Ministry of Finance website. However, many interviewees do not see the availability of this information as having achieved the intended result as it did not attract broad press coverage, and was not extensively used by transparency campaigners (Shaxson *et al.* 2008b). Above all, as the World Bank (2007) recognised, it has not led yet to a clear decline in corruption, at least as captured by perception-based measures.

As a matter of fact, Angola's home-grown, 'gradualist policies of domestic change at its own pace' (Vines 2008) have contributed to the relative progress that has been made in Angola so far. Among the many changes, are the much lauded 2008 legislative elections that were held in September, the first since 1992, which commentators argue, has given the ruling party a 'new' legitimacy. There has also been some progress in terms of the progressive realisation of human rights. There are

23 In an interview with the author on 11 September 2009, one senior British politician also argued that, despite the fact that the United Kingdom has limited power when it comes to regulating companies operating abroad because of the transnational nature of their activities, the government had to stop dictating rules and start leading by example.

now more children in secondary schools; more women with access to healthcare; better trained civil servants in crucial departments such as health and education; also, the government is reporting on the Millennium Development Goals.[24] The government has also taken a first step in addressing the issue of economic security through its 'Angolanisation' policy, an effort to involve Angolans in the oil industry, to ensure that a certain proportion of the work at all levels is secured among Angolans (Govender and Skagestad 2009: 16).[25] Again, many highlight the fact that the main drivers of the government's change in attitude towards transparency and other reforms are its standing in the international scene, foreign direct investment and the intention of the MPLA to rule for many more years to come,[26] rather than the 'pressure' exercised by the international community.

Regardless of this fact, there remains a lot to be done. Many local and external actors alike have denounced what some refer to as 'the privatisation of the state'. In various recent open letters, several members of local civil society groups have criticised the extent to which public officials and the president's family members hold shares in, and own, various private sector companies (Marques 2009b, c; Macedo *et al.* 2009; see also Messiant 2001; Global Witness 2009a). This presupposes that some preconditions need to be met, one of which is the end of the 'promiscuity' of public office holders in mixing their private business interests with official duties, as recognised by the president himself in a speech given at the opening of the XI Extraordinary Meeting of MPLA's Central Committee, on 27 June 2008 (cited in Marques 2009c). The privatisation of the state continues to contribute to the weakening of Angolan civil society, restricting its capacity to act as the government's watchdog, as is the case in Norway, for instance, and further complicates the state–business–society power relations (Messiant 2001; Peclard 2008). Furthermore, it renders donor funding almost unnecessary, as the elite are able to rely on private sources of funding to support their reportedly excessive lifestyle.

The analysis tends to lead to the fact that many of these transparency initiatives 'don't simply touch reality, problems, life' (cited in Govender and Skagestad 2009: 26). It also implies that further 'formulas' for solving Angola's governance issues might only work under certain conditions as spelled out below.

24 Interview with the author on 24 July 2009. This view is also supported by other external observers and some Angolans. Vines *et al.* (2009), in their study on Asian National Oil Companies in Angola, asserted that Angola's rulers have had new priorities since the elections in 2008. According to them, rapid post-conflict infrastructural development is becoming less pressing and delivering on some of the MPLA's election promises such as diversification of the economy away from its dependence on oil and producing better services in health and education is higher up the agenda (Vines *et al.* 2009: 49-50).

25 This policy has a few shortcomings, however. In particular, it has been argued that it does not benefit the neediest but instead Angola's elites (see Paulo 2006).

26 Perhaps it should be remembered that Angola's President, José Eduardo dos Santos, is Africa's second-longest serving leader after Muammar Gaddafi of Libya, following the death of Gabon's President Omar Bongo in June 2009 after almost 43 years in power.

Some lessons learned

The last section provided an understanding of the reasons why transparency campaigns and initiatives have had little (positive) impact in Angola. This section, on the other hand, will attempt to suggest ways in which some of the lessons learned from that experience can be used in the future. Principally, it argues that the success of further policies will depend on a number of issues that need careful consideration, and these are, inter alia, Angola's complex context, the extent of local ownership and local–global interconnections.

First, consideration of each country's specific context is of vital importance. The colonial history of African countries and their different post-independence experiences should be closely examined. In particular, special attention should be paid to the way in which each country entered into peace since, as Polly Ng and Philippe Le Billon argued, 'the nature of conflict termination is influential on how oil governance and political regime may affect the aftermath of civil war'. In their 2007 article on post-conflict oil governance in Angola, they put it that the absence of specific conditions regarding resource partitioning and governance issues that initiated and perpetuated the war in the peace agreements signed by the belligerents allowed the MPLA to use its decisive military victory against UNITA to further consolidate its power without making any concessions for effective change (Ng and Le Billon 2007), change that would have otherwise instigated political accountability.

Likewise, it should be recognised that the success of any policy intervention to address the 'resource curse' requires the adoption of a common approach which will not permit African leaders to 'outmanoeuvre' (Ellis 2005 cited in Pegg 2005) the international community. In the Angolan case, high oil revenues and international policy incoherence—sometimes due to short-term energy interests—made it possible for Angolan rulers to withstand international pressure, pressure mostly undermined by certain foreign governments' and firms' actions *vis-à-vis* Angola.

The method of policy intervention is equally relevant. There is a certain mistrust of 'Western' policies among Angolans, especially given that the adoption by IFIs of 'good' neo-liberal institutions has failed to create the intended result of sustainable economic growth in Angola as in many other 'third world' countries. The relationship appears to have recently flourished, most notably with the World Bank loans agreement of US\$1 billion to assist with the country's economic diversification (Corkin 2009), and the IMF loans agreement of US\$890 million to help alleviate the nation's cash flow pressures (BBC 2009).[27] However, judging by the Angolan officials' enthusiasm and characterisation of this change as a 'victory' for the country and its people (cited in BBC 2009), it would seem that this is very much perceived as confirming Angola's 'power' and strategic importance in the international econ-

---

27   The IMF loans particularly—which can be construed as external recognition and indeed legitimation of Angola's rulers at international level—have been strongly criticised by anti-corruption groups on the basis that they risk condoning corruption in Angola (see for instance Global Witness 2009b).

omy. It would therefore appear that pressure and/or isolation or again a 'naming and shaming' strategy is not always the best approach, rather that Angolan rulers would prefer to be treated and constructively engaged as equal partners. An attempt to impose policies through pressure or isolation could incite the ruling elite to continue to take what Shaxson *et al.* (2008a) have referred to as an 'à la carte' approach to policy reforms, choosing ideas which they might think fit their objectives, and rejecting others which are undesirable.

Linked to the previous point is the issue of local ownership. As Donais (2008) explained, at its core, 'the discourse around ownership revolves around fundamental questions of agency: who decides, who controls, who implements and who evaluates'. This suggests that, for any successful transformation of the 'curse' into a 'blessing', future policies should have at their core the enhancement of Angolans' capacity; capacity that will enable them to become agents and guarantors of their own security while reducing their dependence on other (external) actors, therefore instilling in them a sense of inclusiveness and participation. It also requires a needs-based approach in such a way that international standards are reconciled with local realities and needs.

A stakeholder approach is necessary to establish the roles and influences of each player involved in the oil sector and its governance. This requires the recognition that the oil curse is a global political problem that needs to be tackled in Africa by African societies, but also in Western capitals. Blaming greedy African leaders solely without considering the 'extraversion' of African economies will not help address the structural causes of the problem. For instance, an analysis of the responsibilities of national and local governments, domestic and foreign oil firms and service contracts, foreign and local banks, foreign export credit agencies to cite a few actors, has the potential to provide policy-makers with a better picture on to how and who to engage to bring about positive change.

Summary

This chapter looked at the international response to the 'resource curse' in the Angolan context. It purported to examine the lessons learned from the experience of transparency campaigns particularly, to assess the suitability of a 'Western' approach to solving the 'resource curse' that is allegedly persevering in Angola. We started with a brief overview of the role that oil has played in the conflict, and the extent to which it impacts on human security in post-war Angola. We showed that oil has been used by the ruling party to secure international backing and finance its war, and also discussed the ways in which oil revenues are being used to fund Angola's post-war reconstruction, often excluding the poor and needy, while empowering further the rich elite.

In response to this challenge, the international community proposed various petroleum-related measures which were expected to generate 'trickle-down' effects of oil revenues. Among such measures were transparency initiatives which, proponents say, were intended to bring about political accountability. In Angola, however, these initiatives failed to have the intended outcome. The sentiment among both local and external actors, as this study demonstrated, is that there have not been enough external and internal incentives to influence the government's actions in the intended way. Rather, the incentives available allowed the Angolan regime to move from a state of relative weakness to one of strength.

By adopting a short-term strategy and by failing to acknowledge the interconnectedness of the political, social and economic aspects of the governance systems in Angola, the international community has failed to integrate a holistic human security model in its approach to solving the many challenges that post-war Angola has been facing and, in turn, has fallen short of addressing the root causes of the inequalities and conflicts that are entrenched in Angolan society.

Nevertheless, these failures, as perceived, understood and interpreted by both local and external observers, have provided useful lessons for future policy-making on Angola. Most importantly, we found that considering the rather opaque Angolan context in its entirety is crucial. In particular, a close examination should be made of the multi-layered feature of the state, its relationship with society, business and the international community.

The study also raised some relevant questions for future policy-making. If the Angolan state—like many other African oil states—is not a 'weak', nor a 'strong' state, but a 'successful failed' state, what are the policy implications, especially in terms of human security? What role, if any, do non-traditional, non-state, local and transnational actors such as churches or multinational oil companies play in influencing such a state's actions? What role can they actually play in contributing to the practical attainment of human security? For instance, the recurrent theme of 'dialogue' in interviews conducted so far and some previous studies reveals that there is a certain demand for these actors, especially foreign oil companies, to engage more constructively with local governance issues. What are the possible areas of engagement, and how could such an engagement translate into positive change?

I posit that perhaps the best policies will be those that take a 'people-sensitive', integrated approach to the issues at stake: they must advance Angolans' priorities, support and strengthen their local coping strategies and those strategies that consider the global–regional–local power relations.

Bibliography

Aguilar, R. (2005) *Angola: Getting Off the Hook* (Country Economic Report; Stockholm: International Development Cooperation Agency SIDA).

Alexander, K., and S. Gilbert (2008) *Oil and Governance Report: A Case Study of Chad, Angola, Gabon, and Sao Tome é Principe* (Cape Town: Idasa).

Amnesty International (2009) *Angola: Forced Evictions on a Mass Scale* (London: Amnesty International).

BBC (2009) 'Angola secures IMF loan agreement' BBC News, 29 September 2009; news.bbc. co.uk/1/hi/business/8281639.stm, accessed 24 September 2010.

Cain, A. (2007) 'Housing Microfinance in Post-conflict Angola: Overcoming Socioeconomic Exclusion through Land Tenure and Access to Credit', *Environment and Urbanization* 19: 361.

Christian Aid (2003) *Fuelling Poverty: Oil, War and Corruption* (London: Christian Aid).

Cilliers, J. (2000) 'Resource Wars: A New Type of Insurgency', in J. Cilliers and C. Dietrich (eds.), *Angola's War Economy: The Role of Oil and Diamonds* (Pretoria: Institute of Security Studies).

Collier, P. (2000) 'Doing Well Out of War: An Economic Perspective', in M. Berdal and D. Malone (eds.), *Greed and Grievance: Economic Agendas in Civil Wars* (Boulder, CO: Lynne Rienner).

—— and A. Hoeffler (1998) 'On Economic Causes of Civil War', *Oxford Economic Papers* 50: 563-73.

Corkin, L. (2009) 'Angola's Current Economic Prospects: Oil Curse or Blessing?' Real Instituto Elcano (ARI); www.realinstitutoelcano.org/wps/wcm/connect/89ae5a804f018ba2bb1cff 3170baead1/ARI4-2009_Corkin_Angola_Economic_Prospects_Oil.pdf?MOD=AJPERES& CACHEID=89ae5a804f018ba2bb1cff3170baead1, accessed 24 September 2010.

Council on Foreign Relations (2009) 'Africa Needs Governance and Globalization' 1 April 2009; www.cfr.org/publication/18954/africa_needs_governance_and_globalization.html, accessed 24 September 2010.

Davies, M. (2009) 'China's Involvement in Angola: Mutually Beneficial or Commercial Pragmatism?', *The China Monitor* 38 (March 2009).

De Queiroz, M. (2006) 'Angola: Peace in Cabinda, the Enclave Between the Two Congos'; allafrica.com/stories/200906220026.html, accessed 2 July 2010.

Donais, T. (2008) 'Understanding Local Ownership in Security Sector Reform', in T. Donais (ed.), *Local Ownership and Security Sector Reform* (Geneva: Geneva Centre for the Democratic Control of Armed Forces DCAF).

Farouk, A., T. Søreide and A. Williams (2008) 'Grand Corruption in the Regulation of Oil', U4 Anti-Corruption Resource Centre; www.U4.no, accessed 2 July 2010.

Ferreira, M. (2008) 'China in Angola: Just a Passion for Oil?', in C. Alden, T. Large and R.M. Soares de Oliveira (eds.), *China Returns to Africa, a Rising Power and a Continent Embrace* (London: Hurst Publishers; New York: Columbia University Press).

Fisas, V. (2009) *2009 Yearbook on Peace Processes* (Barcelona, Spain: Icaria Editorial/School of Peace Culture, UAB).

Foley, C. (2007) 'Land Rights in Angola: Poverty and Plenty' (HPG Working Paper; London: ODI).

Global Witness (1999) *A Crude Awakening: The Role of Oil and Banking Industries in Angola's Civil War and the Plunder of State Assets* (London: Global Witness).

—— (2002) *All the Presidents' Men: The Devastating Story of Oil and Corruption in Angola's Privatised War* (London: Global Witness).

—— (2004) *Time for Transparency* (London: Global Witness).

—— (2008) *StatoilHydro's Libyan 'Corruption' Scandal Shows Need for Oil Industry Disclosure Laws: Troubling questions remain about oil deals in Libya and Angola* (London: Global Witness).

—— (2009a) *Private Oil Firm's Shareholders Have Same Names as Top Angolan Government Officials* (London: Global Witness).

—— (2009b) *IMF Risks Condoning Corruption with New Loan to Angola* (London: Global Witness).

Gomes Porto, J. (2003) 'Cabinda: Notes on a Soon to be Forgotten War' (African Security Analysis Programme, Occasional Paper 77; Pretoria: Institute for Security Studies).

Govender, S., and M. Skagestad (2009) *Civil Society and Oil for Development in Angola: Ways to Enhance Strategic Cooperation among Non-state Actors* (Cape Town: Idasa).

Hodges, T. (2007) 'The Economic Foundations of the Patrimonial State', in P. Chabal and N. Vidal (eds.), *Angola: The Weight of History* (London: Hurst & Company).

Honwana, A. (2002) 'Negotiating Post-War Identities: Child Soldiers in Mozambique and Angola', in G. Bond and N. Gibson (eds.), *Contested Terrains and Constructed Categories: Contemporary Africa in Focus* (Boulder, CO: Westview Press).

Human Rights Watch (2003) *Forgotten Fighters: Child Soldiers in Angola* (New York: Human Rights Watch).

—— (2004a) *Some Transparency, No Accountability: The Use of Oil Revenue in Angola and Its Impact on Human Rights* (New York: Human Rights Watch).

—— (2004b) *Angola: Between War and Peace in Cabinda* (Briefing Paper; New York: Human Rights Watch).

—— (2007) *'They Pushed Down the Houses', Forced Evictions and Insecure Land Tenure for Luanda's Urban Poor* (New York: Human Rights Watch).

—— (2009) *'They Put me in The Hole': Military Detention, Torture and Lack of Due Process in Cabinda* (New York: Human Rights Watch).

Imbondeiro (2008) 'Interview with the Vice-Minister of Education, Mpinda Simão', *Imbondeiro* (Official Magazine of the Embassy of Angola to the US), Summer 2008; www.angola. org/newsletter/Imbondeiro.pdf, accessed 24 September 2010.

International Centre for Transitional Justice (2009) *Southern Africa Regional Assessment Mission Report: Angola* (New York: International Center for Transitional Justice).

International Crisis Group (2003) 'Dealing with Savimbi's Ghost: The Security and Humanitarian Challenges in Angola' (Africa Report No. 58; Brussels: International Crisis Group).

Kolstad, I., and A. Wiig (2009) 'Is Transparency the Key to Reducing Corruption in Resource-Rich Countries?', *World Development* 37.3.

——, A. Wiig and A. Williams (2009) 'Mission Improbable: Does Petroleum-related Aid address the Resource Curse? *Energy Policy* 37: 954-65.

Lari, A., and R. Kevlihan (2004) 'International Human Rights Protection in Situations of Conflict and Post-Conflict: A Case Study of Angola', *African Security Review* 13.4: 29-41.

Le Billon, P. (2000) 'The Political Economy of Resource Wars', in J. Cilliers and C. Dietrich (eds.), *Angola's War Economy: The Role of Oil and Diamond* (Pretoria: Institute of Security Studies; www.issafrica.org).

—— (2001) 'Angola's Political Economy of War: The Role of Oil and Diamonds, 1975–2000', *African Affairs* 100: 55-80.

Mabeko-Tali, J. (2001) 'La Question de Cabinda: Separatismes éclatés, habiletés Luandaises et Conflits en Afrique Centrale', *Lusotopie*, 2001: 49-62.

—— (2008) 'Entre économie rentière et violence politico-militaire: la question cabindaise et le processus de paix angolais' *Politique Africaine* 110: 65-83.

Macedo, F., F. Lopes Veira, J. Pinto de Andrade, L. Araujo, W. Tonet and X. Jaime Manuel (2009) Open Letter to Hillary Clinton, English Translation, 7 August 2009; www.africafiles.org/ article.asp?ID=21537, accessed 24 September 2010.

Macmillan, J. (2005) ' "The main institution in the country is corruption": Creating Transparency in Angola' (Stanford University; iis-db.stanford.edu/pubs/20814/Corruption_ transparency_Angola1_No36.pdf, accessed 24 September 2010).

Maidment, P. (2008) 'Angola Leapfrogs Nigeria as Africa's Largest Oil Producer', Forbes. com, 15 May 2008; www.forbes.com/2008/05/15/nigeria-angola-oil-biz-energy-cx_pm_0515nigeria.html, accessed 24 September 2010.

Marques, R. (1999) 'The Lipstick of Dictatorship', *Agora Newspaper*, 3 July 1999.

—— (2004) 'An Angolan Perspective', presentation at a conference on *Oil Revenues: From Curse to Blessing in Developing Countries? Challenges to Governments, Companies and NGOs*, Stavanger, Norway, 9 December 2004.

—— (2006) 'The Power of Oil and the State of Democracy in Angola', a public lecture organized by the Human Rights Program, Harvard Law School, Cambridge, MA, 17 October 2006.

—— (2009a) 'Angola: Mass Media—Hegemonic Power or Power to be Subverted?'; allafrica. com/stories/200901090744.html, accessed 5 July 2010.

—— (2009b) 'The Business Activities of the Attorney-General of the Republic', Open Letter to the President of the Republic of Angola, August 2009; makaangola.com/wp-content/uploads/Letter-to-the-President-of-Angola.pdf, accessed 24 September 2010.

—— (2009c) 'Corruption as a Prerequisite for Contracts with the Government: Legal Doubts over Thales' Angola Deal', Open Letter, September 2009; www.africafiles.org/article. asp?ID=21869, accessed 24 September 2010.

Messiant, C. (2001) 'The Edouardo Dos Santos Foundation: Or How Angola's Regime is Taking over Civil Society', *African Affairs* 100: 287-309.

—— (2007) 'The Mutation of Hegemonic Domination: Multiparty Politics without Democracy', in P. Chabal and N. Vidal (eds.), *Angola: The Weight of History* (London: Hurst & Company).

Murison, K. (ed.) (2004) *Africa South of the Sahara 2004* (London: Europa Publications, 33rd edn).

Newitt, M. (2007) 'Angola in Historical Context', in P. Chabal and N. Vidal (eds.), *Angola: The Weight of History* (London: Hurst & Company).

Ng, P., and P. le Billon (2007) *'Post-Conflict' Oil Governance: Lessons from Angola?* (Copenhagen: Danish Institute for International Studies DIIS): 8.

Paulo, M. (2006) 'Angolanisation: A Hindrance in the Development of Angola?'; www. pambazuka.org, accessed 5 July 2010.

Peclard, D. (2008) 'Les Chemins de la "Reconversion Autoritaire" en Angola', *Politique Africaine* 110: 5-20.

Pegg, S. (2005) 'Can Policy Intervention Beat the Resource Curse? Evidence from the Chad-Cameroon Pipeline Project', *African Affairs* 105/418: 1-25.

Prunier, G., and R. Guisselquist (2003) 'The Sudan: A Successfully Failed State', in R. Rotberg (ed.), *State Failure and State Weakness in a Time of Terror* (Washington, DC: The World Peace Foundation/The Brookings Institution Press).

Reno, W. (2002) 'The (Real) War Economy of Angola', in J. Cilliers and C. Dietrich (eds.), *Angola's War Economy: The Role of Oil and Diamond* (Pretoria: Institute of Security Studies).

Ross, M.L. (2003) 'Oil, Drugs and Diamonds: The Varying Roles of Natural Resources in Civil War', in K. Ballentine and J. Sherman (eds.), *The Political Economy of Armed Conflict: Beyond Greed and Grievance* (Boulder, CO: Lynne Rienner).

—— (2006) 'A Closer Look at Oil, Diamonds, and Civil War', *Annual Review of Political Science* 9: 265-300.

Samset, I. (2009) *Natural Resource Wealth, Conflict, and Peacebuilding* (New York: Ralph Bunche Institute for International Studies, Program on States and Security).

Shankleman, J. (2006) *Oil, Profits and Peace: Does Business Have a Role in Peacemaking?* (Washington, DC: United States Institute of Peace).

Shahrbanou, T. (2005) 'Human Security: Concepts and Implications with an Application to Post-intervention Challenges in Afghanistan' (Les Etudes du CERI 117–18; Center for Peace and Conflict Resolution, Sciences Po; www.ceri-sciencespo.com/publica/etude/etude117_118.pdf, accessed 24 September 2010).

Shaxson, N. (2008) 'Oil for the People: A Solution to the "Resource Curse" ', unpublished.

——, J. Neves and F. Pacheco (2008a) *Drivers of Change, Angola* (Final Report; London: Department for International Development DFID).

——, J. Neves and F. Pacheco (2008b) *Drivers of Change, Angola—Position Paper 1: Strengthening Public Institutions* (Final Report; London: Department for International Development DFID).

Soares de Oliveira, R.M. (2007a) 'Business Success, Angola-Style: Postcolonial Politics and the Rise and Rise of Sonangol', *Journal of Modern African Studies* 45: 595-619.

—— (2007b) *Oil and Politics in the Gulf of Guinea* (New York: Columbia University Press).

Sogge, D. (2006) *Angola: Global 'Good Governance' Also Needed* (Working Paper; Madrid, Spain: FRIDE).

—— (2009) 'Angola: "Failed" yet "Successful" ' (Working Paper; Madrid, Spain: FRIDE).

Stites, E., and J. Leaning (2002) *Human Security in Angola: A Retrospective Study* (Boston, MA: Harvard School of Public Health).

Transparency International (2008) *Promoting Revenue Transparency: 2008 Report on Revenue Transparency of Oil and Gas Companies* (Berlin: Transparency International).

Tvedten, I., A. Orre and R. Bakke (2003) *Angola 2002/2003: Key Development Issues and Democratic Decentralisation* (Bergen, Norway: Chr. Michelsen Institute, Development Studies and Human Rights): 10.

UNDP (United Nations Development Programme) (2008) 'Human Development Report 2007–2008: Angola'; www.undp.org.

UNICEF (United Nations Children's Fund) (1999) *Progress of Nations 1999* (New York: UNICEF).

Velulescu, D. (2008) *Norway's Oil Fund Shows the Way for Wealth Funds* (Washington, DC: International Monetary Fund).

Vidal, N. (2007) 'The Angolan Regime and the Move to Multiparty Politics', in P. Chabal and N. Vidal (eds.), *Angola: The Weight of History* (London: Hurst & Company).

Vines, A. (2008) *Angola: Looking Beyond Elections* (Paris: European Union Institute for Security Studies).

——, L. Wong, M. Weimer and I. Campos (2009) *Thirst for African Oil: Asian National Oil Companies in Nigeria and Angola* (London: Chatham House).

Wanduragala, R. (2000) '. . . Meanwhile the Children Suffer', in *Angola: A Tangled Web: Many Players in a Complex War* (Milton Keynes, UK: World Vision UK).

World Bank (2007) 'Angola: Country Assistance Evaluation' (Report No. 39829; Washington, DC: World Bank).

10

Coltan mining and conflict in the eastern Democratic Republic of Congo (DRC)

Miho Taka

Centre for Peace and Reconciliation Studies, Coventry University, UK

The second Congolese war between 1998 and 2003 has put a spotlight on the supply chain from coltan mines in the eastern Democratic Republic of Congo (DRC) to high-tech electronics goods, such as mobile phones. In the DRC, coltan (columbite–tantalite) is largely mined in the provinces of North Kivu, South Kivu and Maniema in the eastern part (Cuvelier and Raeymaekers 2002a). Tantalum, the mineral extracted from coltan, is resistant to heat and corrosion and has particular ability to store and release electrical energy (*Mining Journal* 2007). Owing to this ability, about half the tantalum consumed each year is used by the electronics industry. Tantalum is processed and made into powder or wire form to manufacture very small capacitors for various devices in telecommunications, data storage and implantable medical devices. In addition, tantalum is used to manufacture super alloys and jet engines.

Tantalum is usually traded with long-term contracts between buyers and mines rather than in the international metal market; however, spot markets exist especially when demand for tantalum is high (*Mining Journal* 2007). The second Congolese war coincided with the coltan boom in 2000, during which the spot price for tantalum increased tenfold owing to the shortage of tantalum (Cuvelier and Raeymaekers 2002a; Jackson 2003). Although the world's largest tantalum supplier, Talison Minerals from Australia, has been supplying about a third of tantalum

(Mineweb 2008), the DRC is considered to have 80% of the world's tantalum reserve (Global Witness 2004).

The exploitation of various natural resources, such as tantalum, in the DRC during the second Congolese war drew attention from the international community and initiated numerous investigations into the link between natural resources and conflict. Most studies support the view that natural resources finance and motivate conflict (Raeymaekers 2002; Hayes and Burge 2003; Global Witness 2004; Snow and Barouski 2006). This view triggered different actions. These include sanctions by the UN, campaigns against 'blood coltan', such as 'No Blood on My Mobile Phone' by Belgian NGOs, and supply chain management of coltan by the business community.

In spite of numerous investigations, campaigns and actions that took place to address the issue of 'blood coltan', the situation remained fundamentally unchanged and the same issue was highlighted again when the fighting intensified in the eastern DRC in 2008. Although the price of coltan never recovered to the level of the coltan boom, mining and trading of coltan, as well as cassiterite and wolfram have been major economic activities in the eastern DRC (Garrett and Mitchell 2009). While it is difficult to estimate the amount of coltan exported from the DRC, the above-mentioned Talison Minerals suspended its tantalum mines because of weak demand, partly caused by cheap supply from the DRC (Mineweb 2008).

The situation in the eastern DRC is often explained as a consequence of failed or fragile states, where phenomena such as 'new wars' and a complex trans-border shadow economy proliferate; thus, posing human security threats. This chapter, therefore, provides a case study on coltan mining and conflict in the eastern DRC, as a human security case study. The case study highlights not only the degree of human insecurity in the DRC, but also issues relevant to an increasingly popular political economy of conflict discourse, and the current debates over the nexus between conflict, security and development. In so doing, the case study also illustrates how human insecurity in coltan mines in the eastern DRC interconnects with consumers worldwide through globalised trade chains.

The aim of this chapter is to analyse the efficacy of the international response to the issue of coltan mining, which largely focuses on boycotting 'blood coltan' through due diligence, in an effort to break the link between coltan mining and violence in the eastern DRC. The following section provides an overview of the human insecurity situation in the eastern DRC, in order to provide the context for coltan mining. This is followed by a section examining particular human security impacts of artisanal coltan mining. Then, the next section reviews the research conducted on coltan mining and trade to crystallise prevailing views on the link between coltan mining and trade, and conflict. The subsequent section analyses various responses and activities on the issue of coltan mining and the concluding section discusses the efficacy of such responses.

Human insecurity in the DRC

The DRC has gone through two major wars between 1996 and 1997 and between 1998 and 2003. An estimated 6 million people have died since 1998, largely because of lack of access to basic healthcare, sanitation, adequate nutrition and infrastructure, especially by being displaced (Caritas Australia 2008). There are about 1.15 million internally displaced persons (IDPs) and 300,000 refugees in neighbouring states, and sexual violence is widespread (UNHCR 2008). The frequent and continuous displacement of the population is coined 'pendulum displacement' by aid workers (IRIN 2007). While the population needs protection from various threats, they actually face threats from the very agencies which are supposed to protect them. There are numerous allegations that a number of UN Mission in Congo (MONUC) personnel sexually abused girls in the DRC (IRIN 2006), and traded their arms with rebel groups in exchange for minerals from the DRC (Escobales 2008). Although the latter significantly hinders the disarmament process in the DRC, there have not been adequate investigations into the allegations (Escobales 2008).

The country is described as the 'world's worst humanitarian crisis' by UN agencies (International Crisis Group, c. 2008) and ranks 168th out of 177 countries in the 2007/2008 Human Development Index (UNDP 2008). The DRC state's inability to provide security, protection of property, basic public services and essential infrastructure is indicative of the country's position as the world's 6th most failed state among 50 other failed states (*Foreign Policy* 2008). Similarly, the World Bank ranks the regulatory environment for business and investment in the DRC as 178th out of 178 states (World Bank 2007).

The current human insecurity situation is not simply a consequence of the two wars nor merely a Congolese problem, as many of the historical events in the DRC and its neighbouring countries since colonial days are inextricably interconnected. However, the focus of this chapter is not to discuss the history and international relations of the DRC, and this section continues with a briefing on the four main armed groups and their political agendas, which operate and affect human security in the eastern DRC.

First, the FDLR (Democratic Forces for the Liberation of Rwanda) is an armed group established in 1999, consisting of the remaining Rwandan refugees and their families, including *genocidaires* (those guilty of taking part in the genocide and hostile to the new Rwandan regime), from the 1994 Rwandan genocide. The FDLR is still determined to return to power in Rwanda, but claims that it demands a political dialogue with the Rwandan government rather than having a war (Fessy and Doyle 2009). According to its website, the FDLR identifies itself as a political organisation, and claims to have aims to 'establish a regime based on universal principles, promote moral values, end wars and establish peace in Rwanda and in the region' (Chatham House 2009: 6). With an estimated 6,000 to 7,000 fighters and operations in North and South Kivu, the FDLR uses harsh training and ruthless punishments in order to retain its members (Chatham House 2009: 6). Although it uses violence when threatened, it acts 'as a state within a state' generally (Chatham House 2009: 7).

Second, the CNDP (National Congress for the Defence of the People) was formed in order to address three key issues for the Congolese Tutsi population, often called Banyamulenge, in the area (Mills 2009). These issues are 'the right of return of dispossessed Congolese Tutsi, the safeguarding of their national identity, and the disarmament of the genocidaires'. The group of people known as Banyamulenge in South Kivu migrated from Rwanda in the 19th century (Takeuchi 2004). There is also another group of people called Banyarwanda in North Kivu, who were forced to migrate from Rwanda by the Belgians after 1930, and there are Rwandan refugees who left during the crisis in Rwanda after 1962. The Banyarwanda had privileged positions and power in the eastern DRC during the Mobutu era; however, they were opposed by other Congolese at the end of the Mobutu era. Both groups are often regarded as foreigners as they speak Kinyarwanda, the language of Rwanda.

In 1994, the Rwandan genocide created a large number of Rwandan Hutu refugees in the eastern DRC, and their refugee camps were armed and highly politicised. This has been a security concern for Rwanda and also for the Banyamulenge as they have been attacked by the Hutu refugees (Takeuchi 2004). After some of the Banyamulenge launched an armed rebellion in 1996, the Congolese assembly decided to dispossess people of Rwandan origin of their citizenship. While the new constitution guarantees their citizenship, these Kinyarwanda speaking Congolese people are ethnic minorities and face challenges in the political space.

Third, the Mayi-Mayi coalition of PARECO (Coalition of Congolese Patriotic Resistance) is considered to be an indigenous resistance force against foreign armed groups, particularly resisting the Tutsi's presence in the DRC (Spittaels and Hilgert 2008).

Fourth, the Congolese national army, FARDC (Armed Forces of the Democratic Republic of Congo), is also blamed for plunder, rape and exploitation of natural resources (Global Witness 2008a).

Impact of coltan mining on human security in the eastern DRC

It is necessary to understand the eastern DRC context as described in the previous section and the artisanal nature of coltan mining in the eastern DRC, in order to appreciate the impact of coltan mining. Artisanal mining is widespread in developing countries, particularly in Africa (*Materials World* 2005). It is often an 'industry of last resort' when there are no other alternatives to earn income, and is an illegal or irregular activity, which exploits miners, including women and children, and is hazardous in terms of health and safety (*Materials World* 2005).

In the eastern DRC, artisanal coltan mining occurs in rivers, opencast or underground, and soft rock deposits (Levin 2008; Garrett 2009). The process includes removing the vegetation and the surface, digging out stones and rocks containing coltan, crushing the stones and washing them in water in order to remove impurities (Hayes and Burge 2003; Levin 2008). Most of mines in the areas are only suitable for artisanal mining because of the soft rocks (Garrett 2009; Garrett and Mitchell 2009).

The environmental impact in the area, especially in the Kahuzi-Biéga National Park, where 75% of the coltan deposits are located (Levin 2008), is significant (Redmond 2001; Moyroud and Katunga 2002; Garrett 2009). These include forest clearance for mining, making mining camps and tools, and cooking; pollution of streams from washing minerals and tailings; the change of biodiversity from eating bush meat; illness caused by sewage; and loss of biodiversity. The unprotected land surface also causes landslides.

There are also considerable socioeconomic impacts from coltan mining (Pole Institute 2002). Since much of the local population including children, have moved to mining, or in some cases are forced to mine, especially during the coltan boom, agricultural production has declined and caused a food crisis. Similarly, school attendance has declined and livelihoods changed. Health and safety issues are the main concern in the mines because of accidents and respiratory illness from the dust. In mining areas, social problems of drinking, drugs, crime, prostitution, sexual abuse, HIV/AIDS and sexually transmitted diseases have increased.

Human insecurity in the eastern DRC is manifested by the engagement of the local population in dangerous artisanal mining, the 'industry of last resort'. Artisanal mining can provide a quick, or the only, livelihood for the local population in the insecure and unstable environment, and does not require any capital or education (Durban Process 2006).

Analysis of the link between conflict and coltan mining and trade

Awareness of the link between exploitation of various natural resources and conflict in the eastern DRC has prompted a number of studies. The most influential study has been the reports of the Panel of Experts on the Illegal Exploitation of Natural Resources and Other Forms of Wealth of the Democratic Republic of the Congo (UNSC 2001a, b, 2002a, b), commissioned by the UN Security Council in order to examine the exploitation of natural resources in the DRC.

In the first report (UNSC 2001a), the link between illegal exploitation of natural resources in the DRC and conflict was identified in terms of financing and sustaining the war efforts of armed groups. The study was significant in highlighting the role played by private companies in sustaining this vicious cycle of conflict, by cooperating to export these resources. The study (UNSC 2001b) also suggested that the exploitation of natural resources has gradually shifted to become the 'primary motive' for Rwanda and Uganda although they initially invaded the DRC for security reasons. Furthermore, the interim report (UNSC 2002a) stated that the trade of conflict resources had been continuing and the system of natural resource exploitation was established during the war. The view from these studies can be supported by the popular 'resource curse' discourse which links natural resources rent and conflict (Collier and Hoeffler 2005; Lalji 2007)._

A study by an NGO (Raeymaekers 2002) also claims that the motivation for the conflict has changed from political to economic, and warring parties are fighting over the control of resources. The plundering of resources is organised by privatised networks of army officers, armed groups and international companies, in order to enrich themselves and finance the conflict. Within this 'network war', an emerging political economy, the conventional state boundaries and sovereignty or the distinction between legal and illegal economy are not relevant. The report cites the term, 'emerging complexes', rather than 'complex emergencies' to describe the situation in the DRC, referring to Mark Duffield (2001). In these 'emerging complexes', the participants have linked the local war economy with global economic networks to obscure the division between governments, armies and individuals.

The view in which natural resource exploitation finances and motivates the armed groups (although there have been some underlying political issues among them, including ethnicity, citizenship and land) has been largely shared by many other studies and reports (Hayes and Burge 2003; Global Witness 2004; Enough 2009). For that reason, the role of private companies in fuelling and sustaining conflict in the eastern DRC has been widely discussed. The business partnership between military and private companies, in which private companies assist in exploiting, transporting and marketing the natural resources from the DRC, is described as 'military commercialism' in some studies (Dietrich 2000; Cuvelier and Raeymaekers 2002a; Raeymaekers 2002; Amnesty International 2003). Within the 'military commercialism', 'the maintenance of insecurity has become a primary source of enrichment' and strategy (Raeymaekers 2002: 9).

While agreeing with the view that natural resources such as coltan motivates and finances conflict in the DRC, research using an ethnographic approach (Jackson 2003: 1) argues that coltan mining has become the most important means for local people to survive. The research looked at the price increase and crash of coltan, and has found out that the price crash did not stop the trade in coltan but intensified the control of 'war entrepreneurs'. This is because armed groups 'turned inwards to the territory they control, capitalising—personally as well as collectively—on the rich resources available' when the war arrived at a deadlock.

There have been a few other studies with different views which attempt to embrace the broader DRC context. For example, a recent study (Garrett and Mitchell 2009) maintains that the mineral resource exploitation in the eastern DRC is a symptom of insecurity and governance failure. Rackley (2006) also criticises the simplistic view that puts all blame on the mineral resources for conflict in the eastern DRC, on the basis that the view ignores the governance crisis in the DRC. Without effective governance, the forms of predation by the civil and military administration have been so pervasive that they occur 'in many spheres of human exchange, down to the basic subsistence practices of Congolese farmers' (Rackley 2006: 420).

In addition to analysing the link between conflict and mineral resources in the eastern DRC, some studies have been conducted in order to examine the trade chain of mineral resources from the eastern DRC. These studies confirm that the trade chain of minerals is highly complex, and involves numerous actors (Hayes and Burge 2003; Jackson 2003). Coltan is mined by diggers with artisanal methods, largely in North Kivu, South Kivu and Maniema, brought to local traders by porters, sold to trading posts in larger cities, sold to international traders and then exported abroad by transport companies (Cuvelier and Raeymaekers 2002a; Amnesty International 2003; Hayes and Burge 2003; Global Witness 2004). If not directly exported from trading posts in Goma or Bukavu (province capitals of North Kivu and South Kivu, respectively), coltan often crosses borders to Rwanda—from Goma to Gisenyi (the western province of Rwanda) and from Bukavu to Cyangugu (south-western province of Rwanda)—is brought to Kigali, the Rwandan capital, and then exported abroad, often through Mombasa or Dar es Salaam (DFID 2007; INICA 2007a; Garrett and Mitchell 2009).

Responses to the coltan mining issues

Analysis of the link between conflict and coltan mining and trade has influenced responses to the issue significantly. Most actions are positioned around boycotting coltan from particular areas, ranging from rebel-held areas in the eastern DRC to the central part of Africa, in order to cut off the financial resources of armed groups. This is because the prevailing view considers coltan as a key driver for the conflict, and it is the most appealing method for public relations (Hayes and Burge 2003).

Responding to pressure, many mobile phone companies, the end-users of tantalum, published statements regarding their supply chain management of coltan on their websites.[1] The telecommunications industry collectively has created a Supply Chain Working Group.[2] Moreover, two of the world's largest tantalum processing companies have published statements on their websites, one affirming that its tantalum is sourced from the company's own mines, Australia's Talison Minerals and Mozambique's Noventa (Cabot Corporation 2008), and the other affirming that

---

1 For example, Nokia (2006) mentions its awareness of the issue of Congolese coltan, and explains that the company has asked its suppliers to avoid purchasing tantalum from the DRC. Similarly, Vodafone (2008a, b) states that it does not produce mobile phones and, hence, it has a limited influence over the supply chain of tantalum. It clarifies that its supply chain management strategy is to engage directly with its first-tier suppliers, who will also do the same.

2 The Global e-Sustainability Initiative (GeSI).

the company does not source any tantalum originating from the DRC 'knowingly' (H.C. Starck 2008).[3] These efforts around supply chain management appear to be public relations exercises by the companies since they are only responsible for their first-tier suppliers, and it is their suppliers that are responsible for their suppliers further down the supply chain (Vodafone 2008b).

There is also a pressure for companies to implement due diligence when trading with tantalum. NGOs such as Global Witness (2008b) call for due diligence by the companies and Enough Project (2009) demands transparency on the supply chain; governments are also trying to develop measures for due diligence. One example is the Congo Conflict Mineral Act of 2009 (Open Congress 2009), by the US government. The act intends to create due diligence guidance for mineral-using companies on the basis of the planned investigation, and obliges mineral-using companies to reveal which mine their minerals are sourced from. Besides, the act proposes to improve the livelihood and situation of the mining communities.

The UN has been trying to break the link between coltan and the conflict through sanctions and an arms embargo, and also named 85 companies in its report (UNSC 2002b) that are considered to be in breach of the OECD Guidelines for Multinational Enterprises.[4] This has been followed up by some NGOs, and in two cases, a UK-based mineral trading company, Afrimex (Global Witness 2007), and a British air cargo company, DAS Air (RAID 2008), complaints were made to the National Contact Point in the UK, under the Specific Instance Procedure of the OECD Guidelines. While these efforts by NGOs have achieved rulings to support the allegations, the OECD Guidelines do not have any enforcement mechanisms.

There have been some efforts to establish certification schemes for coltan in order to support supply chain management and due diligence. The German government is financing a pilot initiative to create a mineral fingerprint for coltan by collecting and analysing data from coltan mined in various locations so that the source of tantalum can be identified (Reuters Africa 2008). The Congolese government plans to use this data in order to develop a certification process for coltan (Reuters Africa 2008), similar to the Kimberley Process Certification Scheme.[5] The government hopes to increase revenues from coltan and control the areas by con-

3 US-based Cabot Corporation, Germany's H.C. Starck and China's Ningxia were predicted to use 70% of the tantalum consumption in 2008 which was estimated to be 2.6 million kg (Mineweb 2008).

4 The OECD Guidelines for Multinational Enterprises are voluntary principles and standards for business activities with regard to human rights, disclosure and combating bribery (see www.oecd.org/daf/investment/guidelines, accessed 7 July 2010).

5 The Kimberley Process Certification Scheme (KPCS) aims to cease production and trade in diamonds from conflict zones so that the diamond trade does not finance violence and conflict. KPCS is a joint initiative of governments, industry and civil society launched in 2003, and its members represent approximately 99.8% of the global production of rough diamonds. With this scheme, international shipments of rough diamonds must have a Kimberley Process certificate to certify that they are not from conflict areas (see www.kimberleyprocess.com, accessed 6 July 2010).

trolling coltan mining and trade through licences, centralised control and certification (Reuters Africa 2008).

Finally, some studies recommend formalising or regulating coltan mining and trade. Regulation of the sector is encouraged by studies that acknowledge the difficulty of boycotting Congolese coltan, owing to the complex supply chain and the prevalence of smuggling of coltan (Hayes and Burge 2003; Jackson 2003). A recent study (Garrett and Mitchell 2009), which recognises the governance failure and insecurity in the eastern DRC, does not see the boycott of coltan from the DRC as a viable option. This is not only because it is difficult to implement any control mechanisms for the supply chain, but also because the issues of governance and security have to be addressed in coordination with the issue of coltan mining and trade. The study suggests that it is essential to coordinate measures in three areas: namely, engaging with and formalising the coltan trade; security sector reform; and reforming and strengthening Congolese state institutions.

Discussion

There are three key questions to discuss on the responses and activities with respect to coltan from the eastern DRC, founded on the studies conducted on the link between conflict and mining and trade of coltan, reviewed in the previous section. First, is it technically feasible to boycott coltan from rebel-held areas in the eastern DRC? The complex nature of the coltan supply chain has been identified as the difficulty for implementing any supply chain management or due diligence measures (Hayes and Burge 2003; Jackson 2003). However, the fundamental problem for a boycott of coltan from rebel-held areas is the extent of the informal economy in the region as illustrated in the following.

As a result of the crash in coltan price and pressures from the international community to boycott Congolese coltan, a number of multinationals have decided to stop their operations in the Kivus (Cuvelier and Raeymaekers 2002b). This had a significant impact, in which the traditional trading posts have been marginalised and a small group of business people with close relations with the Rwandan government have replaced the traditional trading posts (Cuvelier and Raeymaekers 2002b). Despite the withdrawal of these multinationals from the Kivus, coltan from the eastern DRC continues to be supplied widely to the international market. In 2008, Talison Minerals (previously Sons of Gwalia), which used to supply about a third of the world's supply of tantalum, suspended mining of tantalum, based on weak demand owing to the financial crisis and the cheap supply from the DRC (Mineweb 2008), as mentioned above.

A study on regional trade in natural resources (DFID 2007) estimates that more than half of exports from the DRC are not officially recorded, owing to under-declared exports for tax evasion and lack of capacities and weak governance within the state institutions. The degree of informal operation within the mining and trade sector encourages illegal operation since legal operations are more difficult to carry out (DFID 2007). This corresponds to the Doing Business ranking by the World Bank (World Bank 2007), mentioned above. In addition, widespread corruption or predation by the civil and military administration in virtually all areas of activities (Rackley 2006) does not allow any measures to control coltan from the eastern DRC, particularly when there are buyers who do not have to consider their reputational risks, including mafia networks and rogue companies (Raeymaekers 2002).

As a result of the overwhelming informal economy in the DRC, it is not only unfeasible to implement a boycott of coltan from the eastern DRC, but if implemented, the trade would continue in a more opaque manner and/or in different locations (Pole Institute 2002).

Second, whether boycotting coltan from rebel-held areas in the eastern DRC would break the link between conflict and coltan mining and trade, as many studies and reports advocate, has to be considered seriously. This hypothesis is based on eliminating the financial resources of armed groups, but can be challenged when considering two factors. To begin with, there are complex long-term political issues underlying the conflict in the region as some studies recognised (Moyroud and Katunga 2002; Jackson 2003; Putzel *et al.* 2008; Spittaels and Hilgert 2008). The governor of North Kivu clearly disagrees with the view that various armed groups simply fight over mineral resources, and explains the current situation as an accumulation of very poor management in the DRC over several decades (IRIN 2004).

The political agendas of the rebel groups, the FDLR and the CNDP, remain largely unresolved although the CNDP has been transformed into a political party and its soldiers have recently been integrated into the Congolese national army. While disarmament, demobilisation and reintegration (DDR) of the FDLR has often been advocated in order to solve security issues in the eastern DRC, this would not be successful without diplomatic exercises; namely continuous efforts to open up political space within Rwanda, through dialogue (Chatham House 2009). In addition, many of the FDLR members have been living in the DRC for more than a decade, and are assimilated into communities (Chatham House 2009); therefore, it is not realistic to expect them to simply repatriate.

The political agenda of the CNDP also has to be considered genuinely as it is doubtful whether it can participate in and contest political debates in the DRC as an ethnic minority group (Takeuchi 2004). It is crucial to promote diplomatic efforts with Rwanda given increasing migration from Rwanda to the eastern DRC, where the land issue has already been creating tensions (ICG 2009), and military support from Rwanda to the CNDP (UNSC 2008). The necessary processes of DDR and security sector reform (SSR) will not succeed without the cooperation of Rwanda. Donors' unconditional aid for Rwanda should also be questioned (McGreal 2008).

The second factor is the financial resources of rebel groups. Recent UN research (UNSC 2008) has revealed that armed groups, such as the CNDP and the FDLR, have well-established networks outside the DRC. With regard to financial resources, the FDLR, as well as the Congolese army, controls a large portion of the trade in coltan, gold, wolfram and cassiterite, and some of these commodities are exported through formally licensed trading posts in Goma and Bukavu. The CNDP receives income from the mines, tax from the border customs posts, land and cows, and external financing. The study has also found some evidence to show support from the Rwandan government to the CNDP. While revenue from mineral resources is crucial income for the rebel groups, they can also finance themselves from external and diversified financial sources. Thus, boycotting minerals from the area is not likely to have a decisive impact in breaking the link between conflict and minerals.

Moreover, contrary to the good intention of boycotting coltan from the area, boycotting is likely to have a negative impact on human security of the local community. Some studies argue that coltan mining and trade is one of the very limited livelihoods available for the local population and a boycott would harm the local community that has already been suffering great human insecurity (Pole Institute 2002; Jackson 2003; Johnson and Tegera 2005; Garrett and Mitchell 2009). In fact, more than a million people are considered to depend on artisanal mining in the Kivus since most other industries have been destroyed by long-term insecurity in the area (Garrett and Mitchell 2009). In addition, there is concern among local traders that the proposed mineral fingerprint system for coltan would destroy the industry, as the system would increase the price of coltan and reduce the competitiveness of Congolese coltan (Reuters 2008).

The critical issue is that coltan mining and trade has not been benefiting the local population, only the traders who have access to the international market and international buyers (Pole Institute 2002; Johnson and Tegera 2005; Garrett and Mitchell 2009). While coltan mining is not identical to the brutal 'blood diamond' situation, revenues from coltan have not been fairly distributed and artisanal miners face harsh and dangerous working conditions (Garrett and Mitchell 2009). It is, therefore, not a problem of the illegality of mining and trade but the absence of human rights and socioeconomic benefit for the local population (Johnson and Tegera 2005). The weakness of the 'conflict driven by the minerals' view is that it misjudges the complexity of war economies and neglects the fact that the systems of mineral exploitation, created during the war, persist beyond any peace processes (Garrett and Mitchell 2009). For these reasons, it is not effective to boycott coltan from the area, but necessary to reorganise (Pole Institute 2002; Johnson and Tegera 2005) and/or formalise the sector (Garrett and Mitchell 2009).

Given the recommendation above, the third question is the feasibility of formalising the mining sector in the eastern DRC. According to the current Mining Code in the DRC, which was enforced in 2002, all deposits of minerals belong to the DRC state (INICA 2007b). Artisanal miners are supposed to apply for one-year artisanal mining rights and mine in the deposits specified for artisanal mining. However, they need to pass a written exam, receive training and follow various obligations, including restoration of the land that they had mined (INICA 2007b).

The Mining Code has been criticised, in terms of encouraging fraud, because it imposes unrealistic conditions on artisanal mining rights, when an increasing population rely on artisanal mining for their livelihoods as a result of displacement, loss of livelihoods and infrastructure from the conflict (INICA 2007b). Consequently, the specified timetable for application in the Mining Code has not been adhered to (Johnson and Tegera 2005).

It is probably not difficult to amend the Mining Code to address the problem above and formalise the mining sector. However, considering existing cross-border trade networks (MacGaffey 1991; Putzel *et al.* 2008), efforts to formalise the sector have to be coordinated regionally, probably using a regional initiative such as the International Conference on the Great Lakes Region.[6] Nonetheless, the challenge is to reorganise the sector, in order to enhance social accountability in the mining and trade of coltan (Pole Institute 2002) for sustainable peace and development, since some of the trading posts are already officially licensed and conducting legal trade at present (DFID 2007; Garrett and Mitchell 2009). As some studies point out, the system of coltan exploitation has been unaffected by any peace processes; the same actors or networks continued to be involved since the Congolese wars (Garrett and Mitchell 2009). In order to reorganise the sector, strengthened governance, particularly the judicial system, and diplomatic efforts to negotiate with neighbouring countries will be crucial.

This case study, through evaluating the efficacy of the international response to the issues of coltan mining, has highlighted the weakness of the simplistic 'conflict driven by the mineral' view because of the underlying complexity within the human security construct. While conducting research in this area encounters a number of technical constraints, further research integrating broader disciplines to achieve a more holistic understanding of the human security construct in the area is essential for the pursuit of sustainable peace and development.

Bibliography

Amnesty International (2003) *Democratic Republic of Congo: 'Our Brothers Who Help Kill Us'—Economic exploitation and human rights abuses in the east* (AI Index: AFR 62/010/2003; London Amnesty International).

Cabot Corporation (2008) 'Cabot Position on Tantalum and Coltan and the Democratic Republic of Congo'; www.cabot-corp.com/Tantalum/GN200809161037AM6983, accessed 24 September 2010.

Caritas Australia (2008) 'Forsaken Voices: Desecration and Plunder in the Democratic Republic of the Congo 2008'; www.caritas.org.au/AM/CM/ContentDisplay.cfm?ContentFileID=214&MicrositeID=0&Fusepreview=Yes, 24 September 2010.

Chatham House (2009) *'Transcript: Entrepreneurs of Violence: Rebel Groups and Militias in Africa'* with R. Cornwell, D. Zoumenou, P. Roque and H. Boshoff (London: Chatham House).

Collier, P., and A. Hoeffler (2005) 'Resource Rents, Governance and Conflict', *Journal of Conflict Prevention* 49.4 (August 2005): 625-33.

6 www.icglr.org (accessed 7 July 2010).

Cuvelier, J., and T. Raeymaekers (2002a) 'Supporting the War Economy in the DRC: European Companies and the Coltan Trade—Five Case Studies' (IPIS Report; Antwerp, Belgium: IPIS [International Peace Information Service]).

—— and T. Raeymaekers (2002b) 'European Companies and the Coltan Trade: An Update Part 2' (IPIS Report; Antwerp, Belgium: IPIS).

DFID (Department for International Development) (2007) 'Trading for Peace: Achieving Security and Poverty Reduction through Trade in Natural Resources in the Great Lakes Area' (Research Report; London: DFID).

Dietrich, C. (2000) 'The Commercialisation of Military Deployment in Africa', *African Security Review* 9.1; www.iss.co.za/pubs/ASR/9No1/Commerciallisation.html, accessed 25 February 2009.

Duffield, M. (2001) *Global Governance and the New Wars: The Merging of Development and Security* (London: Zed Books).

Durban Process (2006) 'Campaign Report' June 2006; obtained from the former Durban Process Officer, 18 November 2009.

Enough (2009) 'A Comprehensive Approach To Congo's Conflict Minerals: Strategy Paper'; www.enoughproject.org/print/1736, accessed 28 May 2009.

Escobales, R. (2008) 'UN peacekeepers "traded gold and guns with Congolese rebels"', *The Guardian*, 28 April 2008;www.guardian.co.uk/world/2008/apr/28/congo.unitednations, accessed 10 September 2009.

Fessy, T., and M. Doyle (2009) 'From rebel-held Congo to beer can', BBC News, 9 April 2009; news.bbc.co.uk/1/hi/world/africa/7991479.stm, accessed 12 May 2009.

Foreign Policy (2008) 'The Failed States Index 2008'; www.redri.org/new/images/archivos/failed_states_2008.pdf , accessed 24 September 2010.

Garrett, N. (2009) 'Mining The Peace', *The Equatorial Press*, 15 February 2009.

Garrett, N., and H. Mitchell (2009) *Trading Conflict for Development: Utilising the Trade in Minerals from Eastern DR Congo for Development* (London: Resource Consulting Services).

Global Witness (2004) *Same Old Story: A Background Study on Natural Resources in the Democratic Republic of Congo* (London: Global Witness).

—— (2007) 'Afrimex (UK) Democratic Republic of Congo: Complaint to the UK National Contact Point under the Specific Instance Procedure of the OECD Guidelines for Multinational Enterprises'; www.globalwitness.org/media_library_get.php/356/afrimex_ncp_complaint_en.pdf, accessed 2 February 2008.

—— (2008a) 'Control of Mines by Warring Parties Threatens Peace Efforts in Eastern Congo', Press Release, 10 September 2008; www.globalwitness.org/media_library_detail.php/663/en/control_of_mines_by_warring_parties_threatens_peak, accessed 24 September 2010.

—— (2008b) 'Recommendations on Due Diligence for Buyers and Companies Trading in Minerals from Eastern Democratic Republic of Congo and for their Home Governments', November 2008; www.globalwitness.org/media_library_detail.php/681/en/recommendations_on_due_diligence_for_buyers_and_co, accessed 24 September 2010.

Hayes, K., and R. Burge (2003) *Coltan Mining in the Democratic Republic of Congo: How Tantalum-Using Industries Can Commit to the Reconstruction of the DRC* (Cambridge, UK: Fauna & Flora International).

H.C. Starck (2008) 'Statement of the Company on the Use of Tantalous Raw Materials from the Democratic Republic of Congo (DRC)', 17 November 2008; www.hcstarck.com/pages/2740/drc_statement_en2.pdf accessed 4 July 2009.

ICG (International Crisis Group) (2009) 'Congo: Five Priorities for a Peacebuilding Strategy', *International Crisis Group Africa Report* 150 (11 May 2009).

—— (c. 2008) 'Democratic Republic of Congo'; www.crisisgroup.org/home/index. cfm?id=1174&l=1, accessed 12 February 2008.

INICA (Initiative for Central Africa) (2007a) *Natural Resources and Trade Flows in the Great Lakes Region, Phase 1 Report* (Kigali, Rwanda: INICA).

—— (2007b) *Natural Resources and Trade Flows in the Great Lakes Region, Annexes* (Kigali, Rwanda: INICA).

IRIN (2004) 'DRC: Interview with Eugene Serufuli, governor of North Kivu Province', UN Office for the Coordination of Humanitarian Affairs, 22 July 2004; www.grandslacs.net/ doc/3100.pdf, accessed 3 July 2009.

—— (2006) 'Democratic Republic of Congo (DRC): MONUC Troops among the Worst Sex Offenders', 28 August 2006; www.irinnews.org/report.aspx?reportid=60476, accessed 10 September 2009.

—— (2007) 'DRC: "Pendulum displacement" in the Kivus', 1 August 2007; www.irinnews.org/ PrintReport.aspx?ReportID=73524, accessed 13 July 2009.

Jackson, S. (2003) 'Fortunes of War: The Coltan Trade in the Kivus' (Background research for HPG Report 13; London: ODI).

Johnson, D., and A. Tegera (2005) *Digging Deeper: How the DR Congo's Mining Policy is Failing the Country* (Goma, DRC: Pole Institute).

Lalji, N. (2007) 'The Resource Curse Revised: Conflict and Coltan in the Congo', *Harvard International Review* 29.3 (Fall 2007): 34-37.

Levin, E. (2008) 'Environmental Issues Related to Artisanal Mining in the Kivus', slides for Finnwatch Helsinki Seminar, 21 January 2008; slideshare.net/estellelevin/environment-asm, accessed 13 May 2009.

MacGaffey, J., with V. Mukohya, R.W. Nkera, B.G. Schoepf, M.m.M.y. Beda and W. Engundu (1991) *The Real Economy of Zaire: The Contribution of Smuggling and Other Unofficial Activities to National Wealth* (London: James Currey).

McGreal, C. (2008) 'Why Rwanda Holds Key to Ending Bloodshed', *The Guardian*, 3 November 2008.

Materials World (2005) 'Artisanal Mining: A Family Affair', *Materials World*, April 2005: 33-35.

Mills, G. (2009) 'Guerrillas in the Congo's Midst: What is General Nkunda up to?', commentary; www.rusi.org/go.php?structureID=S4625FEA9CB719&ref=C490DF0DF45B68, accessed 10 February 2009.

Mineweb (2008) 'Indefinite Shutdown for World Top Tantalum Miner', 26 November 2008; www.mineweb.com/mineweb/view/mineweb/en/page43?oid=73815&sn=Detail, accessed 27 November 2008.

Mining Journal (2007) 'Tantalum: A Supplement to Mining Journal', *Mining Journal*, special publication, November 2007.

Moyroud, C., and J. Katunga (2002) 'Coltan Exploitation in Eastern Democratic Republic of the Congo (DRC)', in J. Lind and K. Sturman (eds.), *Scarcity and Surfeit: The Ecology of Africa's Conflicts* (Pretoria: Institute for Security Studies).

Nokia (2006) 'Our Position: Tantalum/Coltan'; www.nokia.com/A4230065, accessed 15 November 2007.

Open Congress (2009) 'Text of S.891as Introduced in Senate: Congo Conflict Minerals Act of 2009'; www.opencongress.org/bill/111-s891/text, accessed 28 May 2009.

Pole Institute (2002) 'The Coltan Phenomenon: How a rare mineral has changed the life of the population of war-torn North Kivu province in the East of the Democratic Republic of Congo' (Goma, DRC: Pole Institute).

Putzel, J., S. Lindemann and C. Schouten (2008) 'Drivers of Change in the Democratic Republic of Congo: The Rise and Decline of the State and Challenges for Reconstruction: A Literature Review' (Working Paper No. 26; London: Crisis State Research Centre, Development Studies Institute).

Rackley, E.B. (2006) 'Democratic Republic of the Congo: Undoing Government by Predation', *Disasters* 30.4: 417-32.

Raeymaekers, T. (2002) 'Network War: An Introduction to Congo's Privatised War Economy' (IPIS Report; Antwerp, Belgium: IPIS [International Peace Information Service]).

RAID (Rights & Accountability in Development) (2008) 'Government Condemns British Aviation Company for Fuelling Congo's War', 21 July 2008; www.reports-and-materials.org/RAID-press-release-re-DAS-Air-21-jul-2008.doc, accessed 25 July 2008.

Redmond, I. (2001) 'Coltan Boom, Gorilla Bust: The Impact of Coltan Mining on Gorillas and other Wildlife in Eastern DR Congo' (Report for the Dian Fossey Gorilla Fund Europe and the Born Free Foundation; London/Horsham, UK).

Reuters (2008) 'Rights Group Wants Congo "Conflict Mineral" Tracing', *Mining Weekly Online*, 1 April 2008; miningweekly.com, accessed 25 March 2008.

Reuters Africa (2008) 'Congo to Begin Coltan Certification in 2009: Minister', 25 March 2008; africannewsanalysis.blogspot.com/2008/12/congo-to-begin-coltan-certification-in.html, accessed 23 August 2010.

Snow, K.H., and D. Barouski (2006) 'Suffering in the Democratic Republic of Congo: Behind the Numbers', Z Magazine Online 19.7-8; www.africafiles.org/article.asp?ID=12319, accessed 2 April 2009.

Spittaels, S., and F. Hilgert (2008) *Mapping Conflict Motives: Eastern DRC* (Antwerp, Belgium: IPIS [International Peace Information Service]).

Takeuchi, S. (2004) 'Toubu-Kongo to iu funsou no kaku' ['The Eastern DRC as the Core of the Conflict'], *Africa Report* 39: 38-42.

UNDP (2008) 'Indicator Tables HDI 2007/2008'; hdr.undp.org/en/media/hdr_20072008_tables.pdf, accessed 6 March 2008.

UNHCR (2008) *UNHCR Global Appeal 2008–2009* (Geneva: UNHCR).

UNSC (2001a) 'Report of the Panel of Experts on the Illegal Exploitation of Natural Resources and Other Forms of Wealth of the Democratic Republic of the Congo' (S/2001/357, 12 April 2001; New York: UNSC).

—— (2001b) 'Addendum to the report of the Panel of Experts on the Illegal Exploitation of Natural Resources and Other Forms of Wealth of the Democratic Republic of the Congo' (S/2001/1072, 13 November 2001; New York: UNSC).

—— (2002a) 'Interim Report of the Panel of Experts on the Illegal Exploitation of Natural Resources and Other Forms of Wealth of the Democratic Republic of the Congo' (S/2002/565, 22 May 2002; New York: UNSC).

—— (2002b) 'Final Report of the Panel of Experts on the Illegal Exploitation of Natural Resources and Other Forms of Wealth of the Democratic Republic of the Congo' (S/2002/1146, 16 October 2002; New York: UNSC).

—— (2008) 'Final Report of the Group of Experts' (S/2008/773, 12 December 2008; New York: UNSC).

Vodafone (2008a) 'Industry Partnership: Coltan'; www.vodafone.com/start/responsibility/supply_chain/sector_partnership/coltan.html, accessed 5 March 2008.

Vodafone (2008b) 'Supply Chain'; www.vodafone.com/start/responsibility/supply_chain.html, accessed 5 March 2008.

World Bank (2007) 'Doing Business 2008 Congo, Dem. Rep.: A Project Benchmarking the Regulatory Cost of Doing Business in 178 Economies' (Doing Business Project; Washington, DC: World Bank Group).

Section IV
Human security, relations and community

11

Neurons and nations
Attachment and human security

Marci Green
University of Wolverhampton, UK

Love. Not *all* one needs, of course, but important for one's security and well-being. When it is 'there' for us, in appropriate ways, we feel grounded in the self, and secure in our being with others. But, when it is denied, disrupted, betrayed or broken, we suffer its loss. That loss, then, has to be managed.

The means by which we manage unwanted loss turns on many things: our past experiences of loss and sense of self-security, the conditions in which the loss occurred, our ability to make sense of the heart's rupture, and the presence of sympathetic family and friends as we process our pain. These others are witness to our grief, and can join in the public rituals to mark the passing of loved ones. But, when the mourners depart, we are left to ourselves and the absence we now carry.

The impact of unwanted loss and separation on an individual's emotional health and development is a fundamental theme of attachment-oriented research and psychotherapy. But not exclusively so. Those who work in human rights, humanitarian aid, conflict, development, migration, poverty and health, do not have to be told of the trauma that *unwanted* loss entails. Indeed, that knowledge has informed the emerging discourse on human security. But, whereas therapists engage directly with clients who have experienced trauma from loss, professionals in the field of human security look more to its systemic causes—in, for example, extreme and routine violence, institutional relations, group conflict and persistent inequalities in the distribution of resources.

The differences between these two discourses are a product partly of interest, partly of emphasis, partly of subject matter and analytical perspective, and partly the sociopolitical conditions in which each is embedded and from which each has evolved. Over time, these differences have accumulated like so much matter at a boundary fence; we may nod across the divide to a friendly neighbour, but then retreat back to our intellectual homes. Yet, the fence sits on common ground, and it is that shared space with which this chapter is concerned. In particular, it argues a place for attachment theory—a *relational* model of the mind and emotional development—in the terrain of human security. In exploring this terrain, it is useful to first consider three features of the human security approach which speak directly to the principles of attachment: its conception of human need; its view of human agency; and its understandings of the relations between people and their social environments. Some basic themes of attachment theory will then be introduced in order to consider their contribution to human security discourse.

Human need, human capacity and the relational environment

The perspective of human security that has evolved since the mid-1990s has embraced the principles that real security is more about people than territory, that the security of persons, families and communities are a prerequisite for security within and across nations, and that numerous risks to security are generated by, and through, mainly structural conditions and processes in the public arenas of social networks, neighbourhoods, cultural systems, nations, states and regions in which populations are enmeshed. It is the great virtue of the human security approach that it has shifted and widened the focus of earlier security paradigms, a shift facilitated and nourished by interdisciplinary research.

'Individuals and communities' are the primary referents of a human security approach. In the various United Nations and research centre publications, the discussions are conceptually grounded in the lived experience of populations made *in*secure—those who struggle to be *free from* those fears and wants created by both routine arrangements and extraordinary events. Discussions also recognise that human security requires *freedom to* exercise choice, to assert rights safely, and to create and maintain opportunities necessary for well-being. The human security approach, therefore, is about both enablements and constraints (Luckham 2009).

Thus, at the heart of the human security approach is a concern with the conditions that diminish or enhance the expression and satisfaction of ordinary human needs. As a focus which guides new thinking about security, it is essential, but vague. It begs understanding of several issues. For one thing, 'needs' are often conceptualised in relation to material, social, cultural and political resources; if these resources are routinely available, our freedoms are enabled (but not guaranteed). It follows, then, that if these resources are denied, then security is at risk. This is a substantial reading, but incomplete, for while these are the collective resources on which physical survival depends, people need more to feel secure. The integrity of self is one of those needs. The integrity of our attachments and affectional bonds is another. These two are inextricably linked. *If these two basic needs are met, then people have the internal, emotional resources that help them to manage trauma and its effects.* But, if these needs remain unfulfilled, or are marginalised in, say, efforts to secure physical and power resources, then our current and future security is fragile. This is because the personal experience of unwanted separation and loss of attachments—which undermines self and sociality—can induce trauma. If unresolved, it may have collective as well as individual consequences (de Zulueta 1993, 2004).

Another ambiguity resides in the concept of 'individual'. As one of the key referents of the human security approach, its value is fundamentally moral. Analytically, however, it is weak. It reveals little about our subjective qualities as *agents*, both individual and collective. Certainly, external conditions shape the fortunes and failures of individuals and communities, but more fundamentally, they influence agency—our capacity to 'make things happen': to love, to hate, to empathise, to exercise reason, to regulate emotion, to mobilise restraint or do harm, and to choose between creativity and destruction. While human security writers do address (mainly collective) agency in the processes of, say, resisting infringements to freedom, in bargaining over resources, in reclaiming social spaces, the concept 'agency' from an attachment perspective does several things: for one thing it opens to enquiry those *internal states* of the mind that mobilise our actions and links them to our relational environment (human security from the 'bottom up', from the 'inside out'). Second, 'agency'; is both individual *and* collective, as are the actions it initiates; these can be productive or damaging. Third, it concentrates our thinking about *what it means to be human.*

Partnered with the concept of agency is 'structure', conceived by sociologists as stable and enduring patterns of behaviour, rules and resources. In the human security research, these structures are examined in several domains: socioeconomic and political systems; culture; institutional relations; neighbourhood networks; and familial relationships.[1] The connections among them are situational and complex, but researchers are mapping them with considerable success. More challenging, however, are our efforts to comprehend the relations of structure to agency—the 'parts' of society to its 'people'. It is the quality of those *relations* that shape our security. In the human security literature, colleagues are clearer about the fact of their connection, than we are about its dynamics. We find it easier to calibrate the external risks to security than to grasp their subjective meaning. We can name the constraints to security, but the enablements are harder to identify; this derives partly from the fact that the foundations of our security reside as much in the soft tissue of the human brain as they do in the structures of society.

---

1 Derek Layder, a social theorist, has developed a conceptual framework which helps identify the properties of, and relations among, distinctive but interrelated social domains. His work refines and extends the value of the structure/agency dualism (Layder 1997).

How, then, can we comprehend the nature of human need, the qualities of human agency, and the relations of agency to wider structures and processes in ways that can help us address the human aspects of human security, that ground security in the human condition? As a sociologist working in the field of attachment, I believe that the principles of attachment theory can serve this purpose.

Principles of attachment theory[2]

According to attachment theory, a condition of healthy emotional development is one's security of attachments. Attachments are very particular kinds of affectional bond in which we invest our physical and psychological safety. According to John Bowlby, the originator of attachment theory, attachments matter throughout life. However, the first three years of life are especially important for the emotional health and development of human beings. These formative years are crucial as our early experiences with our 'attachment figures' (primary caregivers) will influence brain development, shape an emerging sense of self, and create an internal, psychological map by which individuals navigate their future intimate, peer and public relationships.[3]

Since the 1940s, Bowlby and colleagues have been developing this relational model of development, a model now supported by neuroscience. They argue that human beings, like other primates, are born biologically predisposed to attach to their primary caregivers, and seek these attachments as a condition of self and species survival. However, what is distinctive about human beings is that our brains mature largely outside the womb. The brain, therefore, is a social organ, hard- and soft-wired through early communication with those to whom we attach. This means that development of the brain entails specific, neurological, chemical and relational processes that depend on experience (Karr-Morse and Wiley 1997; Siegel 1999; Gerhardt 2005; Cozolino and Walker 2008; Cozolino 2009). The brain becomes organised in relation to its environment, and forms patterned ways of thinking and behaving about self and others. Human development, therefore, is a product of both nature and nurture.[4]

2 Much of the material in this section on attachment theory has been adapted from my introductory chapter to the edited volume, *Risking Human Security: Attachment and Public Life* (Green 2008).
3 Holmes (1993) provides a helpful survey of the emergence and key themes of attachment theory.
4 A key feature of establishing attachment for the infant, is a process called 'attunement', in which infants and caregiver interaction come to 'match inner states', through sounds, verbal and facial expressions and touch. One of the primary functions of attunement is that it helps form the capacity within the infant/child to regulate emotion. Failure to attune and securely attach may undermine the ability to regulate one's emotions and result in aggressive behaviour towards self and others.

Within the first year of life, infants establish a hierarchy of attachment figures—those who an infant recognises as a source of security, and to whom they turn to have their attachment needs met. These needs are perfectly ordinary. Primary among them are to be valued, kept safe, soothed, loved and held favourably in the mind of one's attachment figure. If these needs are met in appropriate ways, the infant can develop a trust in the 'thereness' of those on whom its survival depends. This is because the caregiver(s) has established for the infant, both a 'secure haven' (a place to return for comfort and safety when fearful) and a 'secure base' (the point of reference from which to explore the environment). Such infants—and the child and then adult they will become—are 'securely attached'; they are able to form close friendships in childhood and, as adults, are likely to manage intimate relationships flexibly and with reasonable confidence, and process the ordinary strains and stresses of living (Karen 1994: 443). Above all, they are able to be attachment figures for the next generation.

If, however, our attachment needs have not been met in appropriate ways (through inconsistent, chaotic or frightening care-giving; disruption of care; neglect or abuse; and unwanted separation and loss), a child's sense of self and her or his relational abilities may be damaged. In these cases, the child's attachment patterns are deemed to be 'insecure' or 'failed'. Among the consequences of insecure attachments are patterned ways of behaving such as a distrust of one's ability to survive and get one's needs met, self-harm, an inability to parent and give appropriate care, and violence towards others. Certainly, there are degrees of insecurity, and the ability to predict later behaviour on the basis of early attachment insecurities varies.[5] Then, too, we may later form relationships with others who provide us with comfort and love. These new attachments may afford some psychological protection against the effects of earlier attachment traumas. However, they are a poor substitute for the earliest, formative attachment figures. In this sense, not 'any' carer 'will do'.

One of the distinctive features of attachment theory is that attachments matter through life. Human beings are inherently social and we depend on others to meet our emotional needs 'from cradle to grave' (Bowlby 1998: 62). So, while the first few years of life are essential for the formation of the brain and personality, both the need for, and experience of, attachment, will influence our relational capacities throughout our lives. As we mature, the nature of our needs will ordinarily change, but our need for others will remain. Even securely attached adults seek proximity to others, especially in moments of distress. Proximity-seeking is what we mean by 'attachment behaviour'. It is mobilised as a healthy response to, say, unwanted

---

5 Some of the strongest correlations between childhood attachment experiences and behaviour patterns are identified in studies of 'disorganised' attachments. In the case of 'insecure-disorganised' attachment patterns, early experiences of chaotic, disorganised or frightening behaviour by the caregiver is a strong predictor of a disorganised developmental pathway and a predisposition to disruptive and aggressive behaviours (see Lyons-Ruth and Jacobvitz 1995).

separation and loss, and other threats to our emotional and physical well-being. Far from being 'childish', our need for others is a quality of our humanity.

Another distinctive feature of this approach is that it is relational. This means several things. First, while infants are born biologically predisposed to seek attachments, it is the *experience* of both intimate and wider social relationships that will shape our inclinations and ability to trust, to empathise, and to give and receive love. Second, while the need for attachment is universal, communities and societies will vary in the social arrangements by which these needs are met. Attachment research recognises that there can be more than one attachment figure within our network of affectional bonds; this said, in times of perceived danger, we will still seek out those particular figures in whom we can invest our safety. Third, attachment dynamics are generationally related, in the first instance through our patterns of parenting. Researchers have found that the attachment patterns that inform parenting behaviours largely match the attachment patterns that emerge in one's children.

Furthermore, the patterns may also be transmitted through culture. Culture, among other things, is the repository of norms, values and expectations on which we draw to represent and evaluate experiences, and guide our conduct. It informs, for example, our judgements about appropriate parenting (through, say, childrearing conventions) (Miller 1987). Culture is also a collection of sense-making solutions to the problems of living. Communities that have experienced prolonged assaults to their physical and psychological integrity might evolve new solutions that reshape the culture; theoretically, the collective experience of violence in one generation may furnish a culture of violence for the next.

In another important sense, attachment theory is relational. It recognises that, since human development depends on early relational experiences, the social environments in which these experiences accumulate must also be understood. Most attachment theory and research focuses on our first and, largely sensual, environment, which is created through intimate exchanges with the caregiver. (It is within this environment that some of the most profound losses can occur.) The infant brings to the exchange its raw attachment needs. Carers, of course bring more: their emotional capacity to respond to an infant's needs (which is shaped by their own early attachment experiences); their understanding of an infant's needs (influenced by childrearing conventions and their particular family culture); their access to resources such as time, food, clothing and shelter; and their ability to trust in the continuity of life's structures and meanings (Marris 1996, 2008). Thus, the carers' ability to be 'there' for an infant is a product partly of their psychological resources, and partly the wider socioeconomic, cultural and political environment in which care-giving is organised and delivered. Unfortunately, these wider systemic conditions are peripheral to the work of most attachment theorists and practitioners.[6] In this respect, the human security discourse can extend the purview of attachment theory by exposing the range of systemic threats which undermine our security.

6 There are notable exceptions (see, for example, de Zulueta 1993; Marris 1996, 2004; Purnell and Shubinsky 2008; Arnold 2008).

Claiming the common ground

As we comprehend the connections between self and society, agency and structure, we can expose the common ground on which attachment theory and human security reside. As neighbours, our relations are pretty congenial, but our concerns and understandings will be better served when we dismantle the boundary fence. This can be illustrated in four substantive themes that thread through both discourses: grounding security in lived experience (a 'micro' approach); conceptions of freedom; the structures of inequality; and the dynamics and cycles of violence.

Security in lived experience

A human security approach links nation with neighbourhood. In so doing, it embraces the view that national security and human security are part of a piece, however fractured that piece might be. Here lies a key challenge for human security because sustainable security depends on harmonising people's lived experiences, the particularity of their interests, and the systems that organise and govern how those interests are mobilised and expressed. Understanding the needs of people at risk invites a micro-perspective to which attachment theory can contribute. It is micro by nature, with its focus on those intimately lived relationships which first shape the brain and our emotional capacities and, thereafter, our public conduct. So, to nations and neighbourhoods we can add another domain—those neurological processes and patterns of the brain.

Freedom

The human security discourse is anchored in the recognition of human needs and wants. Meeting these needs is conditioned by our freedom from wants and fears, and our freedom to express our agency to secure the means for our material, social and psychological survival. This is a reading of security that is informed by the principles embodied in the conventions and protocols on human rights. Attachment theory moves beyond *recognition* by *understanding* our psychological needs more deeply: to be loved, valued, and kept physically and psychologically secure. To meet these needs we must be free from risks to our attachments and affectional bonds; and be free to trust in the 'thereness' of others. To the list of human rights, perhaps we should add the right to make and maintain secure attachments—however difficult in reality this may be to achieve.

Inequality

Luckham (2009) argues that the poor, the vulnerable and the dispossessed are predisposed to *in*security. They are the least able to mobilise resources and defend their interests when threatened. Human security researchers recognise that those who are systemically vulnerable are not a homogeneous group, as intra-community and familial relations of authority and power may also be unequal. For example, gender relations in communities and families, though structured through roles and norms, put women at risk—from domestic violence, sexual assault, and on assaults on their personal and public integrity. Attachment theory enhances our understanding of inequalities as a source of insecurity, by exposing the most unequal relation of all, that of infant to caregiver. Abuses by caregivers of their power over children can be largely concealed, and culturally condoned, so the child comes to suffer without witness. Given the potential links between private suffering and public violence, this recognition warrants an addition to a human security agenda—that we 'put children first'.

Violence

Threats of violence are both extraordinary and routine, and derive from many sources. Conflicts over material and social resources, power, religious beliefs, political ideologies and communal identities may erupt in violent form. The expression, management and resolution of violent conflict have preoccupied human security writers in illuminating the dynamics of violence and devising community interventions in conflict settings.

Conflict, of course entails unwanted separation and loss. So, too, do ecological disasters, disease, poverty, dispossession, migration and human trafficking. These losses accumulate as our loved ones and friends are killed or dispersed, our homes levelled, our livelihoods destroyed, our social networks dismantled, our places occupied, our identities dissolved and our hope diminished as we struggle to stay alive. Much humanitarian aid work, for example, is devoted to rebuilding those material infrastructures which communities need to survive. Pipelines, water wells, canvas, corrugated iron, bricks and mortar are very much the hard substance of reconstruction. For attachment theorists, however, we must also be mindful of the soft fabrics and rhythms of bereavement and grief. They are no less essential for recovery and repair.

As a sociologist working with attachment insights, Peter Marris has long explored the nature and impact of unwanted separation and loss of our attachment figures (Marris 1974, 1996, 2004, 2008). Underpinning his work is a belief that the self always searches for meaning, and when the continuity of meaning is disrupted or destroyed, our psychological integrity may dissolve. He writes,

> The loss of a crucial attachment is not simply the loss of a relationship, but the loss of all the assumptions and everyday habits that depended on it. This is especially true when the loss is untimely and unforeseen. 'The bottom fell out of my world,' as one young widow once told me. The whole structure of meaning that sustained her life had fallen apart (Marris 2008: 21).

In much of his writing, Marris focuses on the strains to attachments that arise from environmental disaster and economic change.

> It is hard to give a child love and attention when you are constantly anxious about the basic necessities food, water, medicines, and shelter. The search for employment divides families and draws them away from home. Parents no longer represent reliable models of social competence and self-respect (Marris 2008: 30).

These strains have consequences. Among them, Marris argues, is the search for meaning in new places.

> The young people, alienated by their parents' demoralisation and preoccupation with trying to make ends meet, will begin to look for a sense of meaning and self validation in peer groups that reject the humiliations and defeats their parents have endured. They may look for status in gangs, and power through violence and the illegal economy . . . This alienated generation is also attracted towards ideologies that offer an escape from the bewildering uncertainties and powerlessness of their circumstances (Marris 2008: 30-31).

Thus, parents who are unable to provide a secure haven and secure base are likely to compromise the attachment security of their children. In struggling to manage their loss, and the meanings those attachments sustain, those children who feel consistently powerless might become adults who seek power over others. The insecure of one generation might create the threats to security for the next (Miller 1990).

From aspiration to intervention?

Many of the ideas of attachment theory are intuitive; its contours are familiar and keenly felt. We do not need to be schooled in attachment principles to know that attachments matter, but the theory can help us understand *why*. How, then, might we use this knowledge?

Psychotherapy is one process which offers individuals the chance to comprehend their attachment history and develop a sense of self with which they can comfortably live. Through this intimate, usually one-to-one mode of engagement, the client and therapist work together to build a secure base from which the client can come to know, and change, her or his painful self-understandings and patterns of relating with others.

Attachment-informed professionals also work with families, communities and organisations: for example, they help carers develop their parenting skills; support teachers hoping to understand their pupils struggling to learn; provide therapeutic and social support for people displaced by violent conflict or economic migration;

and inform policy-makers of the attachment issues entailed in the sense of loss that often accompanies the experiences of change (Marris 1974; Woodward 2008).

Of course, these attachment-based therapies and interventions occur in largely stable environments: a clinician's study, a community centre or an office. But, what is their value when *in*stability prevails, when studies, corners and desks have been demolished and losses have accumulated? I believe that their value is undiminished since we need witness to our suffering, in whatever conditions and whatever the source. That said, it is important to recognise that the scale and magnitude of collective suffering has situation-specific qualities which demand a range of imaginative responses, however overwhelming that task can be. So much thinking about human security is aspirational, a characteristic that is both understandable and frustrating. Is it possible, then, to apply the insights of attachment theory and therapy in ways that translate aspirations into interventions? At this stage, we are just beginning.

In her analysis of communities in conflict, Leaning adopts a human security model which highlights three attachment components: to home, to community and to a belief in the future (Leaning and Arie 2001; Leaning 2008). Each component is a potential juncture at which physical and psychological security may be breached, and over which both the *fear* and *impact* of loss can encourage and sustain violence. Drawing on numerous examples since the Second World War, Leaning identifies the ways in which these three components are threatened in pre-conflict, conflict and post-conflict settings. Critical of the ways that governments and international agencies, in their assessments of war and its effects, have routinely ignored their importance, she argues that at each phase, opportunities must be sought 'to enhance attachments and mitigate the loss' (Leaning 2008: 147).

Writing about the risks to security from economic development strategies, Marris claims that a common tendency in development programmes is to focus on the provisions of material resources as a route out of want. These resources are treated as so many interchangeable and replaceable units of consumption. While they are essential to life, they are qualitatively different from the resources that social networks provide; it is through these networks that the *particularity* of attachments and affectional bonds are developed and sustained. To ignore the difference between the two kinds of resource and privilege purely market-models in development programmes is to risk psycho-social instability. Working with and through these relational bonds by, say, small-scale cooperatives, micro-lending arrangements and new technologies adapted to the conditions and needs of local populations, lessens those risks (Marris 2004: 81-83).

The most productive resources for communities in crisis are the people themselves. Of course, communities are not inherently benign. Neither do they necessarily accord attachments the value they require. In these cases, all the more reason to create the social and psychological spaces in which attachments can emerge and be sustained over long periods of time (Marris 2004: 77-78). After all, the energy required to rebuild homes, schools and hospitals turns so much on whether people are affectionally connected and feel hopeful enough to believe that the effort is worthwhile. Marris cites examples of the aftermath of a mining disaster in Aberfan, Wales, and the Tsunami in coastal villages of Sri Lanka, making the case that their post-disaster recovery was substantially enhanced by the local populations' ability to direct their own recovery and collectively grieve the losses they have sustained—processes that aided recovery despite, not because of, the policies and practices of agencies called in to assist (Marris 2008: 25-27).

Whatever the source of conflict in groups and communities, the exercise of individual and collective agency in managing unwanted separation and loss turns ultimately on our sense of self and relational abilities. Attachment theory argues that these emerge in the first years of life—in the intimate exchanges between infant and caregiver, whatever the setting—in a house on a quiet street in an orderly neighbourhood or in a makeshift tent in a refugee camp. The need to make attachments is a universal principle of human emotional development, but the *quality* of our attachment *experiences* will shape the direction that development will take. An attachment-sensitive human security agenda that understands the importance of love and the experience of unwanted separation and loss, both 'in the beginning' for the child, and then throughout life, is one that anchors our collective security in the conditions that make us human.

Bibliography

Arnold, E. (2008) 'Unsettling Policies: Unanticipated Consequences for Migrant Afro-Caribbean Families', in M. Green (ed.), *Risking Human Security: Attachment and Public Life* (London: Karnac): 53-70.

Bowlby, J. (1998) *A Secure Base: Clinical Applications of Attachment Theory* (London/New York: Routledge).

Cozolino, L.J. (2009) *The Neuroscience of Human Relationships: Attachment and the Developing Social Brain* (New York: W.W. Norton).

—— and M. Walker (2008) 'The Social Construction of the Human Brain', in M. Green (ed.), *Risking Human Security: Attachment and Public Life* (London: Karnac): 3-18.

De Zulueta, F. (1993) *From Pain to Violence: The Roots of Human Destructiveness* (London: Whurr).

—— (2004) 'Human Violence is a Preventable Disease', in M. Green (ed.), *Attachment and Human Security* (London: Karnac): 99-118.

Gerhardt, S. (2005) *Why Love Matters* (London/New York: Routledge).

Green, M. (2008) *Risking Human Security: Attachment and Public Life* (London: Karnac).

—— and M. Scholes (2004*) Attachment and Human Survival* (London: Karnac).

Holmes, J. (1993) *John Bowlby & Attachment Theory* (London/New York: Routledge).

Karen, R. (1994) *Becoming Attached* (New York: Warner).

Karr-Morse, K., and M. Wiley (1997) *Ghosts from the Nursery: Tracing the Roots of Violence* (New York: Atlantic Monthly Press).

Layder, D. (1997) *Modern Social Theory* (London: UCL Press)

Leaning, J. (2008) 'Human Security and Conflict', in M. Green (ed.), *Risking Human Security: Attachment and Public Life* (Karnac: London): 125-49.

—— and S. Arie (2001) *Human Security: A Framework for Assessment in Conflict and Transition* (Working Paper Series 11.8; Cambridge, MA: Harvard Center for Population and Development Studies).

Luckham, R. (2009) 'Introduction: Transforming Security and Development in an Unequal World', *IDS Bulletin* 40.2 (March 2009): 1-10.

Lyons-Ruth, K., and D. Jacobvitz (1995) 'Attachment Disorganization: Unresolved Loss, Relational Violence, and Lapses in Behavioural and Attentional Strategies', in J. Cassidy and P.R. Shaver (eds.), *Handbook of Attachment: Theory, Research, and Clinical Applications* (New York: Guilford Press): 520-54.

Marris, P. (1974) *Loss and Change* (London: Routledge).

—— (1996) *The Politics of Uncertainty: Attachment in Private and Public Life* (London/New York: Routledge).

—— (2004) 'Attachment and Social Policy', in M. Green and M. Scholes (eds.), *Attachment and Human Survival* (London: Karnac): 71-83.

—— (2008) 'Attachment and Loss of Community', in M. Green (ed.), *Risking Human Security: Attachment and Public Life* (London: Karnac): 20-33.

Miller, A. (1984) *Thou Shalt Not Be Aware: Society's Betrayal of the Child* (New York: Meridian/New American Library).

—— (1987) *For Your Own Good: Hidden Cruelty in Child-Rearing and the Roots of Violence* (London: Virago).

—— (1990) *The Untouched Key: Tracing Childhood Trauma in Creative and Destructiveness* (London: Virago).

Purnell, C., and K. Shubinsky (2008) 'Seeking Asylum: The Struggle for a New Secure Base', in M. Green (ed.), *Risking Human Security: Attachment and Human Survival* (London: Karnac): 71-86.

Schore, A.N. (1994) *Affect Regulation and the Origin of the Self: The Neurobiology of Emotional Development* (Hillsdale, NJ: Erlbaum).

Siegel, D.J. (1999) *The Developing Mind: How Relationships and the Brain Interact to Shape Who We Are* (New York: Guilford).

Woodward, J. (2008) 'Enabling Change', in M. Green (ed.), *Risking Human Security: Attachment and Public Life* (London: Karnac): 151-70.

12

From security barriers to reconciliation?
Co-existence as a prerequisite of human security

Sarah Green and Alan Hunter

Centre for Peace and Reconciliation Studies, Coventry University, UK

> Your neighbour is your other self dwelling behind a wall. In understanding all walls shall fall down (Kahlil Gibran 1883–1931).

Walls became iconic in 20th-century history: the Warsaw ghetto; the Berlin Wall; Nicosia; the Palestinian territory. Security architecture is the physical embodiment of fear, threat and conflict, but also of protection. Walls, indeed many forms of barriers, may sometimes be a necessity and they may save lives, but we suggest there is also a need to look for other ways of managing threats of violence, questioning the legitimacy of safety construction as a response to sectarian violence and as a means of dealing with conflict. Interface barriers may provide physical safety while, at the same time, they increase the divide between 'us' and 'them', both physically and mentally. Our paper examines this duality, specifically in the context of what have become known as 'interface areas', parts of Belfast where hostile communities live geographically very close to each other. We also discuss how a government policy paper approaches these issues, and end with some conclusions.

Underlying the discussion is the question of coexistence, and its place in an overall concept of human security. It is a core tenet of human security that peace is a prerequisite for a free and productive life; that is, citizens must enjoy freedom from the fear of violence. There is a well-worn analysis in peace studies that the term peace can refer simply to an absence of violence ('negative peace') or it can refer to a more ambitious project of peace with social justice, prosperity and other public goods. Following the South Africa transition, there has also been much study of 'reconciliation' between former warring factions, as another prerequisite for any kind of peace and hence human security. However, developments in many countries have shown that it is probably more realistic to attain some form of coexistence rather than the more ambitious, 'positive' goal of reconciliation. Thus a spread of terms has evolved to analyse different levels of relationship between communities, especially in protracted social conflicts and 'post-conflict' environments. At one end of the spectrum is the ceasefire, or temporary cessation of organised direct military action. Later, a society may move to some degree of civic life, with a political framework, even if communities barely meet: there is a tacit or explicit agreement to live in the same territory without, for the most part, engaging in armed attacks. This can lead to a variety of situations termed 'coexistence'. At the other pole, some societies, probably after several generations have passed, might reach a state of reconciliation where, for the most part, historical grievances are defused, forgotten if not forgiven, and communities interact on something like an equal footing. This paper focuses on a situation that lies somewhere in the complex middle ground of this range.

The Good Friday Agreement/Belfast Agreement (GFA/BA) was signed on 10 April 1998, after several hundred years of intermittent conflicts, and some three decades of 'the Troubles' modern incarnation in the late 1960s, intensified by Bloody Sunday in 1972. The GFA/BA was signed by the UK and Irish governments; endorsed by the majority of political parties and paramilitary groups; and approved in a referendum held in Northern Ireland. Among many complex provisions regarding power-sharing, release of prisoners and other matters, all parties committed to use 'exclusively peaceful and democratic means' thereafter. However, the terms of the GFA/BA were still not fully implemented in 2009, 11 years after the signing (Northern Ireland Office 2009). In March 2009, the group known as the Real IRA (RIRA), a splinter faction of the Irish Republican Army (IRA), claimed responsibility for the murder of two young British soldiers, Patrick Azimkar and Mark Quinsey.

The Orange parades, mainly held in July and August, are an annual reminder of past conflicts, and a potential for violence. Since 2000, many of these events have been conducted in a relatively peaceful manner, but the celebrations in 2009 were marred by violence. In the Ardoyne area of north Belfast, police came under fire from at least one gunman. Alistair Finlay, Assistant Chief Constable, later stated that there were people in the crowd with 'murderous intent', individuals impetuously determined to cause trouble for the Protestant community and the Police Service of Northern Ireland (PSNI) (McAleese 2009: 2). Pictures from this recent outbreak of violence show the PSNI dressed in riot gear as they were attacked by petrol bombs, fireworks, bricks and stones. Images from 2009 resembled a scene from 'the Troubles' rather than 'post-conflict' Belfast. Psychological and political barriers separated the two communities: the burden of history remained as the two sides, including politicians, had not yet found a way to deal with the past, sectarianism, issues of law and order, justice and victimhood (Powell 2008).

The psychological and political barriers persisted as well as purpose-built physical walls (Liechty and Clegg 2001). Instead of being demolished, the construction of barriers and other security architecture continued as we see in this chapter: living amid such realities, people in Belfast have largely developed an 'avoidance syndrome' when thinking about the physical and mental separation between the two communities. Reconciliation and harmonious civic relationships seem a far distant prospect. Is coexistence a more reasonable goal?

In definition, 'coexistence' means to exist together, in time or place, in mutual tolerance (*Oxford English Dictionary*, 11th edn); to learn to recognise and live with difference (Rupesinghe 1999); to have a relationship between persons or groups without trying to destroy the other (Kriesberg 2000); and to interact with a commitment to tolerance, mutual respect and the agreement to settle conflict non-violently (Brandeis University 2006). It relates to a state in which two or more groups are living together while respecting each other's differences and resolving their conflicts non-violently (Weiner 2000). At the heart of coexistence lies the awareness of and, possibly grudging, tolerance of difference. This awareness can relate to an individual or group's religion, ethnicity and political affiliation. Such identities may be the cause of conflicts, contribute to the causes of conflict, or become hardened as conflicts develop. Coexistence, however, reduces the probability that identity group divergences will escalate into a destructive or intractable conflict (Brandeis University 2006).

Coexistence can exist before and after violent conflict (Kriesberg 2000). Coexistence is dynamic rather than static, and has a tendency to fluctuate depending on the level of social interaction. One can theorise two categories of coexistence, active and passive. Active coexistence can be defined as a state in which diversity and difference are actively accepted by individuals and groups; whereas passive coexistence is a state which simply involves the toleration of other individuals and groups to the extent that groups can live together without killing each other (Afzali and Colleton 2003). The value of coexistence can therefore be thought of in terms of bringing communities away from violence towards some level of social cohesion, whether that is active acceptance or constrained tolerance.

In the wake of violent protracted conflicts, the core principles of coexistence may generate the need for change. Much scholarly writing on coexistence focuses on its basic tenets: the recognition of difference, non-violence and the worth of the 'other'. For instance, there is a need to address past wrongs, a need for justice and forgiveness, a need to build/re-build communities and fundamentally the need for an equitable community structure and system (Cohen 2001). Strategies for implementing such work encompass conflict management, post-conflict reconstruction and conflict resolution. In sum, the concept of coexistence functions as a framing mechanism, an umbrella term for which other types of peace work can be discussed (Cohen 2001). In theory, the inclusivity of the coexistence framework and approach means that cross-sectoral and multi-level efforts are adopted in order to prevent, reduce and eliminate violence by moving away from conflict to passive coexistence, then to active coexistence, to the deepening of peace and to the creation of sustainable peace. That is the theory. As a result, it is perhaps difficult even to talk about active coexistence in Belfast when events of 2009 caused so much strife and despair.

Barriers of safety and separation

Good fences make good neighbours (Robert Frost 1914).

Following renewed outbreaks of 'the Troubles' in 1968, the British Army entered Northern Ireland in 1969. As part of their mission was supposed to be the protection of Catholic communities, they constructed an emergency short-term response to separate the Protestant Shankill Road community and the Catholic Falls Road community. It was probably the first in Northern Ireland since the 1930s. This 'temporary' barrier was initially a reel of barbed wire but, after a short period of time, separation became a widely accepted and long-term reality for both communities (Jarman 2008). Following this initial construction, interface barriers were erected all over Belfast, soon escalating to metal fencing and steel sheeting (Jarman 2008). As the years have passed, the citizens of Belfast have become accustomed to more elaborate separation structures, many of which are six-foot-high brick walls with steel fencing placed on top. One can often find intricate designs incorporated into the brick or a row of trees to shield the starkness of the wall. The permanent nature of such barriers has become the norm. Even some newly developed, 'post-conflict' housing estates resemble wartime compounds, surrounded by 18-foot-high brick separation barriers.

In Belfast's city centre, with its boutiques, shiny department stores and wine bars, all separation barriers have been demolished (Jarman 2008). In contrast, not a single barrier has been removed from Belfast's interface residential areas. The reasons for the construction of the barriers still remain the same: to separate interface areas, the places where Catholic and Protestant communities intersect. The Northern Ireland Office (NIO), in liaison with the PSNI, officially authorise the construction of the barriers as a response to various sectarian security problems that range from the throwing of stones, to petrol bombs and missile attacks (Jarman 2007).

Many other barriers are, however, constructed in a rather secretive way. The avoidance of acknowledging the diversity of the barriers suggests that there is official approval of the continuing requirement for security barriers as part and parcel of Belfast's landscape and environment (Jarman 2008: 27). Many of the 'unofficial' or 'non-NIO' barriers are built as part of regeneration projects. As a result, architects have to consider and incorporate the territorial boundaries during the design and execution of each development. As such, in recent years, regeneration projects have secretively facilitated and increased the levels of separation and division (Jarman 2008). These designs, which have been approved by the NIO and the Northern

Ireland Housing Executive, are not categorised or recognised as an official interface barrier. Consequently, it is difficult to calculate the precise number and extent of interface barriers around Belfast: first, owing to the inadequate framework used to classify and determine what constitutes an interface barrier; and second, because of interpretation and uncertainty concerning where one barrier stops and another starts.

Interface barriers are now synonymous with Belfast, increasingly becoming a hot spot for conflict tourists and a heaven for community artwork. During Easter 2009, the infamous wall that separates the Falls district from the Shankill district was painted for the first time. Previously, the 12–14-foot-high wall with metal sheets and fencing was covered in names and messages as well as being peppered with marks from assault rifle rounds, Magnum rounds and scorch marks. The vision of this project was to bring talented individuals together, regardless of creed or ethnic difference, to paint messages of peace and acceptance. The project displays a colourful array of design and creativity; a stark contrast to the mostly aggressive nature of the murals that can be found only a few streets away.

Interface communities in Belfast

So, what are interface communities in modern Belfast? Jarman cites the following definition: 'the intersection of segregated and polarised working class residential zones in areas with a strong link between territory and ethno-political identity' (Jarman 2005: 9). Some research suggests that these communities have become even more geographically defined recently than in the 1960s and the use of barriers to avoid hostility with the 'other' has had little success. A PSNI report from one community states that inter-communal violence has continued even after the barrier was put in place.[1] Although some interface communities have experienced improvements due to relatively minimal levels of tension and hostility, other communities have suffered an increase in disorder and violence. The periodic nature of improvement and decline relates to issues of political unrest, marching during parades, rioting, protests and issues surrounding policing. On top of this, low to high level sectarian violence has become a permanent part of daily life that is both anticipated and expected. The cycle of violence and segregation is supported by high levels of poverty, low levels of educational achievement and constant feelings of fear and besiegement.

Still, the diversity and complexity of interface areas is ever-changing. Jarman's description cited above might now be considered rather limited. Interface communities are a result of continual conflict in Belfast. 'Interface areas are not a static phenomenon, nor a purely historical legacy of "the Troubles". Rather they are a dynamic part of the social fabric of a community that is highly polarised and

1 www.psni.police.uk (accessed 7 July 2010).

extensively segregated' (Jarman 2005: 18). This is because, throughout Belfast, an increasing number of new interfaces have appeared that do not correlate with the stereotypical model. For instance, unrest and sectarian violence has taken place in the intersection of middle-class residential areas; public or social spaces and town centres and shopping precincts. The presentation of the same distinctive characteristics (segregation and sectarian violence) as the aforementioned stereotypical, segregated, working-class, residential interface areas, means that Belfast harbours deeper levels of separation than one initially notices. Jarman (2005: 10) argues therefore that a broader understanding of interfaces is needed, which relates to the sectioning of two or more spaces which are controlled, challenged or declared by members of different ethno-national groups. And, at the centre of a new or not so new interface, is the fear, threat or actuality of violence that successfully replaces any remnants of peace.

The battles for territory reflect the centuries-old 'normality' that survival depends on the rejection of the 'other', an action that is intensified by feelings of fear and mistrust that, no matter how deeply hidden, are passed down through family generations. It is the generational continuity of rejection, and the emergence of new interfaces, that still make territorial definitions so significant in the city. To the outside eye, this definition is most visible in the underdeveloped working-class communities that express detachment from the rest of contemporary Belfast, though separateness is a fact in many other city environments. Altogether, it is extremely easy for individuals to become increasingly cynical and fearful about the 'other'.

The fragmentation of Belfast's societal structure means that it is extremely difficult for the younger generation at the interface to attain a life with better prospects. As a result, the sense of belonging and security within the group dynamic is tremendously strong, making it difficult for young adults to move beyond their familiar comfort zone. These young individuals can be overwhelmed with the feeling that the rest of European society is moving forward while they are being left behind. In 2009, fencing surrounding a new housing development on Falls Road was scrawled with questions such as: 'why are we forgotten?' and 'why them and not us?' It is hardly surprising therefore that frustration, anger and anxiety turn into everyday emotions for many individuals in these communities. Resentment and disappointment mean that individuals are always looking for someone to blame. The majority of young Catholics and Protestants living in interface communities feel that their role is to protect their community from an invasion that would result in the challenging of their cultural identity. This can unfortunately leave young adults open to negative manipulation by others. In summer 2009, it was reported that children were sent text messages to urge them to join the riots. The violence that continued for three nights saw a total of 200 youths take part, including children as young as ten years old. It is reported that these young individuals felt threatened by the police presence and tried to violently force the PSNI out of their community (Ellison 2009).

In sum, 'interfaces are where fears turn into bricks and mortar' (Morrow 2008: 3). And the normality of building a barrier instead of tackling deep-rooted fears means that the never-ending cycle of sectarian attacks and consequent separation barriers supports the feelings of fear and mistrust of the 'other' that caused the problem in the first place.

It could be said that interface communities are in the most minimum state of coexistence, as the number of sectarian and reprisal killings has dramatically decreased in the past few years. This is already a great improvement, but it does not allow one to conclude that interface communities are coexisting in a positive way. Probably only a select few interface communities actively coexist, where acceptance of difference and respect for diversity are actively embraced. Several interface communities are sometimes in a state of passive coexistence, because of the fairly consistent absence of violence. However, rarely do these communities move beyond passive coexistence to a state of active coexistence. In contrast, some interface communities have not even reached the stage of passive coexistence because of the continual presence of violence.

At a given time, the communities categorised as 'passively coexisting' do have the ability to tolerate what they see as the 'other'. However, this tolerance can all change rather quickly. It appears, therefore, that this dramatic and sometimes impromptu shift is often the fault of a small percentage of individuals. As a consequence, the change in levels of toleration leads to not only inter-community but also intra-community tensions. Whether or not this low level of toleration is due to the presence of interface barriers is an extremely significant question: for the sake of passive coexistence, should the barriers remain, or do the barriers prohibit passively coexisting communities to move forwards to a state of active coexistence?

Safety and separation: two cases

In order to aid this present discussion, it is appropriate to cite an example of the ways in which interface barriers are put in place. In the summer of 2006, a house situated on the Catholic Old Throne Park Road in the north of Belfast was attacked with a petrol bomb and set alight. The loyalist youths who were responsible for this attack accessed the Catholic estate through the open grounds of Hazelwood Primary School, an integrated school which is positioned between the Protestant White City estate and the Catholic Old Throne estate. As a result, in May 2007, plans were put forward to build a 25-foot-high barrier that would run straight through the school grounds in order to separate the two estates. The plan, decided and announced by the NIO, came a few weeks after Peter Hain, then Secretary of State, insisted that the government was committed to beginning the process of removing barriers that were seen to be dividing communities in Belfast. It was in the context of this statement that the formation of the new devolved government symbolised an era of power-sharing.

The plans, which were announced some nine months after the attack, divided residents and parents who were previously coexisting in a peaceful manner. Many thought that the 25-foot-high barrier was not really necessary as the incident was an isolated attack basically due to antisocial behaviour. They hoped that other walls in the area could, in the not so distant future, be removed. All in all, the general consensus reflected that recreational violence by youths was the problem, and the barrier, as a means of providing safety, did not tackle this problem. Many members of both Catholic and Protestant communities felt that there was a real need to try other means of tackling and challenging such behaviour rather than the placement of a wall. Unfortunately, however, this view was entirely overlooked as the construction went ahead in 2007.

In this instance, members of the community felt safe and did not feel that the barrier was truly needed. The barrier was the result of an automatic response on the part of the NIO who did not appear to conduct an individual assessment of the attack. As such, neither members of the community nor the headteacher of the primary school were consulted about what they thought would be appropriate action. What is even more disturbing is the fact that this integrated school, the only one in the north of Belfast, for many, symbolised the future direction of education in an attempt to build a shared future for society. In addition, this particular interface community could be classified as a unique example of a community actively coexisting, a claim which is supported by an interview published in *The Guardian*, which, after interviewing two parents about the construction of the wall, reported that parents from both communities shop and socialise together on a regular basis (Oliver 2007). The reality of the matter is that the wall and separation could threaten this cohesion.

It makes one wonder at the motives behind the NIO's decision to authorise the construction of this particular barrier. On the one hand, the automatic response and perhaps zero tolerance means that an attack such as this, which could have been a lot more serious than it actually was, justifies the wall as safety and security against future attacks. On the other hand, the isolation of the attack, lack of evidence of an ongoing threat and the views of the community do not appear to have been remotely considered. Ultimately, it constitutes the reality that building a barrier is considered to be an appropriate, normal and routine reaction to a sectarian attack. And while the barrier may or may not provide safety and security, at the same time, it starkly reinforces the divisions that this particular community were successfully moving away from.

As another example, the iconic barrier between the Falls and Shankill estates was the first blockade to be put in place by the British Army in 1969: it is now celebrating 40 years. Although levels of violence are vastly lower than during 'the Troubles', it seems that residents still feel that great protective caging is necessary. A survey commissioned by the US-Ireland Alliance in January 2008 gauged the opinions of residents within this community. The overall intent was to ask residents living in interface areas for their views on the barriers. The survey questioned a total of 1,037 residents of the Falls and Shankill, Antrim Road and Tigers Bay, and Short Strand and Templemore Avenue interfaces. It concluded that there was a 'strong agreement that the walls serve to help residents feel safer by keeping the communities separated' (US-Ireland Alliance 2008).

In the same study, residents were asked if they felt that it would be a good idea to remove the walls. Curiously, 81% of the residents were in favour. This statistic can then be broken down to reflect that 21% said that the walls could be taken down now, whereas 60% said that the walls could be taken down, but not straight away, only when the situation is safe enough (US-Ireland Alliance 2008). The findings suggest therefore that many residents feel that the separation of the two communities is a positive, safe and practical aspect of an interface barrier, with the overall majority suggesting that at the present time it is not safe enough to begin the removal of the barriers.

It seems then that many interface communities have become extremely attached to their barrier of safety and protection. It is, however, questionable what impact the construction of barriers, aimed to reduce violence and increase feelings of safety and security, actually has, beyond creating a bold and symbolic statement of the unwanted 'other'. This is especially the case as the PSNI questions the legitimacy and effect of barriers, stating that inter-communal violence often continues even after the barrier has been put in place.[2] Not only this, but the presence of a barrier also becomes a target for violence as individuals can physically hide behind the wall to throw stones or missiles, where they would not necessarily have the courage or confidence to do so if they came face to face with their 'enemy'. Barriers can therefore provide a negative sense of safety, a psychological barrier, as they symbolise the unknown and hostile nature of the 'other', while, at the same time, encouraging individuals to be aggressive.

The presence of interface barriers creates a physical barrier of separation between two communities. And separation is endemic within Belfast's society. There is, therefore, an urgent call to officially begin a process of engaging with interface communities, and it is through this sensitive dialogue that those who are the most affected can decide when and how the barriers can finally begin to be removed. As this research has suggested, one major problem is the official acceptance and construction of barriers. In part, there is a need for the NIO to develop a long-term strategy that focuses on tackling sectarian and antisocial behaviour, the very problems that persuade officials to order the construction of the barriers in the first place. This strategy ought to aim to restrict further barriers as a means of dealing with sectarian violence and provide an accessible framework for the removal of existing barriers.

There will, however, be various conditions that need to be met in order for an effective process of removal to begin. Aspects of safety ought to be at the centre of this discussion in order to encourage members of each community to feel confident. The following suggestions reflect the need for confidence and safety at the interface: a continued period of political solidarity; a sustained period of a considerable decrease in sectarian violence at the interface; necessary contact and dia-

2 www.psni.police.uk (accessed 7 July 2010).

logue between Protestant and Catholic community leaders; an increased level of confidence in the PSNI; continuous cross-community work; more effort involving the regeneration of interface areas; and an increase in community work with young people at the interface in order to tackle antisocial behaviour. Even though these are only suggestive measures, it is only through this level of involvement that interface residents will begin to feel that the outcome of the process will be a long-term improvement in safety, quality of life and, during this process, will aid coexistence.

The removal of interface barriers would symbolise a step forward towards a shared future. It would be a sign of a transformative effort to enable Belfast to become an integrated and pluralist entity, where communities are actively coexisting and celebrating individuality and diversity. As a point of departure, it is necessary to accept that the barrier, as a means to provide separation, could enable communities to passively coexist, because the physical structure aids the toleration of the 'other'. It is also necessary to accept that the presence of a wall makes it difficult for many interface communities, who are in a state of passive coexistence, to move beyond to active coexistence. In Belfast, the wounds of sectarianism are slow to heal; overall, an interface barrier, as an obstacle to positive coexistence, does not allow healing to begin.

Government policies: A Shared Future

In 2005, *A Shared Future* (ASF) was published by the Office of the First Minister and Deputy First Minister (OFMDFM) with a Foreword by the Secretary of State for Northern Ireland, with the intention of establishing 'over time, a shared society defined by a culture of tolerance: a normal civic society in which all individuals are considered as equals' (OFMDFM 2005: 1.2.1). There were significant policy aims which included: 'to reduce tension and conflict at interface areas' (OFMDFM 2005: 1.2.2). ASF was a breakthrough in that the government recognised the importance of its decisions and agendas towards creating a shared future. As such, ASF identifies various concerns about life at the interface in connection to broader society as well as acknowledging the dynamics of intra- and inter-community conflict. It states that, 'conflict at interface areas is the tragic symptom of a systemic lack of trust rather than the sole cause or evidence of it' (OFMDFM 2005: 1.4.1). It continues to say that 'building trust involves everyone, including political and civic leadership and institutions of government. It should not be expected to emanate from violent interfaces alone' (OFMDFM 2005: 1.4.1). As with any approach or effort that seeks to achieve social cohesion, ASF is challenging. This is because it promotes integration throughout all sectors of Northern Irish society. As this is its major aim, ASF recognises that, in order to achieve this target, more community relations and peace work needs to be done at the interface because of the severity of segregation, fear and mistrust. As a result,

> reducing tensions at interface areas must go beyond the 'band-aid'
> approach. It requires a combined short, medium and long-term approach
> that is earthed in encouraging local dialogue and communication, the
> sharing of resources, which is set in a wider context of social and eco-
> nomic renewal (OFMDFM 2005: 2.3).

ASF reflects that conflict prevention, management and transformation are necessary and there is a need for agencies to work together at the interface, providing a
holistic approach to issues of violence and segregation. Otherwise, it is understood
that major responsibilities will lie with those who live at the interface. The need
for a holistic approach with wider statutory and government support is voiced in
another document, approved by both Belfast City Council and ASF, which sets out
detailed suggestions about the function of statutory agencies and the requirement
of policies that can directly help interface communities:

> We need a commitment at the heart of Government to address the regen-
> eration of interface communities both strategically and comprehensively.
> This means placing interfaces in the Programme for Government as this
> connects so many themes of Government planning including tackling
> disadvantage, making people healthier and promoting comunity safety,
> education, skills-development and employment (BIP 2004: 24).

ASF recognises this suggestion and acknowledges that there is a need for 'the development of a coherent long-term strategy to address the needs of interface areas and
communities both through government plans and priorities and through strategies
developed by local bodies, such as Belfast City Council' (OFMDFM 2005: 2.3.4).

At the interface, it can be recognised that there is a need to move beyond conflict
management to conflict transformation. ASF therefore commits to the following:
'supporting communities in these areas to transform conflict remains an important priority for Government' (OFMDFM 2005: 2.3.3). It also agrees that 'a more
coherent longer-term approach is needed to tackle the problems of interface areas
(and those areas at risk of becoming flash points)' (OFMDFM 2005: 2.3.5). 'This is
best taken forward as part of a more integrated local planning framework, led by
local councils in collaboration with key agencies and other stakeholders' (OFM-
DFM 2005: 2.3.6) and

> the triennial action plan will provide detail of such an integrated plan-
> ning framework: it will look at a range of interventions to address strategi-
> cally the issues at interface areas, including specific action in other areas,
> including those in rural communities, potentially at risk of becoming
> 'interfaces' (OFMDFM 2005: 2.3.7).

The extracts do reveal extremely positive and transformative strategies for interface communities in Belfast. However, four years have passed since ASF and its
strategies were announced, yet the findings of our research suggest that the level
of violence and segregation at Belfast's interface communities has hardly changed.
Why is this so? For the sake of coexistence at the interface, it is now crucial to implement the ASF proposals with the intention of tackling pressing interface issues. One

of the major areas is the need to address the constant drawbacks and difficulties faced by these communities. Throughout this research it has appeared that cycles of violence relate closely to poverty, restricted prospects and facilities, as well as sectarianism and its ramifications. As a result, there is a need to develop policies with a detailed understanding of interface concerns to address the direct effects and disadvantages of violent conflict; the limited facilities for communities at the interface; and the problems exacerbated during social and economic downturns.

The recurring theme of sectarian violence closely connected to antisocial behaviour by young people at the interface needs to be resolved. There appears to be a culture of violence throughout Belfast. As a means of stopping this cycle, more progression routes are needed for young adults that are both the problem and the solution to coexistence at the interface. The solutions to tackle these issues ought to be flexible, innovative and ever-changing. More support for interface and youth workers is needed from the Department of Education's Youth Service, who, in actual fact, ought to be providing a leading role for change at the interface.

For interface communities who live in the aftermath of protracted violent conflict, where sectarian attacks and violence are still everyday occurrences, it is difficult to visualise what peace would be like. For this reason there is a need to create a vision for interface areas. This ought to be a long-term plan that focuses on the regeneration and development of their physical environment. Every year millions of pounds are spent on the development of Belfast's city centre, to include new hotels, multi-storey car parks and rows upon rows of outrageously large shopping precincts. Members of interface communities feel marginalised, which intensifies an overwhelming sense of despair. Short-, medium- and long-term investments outside the city centre would therefore increase morale and trust (in the government and other bodies) at the interface.

Conclusions

> Strength and wisdom are not opposite values (Bill Clinton addressing members of Catholic and Protestant communities in Belfast, 1995).

Interface barriers are still seen, by numerous parties, to be necessary peacekeepers. But, the barriers that cause separation do not allow Protestant and Catholic communities to interact and are a threat to positive coexistence at the interface. Having applied the theoretical concept of coexistence to Belfast's interface communities, this research can conclude that removal of the barriers might aid coexistence for these communities in Belfast, but only if removal is done in a *sensitive* and *secure* way with local agencies.

The emergence of new areas that can be classified as interfaces shows that separation is not just at a barrier. The stereotypical model of working-class communities separated by physical barriers is no longer viable. Belfast's depth of segregation is unclassifiable, uncharted. Understanding this new reality is actually a daunting prospect; nevertheless, it is one that needs to be tackled and transformed.

Efforts to achieve coexistence are successfully carried out by some local community groups; however, funding and financial problems pose a threat for the future of their work. This is especially frustrating as the 25-foot-high wall built through the grounds of Hazelwood Integrated Primary School, which was considered entirely unnecessary by many, cost an estimated £100,000. Such sums are rarely made available for grass-roots work.

Government policies, as an approach to generate social cohesion at the interface are generally unsuccessful because they are not implemented. This is due to the lack of commitment to address sectarianism, which, in turn, threatens the successful work of many grass-roots organisations.

The great strength of grass-roots leadership has been necessary. This needs to be celebrated and encouraged. It is, however, only because of failing government policies and lack of community relations programmes that leadership at the grass roots has become so strong. This is because it is often said that the government does not truly believe in community relations. This is fundamentally due to the fact that both major political parties, especially the Democratic Unionist Party (DUP), see community relations as a 'soft' policy of social engineering that is associated with some form of defeat, whereby future relations are still categorised as unjust rather than shared. This is why politicians need to find a way to deal with the past for the sake of sustainable peace and a shared future for Northern Ireland.

In order to look towards a shared future, it is necessary for more work to be done at the interface. Although conflict prevention is needed, from this research, it can be recognised that the need for conflict transformation is presently overlooked. If the situation and condition of Belfast's interface communities is to move forward, as the transition from passive to active coexistence would suggest, the problem at hand is not just the abolition of violence, but the ways in which the deep-seated relationships that ignite and perpetuate the violence can be dramatically transformed.

We opened this chapter re-stating the central importance of peace—or at least freedom from fear of direct violence—in a society, and specifically in a vision of humans living in security: human security. The question posed by the situation in Belfast, reflected here, is how this can possibly be achieved in a divided city, where two conflict communities seem far from an eventual ideal goal of reconciliation: an ideal that seems unworkable and unrealisable in the immediate future. A detailed investigation of the interface communities and security architecture encapsulates the duality of a protection-centred mode of politics and indeed city planning. Hard physical divides do provide a measure of security, being an obstacle to missiles and a hindrance to direct confrontations. On the other hand, they can hinder communication, especially when imposed, perhaps unnecessarily, by authorities external to the communities themselves or with inadequate consultation.

To summarise, essential components of a process that would aid the removal of the barriers and increase coexistence are as follows: the safety and welfare of the residents must be at the heart of the process; the strength of grass-roots community work and leadership must be recognised and respected; strong political leadership and appropriate government support are needed; a continuous amount of cooperation and commitment; an effective project manager/management structure with correct levels of reviewing, monitoring and evaluation; the overall approach should be flexible and unique for each interface; and finally, the process should start within wider efforts at coexistence, in a framework underpinned by respect and equality in order to increase social cohesion.

Bibliography

Afzali, A., and L. Colleton (2003) 'Constructing Coexistence: A Survey of Coexistence Projects in Areas of Ethnic Conflict', in A. Chayes and M. Minow (ed.), *Imagine Coexistence* (San Francisco: Jossey-Bass): 3-20.

BIP (Belfast Interface Project) (2004) 'Survey of Membership Needs'; www.belfastinterfaceproject.org/otherpub.asp, accessed 1 July 2009.

Brandeis University (2006) 'Coexistence International'; www.brandeis.edu/coexistence/work/coexist.html, accessed 18 July 2009.

Cohen, C. (2001) 'Working With Integrity: A Guidebook for Peacebuilders Asking Ethical Questions', Brandeis University; www.brandeis.edu/ethics/pdfs/publications/working_pre.pdf, accessed 19 June 2009.

Ellison, W. (2009) 'Police Hot on Trail of Troublemakers', *Belfast Telegraph*, 15 July 2009: 1-3.

Jarman, N. (2005) 'Changing Places, Moving Boundaries: The Development of New Interface Areas', *Shared Space: A Research Journal on Peace, Conflict and Community Relations in Northern Ireland* 1: 9-19.

—— (2007) 'Building a Peaceline: Security and Segregation in Belfast', in S. Hackett and R. West (eds.), *Belfast Ordinary* (Belfast: Factotum Publications).

—— (2008) 'Security and Segregation: Interface Barriers in Belfast', *Shared Space: A Research Journal on Peace, Conflict and Community Relations in Northern Ireland* 6: 21-33.

Kriesberg, L. (2000) 'Coexistence and the Reconciliation of Communal Conflicts', in E. Weiner (ed.), *The Handbook of Interethnic Coexistence* (New York: The Abraham Fund): 182-98.

Liechty, J., and C. Clegg (2001) *Moving beyond Sectarianism* (Dublin: The Columbia Press).

McAleese, D. (2009) 'Police hunt for rioters after a night of shame', *Belfast Telegraph*, 14 July 2009: 1-2.

Morrow, D. (2008) 'A Better Future? Interfaces and the Good Relations Panel', *Belfast Interface Project's Interface Newsletter*, February 2008: 1-3.

Northern Ireland Office (2009) 'Northern Ireland Office: Good Friday Agreement'; www.nio.gov.uk/agreement.pdf, accessed 24 September 2010.

OFMDFM (Office of the First Minister and Deputy First Minister) (2005) 'A Shared Future: Policy and Strategic Framework for Good Relations in Northern Ireland'; www.asharedfutureni.gov.uk/gprs.pdf , accessed 4 July 2009.

Oliver, M. (2007) 'Still Divided', *The Guardian*, 3 July 2007: 4-5.

Powell, J. (2008) *Great Hatred, Little Room: Making Peace in Northern Ireland* (London: Bodley Head).

Rupesinghe, K. (1999) 'Coexistence and Transformation in Asia: Some Reflections', in K. Rupesinghe (ed.), *Culture and Identity: Ethnic Coexistence in the Asian Context* (Washington, DC: The Sasakawa Peace Foundation): 3-37.

US–Ireland Alliance (2008) 'Belfast Residents Asked If Peace Lines Should Come Down'; www. us-irelandalliance.org/wmspage.cfm?parm1=779, accessed 4 July 2009.

Weiner, E. (2000) 'Coexistence Work: A New Profession', in E. Weiner (ed.), *The Handbook of Interethnic Coexistence* (New York: The Abraham Fund): 13-24.

Section V
Human security and responsibility to protect (R2P)

13
Responsibility to protect

Vesselin Popovski

Institute for Sustainability and Peace, United Nations University, Japan

'Human security' and 'responsibility to protect' could be called sister concepts; what brings them together is the focus on people at risk. What makes them different is the broad application of human security and the narrow application of responsibility to protect. Anything threatening human life, human welfare or even human comfort, could be attached to human security, but only very narrowly defined situations, such as genocide, war crimes and crimes against humanity, apply to responsibility to protect. Human security addresses the safety of all people at all times from all possible threats, with no distinction of causes, nature or gravity. Responsibility to protect only applies to the most serious international crimes.

This chapter discusses the commonalities and differences between human security and responsibility to protect. It critically examines the evolution of the concept of responsibility to protect over the last decade, its gradual shift from a norm to a policy, and discusses some current challenges.

Emergence and evolution of responsibility to protect (R2P)

The phrase 'responsibility to protect' (R2P) emerged at discussions preparing the Report of the International Commission on Intervention and State Sovereignty (ICISS) in early 2001 and is attributed to Gareth Evans, former Foreign Minister of Australia and co-Chair of ICISS, who offered it as an attempt to reconcile sovereignty and intervention for human rights.[1] The new language of R2P extraordinarily resolved the existing tensions about humanitarian intervention, such as the exclusive focus on military intervention, the sensitivities of using humanitarian language by colonialists and aggressors in the past and the deadlock in searching for new legal rules to govern intervention (Bellamy 2009). The shift in language from humanitarian intervention to R2P was well accepted at later roundtables, leading to the ICISS Report being entitled *The Responsibility to Protect* (ICISS 2001). A new norm was born, which pinned the responsibility to protect people from mass atrocities on state authorities at the national level and on the United Nations at the international level and ensures that interventions, when they do take place, are done with proper purpose, as a last resort and with proportionate means. While the state whose people are directly affected has the default responsibility to protect, a residual responsibility resides with the broader international community of states. This is activated when a particular state is either unwilling or unable to fulfil R2P; or is itself the perpetrator of crimes or atrocities; or where populations living outside a particular state are directly threatened by actions taking place there. The fallback responsibility requires that in some circumstances action must be taken by external parties to support populations that are under serious threat. The goal of protective intervention is not to wage war on a state in order to destroy it and eliminate its statehood, but to protect victims of atrocities inside the state, embed the protection in reconstituted institutions after the intervention, and then withdraw all foreign troops.

In the same way as human security shifted the concept of security from territorial security to individual people, R2P shifted the attention of scholars and the focus of policy-makers from intervening states to people at risk of atrocities. In the same way as human security came as a useful approach to address existing dilemmas within the UN's three agendas—peace, development and human rights—R2P came to resolve the difficulties with the concept of humanitarian intervention, historically often abused by powerful and aggressive states.

R2P was globally recognised and adopted by the UN General Assembly in its *2005 World Summit Outcome* document.[2] Interestingly, it was one of the few substantive innovations to survive the negotiations at the 2005 World Summit and the final document contained clear, unambiguous acceptance of individual state responsibility to protect populations from genocide, war crimes, ethnic cleansing and crimes against humanity. Member states further declared that they 'are prepared to take collective action, in timely and decisive manner, through the Security Council . . . and in cooperation with relevant regional organisations as appropriate, should peaceful means be inadequate and national authorities are manifestly failing to protect their populations'. The concept was given its own subsection title.

---

1 See Gareth Evans, *Responsibility to Protect: Ending Mass Atrocity Crimes Once and for All* (2008), a full personal account from the creator of R2P offering a detailed analysis of the origin and emergence of the norm.

2 UN General Assembly 2005b: par. 138,139.

In January 2009 the UN Secretary-General issued the report *Implementing the Responsibility to Protect*, the UN General Assembly discussed it in July 2009 and in September it adopted a procedural Resolution A/RES/63/308 taking note of the report and deciding to continue its consideration. A decade of normative and institutional history of R2P has been the subject of profound analysis and recent publications (Bellamy 2008, 2009; Evans 2008). The Global Centre for R2P has been created to coordinate research and advocacy for R2P.[3] The current focus is on attempts to develop R2P from a norm to a policy, or in the expression of Ban Ki-moon from 'words to deeds'.[4]

In summary, R2P reconciled centuries-long tensions between sovereignty and intervention by accepting that there could be very serious conditions, when human life is threatened on a mass scale and domestic measures may not provide enough guarantees. Therefore states should, first, accept that international engagement is necessary and, second, be prepared to act collectively to save human life beyond their borders. Or, to reverse this statement from state-centric to people-centred approach: human life at all time everywhere is an absolute value and should be fully protected from all dangers. Accordingly people would expect their states to offer such protection, but genocide and crimes against humanity are so extremely dangerous, that people need a firm assurance of a higher international order of protection. In other words, sovereignty can be praised and respected at all times, but in situations of genocidal and other mass crimes, which are so ultimately murderous, sovereignty cannot be a barrier for international intervention to save human life. If a state understands its sovereignty as a responsibility to protect people, there won't be a dilemma between sovereignty and intervention; this state will either protect people within its own capacities, or will invite international assistance to help with the protection. In neither case will there be interference against the state's will. If a state does not understand its sovereignty as a responsibility to protect people, moreover when it engages deliberately or is complicit in producing human suffering, its sovereignty can be suspended by sanctions or military force, ideally authorised by the UN Security Council, which represents an intervention against such a state's will.

Human security

R2P came to resolve the controversy between the positive notion of 'humanitarian' and the negative notion of 'intervention' (Popovski 2003). Human security came to resolve the controversy between the human rights tradition, which regards the state as the chief threat to its citizens, and the development tradition, which looks to the

---

3 www.globalr2p.org (accessed 8 July 2010).
4 Annual Address to the General Assembly, 25 September 2007, SG/SM/11182.

state as the chief agent of change for the better. Human security puts the individual at the centre of the debate, analysis and policy[5] and demands that the state acts as a collective instrument to protect human life and promote human welfare. The fundamental components of human security—the security of people against threats to personal safety and life—can be put at risk by external aggression, but also by factors within a country, either human-made, such as abuse of power, poverty, corruption, denial of democracy, or natural, such as floods, earthquakes and tsunamis.

The phrase human security was introduced by the United Nations Development Programme's (UNDP) *Human Development Report 1994*. It attracted attention, because it added—with the word 'security'—some urgency for undertaking actions in otherwise more traditional, slow and gradual efforts to achieve UN goals, such as disarmament, economic development and respect for human rights. In the early 1990s all three global agendas of the UN—peace/security, development and human rights—were in need of some reinvigoration and the concept of human security came exactly on time to boost all three.

First, the concept of peace and security had suffered from its overemphasis on states, not only in international relations, but also in the framework of national security, where the priority to the protection of the state often degraded the protection of the people within the state. This has been recognised and the concept of threats to peace and security evolved gradually to include violence within states, non-military threats, such as infectious diseases and others. Accordingly, human security emerged as useful terminology to exemplify this evolution, recognising that the peace and security agenda has became less territorial, less military and more people-focused. Human security language helped the peace and security agenda to be more comprehensive in terms of scope of threats, and more individual people-centred both in terms of care to victims and in terms of sanctions to individual perpetrators. Human security was not only critical to the traditional security approach, but it also gradually transformed it.

Second, the concept of economic development also faced some dilemmas in the early 1990s; it became clear that pure economic growth or economic aid, disinterested in people's expectations or societal needs and detached from environmental considerations, would be problematic and unsustainable. During the cold war, development projects were often conducted at the expense of the well-being of a large proportion of the people. In Latin America the adoption of neo-liberalist economics widened the gap between the rich and the poor despite the economic growth. Since the states reduced social welfare provisions, this put even more pressure on the disadvantaged and poor. Development schemes during the cold war period tended to ignore people's needs for the sake of the state's economic growth. Human security came at the right time to offer a more 'human face' to economic development, and it was no surprise that the introduction of human security was made by a report called 'human development'.

---

5 One of the best single studies of human security is MacFarlane and Yuen Foong Khong 2006.

Third, the human rights agenda also needed a refreshing stimulus in the early 1990s. It had historically suffered from its state-centrism, had been seen as inefficient in emergency situations, slow, over-dependent on states' compliance, over-focused on abstract universalism, isolationist and missing pragmatic and practical opportunities. Human security, with its re-orientation from states to people, injected a sense of urgency into the human rights world, made it more dynamic, demanded transformation of the operating mechanisms, added a higher pressure for actions and the potential power of the UN Security Council to sanction the violators.

As a result human security not only resolved existing dilemmas in the UN's pursuit of peace, development and human rights but also became the bridge between the three of them. To quote the famous formula set out by Kofi Annan in his 2005 report *In Larger Freedom*: we cannot have peace without development, we cannot have development without peace and we cannot have both without human rights. In short, human security became that single magic expression that could unify the peace agenda, the development agenda and the human rights agenda, and later, gradually incorporate the climate change agenda.

Human security, merging the 'freedom from fear', the 'freedom from want' and the 'freedom to live in dignity',[6] also strengthened the coordination between three sets of institutions in the UN system. Because of its inclusiveness, human security has helped to mobilise actions and accomplish international legal treaties, such as the Kyoto Protocol, the prohibition of landmines, the creation of the International Criminal Court, the Millennium Development Goals and others. It created partnerships among diverse actors of civil society, private sector and governments. Not only practitioners, but also scholars found usefulness in human security; the concept served as an umbrella label for a broad category of research, within which scholars can share and cross-fertilise methodologies, empirical evidence and findings.

Comparing human security with R2P

Human security shifts the territorial or national security of sovereign states to what individual humans need, in total, to feel secure. R2P detaches itself from the problematic 'humanitarian intervention' and shifts the attention from state intervention to the need of people, threatened by atrocity crimes. Human security emerged in 1994 and the R2P in 2001,[7] both driven by the need to place a stronger emphasis on the safety of individual people. The difference is that, whereas human security offers a holistic concern for all people from all threats, with no distinction of causes, nature and gravity, R2P limits its focus to so-called atrocity crimes: genocide, war crimes, ethnic cleansing and crimes against humanity. Both human secu-

---

6   These three freedoms, as separate sections, appeared in Kofi Annan's report *In Larger Freedom* (UN General Assembly 2005a).

7   Both strongly supported by the Government of Canada.

rity and R2P, instead of taking heavily state-centred views in achieving goals such as security, development or prevention of atrocities, demand that more emphasis should be placed on human beings and their needs and experiences. They demand that state policies should avoid negative consequences such as damage to human dignity and well-being. Thus human security and R2P serve as useful analytical devices to explain the ongoing problems of international society and evaluate their threat to individual humans, especially those destabilising factors in human rights protection that can lead to mass atrocities.

Both concepts have been initially criticised for being over-academic and not providing an operational ground for policy or action because of ambiguities in interpretation. However, since the concepts emerged and their objectives in safe-guarding human lives from critical pervasive threats were recognised, they both intended to offer an operational framework for policies to improve the human con-dition and guide actions. One common feature in this process of operationalisation of both concepts is the emphasis on prevention and early warning systems that have to be developed to avoid potential crises.

The large scope of human security, compared with the narrow scope of R2P, has been problematic and recently more scholars on human security have suggested the idea of threshold in applying the human security approach to real case stud-ies (Gasper 2005; Tadjbakhsh and Chenoy 2006). The idea emerged largely as a response to the problems of maximalist versus minimalist definitions of human security. Since the emergence of the concept there has been criticism over the lack of practical use of human security due to its overstretched categories of 'threats' against which the concept proposes to secure human lives. To this broad defini-tion, some proponents of human security responded with a minimalist approach and limited the types of threat in order to make the concept applicable to policy actions. However, by limiting the types of threat that can be regarded as violating human security, minimalists ignored the fact that those threats can be seriously threatening human lives in some cases or can be more threatening in one place than in another place. For instance, the absence of serious political conflict with the existence of extensive poverty in no way makes humans free from threats even in a minimal sense. Human security, as a concept and as an approach, is persuasive only when the broad meanings of freedom from want and freedom from fear are recognised. However, this recognition offers little in terms of operational frame-work for policy actions. The question is how to maintain the conceptual broadness and inclusiveness of human security without jeopardising its applicability.

A similar problem exists for the R2P, but in the opposite direction. R2P applies in a very limited number of situations and the dilemma is how to maintain the nar-row applicability to atrocity crimes without jeopardising the need to protect people from a variety of threats, other than intentional, systematic, genocidal policies. If human security covers all the threats, R2P covers a very limited number of threats. Paradoxically, both concepts may have a similar operational shortage: one can be considered too wide, therefore having little applicability, and the other can consid-ered be too narrow, but also with little applicability.

I would illustrate the difference between human security and R2P with one example, the massive human suffering in the Irrawaddy Delta caused by the devastating Cyclone Nargis in Myanmar in May 2008. The Burmese military government, fearing that foreign assistance may jeopardise its sovereign power, failed to offer initial cooperation with international organisations, governments and NGOs willing to deliver humanitarian aid to people in need. The critical situation and the human tragedy obviously fell entirely within the scope of human security, but also voices were raised about the applicability of R2P. Most of the observers agreed that the situation would not fit into R2P.[8] Interestingly, the initial proposal for R2P offered in 2001 referred to serious harm, including from overwhelming natural or environmental catastrophes as one of the triggers of R2P, should a state prove unwilling or unable to cope with the disaster. But the UN General Assembly in 2005 limited the applicability of R2P to only the four atrocity crimes: genocide, war crimes, ethnic cleansing and crimes against humanity. Unless one could have argued that the Burmese government, by denying international assistance, committed crimes against humanity,[9] R2P would not apply to the Irrawaddy Delta situation. Limiting the scope of R2P to only four crimes helped the General Assembly to reach a consensus; the Summit Outcome adopted the concept of R2P and was celebrated as one of the greatest achievements in human history. But this does not help the victims of both the cyclone and the totalitarian rule in Myanmar.

The human security concept is more practical, more permissive for actions, less grounded in UN resolutions and reports, than is R2P. Although still a victim of misinterpretations, human security is more flexible in finding a compromise between maximalist and minimalist approaches, a middle ground, what I would call a 'threshold of human security tolerance', set in a community of people whose security is under serious threat and reactions to it are urgently required. Communities and groups of people under such a threat can be offered long-term preventive measures to eliminate the insecurities. And here I see a strong potential for common operational ground for human security and R2P: policy-makers and practitioners can identify measures to prevent worsening human insecurity that would also prevent situations from leading to R2P crimes. A human security tolerance threshold, once ascertained, would enable us to identify and specify hot spots of problems threatening human lives, and would effectively serve the purpose of preventing potential R2P situations from escalating to atrocity crimes. Knowing what threatens human lives the most would bring decisions on policy issues and thus provide operational ground for security policy implementation.

The reformulation of territorial security into human security and the replacement of humanitarian intervention with R2P have had profound impacts on how we regard the world, how we organise political and economic affairs, how we run public and foreign policies, and how we relate to fellow human beings from differ-

---

8 Well summarised in a report by the Asia–Pacific Centre for the R2P (2008).
9 Obviously difficult, as crimes against humanity require proof of deliberate intent and planning, they need to be committed as part of a widespread or systematic attack directed against the civilian population.

ent countries and cultures. These two major conceptual developments direct our attention to the fact that the discourse of territorial security is often abused to justify state atrocities against its own citizens, whereas human security is resistant to being conflated into regime security.

R2P and its limits

I will now discuss four major limits of the R2P concept: (1) the scope of applicable situations is limited to four atrocity crimes; (2) international intervention is to be authorised only by the UN Security Council; (3) responsibility to prosecute is not part of R2P; and (4) R2P does not impose obligations on non-state actors.

R2P applies only to international crimes

R2P applies to four situations, genocide, war crimes, ethnic cleansing and crimes against humanity. Ethnic cleansing falls within crimes against humanity; therefore one may say that all R2P situations correspond to the international crimes under ICC (International Criminal Court) jurisdiction.[10] The fact that nothing less than a recognised and condemned international crime falls within the scope of R2P has an advantage and a disadvantage. The advantage is that this helps to build a global consensus behind the R2P. The disadvantage is that it demands a judgement of international criminality in order to render R2P applicable. R2P can be invoked to protect a group of people, only if this group is deliberately targeted as such for extermination—and this is a serious limitation. In a subsequent criminal process, the prosecutors would have time to find hard evidence and persuade judges to pronounce on the existence of international crimes. But when the urgent issue is protection of people at immediate risk, limiting R2P to only recognised international crimes may jeopardise the protection.

R2P, being minimised to the recognised international crimes, is effectively reduced to what has already been established as a norm in the 1948 Genocide Convention, the 1949 Geneva Conventions, its 1977 Additional Protocols, 1998 Rome Statute of the International Criminal Court and other obligations from international humanitarian law and human rights law. The UN General Assembly, in order to reach an agreement in 2005, had to go to the lowest common denominator and sacrificed the novelty of the R2P from the 2001 report. States were persuaded that they were not accepting any more obligations in addition to those they had already accepted in various treaties before, and they agreed with the R2P in the 2005 Summit Outcome document (Art. 138 and 139).

10 The exception is 'ethnic cleansing', which is not a separate international crime. However, it fits perfectly into 'forceful deportation', therefore falling within the scope of one of the 'crimes against humanity'.

There is a choice between a larger scope of situations and less international consensus or a limited scope of situations and broader consensus. I see the risks of going into one extreme or another: to aim at large scope and risk jeopardising an agreement, or to have a global agreement but on such narrowly defined situations that leave many other people at risk with no protection. There will be a sceptical and a proactive R2P lobby and the latter would attempt to apply responsibility to help people at serious risk at any time when a massive number are threatened, not just from atrocity crimes. The sceptical lobby would usually raise its voice against over-reaction and the abuse of R2P for unilateral interventions and would cite the Iraqi invasion in 2003. If we ask what the greater danger is—over-reaction or under-reaction—I think that R2P has not been threatened so much by proactive approaches than by inaction. I would like to see the R2P norm primarily geared at the protection of all people at serious risk, not so much geared towards a broad, but less operational consensus. Many more people died from the international community's inaction, not from over-reaction. The 2003 Iraq invasion was indeed cited as a backlash for R2P, but only incompetent or manipulative writers would consider Iraq to be a case of R2P; the purpose of the 2003 invasion was never to protect Iraqi people from planned mass atrocities by Saddam Hussein against Iraqi people. I would worry less that R2P can be abused sometimes, such as in 2003 Iraq or in 2008 Georgia; I would rather worry if the norm remains on paper and does not help next time a massacre on the scale of 1994 Rwanda or Darfur is being planned.

Whether a particular situation fits into atrocity crimes and falls under R2P would usually have two considerations: victims in need of protection and states in need of global consensus. I would not be overly concerned with the protection of the consensus; I would rather focus on the protection of people.[11] R2P came into existence as an approach that shifts the focus from intervening states to the people in need of protection. R2P emerged to address a particularly difficult case—Kosovo 1999—and its major novelty was in challenging the routine traditional sovereignty approach in state-centric international relations. One needs to remember that, if R2P is about genocide and crimes against humanity, it would often not be consensual and fit smoothly into existing theoretical models. Talks about R2P will always re-emerge when innocent people die and urgent actions are necessary. It will be invoked in various critical politically divisive cases. We need to be prepared to face controversial invocations and debates. This is nothing surprising—genocide is an extreme and controversial situation, and often there might not be a consensus.

I would ask: Would it be better to have a consensus on a norm with a very limited scope of application or to have less of a consensus, but broader opportunities for action? I would answer, that it would be better to save human lives first, no matter how, and after that deliberate whether this was R2P or not, and how it would affect

---

11 I reflected on this in a joint article with Andy Knight (Popovski and Knight 2008) in the
   Edmonton Journal.

the consensus.[12] Let's remember that R2P is first and foremost about saving human lives in distant villages, not so much about rhetorical references in UN resolutions in New York, or diplomatic conferences or politicians' statements. I would like to see less talk about whether UN member states support R2P, rather a development of R2P more in human terms, spelling out the consequences for real people in real life situations. As with human security, R2P should be less about states and more about people.

Security Council resolution is the only authorising option

The second limit of R2P is the request that all collective timely and decisive actions, when states fail manifestly to exercise R2P, should be through authorisation by the UN Security Council. I see this request as a good model of insisting that the UN Security Council lives up to its authority—I believe that exactly because R2P situations are so manifestly atrocious, the UN Security Council cannot remain silent. I would use my earlier reference to the sovereignty and intervention dilemma and paraphrase it as follows: if the Security Council understands its primary role to eliminate threats to the peace under the Charter (as everyone expects it to do) and undertakes R2P measures, these are welcome. But if the Security Council does not live up to its authority and fails to discuss or agree on how to protect people from murderous risks, this should not be the end of R2P. A norm—R2P—cannot be dependent on the good mood of an institution— the UN Security Council. If we agree that R2P is a universal norm, it should have a life outside the committee room in the UN building's basement where 15 ambassadors vote.

The initial R2P concept in 2001 was less bound to Security Council resolutions, it mentioned the General Assembly's option (Uniting for Peace resolution 377), it relied on regional organisations that could act first and seek UN approval ex post facto, and was not even foreign to a 'Kosovo scenario', when states would act collectively through observing the precautionary just war principles: proper purpose, last resort, proportionality and balance of consequences.

Similarly to limiting the scope, limiting the authority to the Security Council in the 2005 document achieved consensus, but sacrificed the novelty—obviously, the Security Council can at any time define any situation as a threat to international peace and authorise sanctions or military force. There is no need for the R2P norm for the Council to do so. The Council imposed sanctions and authorised military force many times before the R2P language appeared: resolution 688 (protecting Kurds in Northern Iraq 1991) and tens of resolutions on Somalia, former Yugoslavia, Haiti and elsewhere in the 1990s. If there is an agreement in the Security Council to act in the face of atrocities, there is theoretically not much of a need to formulate this agreement in R2P language. Conversely, if there is no agreement in

---

12 When I hear that invocation of R2P may break some 'consensus', I remember how India in 1971 invaded East Pakistan or how Tanzania invaded Uganda in 1979 to stop massacres, without worrying much about consensus and without asking Security Council approval.

the Council, R2P would be of little help. But if the Council is guided by the norm of R2P and utilises its language more often in its resolutions, this will be a strong signal of recognition and acceptance.

R2P emerged from a Kosovo scenario as a separate opportunity from the well-known interventions of the Security Council, and it would have been more useful to develop it as an emergency rapid reaction measure, which could be supported by the Council, but could also have a life on its own. The Security Council can, obviously, gain from taking the opportunity to utilise the R2P norm,[13] as it can also take the opportunity to refer cases to the ICC, a body that exists on its own. It would be interesting to regard the R2P very much as a complementary international mechanism—similar to ICC—which is activated when domestic efforts to deal with international crimes fail. In other words, the Security Council has always the first choice to undertake R2P intervention, but if the Council fails to do so, this should not be the end of R2P—there should be other opportunities. The Security Council can gain from utilising the language of R2P, and also R2P can gain from the Council's authorisation.

Responsibility to prosecute (R2P 2)

One should deal with the victims and in parallel one should deal with the perpetrators. R2P does not extend to the responsibility to punish perpetrators and I have strongly advocated for such a responsibility to prosecute, saying that in fact the two should be sides of the same coin.[14] I analysed and established a great deal of commonality between the R2P and the ICC jurisdiction in the sense that both are secondary to domestic efforts to protect or punish. R2P and ICC are activated only when states are unwilling or unable to protect the victims of international crimes, or prosecute the perpetrators of these crimes. Not surprisingly, the strongest advocates of the ICC are also the strongest advocates for R2P—this is visible when comparing the civil society pressure to establish ICC with the civil society pressure to adopt R2P—the coalitions of NGOs to reach the two objectives have very similar memberships. Genocide, war crimes and crimes against humanity necessitate two interconnected tasks—to protect the victims and to punish the perpetrators—and both require substantial derogations of sovereignty, the first with respect to the norm of non-intervention and the second with respect to sovereign impunity up to the level of heads of state.

Finally, both dealing with victims (R2P) and dealing with perpetrators (R2P 2) face similar applicability and operational challenges. Both require sensitive safeguards: the use of external military force to protect civilians inside sovereign jurisdiction must first satisfy legitimacy criteria rooted in just war theory, while the prosecution of alleged atrocity criminals must be balanced against the consequences for the

---

13 The Security Council has referred to R2P in some of its resolutions: 1674 on the protection of civilians in armed conflict; 1706 on the situation in Darfur.

14 I have gone through a detailed analysis on this in Thakur and Popovski 2007: 39-63.

prospects and process of peace, the need for post-conflict reconciliation and the fragility of institutions. Darfur would be a good example to illustrate these challenges with both R2P and R2P (2). As I write this text, neither the victims, nor the perpetrators have been dealt with successfully.

Non-state actors and R2P

R2P imposes obligations on states to act, but does not impose such on non-state actors. Obviously, states come first when it comes to protecting people from massacres. We pay taxes to the state, expecting protection. States are capacitated and empowered to prevent and react to atrocities through all state institutions. To paraphrase a famous Weberian sentence, states have the monopoly to use violence, but they should also have the monopoly to protect people from violence.

However, in the era of globalisation and rising and strengthening civil society, a greater role is to be played by other actors, not just states. For example, rebel forces should respect the laws of war and prevent war crimes in the same way as states are obliged to do. R2P should apply to the government of Sri Lanka, as well as to the Tamil Tigers. It should apply to Hezbollah, as well as to the state of Israel. In case of massive street protests and violence, experienced in some post-elections situations, the opposition parties should also exercise responsibility to protect, by urging restraint by their supporters. Powerful private corporations and international NGOs could also be actors, playing a role for the exercise of R2P in some country-specific circumstances.

R2P and its pillars

R2P, as developed by the 2009 UN Secretary-General's Report, has three pillars. The first pillar is the enduring responsibility of states, willing and able to exercise R2P within their territories without external interference. The second pillar applies to states willing, but unable to protect, and inviting international community to assist them to fulfil R2P. The third pillar deals with states that do not live up to their responsibility, are unwilling to protect people, either because they themselves orchestrate genocidal policies or are complicit in such policies. The third pillar requires timely and decisive collective actions and, where necessary, sanctions or military intervention to protect people from massacres. Such third pillar situations would be rare and exceptional, and I anticipate that most of the actual implementation of R2P would be in the first and the second pillar, not so much in military intervention (Bellamy 2008). But the third pillar will attract more debate, because if everything is normal and states are capacitated and willing to protect, this would usually not raise media attention. The R2P will lead to military intervention only in a very small number of situations, but when this happens, these will be on all TV headlines and all newspapers' front pages.

Regarding R2P as less and less about military intervention, and more and more about strengthening domestic capacities to prevent mass atrocities is in fact bridging the gap between R2P and human security. I anticipate that the second pillar is where most of the attention and efforts will be oriented. States that already possess capacities to protect will not need much, apart from keeping and strengthening these capacities. However, states missing vital capabilities to offer protection to the people in their territory and jurisdiction—in other words, willing, but unable to protect—will need to accept international assistance and gradually, when empowered enough, move to the first pillar.

There might be situations falling between the pillars: for example, if a government is half-unwilling/half-unable to protect. A situation such as Myanmar comes to mind, where the fear of accepting foreign aid was compounded by the incompetence of the government to offer assistance to people at risk. Here is a real test: how to capacitate a government, semi-reluctant to be capacitated? A 'stick and carrot' policy might help: if the government cooperates, the second pillar assistance flows in; if the government manifestly fails to cooperate and put its people at risk, the third pillar—coercive measures—are considered. The third pillar, even if used sparingly, is a powerful instrument, a potential deterrent, a reminder of the arsenal of collective coercion, employed when a state is manifestly failing its responsibility to protect. This deterrent is crucial not only in emergencies to save lives, but also against those contemplating future mass atrocity crimes.

There should be two types of capacity for people's protection: an urgent rapid reaction one, when third pillar action is required in the face of imminent atrocities; and a prevention/rebuilding type of capacity, in the face of less imminent potential threats of atrocities, reflecting more developmental needs of states willing to cooperate with the international community. One problem with the third pillar is that it starts with 'timely and decisive' language, addressing situations when states manifestly fail their responsibilities, but still contains a lot of soft diplomacy and Chapter VI attempts. The question remains how long the victims of potential genocide will have to wait for the international community to exhaust all diplomatic and peaceful means, the mediation, negotiations and other Chapter VI approaches before becoming more robust and employing Chapter VII enforcement. It would have helped to clearly distinguish the measures to be applied under the second pillar—states willing but unable to protect—from the third pillar—states manifestly unwilling to protect. Such a distinction, although not always crystal clear on the ground is important when it comes to capacities and operationalisation. It is one thing to deliver assistance, early warning mechanisms and strengthen the rule of law in states willing to cooperate. It is another to develop capacities internationally and regionally to be utilised against non-cooperative states. Moreover, 'non-cooperative states' may be mild language for *genocidaires*.

Often I notice a lot of caution against the third pillar and desire for R2P not to be seen as a path to intervention. If the General Assembly once and for all decided that R2P is about genocide and crimes against humanity, I don't see why there is so much resistance to forceful responses. R2P is not human security, it is not about usual human rights violations that could be more serious or less serious, and accordingly we can debate whether intervention is needed or not. R2P is, let's remember, about Holocaust, about Rwanda 1994 and Srebrenica 1995. R2P is not about Fidel Castro or Robert Mugabe or Kim Jong-Il, where we can endlessly argue what to do and what not to do, and how to balance sanctions with engagement. R2P is about Hitler, Pol Pot and Milosevic and, if so, I don't understand the voices of anger and caution with the third pillar and forceful intervention. And if we are talking about Hitler and Pol Pot, there should not be much space left for Chapter VI in the third pillar.

The 2009 Report introduced the concept 'narrow, but deep', meaning that the response, though limited narrowly to four crimes, should be comprehensive, utilising all possible existing capacities. This is an admirable desire to use almost everything in the UN arsenal and elsewhere to save people from the horrors of genocide. The problem is that many of these capacities have been created with different threats in mind. Genocide and crimes against humanity occur between powerful perpetrators and powerless victims, and I doubt how useful the traditional conflict resolution mechanisms and Chapter VI will be, originally created to make peace between enemies that are more or less equal in power. Ironically, the 2009 Report talks about moving from 'words to deeds', but the document itself is very 'wordy', repetitive, in some parts too abstract.[15] It would have been more useful to distil from the long list of conflict prevention opportunities only those that are more directly relevant to prevention of atrocity crimes, to make the document less wordy and more focused.

The 2009 Report tries to put prevention first and appeals for the development of early warning and response capacities. But one question to ask is 'preventing what?' Prevention of conflicts generally, for which there is a vast body of mechanisms in the UN? Or does it focus on preventing only atrocity crimes? Preventing conflict generally by addressing the root causes is very similar to the human security concept while preventing genocide and crimes against humanity is a different, more precise and concrete task. R2P should deal with the second task, not with the first. The two tasks can and should obviously advance in parallel, but they are two different tasks and there is no need to confuse them. Some of the examples given in the 2009 Report, when discussing the second pillar empowerment of states to prevent conflict and build capacities, leave the impression that the concern is with general conflict prevention and peace-building, and not so much focus is put on prevention of genocide and war crimes.

When it comes to prevention of atrocity crimes, some specific issues to examine more carefully would be: (1) lack of control over irregular forces or militia; (2) small arms smuggling; (3) military training and whether it is aimed at reducing war crimes; and (4) incitement of hatred or racism. If looking at what has generated the atrocities in Rwanda, the former Yugoslavia and Darfur one can think of such con-

---

15 For example, Point 52 last sentence: 'parallel instruments and possibilities may exist in a number of regions and subregions'.

crete areas of monitoring and reporting, which could have been useful in preventing atrocities. Instead of pointing to concrete areas, the 2009 Report talks generally about conflict resolution, mediation and development assistance, it incorporates too many additional and already developed spheres, rather than creating its own coherent scope of attention. Obviously, armed conflicts may lead to atrocities, but atrocities may happen outside armed conflict too—Cambodia and Rwanda are strong examples. It would have been better to design specific machinery for atrocity prevention, rather than duplicating the machinery of general conflict prevention.

In conclusion: I have defined the scope of similarities and differences between R2P and human security above, and I have analysed the latest development of R2P. I would recommend that the two concepts continue to be shaped and implemented separately, but I would emphasise that, although the beauty is in their diversity, they also have a lot to inform each other.

Bibliography

Asia–Pacific Centre for the Responsibility to Protect (2008) 'Cyclone Nargis and the Responsibility to Protect', Myanmar/Burma Briefing No. 2; www.r2pasiapacific.org/documents/Burma_Brief2.pdf, accessed 8 July 2010.

Bellamy, A. (2008) 'R2P and the Problem of Military Intervention', *International Affairs* 84.4 (July 2008): 615-41.

—— (2009) *Responsibility to Protect: Global Effort to End Mass Atrocities* (Cambridge, UK: Polity Press): 43.

Evans, G. (2008) *Responsibility to Protect: Ending Mass Atrocity Crimes Once and for All* (Washington, DC: Brookings Institution Press).

Gasper, D. (2005) 'Securing Humanity: Situating "Human Security" as Concept and Discourse', *Journal of Human Development and Capabilities* 6.2 (July 2005): 221-45.

ICISS (International Commission on Intervention and State Sovereignty) (2001) *The Responsibility to Protect* (Ottawa: International Development Research Centre).

MacFarlane, S.N., and Yuen Foong Khong (2006) *Human Security and the United Nations: A Critical History* (Bloomington, IN: Indiana University Press for the UN Intellectual History Project).

Popovski, V. (2003) 'The Concept of Humanitarian Intervention', in P. Siani-Davies (ed.), *International Intervention in the Balkans since 1995* (London: Routledge).

—— and A. Knight (2008) 'Putting People Ahead of Protocol', *Edmonton Journal*, 4 June 2008.

Tadsbakhsh, S., and A.M. Chenoy (2006) *Human Security: Concepts and Implications* (London: Routledge).

Thakur, R., and V. Popovski (2007) 'The Responsibility to Protect and Prosecute: The Parallel Erosion of Sovereignty and Impunity', in *The Global Community, Yearbook of International Law and Jurisprudence* (New York: Oxford University Press): 39-63.

UN General Assembly (2005a) 'In Larger Freedom: Towards Development, Security and Human Rights for All' (A/59/2005, 21 March 2005).

—— (2005b) '2005 World Summit Outcome: Resolution Adopted by the General Assembly' (A/RES/60/1, 24 October 2005).

—— (2009) 'Implementing the Responsibility to Protect: Report of the Secretary-General' (A/63/677, 12 January 2009).

14

African police: failing agents of human security

Bruce Baker
African Studies Centre, Coventry University, UK

African police have received external training and equipment programmes for a long time, but only since the late 1990s has there been a concerted effort by donors to radically reconstruct the national police and security systems in order to improve the effectiveness and quality of their service. The need for systemic change was glaring. Not just authoritarian regimes, but elected regimes fearful of opposition and overthrow, looked to the police and security forces to be defenders of their regimes and suppressors of opposition, real or supposed. With their eye on their political masters, it was not surprising that such police forces had little interest in serving the public. And given the police forces' urban location, few vehicles and poor training, they did not have the ability to serve the majority of the population. In Alice Hills's summary, African police forces of the 1990s were quite simply clientelist, corrupt, compliant, 'brutal and stagnant' (Hills 2000: 20, 41). It was not surprising that most people in Africa had negative views of their police force, seeing them as, at best, incompetent and disinterested and, at worst, as predatory and dangerous. They were the source of insecurity and fear.

For millions of Africans state policing was only made worse by civil war and insurrection. Since 1980 at least 26 African states have endured the suffering and destruction of conflict over all or part of their territory: Angola, Burundi, Central African Republic, Chad, Comoros, Côte d'Ivoire, Democratic Republic of Congo, Eritrea, Ethiopia, Guinea, Guinea-Bissau, Kenya, Liberia, Madagascar, Mali, Mozambique, Namibia, Niger, Republic of Congo (Brazzaville), Rwanda, Senegal, Sierra Leone, Somalia, South Africa, southern Sudan and Uganda. In these conflicts the abuses and neglect by the state security forces were often factors in the cause of the rebellions. And police and security force abuses were a large feature of the way many of the conflicts were conducted. The decimated and discredited police forces that emerged from conflict were neither able in themselves to be protectors of the public nor desired by the public to be their protectors. Yet the post-war environment demanded, more than anything else, law enforcement and crime protection. This was because of the surging crime wave fuelled by unemployed but armed ex-combatants seizing un-policed opportunities; those seeking vengeance for war abuses; and large numbers of destitute people fighting for survival over scarce resources. For the task of establishing even the minimal levels of social order necessary for human security and political and economic development, the post-war police were quite inadequate, whether measured in terms of numbers, skills, management, equipment or deployment.

Against this background of police degradation under authoritarian and conflict environments, police reconstruction features as a key priority for those seeking development, reconstruction and good governance in post-transition and post-conflict periods. A very different form of policing and police organisation was required for delivering that element of human security known as personal or citizen security; that is, security from violence, crime and disorder. Put positively, personal security is that which assures people that all the community of which they are part (including the rulers and the powerful) live by the agreed rules governing relationships. Focusing on the protection of people's lives and property, the resolution of their disputes, and the maintenance of the social order is, of course, only one aspect of human security. Yet it is foundational to the broad human security agenda, for it allows access to all the other key services and rights. This explains why personal security is a central concern of poor people. Repeatedly, local communities in the World Bank's *Voices of the Poor* research identified physical insecurity as their *major* barrier to development (Deepa *et al.* 2000).

The actualisation of police reconstruction in Africa to meet the clear need has its roots in the mid-1990s. The end of the cold war and the introduction of multiparty politics in much of Africa provoked widespread interest in development based on security and stability. With security increasingly seen as the essential basis of development, a logical starting point for many aid programmes was the security forces. A major hindrance to development needed to be turned into a major driver of development. Donor concern began with a call for 'democratic policing'—representative, responsive and accountable—as authoritarian states underwent transition to multiparty policies and conflict states reached some sort of peace (Bayley 1995; Heymann 1997; National Institute of Justice 1997). Yet even as the new international policing programmes were developed, the new 'human security' agenda, initiated by the UNDP's *Human Development Report 1994*, began to be influential. Marenin describes these two parallel but distinct discourses:

> one might be called the discovery of the development-security nexus, leading, in turn, to policy discussions on the need by the global community and transnational actors to be involved in peace-building, the pro-

motion of human security broadly defined, and security sector reform (SSR); the second policy stream has centred on and responded to developments in the field of police and policing, including the emergence of international democratic policing regimes, and general approaches to reform and innovation of policing organisations and policing and public security systems (Marenin 2005: 2).

By the millennium both reform streams had converged and been incorporated into the SSR (security sector reform) programmes being rolled out across the continent with donor support. The intent was nothing less than a radical restructuring of policing. Policing was no longer to be focused solely on the security of the regime, but on the security of the citizens. Particular values and standards of service delivery were to be required of the police, including: the protection of human rights; the eradication of corruption, violence and inefficiency; a legitimate, effective and just management structure; and oversight bodies external to the police that ensured discipline. The new objectives and vision are seen in donor discourse and policy documents. According to the Development Assistance Committee of the OECD (Organisation for Economic Co-operation and Development):

> Security is increasingly viewed as an all-encompassing condition in which people and communities live in freedom, peace and safety, participate fully in the governance of their countries, enjoy the protection of fundamental rights, have access to resources and the basic necessities of life, and inhabit an environment which is not detrimental to their health and wellbeing (OECD 2004: 16).

Likewise, the Development Ministers of the OECD explain:

> Security matters to the poor and other vulnerable groups, especially women and children, because bad policing, weak justice and penal systems and corrupt militaries mean that they suffer disproportionately from crime, insecurity and fear. They are consequently less likely to be able to access government services, invest in improving their own futures and escape from poverty (OECD 2005: 11).

According to the UNDP, the main objective of SSR is to bring the security agencies into line with the new human security agenda. Reform is: 'to strengthen the ability of the sector as a whole and each of its individual parts to provide an accountable, equitable, effective, and rights respecting service' (UNDP: 2003).

And the UK's Foreign and Commonwealth Office sets the police firmly within this broad security agenda:

> The police are the gatekeepers of the criminal justice system for many people in developing countries, and often the justice or security institution that most impacts on their everyday lives. Building an indigenous police service that acts in accordance with international human rights and democratic policing norms and the rule of law is therefore a key objective of most PSOs [Peace Support Operations] (FCO 2007: 21).

As consensus has been reached over SSR policy, so the checklist of institutions required to be constructed has been iterated. The influence of the new police restructuring agendas for Africa from 2003 onwards is evident everywhere across the continent (DFID 2003). Governments have signed up to policies and the police have signed up to mission statements that offer not just to 'protect' the state and the regime that controls it, but to 'serve' the people. The new era is frequently symbolised by the re-designation of the police as a 'service' rather than as a 'force'. Complaints desks have opened to ensure that human rights abuses by the police are reported, recorded and prosecuted. New family support units and women's units declare that women will now be treated seriously when they report gender crimes against them. Police community forums have been established to listen to local people's security needs and to draw up solutions along with the police.

Although policies and institutions have been put in place to make the police agents of human security, the practice of policing in Africa has not changed to the degree anticipated. For all the training and money invested in their management structures, few forces in Africa could be regarded as democratic or following a human security agenda. Why? Why have African police forces that are undergoing 'reform' shown so little increased accountability to civilian bodies that monitor their human rights conduct? In contrast, serious and persistent human rights abuses by the police, such as torture and rape of those held in custody, bribe-seeking, collusion with criminals and extra-judicial killings are widespread. Take the example of the Burundi police:

> Despite a number of positive developments, the transformation of the police into a state service that respects human rights and to provide security to vulnerable populations faces important challenges. For example, our national survey results reveal that 14% of the population interviewed identified the PNB [Burundi National Police] as one of the groups responsible for insecurity and human rights violations in their community. In addition, gender-based violence and sexual abuse is a particular concern for police reform (Powell 2007: 13).

The evidence of police not only failing to address human rights abuse, but themselves being perpetrators of abuse, applies not just to countries recently emerging from war and/or authoritarian systems, such as Burundi, but also to countries that have been peaceful, multiparty states for a decade or more, such as Nigeria. For instance, Human Rights Watch (HRW) research documented that:

> Across Nigeria, both senior and lower-level police officers routinely commit or order the torture and mistreatment of criminals . . . Forms of torture documented include the tying of arms and legs behind the body, suspension by hands and legs from the ceiling, severe beatings with metal or wooden objects, spraying of tear gas in the eyes, shooting in the foot or leg, raping female detainees, and using pliers or electric shocks on the penis. In addition, witnesses reported that dozens of suspects died as a result of their injuries; others were summarily executed in police custody . . . A culture of impunity has protected the perpetrators. When

> victims and others have tried to attain accountability they have faced har-
> assment, intimidation and obstruction by the police (HRW 2005).

Kenya, like Nigeria, is also associated with more than a decade of multiparty politics. Yet the Oscar Foundation documented 68 enforced disappearances after police arrests in the first three months of 2009, and 122 extra-judicial killings in January–March 2009.[1] Cumulatively, since 2007, the Oscar Foundation recorded 6,452 enforced disappearances and 1,721 extra-judicial killings by police officers. Its reports are derived from monitoring police activity and conducting a paralegal programme in major urban areas around Kenya. The state's Kenya National Commission on Human Rights, the Independent Medico Legal Unit and the Release Political Prisoners pressure group carried out similar investigations. Fewer than ten police officers have been brought to account for the crimes described in this paragraph.[2] During the ethnic conflicts that erupted nationwide in December 2007, rape was used as a tool of violence. According to the Kenya Police crime records there were 876 rape victims.[3] Many police officers were implicated in rapes and the election violence. The press reported that many women had tried to go to the police with their accusations but on many occasions they found that the police were unwilling to take statements. The police say they are investigating the sexual crimes that were committed during the collective violence, although no officer has been charged despite hundreds of allegations.[4]

More examples could be given.[5] Nigerian policing researcher, Etannibi Alemika, says the overall evidence across the African continent demonstrates that the police forces in most African countries are 'significantly brutal, corrupt, inefficient, unresponsive and unaccountable to the generality of the population' (IDASA 2007).

Police reforms have frequently targeted the recruitment of women and minorities into police forces (Liberia for instance has raised its female police officer ratio to 12% after repeated recruitment drives), yet the evidence suggests that there has been no significant impact on sexual violence and abuse against women and minorities. Indeed reports suggest alarming rates of domestic violence and rape, both reported to the police and unreported, but universally unsuccessfully prosecuted (US Department of State 2008). Reforms have also introduced 'community policing', which is a broad approach to police–public relations by police forces that seeks to mobilise local communities through police-sponsored community policing forums that develop anti-crime strategies in partnership with the police. Yet it has not resulted in policing styled to local needs by local people. Rather, the police have largely sidelined local policing forums and given them little attention (Brogden and Nijar 2005; Baker 2007).

---

1 allafrica.com/stories/200903091176.html (accessed 9 July 2010).
2 allafrica.com/stories/200903091176.html (accessed 24 September 2010).
3 allafrica.com/stories/201004020934.html (accessed 24 September 2010).
4 english.aljazeera.net/news/africa/2008/10/2008102075138816568.html (accessed 9 July 2010).
5 See: www.africanpolicing.org/Country_news.php (accessed 9 July 2010).

The question then arises as to why the human security agenda has not prospered under the reconstructed police. Is it lack of time, education, resources, or are there more structural problems? It is worth remembering that the human security agenda is a normative one, not simply a technical one. It incorporates attitudes of respect and entitlement to human rights for women, minorities and criminals that have previously been lacking; it reorients policing to serving the community rather than government; and to seeing the public as the object of concern not threat. For African policing this requires more than advisers, equipment and money. It requires a very large culture change within an organisation notorious worldwide for resisting change because of its male 'cop culture', hierarchical structure, out-of-sight activities, and political protection and direction. Four approaches have been central to attempts to bring about change that addresses the human security agenda: new rules and training for the police; new supervisory institutions within and outside the police force; vetting and removal of unsuitable officers; and community policing programmes to incorporate the public. Yet each of these four approaches is problematic.

New rules, policy manuals and training

Incorporating the new values into African or any other police forces cannot be done by diktat. Yet, so often peace agreements and new constitutions make assertions that cannot be readily implemented. In Liberia the Comprehensive Peace Agreement called for:

> an immediate restructuring of the National Police Force, the Immigration Force, Special Security Service (SSS), custom security guards and such other statutory security units. These restructured security forces shall adopt a professional orientation that emphasises democratic values and respect for human rights, a non-partisan approach to duty and the avoidance of corrupt practices (CPA 2003: Article VIII).

Likewise the General Peace Agreement of Mozambique 1992 was typical. Its aspirations are admirable: the police were to continue operations during the transition phase, but had to take into account democratic principles internationally established, such as respect for civil, political and human rights of the citizens; action according to the interests of the state; and free from partisan or ideological considerations, or any other kind of discrimination (GPA 1992 Protocol IV/IV; IV/V). The implementation of these, as of other legal documents in other countries, has largely gone unheeded. This is because change in police behaviour requires more than a new constitution, new legislation, re-organised management structures, short training workshops and revised police rules of arrest, detention and use of firearms. The attitudinal and behavioural changes required to realign relationships between the police and the population take time. Police reform is a long-term process that depends for its success on changing the cultural patterns and attitudes embedded in the specific history of a police service. The reality, however, is that reform programmes follow short-term budgets and seek quick results.

Take the example of the Sierra Leone Police. In order for it to meet its intake targets, despite the fact that training facilities had been severely damaged in the war of 1991–2001, the basic course was reduced from six months to 12 weeks, followed by three months of field training. Some of the top executive and middle-ranking police managers received training, but this was largely 'book knowledge', rather than 'the type of proficiency that comes with experience' (Meek 2003). Similar problems emerged from an overview of the donor training initiatives of the Burundian police in 2007. It was found that modules on human rights and behaviour towards the population lasted only a few days out of several weeks of intensive training. Further, even though survey results revealed that women and girls are vulnerable to insecurity and that sexual violence is common, there was no training on the gender dimensions of policing, including police responses to gender-based violence and their role in respecting and enforcing the rights of women and girls. When asked why the police basic training modules did not explicitly address the gender dimensions of policing, an official explained that police training was 'focusing on basics' (Powell 2007: 18-19).

Between 1997 and 2003, 9,253 Mozambique police personnel (46% of the service) were 'retrained', but the measure of success, as so often, was on 'outputs' (attendance at workshops) rather than 'outcomes' (change in behaviour). Not surprisingly those seven years of police reform achieved little in the way of altering the patterns of police management or modernising managerial processes and procedures so that a new democratic police culture could emerge. In addition the issue arose, as elsewhere, that graduates from the training school, armed with the 'new ideas', confronted active resistance from the old generation of police. This resistance to change was partially due to a fear of loss of power and status to the new graduates. An outside assessment of the Mozambique police observes that often change:

> May be possible only through generational change. In the case of Mozambique, since the approach was not to disband the existing police and create a new force afresh, this generational change will be crucial and, by necessity, gradual. It may require at least another decade until the investments in police education will take effect (Lalá and Francisco 2006: 174).

Unfortunately, basing change programmes on short-term training, any more than on new rules and regulations, is not going to achieve a human security agenda within the police.

New supervisory institutions

New oversight and supervisory institutions are also not in themselves sufficient to eradicate police brutality and corruption. Few lodge formal complaints, because of perceived defects in their legitimacy and effectiveness, and institutions often lack the staff and resources to fulfil their mandate adequately and in addition struggle to resist political interference. 'They have little if any impact' (Gyimah-Boadi 2004:

129). As a result, the Global Corruption surveys by Transparency International highlight the police in countries such as Ghana, Zambia, Nigeria and Kenya as among the most corrupt institutions in the country. For example, the Complaints, Discipline and Internal Investigation Department (CDIID) in Sierra Leone was set up to address indiscipline in the Sierra Leone Police. It is true that more than 100 officers were removed from the force in 2001–2006 as a result of public complaints. However, the Inspector General was still lamenting in 2006 that the police were one of the most corrupt institutions in the country: 'We need a complete change in attitude and behaviour'.[6] Keith Biddle, the former (British) Inspector General of the SLP, argues that changing attitudes in police culture, whether concerning corruption, brutality or public accountability is a personnel management problem, not just an operational matter. He says it requires line managers to accept responsibility for those under them rather than leaving it to an HQ department such as the CDIID. Is that going to happen? In his opinion: 'It's a massive culture we've got to change. It's not only stopping corruption. It's changing culture'.[7] Likewise, a member of the Commonwealth Community Safety and Security Project (CCSSP) team, which was the chief agent for post-war police reform, claimed: 'CDIID covers professional standards, but that really should be a local problem not just a HQ concern'.[8] So, despite the presence of this new oversight institution, the practice continues in the SLP of charging complainants fees for paper and pens before obtaining statements from them, while 81% of the public still claim that the traffic police arbitrarily demand money from drivers (SLP 2004).

Police reform in Liberia has introduced a professional standards unit that exists, in their own words, 'To instil discipline in the police—to make sure they conform to the rules and regulations manual'.[9] Yet the unit has just one office—buried in the police HQ in Monrovia—and few even know of its existence. Complaints, it says, 'normally come through the channel of the IG' who acts as the judge after the investigation.[10] Between 2003 and 2007 only one officer was dismissed. Interviewed in 2007 they were quite unwilling to consider that police bribery took place: it was all 'made up stories' by the press.[11] Yet just a few hundred yards from the office, traffic police openly took or asked for bribes from vehicle drivers and police officers moved through the markets taking what they wanted or demanding money for its return. And charges of brutality abound across the country.

6 www.africanpolicing.org/Sierra%20Leone%20Police%20News%20August%202006.pdf (accessed 9 July 2010).
7 Interview with Keith Biddle, Freetown, Sierra Leone, February 2005.
8 Interview with CCSSP adviser, Freetown, Sierra Leone, February 2005. CCSSP was established in 2000 to provide training, support and advice to the police. Funded largely through DFID, the mission of the CCSSP was to 're-establish the Sierra Leone Police as an effective and accountable civilian police service'.
9 Interview with the deputy head of the Liberian Police Professional Standards Department, Monrovia, Liberia, February 2007.
10 Ibid.
11 Ibid.

As regards external oversight, African parliaments, by and large, are ill-equipped to scrutinise or exercise rigorous oversight over public services through parliamentary committees. At best they are consultative bodies for the executive branch. When it comes to security matters parliaments abstain from exercising control, preferring to defer to the executive branch. For instance, a recent report on the security sector in Senegal noted that the oversight function of the parliament is supposed to be carried out by the 30-strong Committee on Defence and Security. However the committee members are conscious of their lack of specialist knowledge compared with defence and security chiefs and therefore do not feel competent to raise questions to the executive and to follow through on their oversight responsibilities in these areas. Further:

> The committee does not meet regularly; its meetings are not open to the public . . . the committee has never initiated legislation on security sector governance or weighed significantly on any specific aspect of its governance . . . The CDS's chairman insisted that in the plenary sessions of the parliament, deputies now and then raise security- related questions and concerns, and call on the government to solve them . . . [However] though the chairman recounted anecdotes of his personal efforts in regard [to combating corruption], no specific initiative of the CDS could be pointed to . . . The committee's powers (investigations, hearings on defence and security issues, close scrutiny of budgetary matters, participation in security or defence policy framing, preparation of any aspect of the Senegalese peacekeepers or visiting them abroad), would give it a consistent role in the overall governance of the security sector. However, none of the many powers of the committee were actually exercised (N'Diaye 2008: 218).

The lesson is that supervisory agencies of the police, internal and external, do not work unless there is the political will. Reform has to go beyond setting up a new institution. They alone will not eradicate corruption and human rights abuses in the police. They will not by themselves bring about discipline for the officers and ensure their integrity.

Vetting and recruitment of officers

The term vetting is defined as a formal process to identify and remove from office individuals responsible for abuses. In some cases, the political situation is such that, though it might be thought necessary by donors, a comprehensive vetting is resisted by the state for reasons of sensitivity, stability or protection of the regime's 'servants'. Thus, Mozambique, South Africa and Sierra Leone chose not to thoroughly vet their police in the transition period. Nevertheless, vetting, deactivation and new recruitment is commonly seen as a useful process for driving forward the sensitivity to human rights by police officers. However its implementation is far from the effective method that is often portrayed.

Take, for example, post-war Liberia. By February 2007, 2,064 of the 3,010 registered in the Liberia National Police had been disqualified on the grounds that they had committed human rights abuses; were political appointees with no qualifications; or, more controversially, had served for more than 25 years or who were over 55 years old. Inevitably in the post-war environment the process of searching for human rights abuses was a very inexact process. The UN police unit in charge did not seek the evaluation of serving officers' home communities. Instead it sent a list of names for comment to human rights NGOs and agencies, few of whom knew much about those who had moved around the country in the war and changed their names. In addition, it put up posters and placed adverts in the newspapers, even though illiteracy is 70% and the total circulation of the capital-based press is only 2,000 readers. The lame explanation given for this weak investigation by an UNPOL vetting officer was: 'It is the best we can do . . . we don't go to the community they grew up in for in-service officers'.[12] Meanwhile the inadequacy and injustice of the process left a lot of disgruntled officers. Many failed simply by being unable to provide sufficient proof of educational qualifications—which is not easy in a country where much of the official documentation has been destroyed. A recent report concludes that the process may have been too hasty and that some human rights abusers in the police were not reported for fear of retaliation, given that there was little protection of the identity of informants. In addition it found that:

> There is some concern that now that the vetting and recruitment process has come to an end, the original vetting functions will be abandoned . . . it is hoped that the vetting functions will be replaced by a professional standards, integrity-enhancing mechanism as part of the regular administrative structure of the police force. However, observers note the existence of major problems within the LNP, particularly concerning endemic institutional corruption, scant institutional knowledge of the way that human rights requirements and Liberian law should underpin and shape operational standards and procedures, and poor leadership from the higher echelons of the force (Fithen 2009: 17).

Similar problems have beset vetting procedures in non-conflict countries, demonstrated in the recent process initiated in Botswana, following the merging of the Botswana Local Police and Botswana Police Service.[13]

A vetting and deactivation process has to be complemented by a recruitment policy. Yet invariably the targeted numbers have little relationship to the numbers needed from an operational point of view to protect the public. Instead they have everything to do with what the donors think can be afforded and sustained by national governments. In summary, getting the right number of suitable officers to implement human rights policy and eschew corruption is a daunting task.

12 Interview with UNPOL vetting officer, Monrovia, Liberia, February 2007.
13 allafrica.com/stories/200906020848.html (accessed 9 July 2010).

Community policing programmes

Police reform invariably adopts a community-orientated approach that seeks to empower local people regarding their own security within a police–community partnership. It is thus a key element to promoting human security. The concept of community policing is based on the principle of coordination and consultation between the police and the public, and on a united assessment of local security needs and on the ways of preventing and curbing crime and insecurity.

Rarely is it questioned that the public will want community policing, but, of course, where there has been a history of police abuse and brutality, citizens may be very wary of the police becoming their 'partners' in securing their communities. Where there is an interest, it may well be that it is the most vocal and powerful local elements that hijack the police community forum committee for personal gain. There are certainly accusations in Africa of community policing forums being controlled by local criminal elements.[14] In other words, there can be very real problems in ensuring such forums represent their communities, assuming that the community is sufficiently homogeneous to be represented by a small group of citizens in the first place.

For their part, police officers may also be reluctant to put much energy into another initiative 'sent down' from HQ. At the very least, local station commanders may be reluctant to stray far from their usual practices or to take on additional responsibilities outside of the station where they prefer to stay. As for the concept that they, as professionals, have anything to learn from the community in regard to strategy or worse, criticism, this meets with incomprehension and resistance in much of Africa. From a station commander's point of view, if such novel ideas have to be implemented, then this can be done by just one of the lowest ranks and not treated too seriously. In other words, community policing does not become a new way of doing things but another duty to perform.

Reform that has been resisted by police in the West (Skogan 2008) is, not surprisingly, resisted in Africa. Ruteere and Pommerolle (2003) found in Kenya that, while the people expected to be included in community policing initiatives, the police regarded the police–public forums as 'too time-consuming and too soft in the context of increasing crime rates'. They simply wanted interaction with the community to provide them with crime intelligence. Kyed (2007) found the same in Mozambique, plus the inclination of the police to use forums as sources of free labour to do the tasks that were onerous to them. My research in Freetown, Sierra Leone, found disillusionment with the lack of police interest in and resources for the partnership. As a result some members of policing forums have set up additional neighbourhood watches to do the 'real' work of crime prevention in their neighbourhoods (Baker 2007). An internal ICTJ (International Center for Transitional Justice) report

---

14 A Sierra Leone police commander in Makeni, interviewed in February 2005, told me: 'We have Neighbourhood Watch but it is not too effective since some of the youth on it are criminals!'

in early 2008 found that there were about 90 community policing forums in Monrovia, but these hardly meet, were badly coordinated, and few people knew about them or the work they were supposed to do.

> The result is that citizens–police relations are so poor that often enraged community people have in the recent past physically attacked police officers, suspecting them of collusion in criminal activity, at crime scenes, and in a few instances outside of Monrovia, citizens have burnt down police posts and badly assaulted police officers (in a few instances leading to the death of officers).[15]

If the police fail to develop new operational structures and embed the principles of community-oriented policing within their own culture and ways of working, community policing is unlikely to be sustained beyond the life of the trainers. A former police commissioner who worked with the United Nations Mission in Sudan (UNMIS), noted in 2006:

> Community policing is a concept little understood in many police cultures and is frequently mistaken to refer to a special squad or department of police which will deal with the community . . . In the Sudan context, a true 'community policing' programme will require a fundamental shift in attitudes by police, government and the communities themselves as well as changes to the law. These things are unlikely to happen quickly (quoted in Rauch and van der Spuy 2006: 48).

With a Kenyan victimisation survey showing that over half of crime victims do not report to the police because they are deemed inefficient, and with respondents believing that one in three crimes is either directly or indirectly attributed to the police themselves, Ruteere and Pommerolle ask: 'What is the relevance—in a context of deep running structurally defined mutual distrust—of a policing strategy such as community policing, the selling point of which is the co-operation between citizens and police forces' (2003: 594).

There are reports that increased cooperation with and empowerment of the public is leading to greater confidence in the police in some parts of Africa. A local commander in the Uganda Police told me in 2004: 'I believe the fear of the police has gone, as people have understood the law and discovered their rights'.[16] And a local unit commander in Sierra Leone told me in 2005: 'When I joined in 1984, the SLP were masters. Now people are masters. It is hard. 24 years ago people were frightened of the police . . . Now we try to be friendly to them'.[17] But, overall, police show a reluctance to see citizens empowered in order to have some control over their own security.

---

15 Reported by the Global Facilitation Network for Security Sector Reform (GFN-SSR), www.ssrnetwork.net/ssrbulletin/liberia.php, accessed 9 July 2010.
16 Interview with the officer in charge, Mityana Police Station, Uganda, March 2004.
17 Interview with local unit commander, Magburaka, Sierra Leone, February 2005.

Conclusion

The most obvious drivers of a human security agenda in Africa, or at least the personal security aspect, are the police. Yet the evidence is that they are actually impeding that agenda. Though they are officially the upholders of the new laws that protect women and minorities; though they are in the front line in protecting people from human rights abuses and arresting those who commit them; though their organisational mission statements are to serve all the people equally; though they are operating programmes that officially promote the empowering of people; they are neither well equipped nor, more importantly, fully persuaded of the task. Where constitutions and legislation and policy initiatives run ahead of the prevailing local culture(s) that police share, for example the rights of criminals, they are not going to be enforced by the police. They do not see themselves as radicals driving through an agenda that is not welcomed by the people with whom they share their lives.

Where an agenda is welcome by the people but not by their masters in political leadership, such as allowing opposition rallies, the police see their first duty as being to the latter. Police reconstruction in Africa will only succeed where there are compelling political reasons, for rulers in Africa (whether elected 'fairly' or not) invariably keep a tight hold on 'their' police to ensure their own survival. The fact is that the first two or three layers of senior management are invariably political appointees—those deemed reliable, loyal friends of the president and his or her government. Talk of making the police accountable to the public for their actions in such a political structure is naïve. If change of any sort is to take place, it takes place because the president has determined that it is in his or her political interests (see Hills 2008).

Police in Africa, therefore, are forces of social conservatism not of social change. They will follow but not lead. The human security agenda will not be delivered by 'training' the police. It will be delivered when human security values have won the argument in the corridors of power and then in the streets and fields of the land. As Seleti (2000) has pointed out, historical legacies of police cultural practices are not easily dispelled by reforms. It may be, as he observes in Mozambique, that such things yield more to public and media pressure than institutional changes or training programmes. The history of social engineering is discouraging.

The experience of UK policing working in other countries and contributing to the introduction of a democratic model of policing (community policing) has shown it often requires a fundamental transformation of moving the police 'from a force to be feared to a service to be valued' (Graham Mathias, formerly of the Metropolitan Police Service, June 2006, quoted in FCO 2007: 48).

Norms in societies change as the argument is won in the marketplace: whether that marketplace is the radio chat show, the TV soap, the street corner, the church or under the village tree. The norms associated with human security have yet to make much impression on policing in Africa.

Bibliography

Baker, B. (2007) 'Community Policing in Freetown, Sierra Leone: Foreign Import or Local Solution?', *Journal of Intervention and Statebuilding* 2.1: 23-42.

Bayley, D. (1995) 'A Foreign Policy for Democratic Policing', *Policing and Society* 5: 79-88.

Brogden, M., and P. Nijar (2005) *Community Policing: National and International Models and Approaches* (Cullompton, UK: Willan).

Comprehensive Peace Agreement (CPA) between the Government of Liberia and the Liberians United for Reconciliation and Democracy (LURD) and the Movement for Democracy in Liberia (Model) and the Political Parties (2003). Full text available at United States Institute for Peace: www.usip.org/files/file/resources/collections/peace_agreements/liberia_08182003.pdf, accessed 24 September 2010.

Deepa, N., with R. Patel, K. Schafft, A. Rademacher and S. Koch-Schulte (2000) *Voices of the Poor: Can Anyone Hear Us?* (New York: Oxford University Press).

DFID (2003) 'Security Sector Reform Policy Brief'; www.dfid.gov.uk/pubs/files/security-sector-brief.pdf, accessed 9 July 2010.

FCO (2007) 'Peace Support Operations. Information and Guidance for UK Police Personnel' (London: FCO).

Fithen, C. (2009) 'The Legacy of Four Vetting Programs: An Empirical Review', International Center for Transitional Justice; www.ictj.org/images/content/1/2/1276.pdf, accessed 9 July 2010.

General Peace Agreement (GPA) for Mozambique (1992). Full text available at Conciliation Resources: www.c-r.org/our-work/accord/mozambique/rome-process.php, accessed 24 September 2010.

Gyimah-Boadi, E. (2004) *Democratic Reform in Africa: The Quality of Progress* (Boulder, CO: Lynne Rienner).

Heymann, P. (1997) 'Principles of Democratic Policing', in National Institute of Justice (ed.), *Policing in Emerging Democracies: Workshop Papers and Highlights* (Washington, DC: US Department of Justice): 9-24.

Hills, A. (2000) *Policing Africa: Internal Security and the Limits of Liberalization* (Boulder, CO: Lynne Rienner).

—— (2008) 'The Dialectic of Police Reform in Nigeria', *The Journal of Modern African Studies* 46.2: 215-34.

HRW (Human Rights Watch) (2005) ' "Rest in Pieces": Police Torture and Deaths in Custody in Nigeria'; hrw.org/english/docs/2005/07/26/nigeri11451.htm, accessed 9 July 2010.

IDASA (2007) 'Conference Summary Report', *Police Reform & Democratisation Conference*, Pretoria, 12–15 March 2007; www.idasa.org.za/index.asp?page=topics_details.asp%3FRID%3D11.

Kyed, H.M. (2007) 'The Politics of Policing: Re-capturing "Zones of Confusion" in Rural Post-war Mozambique', in L. Buur, S. Jensen and F. Stepputat (eds.), *The Security Development Nexus: Expressions of Sovereignty and Securitization in Southern Africa* (Uppsala, Sweden: Nordic Africa Institute; Pretoria: HSRC Press).

Lalá, A., and L. Francisco (2006) 'The Difficulties of Donor Coordination: Police and Judicial Reform in Mozambique', *Civil Wars* 8.2: 163-80; www.informaworld.com/smpp/title~content=t713634578~db=all~tab=issueslist~branches=8.

Marenin, O. (2005) *Restoring Policing Systems in Conflict Torn Nations: Process, Problems, Prospects* (Geneva: DCAF).

Meek, S. (2003) *Policing Sierra Leone* (ISS Monograph 80; Pretoria: ISS).

National Institute of Justice (1997) *Policing in Emerging Democracies: Workshop Papers and Highlights* (Washington, DC: US Department of Justice).

N'Diaye, B. (2008) 'Senegal', in A. Ebo and B. N'Diaye (eds.), *Parliamentary Oversight of the Security Sector in West Africa: Opportunities and Challenges* (Geneva: Centre for the Democratic Control of Armed Forces, DCAF): 203-22.

OECD (2004) 'Security System Reform and Governance: Policy and Good Practice' (Policy Brief; Paris: OECD).

—— (2005) *Fuelling the Future: Security, Stability, Development* (Paris: OECD; www.oecd.org/site/0,2865,en_21571361_34225293_1_1_1_1_1,00.html).

OHCHR (Office of the High Commissioner for Human Rights) (1997) *Human Rights and Law Enforcement: A Manual of Human Rights Training for the Police* (Professional Training Series No. 5; Geneva: OHCHR).

Powell, K. (2007) *Security Sector Reform and the Protection of Civilians in Burundi: Accomplishments, Dilemmas and Ideas for International Engagement* (Ottawa, Canada: The North-South Institute).

Rauch, J., and E. Van Der Spuy (2006) *Police Reform In Post-Conflict Africa: A Review* (Pretoria: Institute for Democracy in South Africa [Idasa]).

Ruteere, M., and M. Pommerolle (2003) 'Democratizing Security or Decentralizing Repression? The Ambiguities of Community Policing In Kenya', *African Affairs* 102: 587-604.

Seleti, Y. (2000) 'The Public in the Exorcism of the Police in Mozambique: Challenges of Institutional Democratization', *Journal of Southern African Studies* 26.2: 349-64.

Skogan, W. (2008) 'Why Reforms Fail', *Policing and Society* 18.1: 23-34.

SLP (Sierra Leone Police) (2004) 'An Investigative Perception Survey on the Performance of the SLP for the First Half of the Year 2004: A Case Study of the Western Area and the Provincial Towns of Makeni, Bo and Kenem' (Freetown, Sierra Leone: SLP).

UNDP (1994) *Human Development Report 1994* (New York: UNDP).

—— (2003) *Security Sector Transformation and Transitional Justice: A Crisis Post-Conflict Programmatic Approach* (New York: UNDP).

US Department of State (2008) '2008 Country Reports on Human Rights Practices'; www.state.gov/g/drl/rls/hrrpt/2008, accessed 9 July 2010.

15

Human security crisis in India
From the fiery field of a conflict zone

Manish K. Jha
Tata Institute of Social Sciences, India

The inception and progression of the concept of human security has been received differently by different disciplines; however, the discourse around it has generated serious interest and engagement by a cross-section of people. Critics claim that human security is nothing more than neologism, which makes no value addition to the existing range of related concepts such as 'human development' and 'human rights'. It is argued that the definition of the concept is abstract and lacks clarity. Existing definitions of human security are extraordinarily expansive and vague, encompassing everything from physical security to psychological well-being. It provides little guidance to policy-makers on its application and to academics on its distinctiveness as a concept (Paris 2001: 88). The arguments of critics notwithstanding, while the concept of human security is not a panacea for all concerns of insecurity and vulnerabilities, it certainly provides a useful framework for analysis and engagement. The discursive and evolving nature of discourse around human security also provides a space to locate the concerns of insecurity of people on the margins within the ambit of human security, without being trapped in the quagmire and definitiveness of the concept.

Though most of the literature traces the idea of human security to the 1945 UN San Francisco Conference, the term came into circulation and debate when it was defined by United Nations Development Programme's (UNDP) Human Development Report (HDR) in 1994.

> The concept of security has for too long been interpreted narrowly: as security of territory from external aggression, or as protection of national

> interest in foreign policy or as global security from the threat of nuclear holocaust . . . Forgotten were the legitimate concerns of ordinary people who sought security in their daily lives (UNDP 1994: 22).

The HDR 1994 defined human security as 'safety from chronic threats such as hunger, disease, and repression as well as protection from sudden and harmful disruption in the pattern of daily life'. The report identified seven components that constitute human security: economic security, food security, health security, environment security, personal security, community security and political security. An inclusive and integrative definition of human security broadly delineates two approaches: namely, protection of the individual from threats due to hunger, disease and natural disasters; and from conflict and violence. HDR 1994 makes a departure from the traditional notion of security and repositions it in terms of freedom: freedom from fear (of violence and conflict) and freedom from want (hunger, deprivation, etc.). Through this, the effort has been made to bring security down to the lives of human beings. In so doing, the discursive economy of human security not only sought to unravel the notion of security from statism and the interstate system, but also attempted to couple security with the concerns of international humanitarianism and human development (de Larrinaga and Doucet 2008: 518).

Subsequently, the Report of the Commission on Human Security 2003 and HDR 2005 focused on growing human insecurity in developing countries and located the discussion against the backdrop of neo-liberal economic policies and practice. However, the Human Security Report 2005 found these formulations expansive and therefore it concentrated on 'violent threats to individuals'. All the human security reports brought out by the Human Security Centre put special emphasis on armed conflict and political violence within the framework of freedom from fear. The 2005 Human Security Report classified conflict into four broad categories: interstate; intrastate (civil); extra-state and non-state conflicts. Elaborating further on conflict and its implication, the report states that over the past decade and more genocide has decreased and given way to 'politicide' and 'democide'. 'Politicide' refers to government 'policies that seek to destroy groups because of their political beliefs rather than their religion or ethnicity' (Human Security Centre 2005: 40). Further, 'democide' includes 'genocide, politicide and other massacres, but also deaths that rise from government actions (or deliberate failure to act) that kill people indirectly (Human Security Centre 2005: 41). It also cautions against the policies and intervention strategies of the state that are couched in terms of combating militancy and terror, but lead to premeditated violence against a section of people or territory. It is through the nexus between the state and non-state actors that the provision of both security and insecurity of individuals and communities is predominantly understood and analysed.

Yet more dimensions of human insecurity are brought to the fore by 'increasing terrorist attacks' and justification for 'global war on terror', which made a violent and brutal return of the discourse of state-centric security.

From unsanctioned, pre-emptive military actions against harbouring states and rogue states and targeted military operations to support the 'war on terror', to extra legal detention centres, state-sponsored assassinations, 'extraordinary rendition', deportation without due process, suspension of habeas corpus and indefinite detention, the contemporary moment certainly does not seem to leave much space for governance with a 'human face' (de Larrinaga and Doucet 2008: 518).

Using the work of Michel Foucault and Giorgio Agamben, de Larrinaga and Doucet outline the duality of sovereign power and biopower by examining not only how the human security discourse participates in defining the conditions of exceptionality, thus enabling the exercise of sovereign power, but also how, in making human life as its target, human security ultimately enacts the human in biopolitical terms.

The chapter discusses the issue of human security in the context of the current crisis facing India. It examines an unfolding of civil war that has been silently played out between the Indian state, the Naxals/Maoists[1] and a government-sponsored, extra-constitutional force called Salwa Judum[2] since 2005. The conflict challenges democratic India, as it has steadily amplified the traditional gulf between the government and the people and worsened the conditions of life of the locals. An enunciation of the above would also reveal the inadequacy of the concept as well as its plausible misappropriation by the state and its institutions under the pretext of ensuring human security, thereby further creating conditions of violence and fear among the people. The chapter then explores the ways by which the agenda of human security can be subverted and manipulated against those it professes to protect. The appeal therefore is towards bringing the state, its institutional apparatus and practices within the ambit of human security apprehensions over ensuring human security.

Underdevelopment misappropriated

India, which is the largest democratic country in the world, has demonstrated its ability to manage varied conflict situations in the past. A tumultuous region, which occupies a prominent place in the global map of conflicts, the Indian state has used a variety of techniques to deal with conflicts. Religion, language, caste, ethnicity and issues of autonomy and sub-nationalism are the fault lines which in varying dimensions feed into a cycle of conflicts in India. Conflicts on communal lines, both violent and otherwise, form one of the most disastrous aspects of the body

1 Naxals/Maoists are those communists who believe in and espouse different ideological trends of Maoism. Starting as a peasant movement in the Naxalbari area of West Bengal, they are now active in different parts of central and eastern India.
2 Militia supported by the state to counter Maoist influence in the tribal areas of Chhattisgarh, India.

politic of India. While historical enmity and current expressions of hatred between Hindu and Muslim communities take the centre stage of communal discourses in India, widespread escalation of violence against the Christian community in several parts of the country has also reached noticeable proportions in the past two decades. The upsetting Gujarat genocide (2002) exposed planned and organised crime against Muslim minorities, with tacit support from the state, and, along with a spate of attacks on churches and priests and the rape of nuns, has highlighted the growing insecure condition of minorities. Besides, several ethnic movements in the north-eastern part of the country organised around the so-called 'feeling of betrayal' by the Indian state where a coercive and manipulated integration of their ethnic territories to the Indian Union is being challenged.

Pervasive mistrust regarding the intent and ability of the state towards security of vulnerable communities is palpable. However, one of the most protracted conflicts in India is known as the Naxalite or Maoist movement. The techniques of government to deal with the Maoist insurgency include aggression by the state that led to a spiral of violence and counter-violence, thereby exacerbating the crisis for human security. This chapter locates the crisis through a case illustration of the Dantewada district of Chhattisgarh state which has a large and culturally rich population of tribal groups. The tribal population belongs to the Maria, Muria, Bhatra, Halba, Dhurwa and Gond tribes who represent 80% of the total population of Dantewada. The district comes under Schedule V of the Indian constitution which binds the government to ensure good governance and safeguard the interests of tribal groups. However, according to the 2001 census, out of 1,220 tribal populated villages, 1,161 had no medical facilities, 214 had no primary school, and the literacy rate was 29% for men and 14% for women. This reality exists despite the fact that there are rich mineral reserves in the area which have attracted several industrial companies in the recent past including mining and power stations.

The influence of the armed Maoist movement, popularly known as Naxalites, envelops 12 states in India. The Indian Home Ministry estimates that 91% of violence in India, and 89% of deaths arising from violence, are the result of Naxalite action (Government of India 2005: 39). Even by the conservative estimate of the Government of India, around 160 districts[3] out of approximately 600 districts of the country are witnessing the influence of Maoism. The so-called 'Naxal infected areas' of India are in tribal belts of about 7,000 villages in approximately 19% of India's forests. It is widely acknowledged that the adoption of privatisation policies has increased inequality and the rural–urban divide in addition to increased exploitation of natural resources, alteration of forest laws leading to the felling of trees and the entrance of exploitative contractors into impoverished communities (Tadjbakhsh and Chenoy 2008: 156). Of these districts, the influence of Maoists is quite high in at least 50 where they are either running a parallel governance system or contesting outright the existence of the state and its agencies. They claim to

---

3 Districts are administrative divisions below the states which look after revenue, law and order and others administrative matters in a decentralised manner.

defend the rights of the poor, especially the landless, *dalits* (members of the lowest caste) and tribal communities. The growth of the Maoist influence is largely attributed to the neglect of tribal interests and aspirations by the state and its agencies. Prior to the Maoist influence in the area, tribal communities encountered harassment from forest officials on a recurring basis, were forced to sell their produce to non-tribal contractors and money-lenders at low rates, and tribal women were at a high risk of sexual exploitation at the hands of money-lenders and contractors. The Maoists claim that they are fighting for tribal people's right to *jal, jangala aur zameen* (water, forest and land) and for this they are organising people for armed struggle. While the causality link between underdevelopment and conflict remains to be fully explored, the sense of injustice and grievances can be appropriated for mobilisation purposes and the increasing influence of Maoists is a testimony to this.

The repeated armed attacks across a growing geographical area led Indian Prime Minister Manmohan Singh in 2006 to describe the Naxalite movement as the 'single biggest internal security challenge ever faced' by India. The influence of Naxalites in the 'red corridor'[4] starts from southern Bihar and passes through Jharkhand, Chhattisgarh, Orissa, Andhra Pradesh and parts of Maharashtra and Karnataka. The Maoists claim to include 600 million people in the 'organisational sweep' of their Dandakaranya[5] 'guerrilla zone' comprising Gadchiroli, Bhandara, Balaghat, Rajnandgaon, undivided Bastar, and Malkangiri,[6] which is headed by a Special Zonal Committee. Their mass organisations, such as Dandakaranya Adivasi Kisan Mazdoor Sangathan and the Krantikari Mahila Sangathan are known at the grass roots as *sanghams*. Besides, the People's Guerrilla Army, popularly known as *dalam*, is an armed unit carrying out the underground activities of the Maoists.

It has been observed that indigenous tribal communities living in these areas are sympathetic towards the Maoists and support their interventions against economic exploitation. If sovereignty, like property, provided prescriptive rights, the Maoists can certainly claim the right to sovereignty in Dantewada by prescription since they took over an area practically unoccupied by the Indian state (Balagopal 2006: 2,184). The main reason for the wide popularity of the Naxalites in the entire forest region abutting the Godavari River in Telangana, Vidharbha and Chhattisgarh, is the protection they gave to the forest-dwellers for cultivation in reserve forests, the substantial increase they achieved in payment for harvesting tendu leaf, and the end they put to the oppressive domination of the headmen and the *patwaris* (land record clerk) (Balagopal 2006: 2,184-85). These achievements, however, have

---

4 'Red corridor' is used to describe the underdeveloped region in the eastern part of India where the influence of Naxalites/Maoists is quite substantive.

5 Extending over an area of 92,200 km², Dandakaranya is an area in east-central India covering the Abujhmar hills in the west and bordering the eastern coasts in the east. It includes parts of Chhattisgarh, Orissa and Andhra Pradesh states.

6 These are administrative districts in the states of Maharashtra, Madhya Pradesh, Chhattisgarh, etc.

co-existed with brute force; the Maoists have killed village headmen, *sarpanches*[7] and others who have opposed them (Sundar 2006: 3,190).

In keeping with their emphasis on militarism, the Maoists proudly list attacks on police stations, especially during 'retaliation week', the 'annihilation' of CRPF (Central Reserve Police Force) personnel, attacks on NMDC (National Mineral Development Corporation) explosives depot, and the killing of 'Salwa Judum goons' (Sundar 2006: 3,191). They have abducted, tortured and executed villagers who they believed were Salwa Judum supporters or their family members. Villagers who left voluntarily or were forced into Salwa Judum camps fear being assaulted or killed by Maoists in retaliation if they attempt to return to their villages. There have been cases of high-handedness by some of the cadres, including extortion of money, recruitment of civilians through intimidation and killings of alleged informants or 'traitors'. This has gradually resulted in widespread resentment of the Maoists. A substantive section of people in the area expressed unhappiness with the Maoists for not allowing activities such as road building in the area, forcing them to attend meetings, making them provide food for the squads, making them give away land and cattle which the Naxalites deemed excessive or forcing them to cultivate land on behalf of the armed squads. However, villagers in the area have claimed that the killing of civilians by the Maoists started only in retaliation to the Salwa Judum.

State-vigilante group nexus and perpetuation of human insecurity

The discontent and despondency regarding the Maoists among a section of the tribal groups was taken advantage of by the state and its agencies and an unlawful gang was formed in a clandestine manner. In June 2005, a state-supported vigilante group called 'Salwa Judum' ('peace mission' or 'purification hunt') was formed in Chhattisgarh (CG),[8] which aimed at eliminating Naxalites. The government of CG described Salwa Judum as 'spontaneous', 'self-initiated' groups of tribal people who want to bring peace in the area troubled by Maoists. However, the evidence suggests that there was prior government planning, including a police video which talks of 'Operation Salwa Judum' initiated from January 2005 onwards, and the Director General of Police (DGP) Chhattisgarh saying that Salwa Judum had been introduced as a 'pilot project' in two blocks of the Dantewada district (*Asian Age* 2005 cited in Sundar 2006: 3,191). The intent of the state is reflected in the 2005–2006 Annual Report of the Ministry of Home Affairs: 'The States have also been advised

---

7 Elected representative at *panchayat* level, democratic decentralisation.
8 Chhattisgarh is heavily forested, with a substantive population of indigenous tribal groups. Tribal communities make up about 32% of the total population of Chhattisgarh. In Dantewada and Bijapur districts, about 79% of the population is tribal.

to encourage formation of Local Resistance Groups/Village Defence Committees/ Nagrik Suraksha Samitis (Civilian Protection Committees) in Naxalite affected areas' (Government of India 2005). Other documents from the Indian Government and district administration show meticulous planning for crafting an organisation such as Salwa Judum. The process of formation of the vigilante group was kept under a veil of secrecy in such a sophisticated manner that it took nearly a year for an otherwise alert Indian media to realise the structure and strategies of Salwa Judum. Though there are numerous accounts about the origin of Salwa Judum, it is quite clear that it has been established to combat the Maoists, and the prime-mover of this was Mahendra Karma, the then MLA (member of the legislative assembly) of the Congress Party and leader of the opposition. Several fact-finding teams have emphatically concluded that by all accounts Salwa Judum is state-supported, state-sponsored and state-organised endeavour that has unleashed an atmosphere of terror rather than bringing peace which was the justification for its inception.

With the active support of government security forces, Salwa Judum members conducted violent raids on hundreds of villages suspected of being pro-Naxalite, forcibly recruited civilians for its vigilante activities, and relocated thousands of people to government-run Salwa Judum camps. They attacked villagers who refused to participate in Salwa Judum or left the camps. This has been countered by equally aggressive Maoist groups and a spiral of violence engulfs innocent people and communities on a recurring basis. In one of its most offensive and aggressive responses against Salwa Judum and state agencies, Maoist retaliation is at its peak in the hinterlands of Chhattisgarh. The tribal people of the area are always on tenterhooks and there are continuous fears of being seen to side with Salwa Judum and the state or with the Maoists; in either of the situations, their life, liberty and security is in jeopardy. An extreme sense of vulnerability and of rampant insecurity is easily discernible through the telling narration of a camp resident:

> We often wonder what sins we committed to be born at this time. Our lives are impossible. Naxalites come and threaten us. They demand food and ask us to help them with information about police movements. Then the police come. They beat us and ask us for information. We are caught between these people. There is no way out (HRW 2008b: 6).

Human rights organisations and other citizens' initiatives and fact-finding teams found overwhelming evidence of direct state involvement in Salwa Judum and the group's involvement in numerous violent abuses. Over a period of approximately four years, government security forces joined Salwa Judum members on village raids, which were designed to identify suspected Naxalite sympathisers and evacuate residents from villages believed to be providing support to Naxalites. They raided hundreds of villages in Bijapur and Dantewada districts, engaging in threats, beatings, arbitrary arrests and detention, killings, pillage and burning of villages to force residents into supporting Salwa Judum. They forcibly relocated thousands of villagers to government-run makeshift Salwa Judum camps near police stations or paramilitary police camps along the highways. They also coerced camp residents, including children, to join in Salwa Judum's activities, beating and imposing penalties on those who refused (HRW 2008b: 7). The Chief Minister of Chhattisgarh has openly declared that 'those in the camps are with the government and those in the forests are with the Maoist' (Balagopal 2006: 2184).

Chhattisgarh police have recruited camp residents including children as special police officers (SPOs), an auxiliary police force, and deploy them with other paramilitary police on joint anti-Naxalite combing operations. This has exposed underage SPOs to life-threatening dangers, including armed attacks by Naxalites, explosions from landmines and improvised explosive devices (IEDs), and Naxalite retaliation killings. Using insufficiently trained, non-professional Salwa Judum cadre for a sophisticated counterinsurgency operation has already proved reckless and deadly. It has resulted in a total breakdown in the rule of law and has given license to impressionable young men to terrorise and kill without cause or justification (Mohapatra 2007: 6). Many SPOs are unemployed tribal youth, who have joined up merely to earn Rs.1,500. A good number of SPOs are minors, which is a blatant violation of child rights. Furthermore, all parties to the conflict (i.e. Maoists, Salwa Judum and government security forces) have engaged children in different capacities that expose them to the threat of harm and death. The unprecedented intensification of the conflict since mid-2005 has also caused considerable displacement, resulted in the destruction of hundreds of schools, and severely impacted access to education for children. Unfortunately, children caught in the crossfire are orphaned, killed and traumatised. Excessive violence against women, including rape, gang-rape and beating, has been reported from different parts of Dantewada district. The situation reiterates the view that rape and sexual abuse of women have often been used as an instrument in conflict situations.

The role of the state in establishing and nurturing a vigilante group with state resources is too obvious to reiterate. The situation of insecurity and forced eviction by SPOs and paramilitary forces has resulted in a large-scale crisis due to the internal displacement of tribal groups. Apart from the official figure of 45,958 villagers displaced and living in camps by the main road, media reports also mentioned that some 40,000 people from the southern part of the district had fled to Andhra Pradesh and other neighbouring areas (Independent Citizens Initiative 2006: 2). By the end of 2007 around 50,000 villagers had been relocated to at least 24 camps in Bijapur and Dantewada districts. As a result of forced dislocation, people have lost their homes, their land and all sources of their livelihood. The odd thing about these refugees is that the majority of them did not come to the camps because they were driven away from their habitations, rather they left their habitations because they were driven into these camps. Mobs of Salwa Judum have gone on the rampage with the paramilitary in tow, forcing villagers to come out and join the camps (Balagopal 2006: 2184). According to the latest government estimates, more than 600 villages with over 3 *lakh* people were shifted out of their homes in an anti-Naxal operation that began in 2005 in southern Chhattisgarh (*The Hindustan Times* 2009). Over half of the 1,354 villages in Dantewada district are now completely deserted.

Different investigative teams have confirmed that the majority of the camp residents came to pre-empt attacks or were forcibly brought in by the security forces and Salwa Judum. Most often, the villagers had to leave mostly in a panic parting with their livestock, grains and household possessions. When one set of people from Manikonta village returned to retrieve their implements to build homes in Dornapal, some 50 of them were kidnapped. The majority, including 20 women, were released and 13 men were brutally killed. The Maoists have justified the killing as 'counter action' (Independent Citizens Initiative 2006: 29). The reign of terror on civilians occurs with absolute impunity. There are many more aspects of rights involved in the Dantewada tragedy: the right to life which includes the right not to live at the mercy of killer gangs enjoying unwritten immunity, the right to struggle for a dignified and decent existence, the right to follow the politics of one's choice, the right not to be neglected, ill-treated and oppressed by the administration, the right not to be put outside the framework of constitutional fundamental rights merely because one participates in or supports militant politics, the very basic right that the society one is living in shall not be criminalised, and so on (Human Rights Forum 2006: 30).

The fact-finding report of a respected Human Rights Organisation, People's Union For Civil Liberties, claims that the Salwa Judum leadership represents,

> those sections of tribal and non-tribal society who have been adversely affected by the Maoist policies, e.g. those in traditional positions of authority within the village, those whose lands have been redistributed, those traders whose profit have been hit by the struggle over tendu patta and forest produce (Navlakha 2006: 2189).

The extent of the human security crisis in this mineral resource-rich area needs to be understood in the light of greater interest shown by MNCs (multinational corporations) and other corporate interests. Dhuragaon village is among ten villages along the Indravati River in Bastar district, whose 12,000-strong population the government is currently attempting to displace (*The Hindustan Times* 2009). By using an archaic land acquisition law, the state plans to transfer these fertile farms in order to set up a steel plant. More often than not, the government is blamed to push through the acquisition procedures deploying deceit and force. People argue that the forced displacement of tribal groups under the garb of a counterinsurgency operation is a part of an incentive package offered by the state to attract more MNCs to the area. The state and market nexus has made the pattern of development-induced displacement a regular phenomenon and it has certainly smoothed the process of possession of land by the MNCs. In 2005, the state government signed deals worth Rs.130 billion with industrial companies for steel mills and power stations, including the Memorandum of Understanding (MOU) signed with Essar in Dantewada and TATA in Lohandiguda.[9] The day following the signing of the MOUs, Salwa Judum began its operation. It would be naïve if one overlooked the reasons behind the apparent coincidence.

9 Essar and TATA are giant industrial corporations.

Does human security matter to the state?

Violence and counter-violence has increasingly become a recurring phenomenon in the lives of the tribal community in and around the area hitherto called the 'liberated zone'[10] by the Maoists. The actors of violence, whether Maoist or the state agencies in collaboration with Salwa Judum, have divided the entire village and families vertically and horizontally; people are forced to demonstrate their allegiance either to the Maoists or to the Salwa Judum. A spiral of vengeance and reprisal has been set in motion, with the Salwa Judum targeting villagers assumed to be sympathetic to the Maoists and the Maoists in turn killing those associated with Salwa Judum with little scope for being neutral. Apart from using the police and paramilitary forces against the Maoists, the state quite often resorts to fragmenting communities by encouraging them to settle scores. The examples of providing arms and extra-legal support to caste militias[11] in Bihar, training a cadre of revengeful ex-Naxalites in Andhra Pradesh and obviously the Salwa Judum in Chhattisgarh illustrate the crisis of human security in different pockets of India.

The state's monopoly over violence and counter-violence by ultra-left outfits has aggravated human insecurity and the biggest sufferers are ordinary villagers who are pitted against each other. The spread of violence in civilian spaces, with proxy wars being fought between the state and non-state actors, has increasingly embattled the civilian population and their human security is witnessing an unprecedented crisis. In village after village in the conflict-torn area, people and communities are divided, each side affronted by the other for the choices they are being compelled to make. The state and Salwa Judum appear to be exploiting the existing fault lines in the traditional tribal societies and villages. Denied of any civil, political and socioeconomic rights, the lives of people have been reduced to the biological minimum. An overarching sense of fear looms large in the entire area, which in turn provides political rationalisation for violence by the state and its agencies. The state plays on people's perceived fear and amplifies or manufactures threats to provide political justification for repression. Fear is detrimental not only to the individuals who experience it directly, but also to society at large. As people's fear of violent crime increases, their confidence erodes regarding the capacity of the state to fulfil one of its most basic obligations: to protect its citizens. Though the plight of people amply demonstrates that 'freedom from fear' and 'freedom from want' is inextricably intertwined in the conflict zone in India, even the minimalist approach of freedom from pervasive threat to people's rights and safety of lives is in jeopardy.

10 The liberated zone is an area where an incipient state has been or is declared to have been established, forcing out the existing state.

11 There has been a history of formation of private caste-based vigilante groups in the state of Bihar. These groups are primarily responsible for protecting the interest of upper caste landed gentry in the rural areas where ultra-left groups are mobilising landless labourers to fight for land, minimum wages and for protesting against all forms of exploitation.

'The sovereign power of the state at times reveals itself as a form of power that is at once inside and outside the law' (Agamben 1998). Schmitt's (1985: 5) famous dictum that 'sovereign is he who decides on the exception' interprets the sovereign as being both without and within the legal order: 'without the law is having the power to decide to suspend the existing legal order in self-defined exceptional circumstances, yet remaining within the law as he whom the juridical order grants the power to suspend its own validity'. A state of exception—which can take the form of an emergency, an insurrection, martial law or war—is a situation in which normal law does not apply, but where the force that law is meant to provide and sanction remains and is enacted by sovereign power (Agamben 2005 cited in de Larrinaga and Doucet 2008). The authority to suspend the law as also the authorisation of its re-establishment in the shape of new norms of intercession renders a section of people hapless and insecure. The layered and complex modus operandi of the state determines people's way of life by conveniently asserting a state of exception and/or a state of normalcy. Invariably, such situations of state of exception are being used in times of international conflict and crisis but there have been innumerable instances when national and federal government takes recourse to state of exception. The legal provisions and scope of authority of the state and its agencies are formed by manufacturing the consent of citizens, and use of state violence comes under the ambit of state of exception.

> Traditionally, State sovereignty and sovereign legitimacy rest upon a government's control of territory, state independence and recognition by other states. The role of citizens is to support this system. The human security approach reverses this equation: the State—and state sovereignty—must serve and support the people from which it draws its legitimacy (Newman 2004: 358).

The human security discourse is expected to question the justification of exceptionality by the state which has been responsible for persistent violence and rupture in the lives of individuals and communities. Though the ardent advocates of human security have been emphatic in suggesting that human security goes beyond the narrow understanding of safety from violent threats, the situation in the tribal hinterland in India depicts that insecurity due to violence and its consequences is a corollary of socioeconomic and political threat to human security where violence has become a cause as well as a consequence of human insecurity. In fact the situation illustrates that the threat of violence is inextricably interwoven with a multitude of other independent human security threats.

Conclusion

While examining the crisis of human security in the tribal areas of Chhattisgarh, one wonders what has made the Indian state so confrontationist after decades of inept handling of the Maoist insurgency. A minute scrutiny and analysis reveals that the tribal people of the area have been the unacknowledged victims of six decades of democratic development when they have been dispossessed and exploited unabashedly by the so-called mainstream and dominant political economy of the state. Unlike other disadvantaged groups, such as *dalits* and Muslims, who have managed to carve out some space for their communities and could have some influence as an interest group in democratic governance, the tribal groups remained imperceptible. The unvoiced community of tribal people has been bearing the brunt of exploitation by moneylenders, traders, contractors and state forest departments in post-colonial India. As the experiences of oppression vary from one group to another and also because of their sparse demographic and geographic profile, it is difficult to organise the community to assert itself as a political interest group. In one place, their main persecutors are forest officials; in another place, moneylenders; in a third, development projects conducted under the aegis of the state; in a fourth, a mining project promoted by a private firm. In the circumstances, it is much harder to build a broad coalition of tribal groups fighting for a common goal under a single banner (Guha 2007: 3305). However, the continued neglect of hilly and forested tribal areas was well suited for guerrilla warfare and the ultra-left groups could challenge the authority of the state in these regions.

> In these remote upland areas, public officials are unwilling to work hard, and often unwilling to work at all. Doctors do not attend the clinics assigned to them; school teachers stay away from school; magistrates spend their time lobbying for a transfer back to the plains. On the other hand, the Maoists are prepared to walk miles to hold a village meeting, and listen sympathetically to tribal grievances (Guha 2007: 3309).

As a result of prolonged neglect and continued alienation from the area and its people, the Indian state does not seem to have the confidence to look closely at the complex issue and make attempts to resolve it peacefully. The state has recourse to reassert its power and authority through confrontation and through escalating 'securitised' efforts. In fact the region is witnessing a twofold tragedy. The first tragedy is that the state has treated its Adivasi (aboriginal) citizens with contempt and condescension. The second tragedy is that their presumed protectors, the Naxalites, offer no long-term solution either (Guha 2007). Besides, the character of the Indian state is such that it demonstrates a propensity to act on the basis of electoral arithmetic where the tribal groups are perceived as apolitical and as a less influential group which faces a leadership crisis, too. The absolute marginalisation of tribal people due to lack of leverage of electoral mobilisation denies them the means to make effective claims on the government and the state and they stand outside the boundaries of political society which dictates the terms of reference for their everyday existence. Over the years, the Indian state has evolved a form of 'democratic authoritarianism' (Jalal 1995: 249), notwithstanding the meticulous observance of the ritual of election. Such an authoritarian and confrontationist approach goes well with the neo-liberal mandate and agenda of the state where it is often seen to be on the side of corporate and market interest.

The state governments that are overwhelmingly dominated by non-tribal groups are signing away tribal land for mining, manufacturing and power projects. In the recent past, the state has been encountering opposition and agitation by tribal people against the acquisition of land for the purpose of so-called advancement of capitalist industrial growth. Sometimes, such opposition is tacitly supported by the Maoists as well. Against this backdrop, it is widely perceived that the neo-liberal state uses the pretext of this counter-insurgency campaign for the eviction of the tribal population in general from the areas which are mineral rich. Once the people have been evicted, it can easily be handed over to the giant companies to set up their industrial units without going through the tedious and controversial processes of land acquisition. Besides, the post-colonial Indian state failed to understand the cultural context and ethos of heterogeneous tribal groups which culminated initially in neglect and afterwards in brutal confrontation. Unable to comprehend the nuances of tribal concerns as also the strategy to deal with the Maoists, the state facilitates the process of lawlessness by setting up *supposedly* community-led vigilante groups such as Salwa Judum which runs a parallel administration in the region. While the state could concentrate all its power and encouragement on vigilante groups against the Maoists, it did not have to be apologetic about or accountable for their deeds. The modus operandi of the state accentuates the crisis of human security and the process of finding a peaceful solution becomes even more remote.

Between the two extremes of valorising war and abhorrence of war lies a middle ground of social reality, which accepts that internal war cannot be prevented until government opts for a peaceful resolution of conflicts (Navlakha 2006: 2189). Human security has been described as many different things: a rallying cry, a political campaign, a set of beliefs about the sources of violent conflict, a new conceptualisation of security, and a guide for policy-makers and academic researchers. Definitional expansiveness and ambiguity are powerful attributes of human security, but only in the sense that they facilitate collective action by the members of the human security coalition (Paris 2001: 102). Human security necessitates that the norms, values and dominant understanding of sovereign power is re-examined and re-evaluated. Human security forces the state to look inward to the 'people from where it draws its legitimacy' (Owen 2004: 377). It is important to locate the situation as a 'critical and pervasive' threat to human security where the responsibility of state and its agencies has to be fixed—who will do it and how it will be made possible is both a crisis and a challenge for human security.

The immediate need is to de-escalate securitisation in the state by discontinuing the state-supported violence in the area and thereafter making a congenial environment for an honest dialogue with the Maoists. As their influence gains strength in most of the underdeveloped tribal areas, it is imperative that human security efforts should pay special attention to 'downside risks' (Commission on Human Security 2003: 8) that threaten human survival. The broad components of human security, 'freedom from fear' and 'freedom from want', are often inherently connected as the source of violence and therefore it is important to deal with them concomitantly. Though the conceptualisation of human security reiterated the correlation between underdevelopment/poverty and violence, the opposite causal association is often ignored. The political agenda of the state, the approach towards law and order and a limited effort to build a peaceful environment for dialogue as a precondition for ensuring human security is more often than not undermined. The history of the modern world is indeed a history of negotiated and mediated settlement and therefore durable human security has to count on the belief and processes of such mediation. Durable human security is difficult to achieve by victory and defeat through military means either by the state or by non-state actors. The standpoint of opposing groups can only be reconciled through a political process of dialogue. The human security discourse transcends state-centric understanding and it requires people throughout society to reassess the threats and measures to address them; however the responsibility of the state needs to be articulated squarely.

Bibliography

Acharya, A. (2001) 'Human Security: East versus West?' (Working Paper Series No. 17; Singapore: Institute of Defence and Strategic Studies).

Agamben, G. (1998) *Homo Sacer: Sovereign Power and Bare Life* (Stanford, CA: Stanford University Press).

Bajpai, K. (2004) 'An Expression of Threats versus Capabilities across Time and Space', in P. Burgess and T. Owen (eds.), 'What is Human Security? Comments by 21 Authors', *Security Dialogue* 35.3: 360-61.

Balagopal, K. (2006) 'Physiognomy of Violence', *Economic and Political Weekly* 41.22: 2183-86.

Chandler, D. (2004) 'The Responsibility to Protect? Imposing the "Liberal Peace" ', *International Peace Keeping* 11.1: 59-81.

Commission on Human Security (2003) *Human Security Now* (New York: Commission on Human Security).

Committee Against Violence On Women (2006) *Salwa Judum and Violence on Women in Dantewada, Chhattisgarh* (Nagpur/Hyderabad: Committee Against Violence On Women).

Dunne, T., and N.J. Wheeler (2004) ' "We the Peoples": Contending Discourses of Security in Human Rights Theory and Practice', *International Relations* 18.9.

Guha, R. (2007) 'Adivasis, Naxalite and Indian Democracy', *Economic and Political Weekly* 42.32: 3,305-12.

The Hindustan Times (2009) 'Chhattisgarh: The War Within', *The Hindustan Times*, 17 August 2009.

Human Rights Forum (2006) *Death, Displacement and Deprivation: The Death in Dantewada* (Hyderabad: Human Rights Forum).

HRW (Human Rights Watch) (2008a) *'Being Neutral is Our Biggest Crime': Government, Vigilante, and Naxalite Abuses in India's Chhattisgarh State* (New York: Human Rights Watch).

—— (2008b) *Dangerous Duty: Children and the Chhattisgarh Conflict* (New York: Human Rights Watch).

Human Security Centre (2005) *The Human Security Report 2005* (Oxford, UK: Oxford University Press).

Human Security Report (2005) *The Human Security Report 2005: War and Peace in the 21st Century* (New York: Oxford University Press).

Independent Citizens' Initiative (2006) *War in the Heart of India: An Enquiry into the Ground Situation in Dantewada District, Chhattisgarh*; www.rightsandresources.org/documents/files/doc_387.pdf, accessed 24 September 2010.

Jalal, A. (1995) *Democracy and Authoritarianism in South Asia* (Cambridge, UK: Cambridge University Press).

De Larrinaga, M., and M.G. Doucet (2008) 'Sovereign Power and the Biopolitics of Human Security', *Security Dialogue* 39: 517-37.

Government of India, Ministry of Home Affairs (2005) 'Annual Report 2005–2006'; www.mha.nic.in/pdfs/ar0506-Eng.pdf, accessed 24 September 2010

Mohapatra, S. (2007) 'Conflict-Induced Displacement in Chhattisgarh', in *Conflict, War and Displacement* (Kolkata, India: Mahanirban Calcutta Research Group).

Navlakha, G. (2006) 'Maoists in India', *Economic and Political Weekly* 41.22: 2186-89.

Newman, E. (2004) 'A Normatively Attractive but Analytically Weak Concept', in P. Burgess and T. Owen (eds.), 'What is Human Security? Comments by 21 Authors', *Security Dialogue* 35.3: 358-59.

Owen, T. (2004) 'Human Security—Conflict, Critique and Consensus: Colloquium Remarks and A Proposal for a Threshold- Based Definition', *Security Dialogue* 35.3: 373-87.

Paris, R. (2001) 'Human Security: Paradigm Shift or Hot Air?' *International Security* 26.2 (Autumn 2001): 87-102.

Roberts, D. (2008) *Human Insecurity: Global Structure of Violence* (Bangalore, India: Books for Change).

Schmitt, C. (1985) *Political Theology: Four Chapters on the Concept of Sovereignty* (Cambridge, MA: MIT Press).

Sundar, N. (2006) 'Bastar, Maoism and Salwa Judum', *Economic and Political Weekly* 41.29: 3,187-92.

Tadjbakhsh, S., and A.M. Chenoy (2008) *Human Security: Concepts and Implications* (London: Routledge).

Tehelka (2009) 'The Jungle Justice of the Trigger Happy', *Tehelka*, 7 February 2009.

Thakur, R. (2004) 'A Political World View', in P. Burgess and T. Owen (eds.), 'What is Human Security? Comments by 21 Authors', *Security Dialogue* 35.3: 347-48.

UNDP (United Nations Development Programme) (1994) *Human Development Report 1994: New Dimensions of Human Security* (Oxford, UK: Oxford University Press).

—— (2005) *Human Development Report: International Cooperation at Crossroads—Aid, Trade and Security in an Unequal World* (New York: UNDP).

16

Local order and human security after the proliferation of automatic rifles in East Africa

Toru Sagawa
Japan Society for the Promotion of Science

The proliferation of small arms, which has received international attention since the mid-1990s (e.g. United Nations 1997), has been a top priority for activities directed at building peace and advancing human security.[1] Although the role of the state in maintaining human security may conflict with its role in building peace, both efforts seem to proceed from a consensus that the state should take the initiative with respect to solving problems involving small arms and eventually hold the monopoly on the legitimate use of violence in a country. Such views rest on a deep-rooted Hobbesian assumption; that is, if violence is not controlled 'from above', people with arms will become addicted to violence, and society will descend into chaos.

Although the topic has received scant attention recently, the ways in which people in a 'stateless society' achieve 'ordered anarchy' in the absence of a formal government has traditionally constituted an area of study in the field of social

---

1 Chapter 8, 'Ways to advance the security of people', of *Human Security Now* (Commission on Human Security 2003), points out eight basic tasks for advancing human security. The first is '[p]rotecting people in violent conflict', and the second is '[p]rotecting people from the proliferation of arms'.

anthropology. This chapter will follow in this tradition and clarify how pastoral peoples in East Africa spontaneously maintained local order even after the inability and unwillingness of the state to protect its subjects resulted in the proliferation of automatic rifles. In addition, I will argue that state-sponsored disarmament tends to increase the public's vulnerability to natural and social changes.

Proliferation of automatic rifles and the disarmament policy in East Africa

Dozens of ethnic groups in the arid and semi-arid areas of East Africa depend primarily on livestock (cattle, camel, sheep, goat and donkey) herding for their subsistence. These pastoralists are among the most marginalised peoples in East Africa and face grave threats to their human security. Approximately 100 years ago, many of these groups were conquered by the military of the (colonial) state governments, which then incorporated them into peripheral border areas. Since that time, few government development policies to improve the lives of people in these groups have been implemented. Instead, governments have established international and domestic borders surrounding the incorporated areas and have regulated movement in and out of these territories without considering issues related to the seasonal movements and social networks of the pastoralists. This policy has disturbed local livelihood strategies, which include migrating, using the abundant land for livestock, and extending trans-ethnic social networks to ensure food security.

In the context of this uncertain environment, drought, starvation and low-intensity conflicts between ethnic groups have frequently characterised the daily lives of people within these areas during the course of history. Indeed, the interaction between wants and fears has resulted in a vicious cycle in which an outbreak of conflict renders previously available resources scarcer by expanding the no-man's-land between opposing groups and disturbing the ability of aid agencies to receive and distribute emergency food provisions. This dynamic also increases the vulnerability of the entire area to natural and social changes. As a result, the danger that conflict will recur is also enhanced.

Exacerbating the effects of the state's misuse of power and the dysfunction in the security sector are the primary causes of conflicts, the struggle for natural resources such as livestock and pasture land, and the traditional culture, which values the use of violence against the enemy. Furthermore, it has been argued that the proliferation of (semi-) automatic rifles such as the AK47 and G3 has increased the seriousness of conflicts during the past 30 years. Since the end of the 1970s, when political upheavals occurred in Uganda (1979), Sudan (1983–2005), Ethiopia (1991) and Somalia (1991–), firearms supplied by developed countries have become widely available to ordinary citizens, especially pastoral peoples in border areas (Mkutu 2008: Chapter 3). It has been estimated that 5 million small arms are being circulated in East Africa, many of which are illegally used by pastoralists (Simonse 2005: 244).

In response to this situation, governments, notably that of Uganda, have frequently intervened in local communities to disarm pastoralists. However, these actions have only added to the confusion because national armies have used force unfairly against target groups and areas that were unevenly chosen, in part because of the political motivations of local elites. As a result, disarmament operations have disturbed the local balance of power, deepened mistrust against the government and increased local demand for firearms (e.g. Small Arms Survey 2007; Sagawa 2010).

However, with the exception of the work of a few researchers and organisations, these failures have not yet received the appropriate critical attention until now. At present, the international community has reached a general consensus that the proliferation of firearms causes violence to flourish, indicating that the state (and 'We') should do something. Indeed, in this view, doing something is better than doing nothing. Many researchers and aid agencies have reinforced this recognition and have reported that, after the introduction of automatic rifles, pastoral societies were inundated with naked violence committed by radical youth using the new arms (e.g. Abbink 2000; Gray *et al.* 2003).

Careful reading, however, reveals that many reports do not rely solely on empirical research for their conclusions, but rest in part on a technology-deterministic way of thinking. I agree with Dave Eaton's assertion that '(t)he gun has been fetishized as a change agent without a balanced understanding having been reached as to its impact' (Eaton 2008: 105). I will use a more empirical approach to analyse how people have addressed the new situation produced by the proliferation of automatic rifles in the area.

The case of the Daasanach

The population of the Daasanach, an agro-pastoral people living in south-western Ethiopia at the border with Kenya and the Sudan (Figure 16.1), numbers about 48,000, only about 0.06% of the total Ethiopian population in 2007. In addition, thousands of Daasanach live in north-western Kenya. They classify four neighbouring (agro-) pastoral groups (the Turkana, the Nyangatom, the Hamar and the Gabra) as *kiz* or the 'enemy' and have been engaged in intermittent conflict with them for more than half a century.

The negative impact of state power constitutes the source of these conflicts. The Daasanach were conquered by imperial Ethiopia in the late 19th century. During the first half of 20th century, the Ethiopian state advanced into the area to demonstrate its authority to British Kenya and to exploit natural resources such as ivory. Toward these ends, the Ethiopian state organised a raiding party consisting of local

Figure 16.1 **The Daasanach and their neighbouring groups**

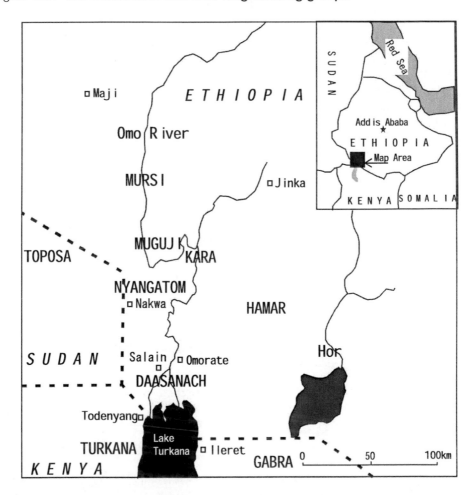

Names in upper case (not oblique) are ethnic groups; place names are upper and lower case; the dotted lines are national borders.

pastoralists, which caused the escalation of hostilities between the Daasanach and neighbouring groups. After the Second World War, however, Ethiopia lost interest in this remote territory and left the area without attempting to mitigate the escalated hostility or collect the firearms. Thus, the situation in this area differs from that of Ugandan pastoral societies, in which government-sponsored disarmament projects have been enforced on many occasions.

Old-type firearms such as muskets were introduced to the area after the state's involvement, and automatic rifles have also been available since the late 1980s. In 2006, 48% of Daasanach adult males ($N = 163$) had rifles, mainly automatic rifles. The Daasanach obtained rifles primarily by bartering with merchants or neighbouring peoples. One automatic rifle could be traded for two adult oxen and 100 bullets could be traded for one female calf in 2006.

In the Daasanach language, *osu* means war or a collective and organised violent attack designed to kill the enemy and raid their livestock. According to interviews I conducted with 174 adult Daasanach males in 2006, adult males went to *osu* an average of 3.4 times, and 67% of adult males had raided the livestock of enemies during previous battles. Although most battles lasted one or two days, more than 100 people have died in large-scale battles. Unorganised small raiding activities (*sulla*) occur much more frequently. Although the data on this situation seems devastating, pastoralists have partially succeeded in their attempts to control the violence. I will briefly describe how the relationship between the Daasanach and the Nyangatom changed after the proliferation of automatic rifles.

The Nyangatom, who are the northern neighbour of the Daasanach, initially obtained automatic rifles from their ally, the Toposa, in south-eastern Sudan during the civil war in the mid-1980s (Tornay 1993). The Nyangatom attacked neighbouring peoples and exterminated three Daasanach villages on the western side of the Omo River in 1988 and 1989. For example, the Nyangatom entered Salain village before dawn and killed hundreds of Daasanach and raided all their livestock during a few hours. In this battle, a few Daasanach observed some Nyangatom continuing to shoot at dead bodies after their bullets had been exhausted. The Nyangatom were also observed after the battle to be on a nearby mound shooting their guns toward the sky and eating livestock meat raided from the Daasanach. After a normal conflict, groups return to their villages as soon as possible after the raiding of livestock lest they be chased. In this instance, however, the Nyangatom remained near the village for a few hours, as if flaunting their overwhelming power to the Daasanach. Looking back at those episodes, the Daasanach say 'The Nyangatom got drunk with Kalashnikovs'. Fearing the power of the Nyangatom, most Daasanach abandoned the land on the western side of the river and emigrated to the eastern side.

In a more forceful response, the Daasanach demanded that the local government supply them with automatic rifles, but this request was refused. Next, the Daasanach visited their eastern ally, the Hor, after learning that the Hor had obtained automatic rifles via eastern routes. In 1991, after most of the adult males had purchased automatic rifles from the Hor, the Daasanach attacked Nakwa, one of the largest Nyangatom villages. Although the Daasanach were not able to achieve military victory in this battle, the attack proved their ability to fight the Nyangatom as equals (cf. Turton 1994).

After the war, many Daasanach gradually began moving to the western side of the river, which remained a no-man's-land, to herd livestock, and the Nyangatom did not mount an organised attack until 2006. Indeed, the Daasanach even moved north and started to live with the Nyangatom in Nakwa during the late 1990s.

Spontaneous attempts to maintain local order

Although the proliferation of new arms temporarily intensified the violence of conflicts, relationships among ethnic groups have not become chaotic. This relied on peoples' spontaneous attempts to prevent the spread of violence and maintain local order in the face of fear and want brought about by violence.

In terms of fear, both parties to the conflict between the Nyangatom and the Daasanach responded to their fears by recognising the balance of power and the dangers of using automatic rifles in mutual attacks that result in serious battles; both groups came to share the wish to avoid the excessive use of violence. Among the Daasanach, there is 'a culture of violence' in which a man who achieves military results in battle is regarded as a 'brave man', and a young man mobilises for war in the hope of becoming a 'brave man'. However, several young men said, 'I became a coward through the battle experiences with Kalashnikovs' and voluntarily decided not to go to war again (Sagawa 2009). Such sentiments have contributed to the deterrence of further conflict.

In terms of want, the Daasanach and the Nyangatom had lived together and shared pasture land to facilitate adaptation to an uncertain environment before serious conflict erupted. They also established amicable individual ties across group boundaries. For example in 2006, 71% of the adult males ($N = 169$) had friend(s) who belonged to other groups, and 41% ($N = 170$) had relative(s) who had married a woman from other groups. Friends and members of kinship groups exchanged goods that were scarce in their own communities (Sagawa in press). After the attacks by the Nyangatom, the no-man's-land expanded, mutual visits were suspended, and resources became more limited. After the attack on Nakwa, the Daasanach women and men started to engage in conversations that reflected and reinforced the atmosphere of war-weariness at a community level. For example, they worried, 'This year, where can we herd livestock?' (because of the reduction of available lands caused by conflicts).

However, fear and want alone will not restore amicable relationships; indeed, they may create vicious cycles that lead to the recurrence of violent conflicts as mentioned above. The shift from hostile to amicable relations must include individual initiatives, what I refer to as 'an aspiration for face-to-face interactions with others'. The Daasanach society had no strictly institutionalised process for improving relationships after the war. Thus, peacemaking requires that an individual visits other groups' territory on his own initiative, risking victimisation by possibly vengeful enemies. Those who are the first to visit the lands of other groups typically have personal ties to a member of the 'enemy' group. These individuals visit their friends and/or kin and experience the hospitality of their hosts. Following their visits, other members also visit, and the inter-ethnic relationship will shift from a peace that is passively maintained through the separation provided by a no-man's-land to a peace that is actively developed through trans-ethnic amicable interactions.

The pastoralists have achieved local order on the basis of the complementary dynamics involving the intra-personal/group push away from fear and want and the inter-personal/group pull towards face-to-face interactions. I refer to this developed order as local order to emphasise that it emerged from the efforts of individuals who shared the physical and mental experiences of want and fear that resulted from violence rather than from the interventions by external forces holding asymmetrical power.

State reconstruction and human security in marginalised areas

With this case in mind, I will now discuss problems with respect to small arms policies. The majority of the international community expects a reconstructed state to monopolise the legitimate use of violence and control the circulation and use of arms in Africa. However, a policy that involves the control of arms from above poses the strong possibility of repeating the marginalisation of pastoralists.

As mentioned above, even though the Daasanach have maintained some measure of amicable relations thus far, international and domestic borders established by governments since the early 20th century have damaged pastoralists' traditional coping strategies and led to the escalation of hostilities between groups. If a policy preventing the influx of firearms from foreign countries relies on strengthening cross-border control and results in stricter restriction on the movement and social networks of the pastoralists, their vulnerability to drought (and thus their want) will increase.

In terms of policies for controlling the possession and use of firearms, we should first consider the many failed disarmament policies that have been initiated since colonial times. Because target groups and areas were determined unevenly and unfairly, disarmed people who were loyal to the government became targets for attack by armed neighbouring groups located beyond the administrative borders.

Given the initial goals of conquest and the more recent disarmament operations, many pastoral peoples have experienced the state as merely a violent and oversized oppressor. Such oppression has been based on and justified by a deep-rooted cultural prejudice towards pastoralists. The majority of citizens in East Africa regard peripheral pastoralists as primitive, savage and warlike. Thus, even if the security sector could be reformed and disarmament operations could be enforced with an 'appropriate' method on an 'appropriate' scale, it is likely that the state would use violence in their relations with disarmed pastoralists because of the prejudice that easily obscures superficial considerations of political legitimacy. We can all too easily provide evidence that naked violence against stigmatised citizens is perpetrated not only by the corrupt governments in Africa, but also by the governments characterised by so-called 'good governance' that have behaved as if they have a right to teach this practice to other governments in Africa. Thus, it is not surprising that pastoralists have concluded from their historical experiences that the proper way to prevent violent interventions from the state (and thus to quell their fear) is to keep firearms, because, as one pastoralist in Uganda said, 'Where there are no guns, they [the state] use the threat of guns' (Knighton 2003).

Conclusion

This chapter described how pastoralists in East Africa, operating under a state without the capacity or will to protect its subjects, restored local order after the proliferation of automatic rifles. I also underscored that disarmament, enforced as part of an effort to enable the territorial state to monopolise the legitimate use of violence, intensifies pastoralists' want and fear. This analysis is the reverse of that derived from a Hobbesian perspective, but is self-evident from the local perspective. This view recognises that the people who know the most about the fear and want brought about by violence are those who have experienced these conditions and they always exercise their agency to address problems within the structural constraints. The Hobbesian state is neither more nor less than an intellectual fiction, and we need to reconsider the types and scales of political unit appropriate for the management of violence.

I do not intend to idealise the subjects of my research. The life of the Daasanach is always in danger from a recurrence of armed conflict. I emphasised their spontaneous practices not because we should regard this area as an autonomous peace-forming unit where interventions are unnecessary, but because the international community needs to recognise the local security unit and consider its role in the process of reforming states. I define the local security unit as a unit in which people's experiences and aspirations for face-to-face interactions with others directly contribute to peace-building and to the advancement of human security. Efforts to establish the territorial state as holding a monopoly on the legitimate use of violence will drive marginalised peoples into the palm of the state's hand. It will not be the end of marginalisation but the perpetuation of it.

Bibliography

Abbink, J. (2000) 'Restoring the Balance: Violence and Culture among Suri of Southern Ethiopia', in G. Aijmer and J. Abbink (eds.), *Meanings of Violence* (Oxford, UK: Berg): 77-100.

Commission on Human Security (2003) *Human Security Now* (New York: Commission on Human Security).

Eaton, D. (2008) 'The Business of Peace: Raiding and Peace Work along the Kenya-Uganda Border (Part I)', *African Affairs* 426: 89-110.

Gray, S., M. Sundal, B. Wiebusch, M.A. Little, P.W. Leslie and I.L. Pike (2003) 'Cattle Raiding, Cultural Survival and Adaptability of East African Pastoralists', *Current Anthropology* 44.1: 3-30.

Knighton, B. (2003) 'The State as Raider among the Karamojong: "Where there are no guns, they use the threat of guns" ', *Africa* 73.3: 427-55.

Mkutu, K. (2008) *Guns and Governance in the Rift Valley: Pastoralist Conflict and Small Arms* (Oxford, UK: James Currey).

Sagawa, T. (2009) 'Why Do People "Renounce War"?: The War Experiences of the Daasanach in the Conflict-ridden Area of Northeast Africa' (Working Paper Series 42; Kyoto: Ryukoku University).

—— (2010) 'Small Arms Issues and the Disarmament Policy: A Case of Local Conflict in East African Pastoral Societies', in M. Kawabata, S. Takeuchi and T. Ochiai (eds.), *Conflict Resolution* (Kyoto: Minerva Shobo [in Japanese]): 221-51.

—— (in press) 'Local Potential for Peace: Trans-Ethnic Cross-cutting Ties among the Daasanach and Their Neighbors', in C.E. Gabbert and S. Thubauville (eds.), *To Live with Others* (Köln, Germany: Köppe).

Simonse, S. (2005) 'Warriors, Hooligans and Mercenaries: Failed Statehood and the Violence of Young Male Pastoralists in the Horn of Africa', in J. Abbink and I. van Kessel (eds.), *Vanguard or Vandals* (Leiden, Netherlands: Brill): 243-66.

Small Arms Survey (2007) *Response to Pastoral Wars: A Review of Violence Reduction Efforts in Sudan, Uganda, and Kenya* (Geneva: Small Arms Survey).

Tornay, S. (1993) 'More Chances on the Fringe of the State? The Growing Power of the Nyangatom', in T. Tvedt (ed.), *Conflict in the Horn of Africa* (Uppsala, Sweden: Uppsala University): 143-63.

Turton, D. (1994) 'Mursi Political Identity and Warfare', in K. Fukui and J. Markakis (eds.), *Ethnicity and Conflict in the Horn of Africa* (London: James Currey): 15-31.

United Nations (1997) 'Report of the UN Panel of Governmental Experts on Small Arms', A/52/298 of 27 August; www.un.org/Docs/sc/committees/sanctions/a52298.pdf, accessed 8 August 2008.

About the contributors

Bruce Baker is professor of African Security and Director of the African Studies Centre at Coventry University, UK. His current research focus is informal and formal policing in Africa and has led to *Multi-choice Policing in Africa* (Nordiska Afrikainstitutet, 2007); *Security in Post-conflict Africa: The Role of Non-state Policing* (CRC Press, 2009) and numerous articles (see www.africanpolicing.org).

Hazel R. Barrett is Head of the Department of Geography, Environment and Disaster Management and Professor of Development Geography at Coventry University. Her research interests focus on health and development issues in sub-Saharan Africa, in particular the socioeconomic impacts of HIV/AIDS on rural communities and, in particular, children.

Nicky Black has worked across the private, public and civil sectors on corporate citizenship issues since 2004. Her research interests include global governance, weak governance/conflict zones and humanitarian action. Trained as a sociologist at Oxford and McGill Universities, Nicky has a PhD in Strategic Management from the University of Waikato, New Zealand. In June 2010 she took up the role of Corporate Citizenship Manager at De Beers, a diamond mining and marketing company.

Marci Green, PhD, is a senior lecturer and Head of Sociology at the University of Wolverhampton. Her earlier published work was on 'Immigration, Race-making and National Identity'. She began working in the field of attachment theory in the mid-1990s, and has since edited two books: *Attachment and Human Survival* (2004) and *Risking Human Security: Attachment and Public Life* (2008).

Sarah Green has an Honours Degree in Religious Studies and Theology and an MA in Peace and Reconciliation Studies. Her most recent research focused on exploring the concept of coexistence and interface communities in Belfast. Sarah is currently a PhD candidate at the Centre for Peace and Reconciliation Studies, Coventry University, UK.

Professor **Alan Hunter** is Professor of Asian Studies and Director of the Centre for Peace and Reconciliation Studies at Coventry University, UK. He was formerly Associate Director of the Applied Research Centre in Human Security at Coventry University and has taught peace studies, religious studies and Chinese studies in the UK, the PRC, Hong Kong and Singapore.

Dr **Manish K. Jha** is an Associate Professor at Tata Institute of Social Sciences, Mumbai, India. He did his doctoral on Naxalite movement and caste violence. He has published articles on Human Rights and Human Security, Food Security, Hunger and Starvation, Disaster and Development, Marginalities and Justice, etc. in reputed journals. His research interests includes conflict and human security, social exclusion, development and governance.

Hitomi Kubo is Co-Director of the Concentration in Human Security for the Master of Public Affairs (MPA), Sciences Po, Paris. Her current work focuses on developing the operational aspects of human security and the application of human security for post-conflict peace-building. Recently, she has developed several human security training programmes in collaboration with the United Nations Human Security Unit and the Comprehensive Crisis Management Center (CMC) in Kuopio, Finland.

Dr **Malcolm McIntosh** FRSA is Professor of Sustainable Enterprise at Griffith University, Australia, and Director, Asia Pacific Centre for Sustainable Enterprise. He also holds visiting professorships at the Department of Civil Engineering at the University of Bristol, Centre for Peace and Reconciliation at Coventry, UK, and Sustainability Institute, University of Stellenbosch, South Africa.

Liliane Mouan is a PhD student at Coventry University. Her research focuses on oil sector governance reforms in Angola. Liliane holds an LLB from the University of Buea, Cameroon, and an LLM in International Law and Human Rights from Coventry University's Law School, where she was awarded the Coventry Law Prize as the Best Postgraduate Law Student in 2007.

Vesselin Popovski is Senior Academic Programme Officer at the United Nations University, Japan. He was among the participants in the work of the International Commission on Intervention and State Sovereignty (ICISS) that in 2001 lead to the original report 'Responsibility to Protect'. He wrote chapters for and edited numerous books, such as *International Criminal Accountability and Children's Rights* (2006); *World Religions and Norms of War* (2009); *Human Rights Regimes in the Americas* (2010); *Democracy in the South* (2010); *Building Trust in Government* (2010); and *Engaging Civil Society in Global Governance* (2010).

Deepayan Basu Ray has an international relations and political science background with experience in human security, disarmament and arms control, conflict and emergencies, international aid architecture, and human development. He is currently a Policy Advisor on arms control and development at Oxfam GB. Prior to this, he worked on humanitarian aid and fragile states issues at the Overseas Development Institute and Oxford Policy Management. His previous work experience has also included research and policy analysis on sociopolitical and security issues, human rights and vulnerable groups, ICT and knowledge management for development, and non-traditional threats to security.

David Roberts's most recent monograph on human security is entitled *Global Governance and Biopolitics: Regulating Human Security*. He is convenor and chair of the British International Studies Association Human Security Working Group, external examiner to Coventry University and the Royal University of Phnom Penh, and Senior Lecturer in International Politics at the University of Ulster.

Toru Sagawa is research fellow of the Japan Society for the Promotion of Science. He has carried out anthropological research among East African pastoral societies. He has published several articles on inter-ethnic relations and gender relations of the Daasanach in south-western Ethiopia.

Yasunobu Sato is Professor of the University of Tokyo, Graduate School of Arts & Sciences, Graduate Program on Human Security. He has a PhD in law (University of London 2000) and has practised law since 1984. He worked as legal officer with UNHCR, as Human Rights Officer with UNTAC and as Counsel with EBRD.

Dylan Scudder is completing his PhD at the University of Tokyo while managing his consulting firm, Milestone Inc. He consults and trains companies in Japan on issues related to operating in emerging markets. He also has extensive experience with UNICEF, where he was responsible for screening multinationals against ethical performance criteria.

Miho Taka holds a BA in Education, a MA in Third World Studies, and a Master of Public Administration, and served as country director of a NGO in Rwanda. She is currently a site-split PhD research student at Coventry University and the UN University.

Index